The Elizabethan Courtier Poets

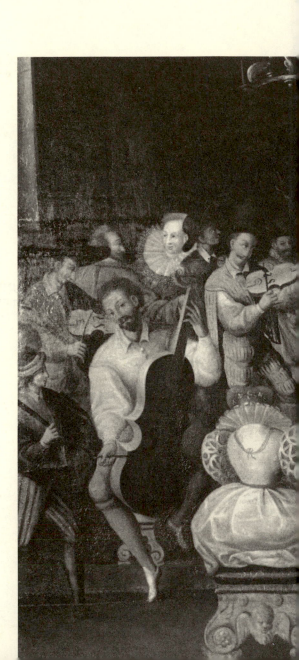

University of Missouri Press

COLUMBIA AND LONDON

The Elizabethan Courtier Poets

The Poems and Their Contexts

Steven W. May

Copyright © 1991 by
The Curators of the University of Missouri
University of Missouri Press, Columbia, Missouri 65201
Printed and bound in the United States of America
All rights reserved
5   4   3   2   1   95   94   93   92   91

Library of Congress Cataloging-in-Publication Data
May, Steven W.
    The Elizabethan courtier poets : the poems and their contexts /
Steven W. May.
        p.   cm.
    Includes bibliographical references and index.
    ISBN 0-8262-0749-9 (alk. paper)
    1. English poetry—Early modern, 1500–1700—History and
criticism.   2. Great Britain—Court and courtiers—History—
16th century.   3. Courts and courtiers in literature.   I. Title
PR535.C69M3   1991   90-40652
821'.309—dc20   CIP

∞™ This paper meets the requirements of the
American National Standard for Permanence of Paper
for Printed Library Materials, Z39.48, 1984.

FRONTISPIECE: "Queen Elizabeth Dancing," courtesy Viscount
De L'Isle, VC, KG, from his collection at Penshurst.

Designer: Liz Fett
Typesetter: Connell-Zeko Type & Graphics
Printer: Thomson-Shore, Inc.
Binder: Thomson-Shore, Inc.
Typeface: Trump Medieval

To the memory of William A. Ringler, Jr.

Contents

Acknowledgments

I am grateful to the editors of *Modern Philology* and *Studies in Philology* for permission to reprint my editions of the poetry of Ferdinando, Earl of Derby; Edward, Earl of Oxford; and Robert, Earl of Essex. The following individuals and archives have kindly granted permission to publish edited transcripts from manuscripts in their collections, as specifically recorded with the accompanying texts in Part II: the owner of Trumbull Add. MS 23, on deposit at the Berkshire Record Office; the Syndics of Cambridge University Library; the Governing Body of Christ Church, Oxford; the Houghton Library, Harvard University; the Henry E. Huntington Library; the Pierpont Morgan Library; the Rosenbach Museum and Library; and the Victoria and Albert Museum.

Most of the research for this book was made possible by a series of summer study grants and a sabbatical leave of absence from Georgetown College. I am grateful as well for support from the Huntington Library, the Southern Regional Education Board, and the Education Commission of the Southern Baptist Convention. A year's fellowship from the National Endowment for the Humanities gave me time to write up the results of my investigations. For their freely shared expertise I am grateful to a host of archivists and colleagues, and particularly to Katherine Duncan-Jones, W. H. Kelliher, R. H. Miller, and Michael Rudick, who read and commented on parts of this work in progress. J. Timothy Landgrave, Dr. John Blackburn, and Marijean Booske displayed extraordinary patience while compensating for my ignorance of computers. John Shawcross, Sydney Francis, and Dr. William Tighe shared information and offered invaluable advice. Virginia Covington, Jane Lawson, and William Terry Martin helped solve a variety of bibliographical and research problems. I am even more indebted to Arthur J. Slavin for generous guidance extending well beyond the historical questions I originally posed to him. My greatest debt is to the late William A. Ringler, Jr., who encouraged this study from the beginning and shared with me his knowledge of the courtier poets, and whose distinguished career continues to serve as an inspiring ideal of literary sensitivity and scholarly excellence.

Sources and Abbreviations

BL	British Library, London
Bodl.	Bodleian Library, Oxford
C	Chancery
CSPD	Calendars of State Papers Domestic, Elizabeth I (cited by volume and document number)
CSPF	Calendars of State Papers Foreign, Elizabeth I (cited by document and volume number)
DNB	*The Dictionary of National Biography* (1st ed.; reprint, 1921–1922)
E	Exchequer
EETS	Early English Text Society
Folger	Folger Shakespeare Library, Washington, D.C.
HMC	Historical Manuscripts Commission
LC	Lord Chamberlain's
Nichols	John Nichols, *The Progresses and Public Processions of Queen Elizabeth*, 3 vols. (1823; reprint, New York: AMS, n.d.)
PCC	Prerogative Court of Canterbury
PRO	Public Record Office, London
SO	Signet Office
SP	State Papers
STC	*A Short-Title Catalogue of Books Printed in England, Scotland, and Ireland*, 2d ed., 2 vols., compiled by W. A. Jackson, F. S. Ferguson, and Katharine F. Pantzer (London: Bibliographical Society, 1975, 1986)

All references to the Elizabethan New Year's gift exchanges derive
from the following sources:

Year	Document
1559	John Rylands University Library of Manchester, English MS 117
1562	BL, MS Harleian Roll V.18
1563	PRO, C Misc. 3/38
1564	Folger, MS Z.d.12
1565	Folger, MS Z.d.13
1567	BL, Add. MS 9772
1575	Folger, MS Z.d.14
1576	BL, Add. MS 4827
1577	PRO, C Misc. 3/39
1578	Nichols, 2:65–91
1579	Nichols, 2:249–75
1581	Eton College, Berkshire, MS 192
1582	BL, Harleian MS 1644, ff. 7v–11v
1584	BL, Egerton MS 3052
1585	Folger, MS Z.d.16
1588	BL, Add. MS 8159
1589	Nichols, 3:1–26
1597	BL, MS Facs. *672
1598	PRO, C Misc. 3/40
1599	Folger, MS Z.d.17
1600	Nichols, 3:445–67
1603	PRO, C Misc. 3/41

The 1582 record in a copy of the treasurer of the chamber's accounts
lists rewards at New Year's to donors' servants, but arranges them
as in the rolls under such usual headings as "Marquesses and Earles,"
"Busshopps," and so forth. Gaps in the records between 1572 and
1586 are partially filled by records of the New Year's gifts entrusted
to Lady Katherine Howard as entered in BL, Harleian MS 4698, and
BL, Sloane MS 814. Except for the 1582 and 1597 lists, these sources
are described in A. J. Collins's *Inventory of the Jewels and Plate of
Queen Elizabeth I* (London: Trustees of the British Museum, 1955),
249–52.

The Elizabethan Courtier Poets

Introduction

During the reign of Elizabeth, English poetry emerged from its midcentury doldrums to create a national literature of unprecedented excellence. The queen and her courtiers, consumers of all that was best in the new age, served as the primary audience for this artistic flowering. The plays of Lyly and Shakespeare, Spenser's *Faerie Queene*, and lyrics by scores of poets such as George Gascoigne, Samuel Daniel, and Michael Drayton were offered up to this courtier elite as the audience of first importance. No other component of English society could muster a similar prestige or affluence in the service of art. As the center of national patronage, the court directly influenced poetry by its approval or disapproval of individual works and authors. Indirectly, moreover, courtiers influenced out-of-court writers by their example. "Take hede therfore, ye great ones in the Court, . . . take hede, what ye do, . . . For as you great ones use to do, so all meane men love to do."[1] Thus Roger Ascham sized up Elizabethan courtiers as models of behavior for their society. The best-known instance of this power in the age's literary history is no doubt the "sonnet craze" of the 1590s, a direct result of the publication of Sidney's *Astrophil and Stella*. But the development of poetry within the court and the nature of courtier responsibility for its role there have received only fragmentary and imperfect study.

Two obstacles stand in the way of any comprehensive assessment of Elizabethan courtier verse. First, without meaningful and consistently applied definitions of the terms *court* and *courtier* it is impossible to discriminate those who were bona fide participants in the life of the court from hangers-on or mere servants of the court. "Many of the household officers were literally 'courtiers'" under Charles I according to G. E. Aylmer: "they lodged at Court, and when off duty they went away to their country estates." Conyers

---

1. William A. Wright, *Roger Ascham: The English Works*, 220.

Read, however, felt that Lord Treasurer Burghley "was never a Courtier" despite the fact that his "position involved constant attendance at Court." Elizabeth rewarded Spenser with a pension in return for his presentation of *The Faerie Queene* at court, yet David Daiches notes that he "was never the complete courtier," while James Bednarz terms him a "fellow courtier-poet" with Ralegh.[2] John Lyly complained to the queen that she had given him nothing for his service to her; nevertheless, he is termed a courtier without reservation by his foremost critics. Such terms as *court poet, courtly writers*, and *courtier artist* crop up promiscuously in our literary histories, while the social and cultural realities underlying these terms remain largely obscured for want of historically authentic definitions. As we shall see, however, the queen's regulation of her household singled out her courtiers as a distinct and, at the time, readily identifiable social entity. Their status was consistently recognized by Elizabethan aristocrats, to the extent that a meaningful definition can be established.

Once this term has been defined it becomes possible to identify the queen's courtiers and the poets among them. But here we encounter the second obstacle to any systematic study of their verse: for most courtiers, complete and reliable canons and texts have not previously been determined. These authors seldom published their poetry because the writing of verse was considered a questionable practice during at least the first half of Elizabeth's reign. Courtiers gradually modified their attitude toward poetry but not sufficiently to lead more than a few of them to publish their works. As a result, the bulk of courtier verse filtered into the vast, unpredictable network of manuscript circulation. To this manuscript tradition we are wholly indebted for the survival not just of whole poems but of whole bodies of works by individual poets: Sir Robert Sidney's entire canon; the psalms translated by his brother and sister, Sir Philip and the countess of Pembroke; and for most of the verse written by Sir Edward Dyer, the earl of Oxford, and the queen herself. Unfortunately, the manuscripts distorted as they preserved. A canon edited from these anthologies is often quite difficult to arrange in chronological order so that the poet's development can be studied. The manuscripts seldom record circumstances of composition, often the

2. G. E. Aylmer, *The King's Servants: The Civil Service of Charles I, 1625–1642*, 411; Conyers Read, *Mr. Secretary Cecil and Queen Elizabeth*, 20; David Daiches, *A Critical History of English Literature*, 1:175; James Bednarz, "Ralegh in Spenser's Historical Allegory," 51–52.

most interesting and necessary information in the explication of a courtier's work. Worst of all, many scribes gave spurious attributions to the poems they copied, while they often revised the texts at will. As a result, courtier verse poses some of the most difficult editorial problems in English literature. Small wonder that, despite the repeated efforts of highly competent scholars, even such prominent authors as Ralegh, Sir John Harington, and Fulke Greville still await definitive editing. For those courtiers who wrote only sporadically in verse, such figures as Sir Edward Hoby, Sir Francis Drake, Lord Burghley, and Sir William Cordell, for example, no effort has heretofore been made to collect or evaluate their poetry.

The purpose of this study, therefore, is to identify the queen's courtier poets and then to collect, edit, and assess their work within the context of the court which produced it. Unlike most broadly Elizabethan studies, this book is rather strictly confined to the years 1558–1603. Insofar as courtier verse was affected by the climate at court such limits are quite functional since the Elizabethan atmosphere differed greatly from that of the courts which preceded and followed it. There is considerable evidence, for example, that the arbitrary and violent rule of Henry VIII produced a feeling of dread among his courtiers which was but slightly abated during the power struggles of Edward VI's minority.[3] Queen Mary's reinstatement of Catholicism, culminating in the unpopular advent of a foreign and Catholic king consort in 1555, lent a grimly alien and zealous tone to the Marian court. The nature of court life under Elizabeth was generally more humane, less threatening, less intensely ecclesiastical. Its contrast with the reign of Mary I is, however, no greater than with the irresponsible indecorum, even debauchery, of the Jacobean court. Each sovereign controlled the atmosphere of court life, and that atmosphere changed and developed in accord with the ruler's personality so that, with the death of the queen, Elizabethan court life came abruptly to an end.

I have divided this study into two parts in order to preserve the narrative flow of the critical history of courtier verse (Part I), while providing the reader with convenient access in Part II to biographical, canonical, and textual data relating to the courtier poets whose

3. In *The Courtly Maker*, Raymond Southall suggests that the conditions at the Henrician court produced in its verse a dominant tone of depression and insecurity that stemmed from the King's unpredictable personal relations (68–69, and chapter 6, "The Psychology of a Courtier"). Lacey Baldwin Smith blames the ominous atmosphere at court on Henry's lack of emotional control (*Henry VIII: The Mask of Royalty*, 83).

works are analyzed in Part I. Chapter 1 defines the Elizabethan court and its courtiers according to the social criteria acknowledged by the courtier class. I explain as well why such writers as John Lyly, George Puttenham, Edmund Spenser, and a number of others fell short of courtier status. The history of courtier verse occupies Chapters 2–7, followed by the conclusion to Part I. This is primarily a chronological account, although some backtracking occurs in tracing the development of certain genres, especially devotional verse and drama.

Part II answers two fundamental questions: who were the Elizabethan courtier poets according to the criteria established in Chapter 1, and what did they write? Evidence of courtier rank for the following thirty-two poets, with their dates of courtiership, editions and sources of their poetry, and selected texts, is set forth in Part II:

Roger Ascham
Sir Nicholas Bacon
William Cecil, Lord Burghley
Lady Mary Cheke
George Clifford, third earl of Cumberland
Sir William Cordell
Robert Devereux, second earl of Essex
Edward DeVere, seventeenth earl of Oxford
Sir Francis Drake
Sir Edward Dyer
Elizabeth I, queen of England
Sir Arthur Gorges
Fulke Greville
John Harington
Sir John Harington
Sir Christopher Hatton
Sir Thomas Heneage
Mary Herbert, countess of Pembroke
Sir Edward Hoby
Saint Philip Howard, earl of Arundel
Sir Henry Lee
Sir Walter Mildmay
Henry Noel
Sir Walter Ralegh
Lady Elizabeth Russell
Thomas Sackville, Lord Buckhurst
Sir Philip Sidney

Sir Robert Sidney
Ferdinando Stanley, Lord Strange, fifth earl of Derby
Gilbert Talbot, seventh earl of Shrewsbury
Dr. Thomas Wilson
Sir John Wolley

Reliable editions of the verse written by these courtiers as courtiers are available for only a few of them—for Gorges, the Sidney brothers, and most recently, Sackville. In order to make the poetry discussed in Part I more fully and accurately accessible to the reader, I include in Part II full editions of the poems of the earls of Cumberland, Derby, Essex, and Oxford (Clifford, Stanley, Devereux, and DeVere), Sir Edward Dyer, Lady Mary Cheke, Sir Francis Drake, Sir Thomas Heneage, and Henry Noel. In addition I provide new or newly edited texts by Roger Ascham, William Cecil, Queen Elizabeth, Sir John Harington, Sir Edward Hoby, the earl of Arundel, Sir Henry Lee, Sir Walter Ralegh, Lady Elizabeth Russell, Dr. Thomas Wilson, and Sir John Wolley. Part II is thus a representative anthology of Elizabethan courtier verse and a source of new biographical information about many of the poets it treats, with the additional advantage of keeping so much necessary but often bulky material from interrupting the narrative of Part I.

Within its strictly defined chronological limits this study nevertheless surveys only courtier verse, a significant component of the poetry at Elizabeth's court but not the only one. That institution was, of course, entertained by professional, out-of-court poets such as Gascoigne, Peele, and Shakespeare, as well as by writers such as Richard Edwards and John Lyly whose genuine ties to the court failed to elevate them to courtier status. The relationship of courtier verse to other poetry known at court, or to the overall development of Elizabethan poetry, receives only general or passing mention here. The courtiers' output alone is quite enough for one book. With their contribution defined, however, it becomes possible to study in detail the relationships between their works and those of other writers.

PART I

A Critical History of Elizabethan Courtier Verse

1

The Social Organization of the Court

George Peele's *Polyhymnia* provides a detailed, eyewitness account of the 1590 Accession Day festivities honoring the commencement of Queen Elizabeth's thirty-third regnal year. Peele describes "Yoong Essex, that thrice honorable Earle," dressed as was

> . . . all his companie in funerall blacke,
> As if he mourn'd to thinke of him he mist,
> Sweete Sydney, fairest shepheard of our greene,
> Well lettred Warriour, whose successor he
> In love and Armes had ever vowed to be.[1]

The sentiments that Peele attributed to Essex are touching but neither true nor appropriate in light of the actual circumstances. The earl was not mourning for Sidney, he was responding to the queen's intense displeasure over his secret marriage to Philip's widow, Frances. Essex had become indeed Sidney's successor in love, but in doing so he elicited a royal tantrum that was hardly a court secret. Sir Robert Sidney was warned that he had incurred "her Majesties Indignacion, in respect of your Privitie to the Mariage of my Lord of Essex," and in early November the court postmaster, John Stanhope, had observed that if the queen "could overcome her passion against my Lord of Essex for his marriage, no doubt she would be much the quieter." Essex's grief-stricken display in the tiltyard apparently placated Elizabeth, for within a few days of the tournament he was said to have regained her favor.[2] Peele misinterpreted the show because he was not a courtier nor in any demon-

1. David H. Horne, *The Life and Minor Works of George Peele*, 235–36.
2. Edmund Lodge, *Illustrations of British History, Biography, and Manners*, 2:422, 419–20; Arthur Collins, *Letters and Memorials of State*, 1:312. Stanhope wrote on December 9 that the queen's "favour holdeth in reasonable good terms to the Earl of Essex" (Lodge, *Illustrations*, 2:433).

strable way a member of the court circle; thus, even a firsthand account of events at court will not necessarily report what actually happened if the witness did not belong to that elite for whose sake the court existed.

Similarly, recent studies of the style, meaning, and function of poetry at the Elizabethan court rely upon George Puttenham's *Arte of English Poesie* as a virtually oracular guide to all such matters.[3] Unlike the commercial, out-of-court poet George Peele, Puttenham was an aristocrat whose wife, Lady Windsor, held the rank of baroness. Yet he held no court office and his social standing there remains ambiguous. The only courtier known even to mention the *Arte* is Sir John Harington, whose assessment is decidedly negative. Harington rejects the book's central premise, that poetry is an art to be learned, by invoking the opinion of his fellow courtier Sidney, who argued that it was instead a gift of nature. In further support of his rebuttal Harington scornfully observes that Puttenham had "a very slender gift" in poetry himself.[4] The *Arte* then, although written by a gentleman with definite if unspecifiable court connections, does not describe with comprehensive authority how poetry was understood at court nor how it functioned there. The problem is that any Elizabethan could write for or about the court, and while some out-of-court writings reflect a secondhand or temporary understanding of actual court conditions, the majority do not. Meanwhile, however, an authentic literature of the court developed within the institution itself, produced by courtiers whose social status and attendance upon their sovereign gave them firsthand knowledge of the establishment. Their writings reflect the court not as the royal household in general, but as the particular social milieu within it that dominated national patronage and the exercise of political and economic power. Thus, to find out about the actual place of poetry or anything else at the Elizabethan court, it is first necessary

3. Louis Adrian Montrose terms the *Arte* "the central text of Elizabethan courtly poetics" ("Of Gentlemen and Shepherds: The Politics of Elizabethan Pastoral Form," 421). Daniel Javitch relies heavily on Puttenham's testimony in his *Poetry and Courtliness in Renaissance England* but wisely restricts his study to the theoretical rather than actual apprehension of poetry within the court (4). He is less cautious about Puttenham's reliability in "The Impure Motives of Elizabethan Poetry" (225–38), arguing that the book was designed to instruct neophytes in successful courtiership. Heinrich F. Plett seeks insight into court culture from Deloney, Dekker, Gascoigne, and Shakespeare as well as Puttenham in "Aesthetic Constituents in the Courtly Culture of Renaissance England."
4. "A Preface, or Rather a Brief Apologie of Poetrie," in Ariosto, *Orlando Furioso*, 2.

to study that institution and above all its social structure in order to identify the sources of authentic testimony.

Despite the vigor of the "new historicism" in literary studies, such understanding is not readily at hand, in part because of the lack of resources in related disciplines. Professional historians, as G. R. Elton points out, have not yet reached agreement on such basic questions as what the terms *court* and *courtier* mean; with regard to Tudor court personnel, moreover, "their demography has not been written, and even their population . . . has not been defined." R. Malcolm Smuts acknowledges the social dimensions of courtiership in his work on the early Stuart period by including within his definition of the court those "individuals with active social connections to the royal entourage even if they did not enjoy a household post."[5] By focusing more narrowly upon individuals with or without office who personally attended their sovereign on a social plane above that of mere servants of the court, I believe it possible to identify the Elizabethan courtier class as it was understood by contemporaries. These are the issues that must be addressed in order to develop a methodology for understanding what poetry meant or "did" at court.

Studies of European court culture have generally accepted the royal household as a synonym for the royal court, and from an administrative viewpoint this definition is probably workable enough.[6] It is less useful however to students of cultural history because it does not differentiate the mechanisms for dispensing influence and rewards that made the court the center of national culture. In this sense, Queen Elizabeth's court was not her entire household, for that institution was organized into units of widely disparate social rank. Its foremost officer in terms of precedence was the Lord Steward, who supervised twenty departments responsible for the physical well-being of the court. The names of these departments—the pantry, bakehouse, laundry, and woodyard, for instance—indicate the "below stairs" functions headed by the Lord Steward. Above stairs, the Lord Chamberlain's staff attended to the immediate needs of the monarch and courtiers. Waiters, carvers, and sewers

5. G. R. Elton, "Tudor Government: The Points of Contact III. The Court," 211–12. R. Malcolm Smuts, *Court Culture and the Origins of a Royalist Tradition in Early Stuart England*, 10n.

6. Elton, "Tudor Government," 217; Neville Williams, "The Tudors: Three Contrasts in Personality," 147. C. Stephen Jaeger likewise equates the court with the sovereign's household in his study of the development of continental courtliness, *The Origins of Courtliness: Civilizing Trends and the Formation of Courtly Ideals, 939–1210*, 19.

(servers) arranged and served the meals. Sergeants at arms, yeomen of the guard, and gentlemen pensioners kept order at court and guarded the sovereign. Chaplains provided spiritual leadership, assisted by the gentlemen and children of the Chapel Royal. Under the Tudors, of course, chapel personnel also came to perform musical and dramatic entertainments unrelated to their religious duties. The instrumental musicians, sixty to seventy strong by the end of Elizabeth's reign, also provided entertainment for the court.[7] The third great household officer, the Master of the Horse, was primarily responsible for the royal stables, through which he had charge of the queen's coach, litter, and her sixteen footmen, in addition to the horses and their equipment.

The thousand-odd employees of these household departments served the queen with widely varied duties, yet few among them enjoyed regular, face-to-face contact with her. Elizabeth spent nearly all of her time at court in one of two locations within the suite of state rooms, galleries, and private apartments known collectively as the chamber. On ceremonial occasions she sat enthroned in the Presence Chamber where she could be seen, at least, by members of her household staff and anyone else who had gained admission to this part of the court.[8] The Queen was likewise visible, and at times approachable, during her processions to and from chapel services at court. But she spent most of her time in the Privy Chamber, a suite of household accommodations which varied from palace to palace but which always included a main salon and bedchamber, plus withdrawing rooms and a privy gallery, garden, or terrace.[9] Here the queen conducted business, received suits, and socialized with her most intimate attendants: the chief officers of state and household, members of the Privy Chamber staff, royal favorites, and friends. "Going up to court," therefore, conferred little if any social or tangible advantage except upon those who could enter the Privy Chamber to gain personal access to the queen and her closest associates. These persons alone held a status that linked them directly to their sovereign; their rank enabled them, for example, to prefer suits to their fellow courtiers and to Elizabeth herself. Socially and politically, the retinue that waited upon the queen in her chamber was the court. The remainder of the household staff were servants of the

7. E. K. Chambers, *The Elizabethan Stage*, 1:49.
8. Chambers concludes that anyone with a right to attend court could gain admission to the Presence Chamber (*Stage*, 1:14).
9. David Loades, *The Tudor Court*, 45.

court but not courtiers in any meaningful sense of that word. Many household employees kept families and servants at court, in addition to which the precincts of the royal household were routinely infiltrated by numerous interlopers and hangers-on, who were nevertheless denied access to the sovereign and her personal associates.[10] The distinction between Elizabeth's personal associates and the rest of her entourage is acknowledged in a contemporary dispatch which notes that "The Court is at Nonsuch, and the household is near Oatlands, expecting the next remove to be to Otelands."[11]

Elizabeth's monarchical style has been termed "distant" by David Starkey; she avoided familiar mingling with her subjects, and she strictly controlled access to her Privy Chamber.[12] As a result, the social boundaries between genuine courtiers and hangers-on were sharply defined. When Ralegh began to work his way back into royal favor in 1597 after five years of banishment from court, it was noted that "he once spake with the Queen, but not private; comes seldom to court, and then but to the presence" (that is, the Presence Chamber). After gaining his pardon, however, he was said to come "boldly to the Privy Chamber as he was wont."[13] Similarly, when Elizabeth banished Francis Bacon in 1593 for speaking in Parliament against the subsidy bill, the earl of Essex headed the campaign to reinstate him. Essex's account of one audience with Elizabeth defines precisely the courtier's status which Francis had lost and now had to regain. "Your access, she saith, is as much as you can look for. If it had been in the King her father's time, a less offence than that would have made a man be banished his presence for ever. But you

10. For infiltration of the court by "vagabond and other idle persons," including "boys and rascals," see Paul L. Hughes and James F. Larkin, *Tudor Royal Proclamations*, nos. 483, 712, 762. Number 712, a proclamation of July 1589, forbade soldiers and mariners returning from the Portuguese expedition from entering the court. A similar proclamation the next month protests that they had "presumed to repair to her majesty's court" all the same.

11. Richard Broughton to Richard Bagot, May 1593, HMC, 4th report, 336. Contemporary lists of government offices recognize the social dichotomy by grouping the various household departments under the heading, "The Queen's Court or Household" (Society of Antiquaries, *A Collection of Ordinances and Regulations for the Government of the Royal Household* [London, 1790], 250; BL, Add. MSS 34395, f. 82, and 31030, f. 12v). Royal proclamations separate the queen's chamber from her household but then lump both together as the court (Hughes and Larkin, *Proclamations*, nos. 755, 750).

12. David Starkey, "Introduction: Court History in Perspective," 9; Pam Wright, "A Change in Direction: The Ramifications of a Female Household, 1558–1603," 159–60.

13. HMC, De L'Isle and Dudley, 2:244, 286.

did come to the Court when you would yourself; and she should precipitate too much from being highly displeased with you to give you near access, such as she shows only to those that she favors extraordinarily."[14] Presumably, Bacon had been readmitted to the chamber, there to wait upon Elizabeth. The earl's words imply, however, Bacon's restricted attendance in the Presence Chamber, where the queen might choose to recognize him on those semi-public occasions when she presided there. He was apparently excluded from the Privy Chamber, where courtiers fully in the queen's grace enjoyed regular contact with her.

A number of officeholders were routinely in such close contact with the queen as to be ipso facto courtiers. The Privy Council, for example, traveled with the court and met in or near its privy lodgings. Councillors in attendance were thus always courtiers by virtue of their access to Elizabeth even though the principal secretary was formally responsible for communications between queen and council. Many councillors, moreover, held other posts requiring their personal attendance on the sovereign; the Lord Chamberlain and comptroller of the household, for instance, were always council members, along with the Lord Chancellor and Lord Admiral. Elizabeth appointed no one to so weighty a position as the Privy Council before they had established a personal rapport with her, and there is ample evidence that councillors other than the secretary conferred with her privately on a regular basis. It is worth noting in this regard that when Elizabeth finally appointed a clergyman to her Privy Council in 1586 she chose her "little black husband," John Whitgift, archbishop of Canterbury, who had been her confidential spiritual adviser for many years.

Other state officeholders who were Elizabeth's near associates included the Lord Chancellor, as keeper of the Great Seal; the Lord Treasurer, the keeper of the Privy Seal; one or more principal secretaries; and the chancellors of the Exchequer and duchy of Lancaster. Officers of the common law, on the other hand, were not ordinarily courtiers, although exceptions might be found among the masters of requests, who traveled with the court and appear on every bouge of court document (records of food, fuel, and candle allowances). But they did not normally participate in the New Year's gift exchanges, nor did the attorney-general, solicitor-general, nor the chief justices of the queen's bench and common pleas.

Within the household a number of chamber offices tended to

14. James Spedding, *The Letters and the Life of Francis Bacon*, 1:254.

confer courtier status automatically. In addition to the Lord Chamberlain, the Vice-Chamberlain, treasurer of the chamber, and captain of the guard were always highly favored courtiers. The same is true for the ladies, gentlewomen, gentlemen, grooms, and gentleman usher of the Privy Chamber, along with the queen's cupbearer and sewers (servers). The royal physicians, who were first added to the Privy Chamber staff by Queen Mary, retained their prestige at court under Elizabeth, as did the maids of honor, who attended the queen in her Privy Chamber although they were formally stationed in the Presence Chamber.[15] It is tempting to assume that all Privy Chamber officers were courtiers, but that was not quite the case. The joiners of the Privy Chamber earned more than eighteen pounds per year, which compares favorably with the twenty-pound fees of the grooms and gentlewomen chamberers,[16] yet the joiners were socially invisible and there is no evidence that they enjoyed personal contact with their sovereign. The same is true for Robert Balthrope, who was for decades sergeant surgeon of the Privy Chamber.[17]

Within the chamber at large, only a few offices appear to have facilitated courtiership. As were the maids of honor, the gentlemen pensioners were stationed in the Presence Chamber. Fifty of the one hundred members of their band served at court on a rotating basis throughout the year. Their social status was rather above that of most other chamber officers, for only gentlemen of means, able to provide three horses and two servants, were eligible for admission to the band.[18] They amounted to an elite bodyguard which accompanied Elizabeth wherever she went, and they participated in large numbers in the tournaments that entertained the court on the queen's Accession Day and other special occasions. Some of the pensioners at least were prosperous courtiers, to judge from the significant forms of crown patronage bestowed on them. Several received patents of monopoly, the kind of lucrative gift generally,

15. Loades, *Tudor Court*, 56; Wright, "Change," 151. Wright presents a valuable survey of the salaried members of the Privy Chamber staff, demonstrating their usefulness in securing patronage.

16. James and Henry Waller succeeded William Jasper as joiners of the Privy Chamber circa 1595 at a fee of twelve pence per day (PRO, SP 12/255/37). For fees in the Privy Chamber see, inter alia, BL, Lansdowne MS, 3/87, ff. 162–63.

17. Balthrope was appointed to his post by letters patent of May 10, 1559, and was listed among those entitled to remove with the household on progress as late as August of 1589 (BL, Lansdowne MSS 59/22, f. 43v, and 59/25); PRO, LC 2/4 (4), ff. 47, 63v).

18. William Tighe, "The Gentlemen Pensioners in Elizabethan Politics and Government," 17.

but as we shall see not always, reserved for prominent favorites. Thus Brian Annesley, who held two annuities from the crown worth nearly one hundred pounds, received a patent to import steel in August of 1593.[19] Thomas Bedingfield, another royal annuitant, shared a playing card monopoly with his fellow pensioner Ralph Bowes,[20] while pensioners Henry MacWilliam and Robert Colshill shared the patent to write and engross "writs of subpoena in the court of Chancery" with Thomas Gorges and his brother, Nathaniel. Gorges's appearance here is significant because, as a groom of the Privy Chamber, he was indisputably a courtier who enjoyed Elizabeth's particular favor throughout the last two decades of her reign.[21] Other pensioners also appear to have been courtiers, yet it is probably safest to judge their credentials individually rather than as a given of their office.

A third Presence Chamber entity, the esquires for the body, maintained a somewhat ambiguous relationship with the queen. Traditionally, the four esquires were intimate personal servants of English kings. They dressed and undressed their sovereign and slept in his bedchamber. Naturally, the ladies of the bedchamber usurped these duties under Queen Mary and Queen Elizabeth. Each evening, however, control of the court above stairs was relinquished to the esquires during a ritual called the Order of All Night. Thereafter until morning, these officers exercised a command above stairs equal to that of the Lord Chamberlain.[22]

Despite the distancing from the sovereign which a female ruler entailed, at least the more entrenched esquires for the body seem to have been courtiers. Roger Manners and Sir James Marven, or Martin, for example, were esquires from Elizabeth's coronation to her funeral. In 1576, Walsingham assured the Earl of Rutland that "No man can give better information as to how things pass in the Court than Mr Roger Manners." Manners several times described himself as a courtier, and he attested that he had personally moved a suit to the queen in 1587 on behalf of his nephew, the earl of Rutland. As late as 1597 Rowland Whyte, Sir Robert Sidney's confidential agent at court, attempted to enlist Manners's support for Sidney's suit to become Lord Warden of the Cinque Ports. Manners, however, had

19. BL, Cotton Titus MS B.3, f. 233; William Hyde Price, *The English Patents of Monopoly*, 143.

20. Price, *English Patents*, 17.

21. PRO, SP 12/224/91; SP 246/53.

22. Samuel Pegge, *Curialia; or, An Historical Account of Some Branches of the Royal Household*, 12, 16–17.

already pledged his support to another, and he excused himself from a dinner party at the Lord Treasurer's to inform Whyte that the queen had named Lord Cobham to the post.[23] Roger's status as a courtier looks fairly certain, and the same is probably true for Marven, along with such ordinary (that is, regularly attending) esquires as Henry and Robert Knollys, Oliver and John St. John, and Sir Edmund Carey.

Confusion arises, however, in the apparent creation of extraordinary and ad hoc esquires for the body. Thus Ralegh had been appointed to the post extraordinary as early as February 3, 1581,[24] almost a year before he came to the queen's personal attention. In 1595, Robert Parry recorded in his diary that John Salisbury had been appointed esquire for the body to her majesty, and he is referred to as the queen's servant in a Privy Council letter appointing him deputy lieutenant for the county of Denbigh. Similarly, a herald's visitation styles John Lyly, the playwright and author of *Euphues*, "Esq. of the body to Q. Eliz."[25] The problem is that none of these appointments is confirmed by records of court service. The names of Ralegh, Salisbury, and Lyly do not appear among the esquires on the surviving household subsidy rolls nor among those who served at the queen's funeral. Instead, the funeral list names more than a dozen esquires for the body, only five of whom seem to have been ordinary to the office.[26] What this apparently means is that promising hangers-on at court might be appointed esquires extraordinary. Such sinecures without wages allowed them to call themselves her majesty's servants. The list of esquires on folio 47v of the funeral accounts probably names all those who were ordinary, extraordinary, and perhaps those who were esquires in reversion. The remaining esquires in this document seem to have been ad hoc officers who served only on the day of the funeral.

One last Presence Chamber office warrants a glance because it reveals the extent to which even a lowly sounding post might be sought out because it provided access to the queen and her nearest associates. In May of 1597 Sir William Cornwallis wrote Sir Robert

23. HMC, Rutland, 1:108, 213, 153 ("I intend by God's grace to be a courtier till after Christmas"), 185, 325; HMC, De L'Isle and Dudley, 2:254, and see Lisle Cecil John's "Roger Manners, Elizabethan Courtier" (57–84) for a summary of his career as Esquire.

24. Agnes M. C. Latham, "A Birth-Date for Sir Walter Ralegh," 245.

25. Carleton Brown, ed., *Poems by Sir John Salusbury and Robert Chester*, xviii; Albert Feuillerat, *John Lyly*, 504.

26. PRO, LC 2/4 (4), ff. 47v, 63–64.

Cecil "that if god dispose of my old cosen," Francis Cornwallis, groom porter of the Presence Chamber, the post might go either to "the younger" Cornwallis, or to him and Sir William jointly. Cornwallis waxes eloquent upon the advantages of such service: "I may have a poor chamber in Court, and a fire, which my years grow fast upon, and a title to bring a pair of cards in to the privy chamber at ten of the clock at night. So I may be about her majesty, I care not to be Groom of the Scullery."[27] The groom porter apparently had opportunity to associate with the queen in her Privy Chamber, at least on idle evenings when card playing was in vogue. Sir William had been, by his own account, her majesty's servant at court for twenty-six years without office, fee, or suit, and his name does appear on the New Year's rolls in 1581, 1583, 1584, and several times after the date of his petition. When he did sue for an office, this knight was content to share the groom porter's post because it provided regular access to Elizabeth.

To some extent, any office at court that entailed at least occasional direct contact with the queen held out the promise of courtiership. Certainly the pensioners, esquires for the body, and the groom porter had reasonable opportunities to become bona fide courtiers. As we survey the lesser officers of the Presence Chamber, however, and move through the great chamber down to the Lord Steward's department, the likelihood of royal recognition dwindles. If any groom or yeoman did ascend from the scullery to a courtier's social status in the Privy Chamber, the record of that Cinderella story has yet to be discovered and would even so be a most unusual way to preferment.[28] Only the great offices of court and state seem to have guaranteed courtier rank, along with most of the appointments in the Privy Chamber. Beyond these instances, office is an uncertain criterion for determining courtiership. The remaining criteria, furthermore, are so ambiguous that no one of them alone can be used to identify a courtier beyond all doubt.

27. PRO, SP 12/263/75.
28. Sir Robert Naunton affirmed "that the Queen in her choice never took into her favor a mere new man or a mechanic" (*Fragmenta Regalia*, 72). Considerable social elevation was possible, however, in the course of several generations of household service—witness the minor chamber positions held by Lord Burghley's grandfather and father. Members of the Zin-zan (Alexander) family were equerries, grooms, and yeomen of the stables from the reign of Henry VIII, but under Elizabeth they participated in court tournaments and received a patent of monopoly in 1594, and they received a knighthood under King James. See E. K. Chambers, *Sir Henry Lee: An Elizabethan Portrait*, 208, and Price, *English Patents*, 144.

Many Elizabethans who held no household office regularly came up to court and associated personally with the queen. These privileged few belonged to what Wallace MacCaffrey terms the "politically active class": peers, knights, and the more prominent representatives of the county gentry. With the queen and her chief officers of state, this elite wielded all the real power in the land, although they may have numbered only some twenty-five hundred souls.[29] Those who sought access to Elizabeth without belonging to this class might very well fail of their purpose. Thus, a "very great captain," a protégé of the earl of Leicester, was denied entrance to the Privy Chamber because "he was neither very well known nor a sworn servant to the Queen." Leicester complained to Elizabeth, but she had charged her gentleman usher "to look precisely to all admissions into the privy chamber," and she upheld his decision, much to the earl's chagrin.[30] The criteria for admission to the royal presence, then, were sworn service to her highness or the condition of being "well known." This last phrase had two overlapping meanings. Someone might be known to wait upon the queen with her personal permission or else command a sufficiently elevated social rank to be admitted to her presence. Without such credentials, and despite the ease with which all kinds of people entered the precinct of the court, access to Elizabeth herself was difficult or impossible.

For many, perhaps most of those qualified for courtiership, actual attendance at court was so sporadic that they did not consider themselves members of the court circle. The earl of Huntingdon observed in August of 1571 that, while he resided in the vicinity of the court in and around London, he was "but a rare courtyar," meaning that he seldom exercised his prerogative of joining Elizabeth and her associates at court.[31] Sir Francis Vere was likewise too infrequently at court to be styled a courtier, but when there, "no man had more of the Queen's favor," for she "would court this gentleman as soon as he appeared in her presence."[32] This accords well enough with Vere's own account of his reception at court after the "Islands Voyage" of 1597. At his arrival, he supposed that "her Majesty, after her most gracious manner, would talk and question with me concerning the late journey." He adds, "Because I would use no bodies help to give me accesse to her Majesty, . . . I resolved to shew my self to her

29. Wallace MacCaffrey, "Place and Patronage in Elizabethan Politics," 99.
30. Naunton, *Fragmenta*, 41.
31. HMC, Rutland, 1:95.
32. Naunton, *Fragmenta*, 84.

Majesty when she came into the garden; where so soon as she set her gracious eye upon me, she called me to her and questioned with me concerning the journey."[33] On the other hand, Sir Robert Cecil's observation that "My Lord Cobham (since his jorney into Flanders,) is a courtyer" marks Cobham's resumption of his regular court attendance which began in the mid–1590s.[34]

The courtiers who figure in this study were not the occasional sort such as Vere and Huntingdon but the ranking officeholders and that relatively permanent group of courtiers as represented by Lord Cobham whose periodic sojourns at court formed, in aggregate, Elizabethan court society. These individuals spent an appreciable amount of time, often traceable for weeks or months per year, attending court. Those who were household officers necessarily saw the court as their central occupation, yet even courtiers without office looked to the court as an important focus of their economic well-being and social activity. The existence of a regular courtier class was acknowledged by Dudley Carleton when he contrasted his temporary courtiership with that of the habitués accordingly: "I haue beene a Courtier all this weeke. . . . The Queen hath so played the goodefellow amongst vs these hollie dayes at dancings and musick, that the Courtiers (which make her lookes theyr Kalenders), made a coniecture by her goode disposition of goode newes owt of Irland."[35] Carleton's social status allowed him to enter the queen's presence, but he distinguished his temporary sojourn at court from the behavior of those who normally waited there. The continuity of courtiership is affirmed both by many individual life records and by such official documents as that presented in an appendix to Penry Williams's valuable study of the court, a listing of "Principall Gentlmen of value and service that have ben and are usually in Court."[36]

The key criterion in all matters of courtiership was Elizabeth's personal recognition and acceptance. Charles Blount came up to

---

33. Sir Francis Vere, *The Commentaries of Sr Francis Vere*, sig. K1v.

34. John Maclean, ed., *Letters From Sir Robert Cecil to Sir George Carew*, 24. HMC, De L'Isle and Dudley, 2:236, 265–67, 279, 286, 290, 298. Cecil named Cobham among four "other of our Courtiers" in a letter of July 1597 (PRO, SP 12/264/54).

35. PRO, SP 12/274/86, March 29, 1600.

36. Williams, "Court and Polity under Elizabeth I," 282, from PRO, SP 12/269/46–47. A companion list also printed by Williams enumerates "Principall Gentlemen that dwell usually in their contreis." Williams dates the lists to 1598, noting that a contradictory overlapping of some names on both of them qualifies their usefulness. The "in Court" list names the courtier poets Dyer, Gorges, Greville, Ralegh, Sir Henry Lee, and Sir Robert Sidney.

court while still a younger brother of the Lord Mountjoy, yet he caught the queen's eye, received her hand to kiss, and was invited to attend the court.[37] She did much the same for such courtiers as Hatton, Ralegh, John Packington, and Edward Dyer. Presumably, she could have elevated anyone to courtier rank, although she seems never to have admitted anyone below gentry status. And she was quite capable of suspending or demoting her courtiers; Bacon's repulse was equaled or surpassed by the exile she imposed upon many prominent favorites. The sovereign exercised final control over all who waited on her, noble or commoner, and whether or not they held office at court.

On a case-by-case basis, the most reliable means of ascertaining courtiership are firsthand, contemporary accounts of personal association with the queen. In the absence of eyewitness testimony, other criteria must be used to single out the privileged few at court. The pet names Elizabeth bestowed on many of those nearest to her can provide telling evidence of courtiership, albeit most recipients of these nicknames were so prominent at court that their status is beyond question. A few favorites accumulated multiple names: Hatton was her mutton, sheep, bellwether, and lids; Whitgift, her white gift as well as her little black husband. Sir Robert Cecil was her pygmy and her elf. Familiar forms for given names generally indicate the same degree of intimacy as pet names. Elizabeth addressed Frances, countess of Hertford, as "Good Francke" in a letter consoling her for her husband's commitment to the Tower.[38] Sir Thomas Heneage wrote Burghley in 1590 that the queen was loath to allow Sir Edward Norris to take up his command in the Low Countries, "whose service (it seems to me) she likes better to use here than abroad." When, a few years later, Elizabeth wrote Norris an encouraging letter in her own hand it began, simply, "Ned"; he was appointed sewer to the queen by 1598.[39] These nicknames indicate warm, personal ties between Elizabeth and some of her favorite subjects; coupled with attendance at court, they are ordinarily sure signs of courtiership.

For some, courtier status was facilitated or assured by birth.

37. Naunton, *Fragmenta*, 80.
38. PRO, SP 12/254/54.
39. John Lothrop Motley, *History of the United Netherlands*, 3:252. PRO, E 179/70/107. Norris also appears as a sewer to the queen at her funeral (PRO, LC 2/4(4), f. 47v). The queen dined with him at his house at Englefield on progress in September 1601 (Norman Egbert McClure, *The Letters of John Chamberlain to Dudley Carleton*, 1:131).

Peers of the realm were automatically eligible to become courtiers; indeed, it might even be demanded of them. Ferdinando Stanley, heir to the earldom of Derby, was personally summoned to court by Elizabeth "to be fashioned in good manners, mete for one such as he is, and hereafter shall be by course of nature, mete to serve the Realme."[40] The crown retained a special interest in young Stanley because of his family's viable claim to the throne, but this does not alter the fact that the nobility owed their attendance upon the sovereign at court. Even so, nobility alone did not guarantee courtier rank, since a number of peers did not frequent the court. The earl of Shrewsbury seldom got permission to wait upon Elizabeth during the long years he served as guardian of the Queen of Scots. William, Lord De La Warr, and Henry, Lord Morley, avoided the court because of their devotion to Catholicism, just as Baron Vaux and Lord Henry Howard avoided it at times for financial reasons.[41] Accordingly, noble poets were not necessarily courtier poets, and their credentials must be evaluated individually.

Of the remaining criteria for identifying courtiers, the most useful are the New Year's gift exchanges, full or relatively complete records of which have survived for twenty-two of Elizabeth's forty-five New Year's days.[42] These rolls name those persons who were, with a few exceptions, actually known to the queen, so that an alleged courtier whose name never appears on these lists must be viewed with some suspicion. Yet these documents do not identify courtiers alone, and so must be used with caution. Lawrence Stone characterized these records as naming the queen's closest associates, the titled nobility, and great officers of state, the rest being "courtiers pure and simple."[43] Stone observed, however, that Sir Horatio Palavicino belonged to neither of these categories although his name appears on several of the rolls. Unfortunately, the number of other exceptions makes this body of evidence as difficult to use accurately as it is invaluable for identifying those who held undisputed courtier status.

40. William Murdin, *A Collection of State Papers*, 2:124–25.
41. William, third Lord Vaux (d. 1595), wrote Burghley on February 18, 1593, that he had pawned his Parliament robes, yet he came to London when summoned "raggedlie suted and clothed, unfittedst to geve duetiefull attendance on Royall presence" (Sir Henry Ellis, *Original Letters Illustrative of English History*, 3d series, 4:109–10). Howard excused himself from attending court in a letter to Burghley of October 23, 1571, BL, Cotton Titus MS C.6, f. 13v.
42. See the List of Sources and Abbreviations for a complete list of these sources.
43. Lawrence Stone, *An Elizabethan: Horatio Palavicino*, 25.

One prominent group of persons appearing on every gift list can be largely dismissed from the beginning. The Elizabethan bishops always participated in the exchange, yet if they followed the court their presence there was strangely ignored by both the queen and the chief retailers of court gossip. Archbishop Whitgift, of course, was a courtier clergyman during his years on the Privy Council and quite possibly even earlier. The queen's high almoners were bishops who spent at least some significant part of their time at court. Richard Fletcher, bishop of Worcester, urged his translation to the see of London in 1594 on grounds that he would then be near the court "where his presence had become habitual and looked for," undoubtedly because of his years as royal almoner. He was, however, "one of the few" bishops appointed by the queen "to enjoy her real favour and to gain rapid promotion" as a royal favorite. The Elizabethan bishops generally "had ceased to compete for social status with the nobility and leading courtiers but were more closely comparable with the country gentry among whom they worked as diocesans."[44] The bishops' titles on the New Year's gift rolls are ordinarily as impersonal as their relations with their sovereign. They did not follow the court nor maintain a close rapport with Elizabeth.

For some of the lords temporal, as for many of the lords spiritual, the annual New Year's exchange was an obligation of rank rather than proof of courtiership. Roger Woode wrote to the earl of Rutland at Newark Castle on January 7, 1575, that he had given the Lord Chamberlain twenty pounds as New Year's gifts to the queen from the earl and his countess. Woode added that Mr. Manners (no doubt the esquire for the body) "thought it good that you should give 10 *l.* apiece as you did last year." Lord Willoughby dated a letter from Berwick December 28, 1598, and although he could not have been at court for the New Year's exchange, his name appears on the 1599 gift roll as "Governor of Barwick."[45] The examples could be multiplied; they show that for some Elizabethan peers, the New Year's ceremony was an obligation which could be carried out in absentia. Most of these lords and ladies were, no doubt, habitués of the court, yet their names on these lists do not automatically assure us of that.

Meanwhile, many persons who habitually attended court participated in the New Year's exchanges without being genuine courtiers. These included some of the queen's personal servants who

44. DNB, s.v. "Fletcher, Richard"; Felicity Heal, *Of Prelates and Princes*, 240, 244.
45. HMC, Rutland, 1:102–3; HMC, Salisbury, 8:523.

maintained their subordinate social status unlike, say, the Privy Chamber attendants who were ladies or gentlemen as well as servants of the queen. The master cook of the queen's privy kitchen and the sergeant of the pastry are two such officers who regularly appear on the gift rolls and whose duties were supervised by the Lord Steward, not the Lord Chamberlain. In addition, the queen's laundress, many of the instrumental musicians, out-of-court officeholders, and London tradesmen exchanged gifts with Elizabeth. They are classified among the gentlemen and gentlewomen on the rolls, although their names are not usually preceded with a "Mr" or "Mrs" (master or mistress). As MacCaffrey noted with regard to the 1567 household subsidy roll, contemporary records used these titles to indicate the social rank of those who were not otherwise titled. The New Year's lists that observe this distinction usually place the masters and mistresses first in their respective categories, thus indicating the social preeminence of these persons over the untitled participants whose names follow. Unfortunately, some rolls obscure these distinctions by making nearly everyone, or no one, master or mistress.[46] Where the distinctions are made, however, they probably do indicate social status with some accuracy.

George Webster, the master cook, provides an interesting test case of this principle. He appears as plain George Webster on the gift lists of 1562, 1563, 1564, 1565, and 1567, and he probably participated in the exchange in other years for which records are lacking until his death in 1574. His rewards from the crown included a lease to the Chapel of Saint Sepulchre at York, and it is clear from his will that he held other crown leases in that county.[47] Webster's will also reveals much about his social status and the persons with whom he associated at court. Although he undoubtedly worked with his hands, he was nevertheless armigerous; he left to his son a gold ring with his arms engraved on it, and these are neatly tricked in the margin of his will. The bequests for his five daughters were to be paid out of income from his Yorkshire leases. His wife received half his property, including his wagon and three wagon horses. Webster had accumulated ample worldly pelf, yet there is a definite belowstairs tincture to his last will and testament. No one of courtier status is mentioned in this document. William Cocks, yeoman of

---

46. MacCaffrey, "Place and Patronage," 106. Thus John Stanhope and Edward Bashe go untitled in the 1575 list, are masters in 1576, but are demoted again to untitled status in 1578.

47. PRO, SP 12/166, f. 4; PRO, PCC, 37 Martyn.

the queen's pantry, received a furred gown; William Hearne, sergeant painter, a gray horse; and Lewis Stockett, surveyor of the queen's works, a leather jerkin embroidered with gold and pearls. These are the most prestigious recipients of Webster's bequests, his friends and peers. Webster was a prosperous royal servant whose social status fell short of that held by such fellow crown servants as the grooms of the Privy Chamber, sewers, and cupbearers to the queen.

Surveyor of the works Stockett also exchanged New Year's gifts with the queen in 1565, yet the will he drew up in 1578 indicates a social status no more elevated than Webster's. Although he owned houses in Fleet Street, Barking, and Westminster, with other lands and leases, no one mentioned in his will was even associated with the court.[48] As with so many other royal servants, Webster and Stockett were in positions to become courtiers; the social transformation was entirely within the queen's power. But for lack of evidence that they attained this rank, their appearance on the New Year's gift lists indicates only that Elizabeth admitted them to this ceremony along with their betters. The same appears to be true for the sergeants of the pastry and the musicians who are regularly named on the rolls, along with many others classified as gentlemen and gentlewomen.

Many of the participants in those ambiguous categories undoubtedly were courtiers. The queen's physicians, for example, left wills in marked contrast to those of such men as Webster and Stockett. Dr. Richard Master, a regular on the gift lists from the beginning of the reign until his death in 1588, left bequests to Mr. John Stanhope and to five grooms of the Privy Chamber, while naming Robert Cecil the overseer of his will. The social status of the court physicians generally is indicated by their exemption from certain provisions of the sumptuary laws.[49] Mistress Blanche Parry provides another contrasting example of the mixed social strata represented among the gentlemen and gentlewomen named on the New Year's gift rolls. As a lady of the queen's bedchamber from the coronation until her death in 1596, she regularly participated in the New Year's exchanges. Mrs. Parry's will rattles off eight bequests before mentioning anyone below the rank of a knight, by which time she had distributed six diamonds, one hundred pounds, and some odd plate.

48. PRO, PCC, 12 Bakon.
49. PRO, PCC, 34 Rutland; Hughes and Larkin, *Proclamations*, nos. 496, 601, 787.

Hatton, Thomas Knyvet, and Dorothy Stafford of the bedchamber are among her beneficiaries, with Lord Burghley serving as the will's supervisor.[50] Parry's social rank was, on the surface of things, equivalent to that of Webster and Stockett: she was a gentlewoman in Elizabeth's service. But her courtiership, her proximity to the queen, placed her in a social circle that excluded the majority of those who served at court.

Records of court lodgings and food allowances can also be used to identify courtiers, although they are even more ambiguous than the New Year's rolls. Those who had chambers and diets, or bouge of court, as the food, fuel, and candle allowances were called, all tend to be lumped together in contemporary records. A "diet" of 1570, for instance, includes allowances for the Lord Chamberlain, the Master of the Horse, the principal secretary, servants to the maids of honor, and other servants all mixed in with the court locksmith, porters, and "scurers of all sides."[51] Courtiers can be singled out in such documents, however, among those who lacked household offices. Thus a "Boug de Curia" list of January 20, 1575, includes the earl of Oxford, whose office as Lord Great Chamberlain was largely ceremonial and did not ordinarily assure him of a place at court. He appears here, as in a list of lodgings for 1574, by virtue of his high favor with Elizabeth.[52] As his attendance upon the queen waned during the late 1580s, his name disappeared from the records of those who enjoyed free room and board at court. Others named in the list of chambers at court in 1574 include Sir Henry Lee and Mr. Dier (no doubt Edward Dyer), neither of whom held offices that required their attendance on the queen. They were courtiers, however, and provision was made for them.

The gifts which Queen Elizabeth bestowed at weddings and christenings are also useful in identifying those who maintained cordial relations with her. The queen was not particularly fond of weddings. When she blessed a marriage with a gift or her presence it was ordinarily a sign of special favor. If the happy couple were not themselves courtiers, an influential courtier was usually connected with the match in some way. Thus the two pieces of gilt plate she presented to John Baptist's daughter on the occasion of her marriage in 1587 were in recognition of John's service as groom of the Privy Chamber from the beginning of the reign. In 1576 Elizabeth at-

50. PRO, PCC, 16 Drury.
51. BL, Harleian MS 609, ff. 16–17.
52. PRO, SP 12/103/4; BL, Lansdowne MS 18/37.

tended the wedding of a Mrs. Savage who was not herself a courtier but was described as kinswoman to Sir William Cordell, master of the rolls and a courtier of long standing.[53]

Similarly, the queen's gifts at christenings, especially when she agreed to stand as godmother to the child, were also marks of particular favor either to the parents or to some close relative. Granted, a few members of the nobility may have gained this recognition merely as peers of the realm. George, eleventh Lord Audley, for example, was not an active courtier by 1579 when the queen presented a gilt bowl at the christening of his child, and her gift to the infant James VI of Scotland was a purely political gesture. Still, most of the christening records concern courtiers whose ties with the queen are easily confirmed in other ways: Lord Oxford's daughter in 1575, for instance; a child of Henry Knollys, esquire for the body, in 1576; or Dru Drury's daughter in 1586.[54] The christening records are plentiful, and they cluster in the main around those who were nearest the queen at court.

Many of those who participated in court tournaments were certainly courtiers, and it is possible that all of them were, in that a foreigner visiting the court in 1584 was told that no one could compete without the queen's personal approval. "Runners at jousts, tourneys, or such martial feats" were exempted from strict observance of the sumptuary laws, along with the royal physicians and the ladies and gentlemen of the Privy Chamber.[55] Jousting was an expensive aristocratic pastime dominated by noblemen, knights, and gentry of the gentlemen pensioners' status. Nearly all of the known tilters can be connected with the court in some way, although it is not clear that all of them belonged to the queen's immediate circle. From at least 1580 to the end of the reign, the Accession Day tilts at Whitehall every November 17 served as patriotic expressions of the so-called cult of Elizabeth. The queen took full advantage of the propaganda opportunities these spectacular

53. BL, Add. MS 8159; PRO, C Misc. 3/39.

54. John Nichols, *The Progresses and Public Processions of Queen Elizabeth*, 2:274; BL, Add. MS 4827; PRO, C Misc. 3/39; PRO, E 351/542, f. 98v; Drury was a gentleman usher of the Privy Chamber. Constance E. B. Rye lists 102 of "Queen Elizabeth's Godchildren" (292–96) as extracted from the enrolled accounts of the treasurer of the chamber. The total is incomplete and should be supplemented from records of additional christenings appended to most of the New Year's gift rolls.

55. Gottfried Von Bülow, ed. "Journey Through England and Scotland Made by Liupold Von Wedel in the Years 1584 and 1585," 236; Hughes and Larkin, *Proclamations*, nos. 601, 787.

shows provided. In 1600, for instance, she commanded that "great care [be] taken that her Coronacion day [*sic*] be with gallant solemnyties at tilt and turney observed, to the end the embassador of Russia may hold yt in admiracion." The court responded; young Lord Herbert, who had been criticized "for his weak pursuing of her Majesty's favour," was in training at Greenwich by October 24, but whether he did so with Elizabeth's blessing or in hopes of gaining it thereby is unknown.[56] As they entered the tiltyard at Whitehall, the combatants sent their servants to the queen's gallery with speeches and presents for her majesty. Occasionally, the participants addressed Elizabeth in person, for Chamberlain describes how Garret (probably the gentleman pensioner Thomas Gerrard), "delivered his scutchion with his impresa himself and had goode audience of her Majestie and made her very merry."[57] These tilters had good opportunity to become courtiers, if they were not so already, by virtue of their conspicuous endeavors on the queen's behalf.

Crown rewards are ambiguous indications of courtiership because royal patronage was often doled out to persons with neither courtier rank nor demonstrable ties to the court. Scores of household employees petitioned the queen for leases and other rewards through the court of requests, and had their suits granted without so much as a word with the queen or a major courtier. Courtiers' names do not appear in the records of this court as it functioned to hear petitions for royal "grace," since courtiers used instead their direct access to the queen and their fellow courtiers to press their suits. The patents of monopoly are often considered a form of reward largely reserved for courtiers, yet even in the absence of any realistic definition of that term, many recipients were foreigners, merchants, and tradesmen wholly unassociated with the court. Especially during the first two decades of Elizabeth's reign, these patents were designed to encourage or protect new technologies; their use as rewards to courtiers or others to whom the crown was indebted did not become common practice until the 1580s.[58] Crown offices need not denote courtier status either since regional and relatively minor posts, such as wardenships of forests, parks, and manors, were bestowed on persons who chose not to attend court even though their local influence and status might qualify them to do so.[59] Important

56. HMC, De L'Isle and Dudley, 2:486, 489.
57. McClure, *Chamberlain*, 1:172.
58. Price, *English Patents*, 6–8.
59. MacCaffrey, "Place and Patronage," 108–22.

offices, moreover, often entailed duties elsewhere which kept the incumbent away from court. Sir Henry Sidney was absent for all but a few months from 1566 to early 1571 by virtue of his appointment as Lord Deputy of Ireland. Henry, Lord Hunsdon's service as governor of Berwick frequently kept him from serving as a gentleman of the Privy Chamber, just as Huntingdon's presidency of the Council of the North kept him, another highly regarded royal favorite, from waiting in person upon his sovereign.[60]

Records of crown patronage, then, do little more than confirm courtier status when that has been suggested by other types of evidence. Attendance at court was, nevertheless, an expensive occupation, and courtiers stood at the apex of the privileged classes. As a result, nearly all of the most lucrative rewards and honorific offices went to courtiers. Thus while annuities from the crown averaged less than twenty pounds, Lady Stafford's amounted to two hundred; Lord Henry Seymour, sewer to the queen held a three-hundred-pound annuity; and the countess of Kildare's was worth seven hundred pounds. Most of the patents of monopoly granted during the queen's last fifteen years on the throne went to courtiers, along with the larger cash gifts and fee-farm grants, that is, leases obtained for nominal rents. Leases to crown lands in reversion, also "very much a personal grant from the Queen," went primarily to crown servants, including courtiers.[61] The most generous outlays of royal largesse usually benefited courtiers, as might be expected of the queen's closest friends in an age when the sovereign controlled the principal forms of patronage. Nevertheless, even the most fortunate recipients of the royal bounty must be considered individually, as is true for those named on the New Year's gift rolls, lists of court lodgings and diets, and as participants in court tournaments.

These are the most useful criteria for distinguishing true courtiers from the rest of the socially elite on the one hand, and from mere hangers-on at court on the other. In every instance I have found, Elizabethans with genuine ties to the court designate as courtiers only persons who can be easily confirmed as such by these criteria. That is, only persons with status requisite for obtaining personal access to the queen and who actually attended court are

60. Among the offices Lord Hunsdon held at his death in 1596, he listed gentleman of the Privy Chamber and member of the Privy Council as "Matters of honour and pleasure not of profit" (HMC, Salisbury, 6:304).

61. MacCaffrey, "Place and Patronage," 115, 120; BL, Add. MS 22924, ff. 5, 60; McClure, Chamberlain, 1:52; David Thomas, "Leases in Reversion on the Crown's Lands, 1558–1603," 67–68.

termed courtiers by those at court and by their peers. The dowager Lady Russell addressed Sir Robert Cecil, a Privy Councillor and principal secretary, as a "complete courtier" in 1596, adding that she only wished herself well enough to join him in the Privy Chamber. The solid connections with Elizabeth and her circle which Mac-Caffrey established for John and Michael Stanhope are confirmed by Rowland Whyte's assertion in 1595 that "two Stanhopes" had been committed to the Tower, "but not the Courtiers."[62] Sir John Harington described Sir Thomas Heneage, gentleman of the Privy Chamber and treasurer of the chamber, as "an Old Courtier," and William Cecil wrote Sir Thomas in 1569 to express mock-surprise that Heneage's wife, Anne, had not yet "learned how needful patience is in Court," having been "so long a courtier." Mrs. Heneage, a gentlewoman extraordinary of the Privy Chamber at the queen's coronation, appears on every complete New Year's roll until her death in 1593, as well as on the reversionary lease to Copthall, Essex, which Elizabeth granted to the Heneages in 1564.[63] Her status as courtier and Privy Chamber attendant appears certain.

Courtiers without household offices were likewise easily identified by their contemporaries. Henry Percy, earl of Northumberland, began his career at court in the late 1580s. His name first appears on the New Year's rolls in 1588, and he was described in the following year as "a fine gentleman and a wise, and of good courage and begins to be a good courtier." The earl can be traced at court with some regularity throughout the 1590s; in early 1600 the court postmaster termed him "a perpetuall courtier and familiar with Sir Walter Rawley at cards."[64] Sir John Packington provides another example of the extent to which a courtier could participate in the life of the court and reap its benefits without holding significant office. Naunton described him as "a very fine courtier" who supposedly gained his entrée to court when Elizabeth picked him out in a crowd during her 1575 progress and urged him to wait upon her. He first exchanged New Year's gifts with the queen in 1580, and his name also appears on the rolls of 1581 and 1582. Elizabeth nicknamed him her Temperance, and appointed him her deputy lieutenant of Worcestershire from at least 1579 until 1601.[65] She knighted him November 21,

---

62. HMC, Salisbury, 6:546; Collins, *Letters*, 1:359.

63. Sir John Harington, *A Supplie or Addicion to the Catalogue of Bishops to the Yeare 1608*, 122. HMC, Finch, 1:6; PRO, LC 2/4 (3), f. 54; CSPD, 34/44.

64. HMC, Bath, 5:99; HMC, De L'Isle and Dudley, 2:429.

65. Naunton, *Fragmenta*, 69; DNB, s.v. "Packington, Sir John"; PRO, SP 12/133/19, cites Packington sharing the lieutenancy with Sir John Litleton in 1579.

1587, in the course of a visit to Secretary Walsingham's house. Packington also ran at tilt on at least one occasion, and he received a crown lease worth over sixty-six pounds annually in 1583, a free gift of eight hundred pounds from the queen in 1593, and the starch monopoly in 1594.[66] Thus Packington participated in most of the honorific activities and enjoyed most of the advantages a courtier might hope to gain through close association with his sovereign.

Once courtier status had been achieved, the distinction was recognized despite relatively long absences from court. Sir Henry Sidney and the first Lord Hunsdon pursued careers of service to the nation, but careers dedicated as well to the personal service of Elizabeth herself. Both returned to court and resumed their courtiership there after years spent in Ireland and at Berwick. Accordingly, Sidney's *Arcadia*, largely written during his absence from court in 1579–1580, or his brother's lyrics, which may have been composed while Sir Robert was on duty as governor of Flushing in the Netherlands, are nonetheless products of court culture. The same holds true for the poetry written in the Tower of London by such courtier prisoners as Ralegh; Philip, earl of Arundel; and the earl of Essex—the Tower was, after all, a fairly common habitat for courtiers. Verse composed before someone gained (or assumed) courtier status, however, reveals nothing about the court or the condition of poetry there, so that the works written by such poets as Thomas, Lord Buckhurst; the earl of Leicester; Hatton; and Ralegh before they became courtiers are here not of immediate concern.

The thirty-two courtier poets whose output forms the basis of this study are enumerated in the Introduction, with their full credentials as courtiers, periods of courtiership, their Elizabethan compositions, and textual sources set forth in detail in Part II. Their names do not, however, compose an exhaustive list of the Elizabethan courtier poets. The rediscovery of Gorges's full collection of poems in 1940 and of Robert Sidney's lyrics in 1973 show how suddenly a courtier poet can spring fully laureled from the world's manuscript archives. Puttenham named Henry, second Lord Paget (d. 1568), with Oxford, Ralegh, and Sidney among the "new Crew of courtly makers" sprung up under Elizabeth, although none of his output is known today. Camden remembered William Parr, first marquis of Northampton (d. 1571), as "a man very well versed in the

---

66. William Segar, *The Booke of Honor and Armes*, sig. 2N3; PRO, SP 12/166, f. 93v; Price, *English Patents*, 143–44.

more delightfull sort of studies, as Musick, Love-toys, and other Courtly Dalliaunces," while the eighth Lord Mountjoy, sixth earl of Derby, and Sir Robert Cecil are other poets whose works either have not survived or are yet to be identified.[67] In addition, much verse by the identifiable courtiers has been lost. Aside from the untraced volume of his works which Mildmay gave to Harington, the tragedy of *Antonius* that Greville himself destroyed, and Sidney's lost translation of DuBartas, only a fraction of the total canon is likely to be extant for authors who did not collect their own poetry, among them Oxford, Ralegh, Dyer, Stanley, and many of the rest. What has survived, however, is a considerable and varied corpus allowing ample scope for studying the development and role of poetry at Elizabeth's court.

New courtier poets may well be brought to light by means other than the discovery of new poems or attributions, for courtiers are not always easily identified at a distance of some four centuries despite their social prominence at the very apogee of Elizabethan society. An hour or two of immediate observation in that bygone Privy Chamber would reveal conclusively what must otherwise be pieced together from incomplete, often ambiguous records. It is possible that several well-known Elizabethan poets were in fact courtiers, but they have been excluded from this study for want of evidence. One such author is Walter Haddon, a master of requests from the beginning of the reign. In 1567 he published his *Lucubrationes*, many of which are occasional poems which can be dated after 1558. Haddon was well-acquainted with Ascham, Cecil, Thomas Wilson, and Heneage among other courtiers, and he was present at the discussion that led to the composition of Ascham's *Scholemaster*. I am unable, however, to trace Haddon's attendance at court or upon his sovereign. He is not named on any of the New Year's rolls or christening records, nor did his office necessarily confer courtier status.

---

67. George Puttenham, *The Arte of English Poesie*, 61; Camden, *Annals*, 169. Charles Blount, Lord Mountjoy, is credited with a pen which "the Muses stile did mate, / . . . Parnassus knowes my Poet by his looke," according to James Lea's translation of D. F. R. de M.'s *An Answer to the Untruthes* (1589, STC 17132, sig. H3v). As a further indication that Blount was known as a poet, the compiler of Bodl. MS Rawlinson poet. 148, attributed "Amidst the fairest Mountain tops" to both Essex and "L: Mountjoy" before assigning it to Dyer (f. 66). In June of 1599, Lord Derby was "busy penning comedies for the common players," although if any of his plays have survived, they have not been identified as his (Chambers, *Elizabethan Stage*, 2:127). For Cecil's lost poem sung before the queen see pp. 133–34 below.

Similarly, George Puttenham may have been a courtier. Although neither his name nor that of his wife appears on the New Year's rolls, about 1579 he gave the queen his "Partheniades" in verse as a New Year's present. Puttenham's prose tract in defense of Elizabeth's treatment of Mary, Queen of Scots, was royal propaganda no doubt approved if not commissioned by Elizabeth, and for which he was rewarded in 1588 with two crown leases in reversion. His claim to "haue seene forraine Embassadours in the Queens presence" indicates only that he had been admitted to the Presence Chamber when ambassadors, but not necessarily Elizabeth, were there.[68] It is Puttenham's lack of a demonstrable place in court society, the absence of his name from courtier correspondence, records of court lodgings, or other evidence of his attendance which calls his status into question.

A different but even more tantalizing exclusion for want of evidence applies in the case of Sir Francis Bacon. He can be credibly identified as a courtier during the 1590s, and he presented the queen with a sonnet in 1600, yet none of his extant verse can be assigned with confidence to Elizabeth's reign.[69] Bacon's poem may eventually come to light, just as it may become possible to demonstrate that Haddon and Puttenham were bona fide courtiers when they composed their known works. The lives and works of many other poets, on the other hand, are sufficiently known to exclude them from the ranks of Elizabethan courtiers, the assertions in our literary histories notwithstanding.

To what extent, for instance, was Edmund Spenser qualified to describe the Elizabethan court, let alone to prescribe its tastes and values? Would he have been able, for example, to monitor the alleged decline in courtesy there, as Daniel Javitch suggests in his ingenious analysis of the connections between poetry and the ideals of courtly behavior?[70] As a prosperous civil servant resident in Ireland for almost a decade, Spenser necessarily lacked any firsthand understanding of Elizabeth's court as he wrote the first three books of *The Faerie Queene*. For a few months during the winter of 1589–1590 he apparently had the opportunity to associate with courtiers

68. PRO, SO 3/1, f. 153v; Puttenham, *Arte*, xxiii, 291.
69. Thomas Birch, *Memoirs of the Reign of Queen Elizabeth*, 2:438. Bacon's "The world's a bubble" did not circulate until late in the second decade of the seventeenth century, while his translation of Psalm 104, published in 1625, was apparently also a Jacobean composition. See Peter Beal's *Index of English Literary Manuscripts*, vol. 1, pt. 1, 24–29.
70. *Poetry and Courtliness*, 132–34, and chapter 5 passim.

and to meet Elizabeth in a socially subordinate position as the guest of Sir Walter Ralegh. Moreover, what former conditions there might Spenser have used for comparison with the 1590s? Schelling believed that he was "newly come to court" at the time of his problematic association with Sidney and Dyer in the "Aereopagus" discussions, yet his arrival could have amounted to little more than his physical presence there, presumably as a servant of the earl of Leicester.

But even if Spenser had previously been to court and noted that its atmosphere in 1590 was somehow less courteous than it had been before, he would have marked this change only from the standpoint of an outside observer, not as a courtier, for Spenser acquired no discernible entrée to the queen and her circle other than Ralegh. He launched an ambitious campaign to broaden his base of patronage, but despite his expressions of gratitude to various members of the nobility the effort was unsuccessful. When Ralegh fell as a result of the Throckmorton marriage, Spenser's ties with the court simply dissolved. His subsequent complaints about his reception there stemmed primarily from his failure to gain another courtier patron. Spenser's vision of the diverse, complicated milieu of the court was too brief and viewed from too subordinate a position to lend much authority to what little may be inferred about the court from his writings.

At best then, Spenser momentarily penetrated the chamber, establishing a temporary and superficial acquaintance with the queen and her courtiers. As much can be said for perhaps a dozen professional, out-of-court writers, and while it would be pointless to refute every implausible designation of courtier status that has been proposed, an examination of the most compelling claims demonstrates that a more realistic classification can be established for at least some of these writers.

An interesting borderline figure is Richard Edwards, gentleman of the chamber at the beginning of Elizabeth's reign, gentleman of the Chapel Royal by May of 1560, and master of its children by 1561. A year later he received from the crown leases of two rectories in Lincolnshire, and as a further mark of his genteel status he became an honorary member of Lincoln's Inn in 1564.[71] His part in writing and directing dramatic entertainments for the court, along with the verses he addressed to several ladies at Queen Mary's court, prompt-

---

71. Leicester Bradner, *The Life and Poems of Richard Edwards*, 15–20; PRO, SP 12/166, f. 5v.

ed Leicester Bradner to term him a courtier, and Jackson Cope, a "court poet."[72] But do Edwards's accomplishments suggest courtier status? Neither his office in the chamber nor those in the chapel assured him of personal access to Elizabeth. His crown lease could be a sign of personal royal favor, yet it is no different from the rewards doled out to scores of grooms, yeomen, and other household employees. Edwards did not participate in the New Year's gift exchanges nor did he socialize with other courtiers. His position seems to have been that of a respected impresario, musician, and servant of the court rather than a courtier.

By far the most talented playwright with genuine connections at court was John Lyly. During the 1580s he no doubt frequented the chamber to supervise the production of his plays there, and scholars generally term him a courtier.[73] It was probably as Burghley's protégé that, by the early 1580s, Lyly had joined the retinue of his son-in-law, the earl of Oxford, and as late as 1599 Lyly was conversing with Oxford on behalf of the earl's creditors who were trying to recover the debts he owed them.[74] Yet the only evidence that Lyly might have gained independent status at court or recognition from the queen is his appointment about 1588 as esquire for the body. The emptiness of this honor, however, is demonstrated first by Albert Feuillerat's puzzled confession that he could find no mention of Lyly in any such capacity in the Exchequer accounts, and second, by Lyly's own remonstrance to the queen in 1601: "Thirteene yeeres your Highnes servant: but yet nothinge."[75] Lyly had apparently become an esquire extraordinary, without wages or place at court unless called up to substitute for one of the esquires in ordinary. The position allowed him to style himself her majesty's servant, but there is no reason to suppose that he could stroll into the Privy Chamber by virtue of his office or in recognition of his social position. Lyly's case graphically illustrates the queen's crucial role in any meaningful promotion at court, for by the late 1580s his place in society was essentially the same as was Ralegh's in the late 1570s: he was esquire extraordinary, the protégé of capable courtier pa-

---

72. Jackson I. Cope, " 'The Best for Comedy': Richard Edwardes' Canon," *Texas Studies in Literature and Language* 2 (1961): 517.

73. G. K. Hunter, *John Lyly: The Humanist as Courtier*; Gerald Eades Bentley refers to "the courtier and fiction writer John Lyly" (*Shakespeare: A Biographical Handbook*, 120).

74. Hunter, *John Lyly*, 69; Mark Eccles, "Brief Lives: Tudor and Stuart Authors," 87.

75. Feuillerat, *John Lyly*, 196n, 561; Lyly's second petition to the queen.

trons. Elizabeth, however, never took a fancy to Lyly as she had to Walter Ralegh, thereby depriving us of a highly talented addition to the ranks of the courtier poets.

Three other poets, whose claims to courtiership are rather stronger than those of Edwards or Lyly, reveal from different perspectives the kinds of connections at court that cannot be legitimately parleyed into bona fide courtier status.

Thomas Churchyard rendered a variety of services to Elizabeth's court and government from at least 1574 when he was paid for work on both the fortifications and speeches devised for a progress show at Bristol. The following summer he was paid for work on a similar presentation as "Mr Churchyard," and he claimed to have written a Shrovetide show staged at court by Ralegh, Sir Robert Carey, Master Chidley, and Arthur Gorges.[76] A gentleman, undoubtedly Thomas, was enrolled as plain "Churchyerd" on the New Year's gift list of 1575, while in an undated letter to the earl of Hertford, he wrote that he and his wife "wold fayn travell to the cowrtt."[77] In 1576 he carried Privy Council letters to and from Brussels, and in 1584 the council appointed Captain Churchyard as mustermaster at Rochester with the important responsibility of training the local militia to resist a Spanish invasion.[78] It was probably in recognition of these services rather than for his relentless publication of poetry that Churchyard received a royal pension in January of 1593. The patent, worth eighteen pence daily, was apparently gained with the help of Sir John Fortescue and Lord Keeper Puckering. For some unknown reason it had been revoked by 1595, only to be renewed in the amount of twenty pence daily in 1597, this time through the intervention of Dr. Julius Caesar, master of requests.[79]

The irrepressible Churchyard was undoubtedly well known at court; he may even have been known to Elizabeth. What is lacking is any evidence that he was accepted there in any capacity above that of a servant or hanger-on. He is identified in the funeral accounts as "Captaine Churchard gent. wayter," and he apparently served in the

76. *Churchyard's Challenge* (London, 1593, STC 5220, sig. *2); Merrill Harvey Goldwyn, "Notes on the Biography of Thomas Churchyard," 1.

77. J. E. Jackson, "Thomas Churchyard," *Notes and Queries*, 5th ser., 8 (1877): 331. The title page of Churchyard's *Pleasant Conceite* of 1593 states that he presented it to the queen as a New Year's gift at Hampton Court Palace.

78. Goldwyn, "Notes," 12–14.

79. Goldwyn, "Notes," 3–4; Roger A. Geimer, "Spenser's Rhyme or Churchyard's Reason: Evidence of Churchyard's First Pension," *Review of English Studies*, n.s., 20 (1969): 308–9.

chamber as opposed to ad hoc for the day of the funeral alone. If he did so, however, his account of the court ladies in his *Pleasant Conceite* (1593) indicates at what remove he stood from the habitat of genuine courtiers. Churchyard imagines his painter-poet persona going up to court and "peeping throw the Presence Chamber doore" (signature B2). Inside he sees the cloth of state and many noble dames, including five "faire flowers . . . of Dians traine," presumably the maids of honor less one of their usual complement. Dazzled by this sight, he imagines that even finer folk would be found in the Privy Chamber. Finally, Churchyard had accumulated more than sixty pounds in gold by the time of his death, yet his will names no other beneficiaries than his brother George and a George Onslowe of the Middle Temple. Two of the witnesses to his will signed with their marks rather than signatures.[80] Thomas was a royal servant who lacked the social status to be termed a courtier.

A poet who undoubtedly served in the chamber for many years was Lodowick Lloyd, one of the queen's sergeants at arms, sixteen of whom were appointed to wait in the Presence Chamber. Lloyd is best remembered today as the one credited with paying for Spenser's funeral. In 1579 Lloyd's ballad of "Brittishe Sidanen applied by a courtier to the praise of the Quene" was entered in the stationers' register; it survives as well in a number of manuscript copies.[81] Lloyd's identity as a courtier was reiterated in a verse treatise he published in 1586 entitled *Certaine Englishe Verses, presented unto the Queenes most excellent Majestie, by a Courtier* (STC 16617). Lloyd published other verse and was probably responsible as well for the epitaph on William, Earl of Pembroke.[82]

Lloyd's publishers may have termed him a courtier the better to grace their title pages, but Lodowick referred to himself during the 1570s and 1580s as a servant of Sir Christopher Hatton, to whose influence he probably owed his chamber appointment. In 1592 he received a fee farm lease from the crown, followed by other such grants in later years, one of them without fine and in explicit recog-

80. Robert Cole, "Churchyard the Poet," *Notes and Queries*, 3d ser., 6 (1864): 26; Onslowe corrected from Puslowe by Eccles, "Brief Lives," 24.

81. Hyder Edward Rollins, *An Analytical Index to the Ballad-Entries (1557–1709) in the Registers of the Company of Stationers of London*, 29–30. The text was printed from an unidentified manuscript by J. H. [Joseph Haslewood?], in Sir Samuel Egerton Brydges, *The British Bibliographer*, 1:338–39. Other texts occur in Folger, MSS V.a.198, ff. 19v–20, and V.a.399, ff. 32–33; BL, Add. MSS 14965, ff. 6–7, and 15020, ff. 30–32; and BL, Harleian MS 1927, ff. 48–49v.

82. This epitaph is subscribed "L:Ll:" in Inner Temple, Petyt MS 538.10, ff. 1–1v.

nition of his service as sergeant at arms.[83] Lloyd's office was honorable without being one that could readily lead to courtiership. His name does not appear on the New Year's rolls, while in subsidy records from 1589 to 1602, as in the funeral accounts, he is styled plain Lodowick Lloyd (Flud or Floyd), nor are his fellow sergeants termed masters in these documents.[84] He could legitimately call himself gentleman or even esquire, but for want of evidence that he associated with Elizabeth or rose above his subordinate position as Hatton's client, his appellations as courtier must be viewed as printers' fabrications.

A final exclusion from the roll of courtier poets, but one with perhaps the best claim of all, is the Florentine citizen Petruccio Ubaldini. In addition to several Italian poems in his manuscript works, he published in 1596 his *Rime*, a collection of lyrics dedicated to the queen. Ubaldini may have been attached to the Tudor court as early as the 1540s.[85] He had returned to his homeland by 1552 but was established in Elizabeth's household by 1563 as schoolmaster to the soon-to-be-abolished henchmen. After 1565 this post became a sinecure for which Petruccio was regularly paid into the forty-first year of the reign; his absence from these records of payment for late 1599 and 1600, as well as from the 1600 New Year's gift list, indicates that he died in 1599.[86]

Ubaldini first exchanged New Year's gifts with the queen in 1564; his name appears on eleven of the subsequent rolls. Several of his presentations to Elizabeth in the form of Italian treatises on various subjects have survived, along with similar tracts which he dedicated to such courtiers as Hatton and Lord Admiral Howard.[87] The New Year's rolls reveal both Ubaldini's presence at court and his status there, for in the lists which distinguish masters among the gentlemen, he is always plain Ubaldini (or Petritio, Petrochio, and

83. Eccles, "Brief Lives," 80; Huntington, MS EL 3505.
84. PRO, E 179/382/12; E 179/266/13; E 179/70/107; E 179/70/115; LC 2/4 (4), f. 49.
85. Giuliano Pellegrini, *Un Fiorentino alla Corte d'Inghilterra nel Cinquecento, Petruccio Ubaldini*, 13–15.
86. The record of his wages in the treasurer of the chamber accounts for 1579–1580 gives the date of the original warrant (PRO, E 351/542); the records for 1599 and 1600 are in E 351/543, membranes 37 and 53.
87. The DNB (s.v. "Ubaldini, Petruccio") summarizes Petruccio's New Year's gifts among the BL, Royal Manuscripts, and refers to a prayer book of his composition in the Huth Library. Royal MS 14.A.10 is the copy of his tract on the Spanish Armada presented to Howard in 1589, and he presented Royal MS 14.A.11, on the same subject, as a New Year's gift to Hatton in 1590.

so forth), as in 1584 for example, where he appears untitled after a long list of "masters," including Wolley, Dyer, Greville, and Noel. His rank was clearly that of a servant and one who, despite his court office, had trouble maintaining a subsistence-level income. As a result, Ubaldini sought patronage shotgun fashion, as did Churchyard, firing off frequent, even multiple dedications of his works to the queen and her courtiers, as with his *Descrittione del Regno di Scotia* (1588, STC 24480), with its dedication to Hatton, Leicester, and Walsingham. He petitioned Burghley for relief from his debts on several occasions, and he obtained Privy Council letters in 1578 and 1580 protecting him for one year at a time from the "arrests and molestacons" of his creditors.[88]

Ubaldini was apparently retained at court as a professional Italian. In this connection, it is interesting to find him collaborating in 1572 with his countryman Alfonso Ferrabosco in the production of a court masque, and in 1579, writing Italian speeches for another masque.[89] Petruccio was, of course, by no means the only one of his nationality employed at court; besides Ferrabosco there were the Bassano and Lupo families among the royal musicians, the Zin-zan, alias Alexander, family of the stables, and many more. Ubaldini seems to have conscientiously set himself apart, however, by never using one word of English during all his years in England. He always termed himself a Florentine, and all of his letters, manuscript treatises, and books are in Italian. Thus, in Petruccio the queen found a modish accessory to her train, but one whose status remained as subordinate as that of the Italian musicians who performed in her consorts and whose names appear with Ubaldini's toward the ends of the New Year's gift rolls.

If these poets do not qualify as courtiers, they did nevertheless develop genuine ties with the court. Churchyard and Lyly obtained at least nominal offices there, while Edwards, Lloyd, and Ubaldini held salaried posts in the household. To this list might be added Anthony Munday, who served as a messenger of the chamber during the 1580s, and William Hunnis, master of the children of the chapel and supervisor of the royal gardens at Greenwich. These poets spent considerable time within the royal household where they were personally known to various courtiers, if not to the queen herself. Their

88. Pellegrini, *Un Fiorentino*, 24.
89. Chambers reprints Ubaldini's undated letter to the queen concerning an Italian "Commedia" which he planned to present before her (*Elizabethan Stage*, 2:265).

witness to court affairs, then, necessarily carries more weight than that of such out-of-court authors as Gascoigne, Peele, Spenser, and Shakespeare, not to mention Henry Constable, Samuel Daniel, Thomas Watson, and that remaining host of professional writers who wrote for courtiers and the court without being a part of that institution at any level. A useful phrase for differentiating these poets from those who were in some way connected with the court comes from the pen of William Camden, who described Thomas Churchyard as "the poor Court poet."[90] The term *court poet* appropriately identifies servants of the court beneath courtier status who wrote poetry to entertain the sovereign and her courtiers.

Distinguishing the courtier poets from court and out-of-court writers is a necessary first step toward any systematic study of courtier verse in its historical context. Those critics who have identified 'courtly' poets or writers solely as a function of their subject matter obscure our understanding of the past in that anyone could (and did) write about courtly love, courtly manners, and the court in general. It was a large institution and much was imagined and said about it, yet in classifying literature by such criteria we ignore the social realities that make one writer's testimony about the court authoritative and another's merely guesswork or outright fantasy. The key distinctions center upon the courtiers who belonged to the elite circle nearest the queen, and court poets, who were connected with the royal household but socially subordinate to, and physically distanced from, that privileged atmosphere. This latter group formed a unique artistic entity within Tudor society deserving of separate investigation. As for those out-of-court and in the main professional writers who fall into neither category, their impressions of the court were fragmentary if not wholly fictional. The tendency to accept at face value what their works imply about their social standing and knowledge of the court has distorted our interpretation not only of their lives and works but of court culture as well.

90. *Remains Concerning Britain*, 432.

2

Courtier Verse before Sidney

The royal household was the sovereign's personal establishment in both structure and operation, with even its most well-worn traditions subject to change. Thus, upon coming to the throne Elizabeth had retained the band of gentlemen pensioners which her father had instituted in 1539, but she dissolved the royal henchmen in 1565. The tone and atmosphere of the early Elizabethan court were fluid as queen and courtiers adapted its style to the circumstance of a maiden queen who was likewise head of the national, Protestant church. The main implication of this fluidity for the development of courtier verse was the lack of an absolute, preconceived standard of courtliness. What was later hailed as the dawn of English Renaissance lyricism in the works of Wyatt and Surrey found no immediate revival under Elizabeth because her courtiers did not recognize it as a compelling precedent. Courtliness was largely to be devised anew and tailored to the new regime without well-defined models and, at first, without a vibrant or conspicuous role for poetry.

Petrarchan lyricism, a combination of courtly love motifs with amorous verse, especially in sonnet form, is generally designated "court poetry." This kind of verse, however, almost disappeared from English poetry and above all from that written by courtiers between about 1547 and 1570. The queen's translation of Petrarch may date from the early 1560s, but even so the passage she chose from his *Triumphs* is a serious meditation upon God and eternity wholly lacking in amorous overtones. During the first dozen years of her reign, the only definite example of courtier involvement with love poetry concerns Hatton's composition of the fourth act of *Gismond of Salern*, which was performed at court by the gentlemen of the Inner Temple about 1567.

This melodrama, based on a tale from Boccaccio's *Decameron*, unfolds in a world controlled by the pagan gods, particularly Cupid,

41

who destroys both the lovers along with King Tancred. Hatton's "Chore," the chorus that concludes act 4, assures his audience that virtuous lovers are exempt from such tyranny. They are urged to serve their ladies as Petrarch served Laura, or as Diana "loued th'Amazons sonne"; this passage on Diana is followed by a couplet deserving of some further consideration in light of its author's place as a highly favored courtier: "Desire not of thy soueraine the thing / wherof shame may ensue by any meane."[1] Hatton seems to allude here to any lover's sovereign lady, yet the preceding reference to Diana creates an immediate ambiguity given Elizabeth's association with that goddess and the pressures upon her to accept a suitor and marry. The royal response to that pressure was an oft-repeated assurance that, while she would accept the yoke of matrimony for her country's sake, were she a private citizen she would be most reluctant to do so. Hatton's lines not only defend the queen's policy, they stand at odds with the play's emotional momentum which condemns King Tancred for prohibiting Gismond's remarriage.[2] Her choice of an illicit love affair, however, is likewise condemned in the play, which fails in any way to endorse chaste married love as the obvious alternative course of action. The approval of love at a distance uttered by Hatton's chorus forms only a momentary aside to the overall impact of *Gismond*, yet the play did allow this one early Elizabethan courtier to write about love. There is no evidence, however, that it was specifically intended for court performance, or that Hatton helped to select its subject, or determined its treatment beyond his responsibility for act 4. Thus *Gismond of Salern* as a work about aristocratic love was but slightly influenced by a courtier, since none of the four remaining collaborators had definite court connections at the time.

The Older Humanism

Aside from this play, Elizabethan courtiers avoided love as a subject for poetic expression until the early 1570s. Instead, courtier

1. John W. Cunliffe, *Early English Classical Tragedies*, 202, lines 38, 42–43.
2. In *The Queen's Two Bodies: Drama and the Elizabethan Succession* (57–58), Marie Axton argues that the queen's policy was criticized in the play by both Tancred's refusal to permit Gismond's remarriage and by reference to Diana's chaste love for Hippolytus (an allusion granted only four lines in Hatton's chorus). The thrust of this chorus, however, is to applaud chaste, distant love, as represented by both Diana and Petrarch; the queen's oft-stated aversion to marriage dovetails neatly with this sentiment.

verse survived in a distinctively humanist garb by adapting to the circumstances of life at court the functions for poetry that had been developed by English humanists during the 1540s and 1550s. The results violate what has generally been expected from courtiers in both language and subtlety of expression, for this output is primarily in Latin and the messages it conveys are presented in straightforward, unambiguous terms. The agenda included poems addressed privately to friends upon notable occasions, commendatory verses before published books, and eulogies similar to those contributed during the 1550s to the memorial volumes for the Brandon brothers and for Martin Bucer.[3]

What little verse has survived from the queen's early years was composed for the most part by courtiers who had been intensively trained in the classics at Reformation Cambridge. We would hardly expect an enthusiastic cultivation of the amorous lyric to emerge from this background, although just such experimentation was being carried out in the neo-Latin verse of continental humanists. Instead, Ascham, Wilson, and Cecil were disposed by their education to restore authentic Latin and Greek expression in verse or prose and, secondarily, to adapt English style to ancient models and practice.[4] In England, furthermore, the preferred subjects for poetry were moral and religious, so that we might expect humanist verse at court to be devotional in nature or vigorously to espouse the Protestant cause. The court environment, however, modified the humanist agenda at nearly every point. The forthright meanings and cautious conservatism of their output during the 1560s are well represented by the two Latin poems addressed to Elizabeth by Ascham and Wilson.

Ascham's poetic New Year's gift, left unfinished at his death in 1568, emphasizes the peace and stability which the queen's reign has brought to England. Ascham specifically attributes this tranquil state to Elizabeth's womanhood, which he contrasts with the belligerent tendencies of male rulers. She is described as the sole support of true Christianity, from which it would follow that she must

3. Leicester Bradner, *Musae Anglicanae: A History of Anglo-Latin Poetry, 1500–1925*, 19–20.

4. Bradner, *Musae*, 11–13, 33. The overall humanist agenda is described in John M. Berdan's *Early Tudor Poetry* (306ff). Winthrop S. Hudson examines in detail the personal and intellectual background of these men as students of John Cheke and heirs of the program of the "Athenian Tribe" at Cambridge in his *Cambridge Connection and the Elizabethan Settlement of 1559* (chapter 4 and passim).

produce or name a successor to insure that the stronghold of reformed religion not fall prey once more to Catholicism. Upon this
line of reasoning the contemporary clamor for marriage and an heir
to the throne was often predicated. From Ascham's verses, however,
Elizabeth would gather that all was going rather well despite some
threats from foreign parts, most noticeably from Spain and the
"meretrix Babylonica." Instead of encouraging a policy of confronta-
tion or the vigorous promotion of reformed religion, Ascham praises
the moderate, lawful, stabilizing aspects of Elizabeth's rule. Similarly, Wilson's congratulatory "epigramma" (poem 1) presented to
the queen on Accession Day in 1569 is a set piece that celebrates the
success of the house of Tudor with hopes for its continuation, even
augmentation under Elizabeth if the fates can allow so much. The
queen merits eternal life even if she remains single, Wilson affirms,
although she could guarantee herself immortality by becoming a
thrice-happy mother (line 15). The poem leads up to this endorsement of marriage and motherhood, but its tone lacks any sense of
that urgency which marked both private and public discussions of
the succession problem: for Elizabeth to solve that problem would
make things even better than they already are according to Wilson.

Both works addressed to the queen are flattering but only mildly
persuasive; yet it is difficult to find a motivation for courtier verse of
the 1560s beyond flattery and persuasion. Any interest in poetry for
its own sake, let alone the founding of a respectable classical poetics
at court be it in Latin, Greek, or the vernacular, was not at issue to
judge from the works that have survived. The precedent for "informal" cultivation of poetry had been established, of course, by
Wyatt, Surrey, and lesser writers at the court of Henry VIII, since
many of their poems, including their translations from Petrarch,
have no ostensible purpose beyond the amusement of poet and
reader alike. Such expatiation in verse, unprompted by compelling
circumstances, was almost unknown to the earliest Elizabethan
courtier poets. Their caution stemmed from something more than
the fact that Wilson was a merely competent poet and Ascham, a
mediocre one. The restricted, conservative role of humanist verse at
court is clearly indicated by both its contexts and scarcity.

Every item of courtier verse that can be dated to the first dozen
years of the reign was prepared for an identifiable occasion or reader,
or both. Beyond Ascham's New Year's poem, and Wilson's Accession Day offering, there are Wilson's Latin verses in commendation
of Carr's *Demosthenes*, and those congratulating Cecil for his recovery from illness, the elegies for Bishop Jewel by Wilson and Wolley,

and the lines presented to the queen upon her arrival at Theobalds in 1571. These formal Latin compositions were prepared for occasions that seem almost to have justified or even excused a courtier's declining into verse. The example of Wyatt and Surrey notwithstanding, poetry was held in very low esteem by mid-sixteenth-century English aristocrats.[5] Castiglione's *Courtier* is often cited to support the notion that courtiers were expected to write verse, yet Castiglione quickly dismisses any such accomplishment in a passage that endorses the writing of prose as well, with verse largely relegated to so menial a function as the entertainment of the ladies, who "ordinarily love such matters."[6] Furthermore, the *Courtier* is the only sixteenth-century courtesy book with genuine aristocratic credentials to so much as suggest in even an ambivalent fashion that a courtier might compose verse. More than any other influence, it was probably the widespread, negative attitude toward poetry that accounts for the general scarcity of verse and the predominance of Latin occasional works during the first decade and more of Elizabeth's reign.

Early courtier verse in English is more varied in purpose and less formal than the Latin, but it too is almost exclusively occasional. Only eight such works can be positively dated between 1558 and 1570, and Ascham's brief translations from Greek in *The Scholemaster* account for three of these. A fourth is Ascham's poem 1, his praise of Blundeville's translation of Plutarch, which fulfills a more conventional role for early Elizabethan verse than the English works of either Cecil or Elizabeth. Ascham's purpose, of course, was to encourage the dissemination of classical culture; ironically, however, he did so in a poetic medium that violates his own strictures on how that culture should be revived in English, for his verses illustrate Gothic English rhyming at its worst in both meter and rhetoric:[7] Blundeville's words, Ascham writes,

> Doe bryng suche light unto the sense:
> As if I lackt I woulde not lette,
> To bye this booke for forty pense.

5. A good summary of the contemporary attitude is set forth in Richard Helgerson's *Elizabethan Prodigals* (31–32), and in his "The New Poet Presents Himself: Spenser and the Idea of a Literary Career" (*PMLA* 93 [1978]: 894), as also in Edwin Haviland Miller's *The Professional Writer in Elizabethan England* (18–22).

6. Baldassare Castiglione, *The Book of the Courtier*, 71.

7. For the derogatory humanist denotations of the word rhyme as both accentual meter and rhyming words see Derek Attridge's *Well-Weighed Syllables* (93–100).

Such awkward commendation might cast doubt upon Ascham's sincerity here were it not for the fact that lines of much the same quality crop up in *The Scholemaster* in passages adjacent to those that deplore just such versifying as this. A master of lively prose, the Latin secretary was quite unable to revive an authentic classical poetics or to adapt English poetry to a classical style.

The elder Harington's Elizabethan poetry is likewise tied to occasions with the possible exceptions of his translations of Haddon's Latin verses between a husband and wife.[8] The lines he wrote for an unidentified earl, and those for "A boy that should content me wondrous well" (presumably his son, John), must have been elicited by particular circumstances, as was certainly the case with the two poems he wrote to accompany the portrait of Lord Admiral Seymour, a gift he presented to the queen in 1567. This painting, with its eulogistic verses, was especially appropriate for Elizabeth, who had admired Seymour and may well have considered marrying him; however, Seymour's execution stemmed in part from his efforts to arrange just such a match. But if Harington's poetry was elicited by specific occasions, its inspiration and method were anything but stilted and conventional. "None can deeme righte" was translated from book 19 of Ariosto's *Orlando Furioso* with a slight variation upon the original's ottava rima in Harington's *a b a b b a c c* rhyme scheme. His sonnets, both the one on Seymour and "A boy that should content me," are set forth in unique rhyme schemes derived from the Petrarchan sonnet but with variations influenced by terza rima. Harington lacked a university education and made no discernible attempt to clothe his English verse in classical respectability. Although he translated Haddon's Latin verse and published his own translation of Cicero's *De Amicitia*, he apparently did not write verse or prose in the classical languages. Instead, his literary models were primarily Italian, an influence wholly alien to the humanists who dominated courtier verse until the early 1570s.

William Cecil's only poem in the vernacular is sincerely personal but intended for a restricted, non-courtly audience. His poem 1 accompanied the spinning wheel he gave to his daughter, Anne, as a New Year's present in 1567. These rough tetrameters are couched in two stanzas of rhyme royal, a fairly demanding medieval verse form; his rather old-fashioned lines reveal the warmth of personal feelings in Cecil's family life, as the tireless principal secretary urges Anne "only to spynne oon pounde a daye / And play the reste." This is a

8. Ruth Hughey, *John Harington of Stepney*, 2: A 16–17, 5.

genuinely private poem, its kindly, informal tone as well suited to its recipient as it is unlike the Latin verse turned out by other courtiers during this period.

The most imaginative use of poetry in either language during these years is Elizabeth's "The doubt of future foes."[9] Her sixteen lines of poulter's measure were written upon the collapse of the Northern Rebellion late in 1569 or early in 1570: thus her "present joy." It appears that this is a personal distillation into verse of the queen's feelings, elicited by the occasion but private, rather than addressed to a particular reader or audience. Were this the case, her innovative use of poetry as an outlet for personal reflection would set it apart from all the known verses that had been written by her courtiers. However, the circumstances behind this poem's transmission reveal that its end was in fact more calculated than the verses addressed to her by Ascham and Wilson.

"The doubt of future foes" was circulating in manuscript by 1570; eight manuscript copies are known in addition to the version printed by Puttenham in 1589.[10] Presumably, all of these texts derive from the one copied "covertly" by Lady Willoughby from the queen's tablet. Elizabeth, we are to believe, was greatly offended at this invasion of her privacy "and chid [her] for spreading evil bruit of her writing such toyes."[11] It seems unlikely all the same that the culprit suffered any great disfavor for her theft, since it effected a display of royal talent of the kind that Elizabeth often practiced. Her lines express her resolution to govern England, the use of future

9. Leicester Bradner, *The Poems of Queen Elizabeth I*, 4.

10. Bradner (*Poems*, 72) notes that the text in Bodl., MS Rawl. poet. 108, was transcribed about 1570. In addition to the texts he cites, the poem is found in BL, Egerton MS 2642, f. 237v; Inner Temple, Petyt MS 538.10, f. 3v; and in the Ottley Manuscript in the National Library of Wales, described by Peter Beal, "Poems by Sir Philip Sidney: The Ottley Manuscript," 284–95. A ninth text is referred to among the manuscripts of E. P. Shirley in HMC, 5th report, 363. The queen's verses enjoyed a very wide circulation.

11. *Nugae Antiquae*, (1769), 1:58. Lady Willoughby was probably Margaret Willoughby, "maid" of the Privy Chamber at Elizabeth's coronation and gentlewoman of the Privy Chamber on the subsidy roll of 1558–1559 (PRO, LC 2/4 (3), f. 53v; BL, Lansdowne MS 3/87). If so, the story of Elizabeth's composition of the poem reached the Haringtons through an old friend of the family, for Margaret had served Princess Elizabeth at Hatfield along with the elder Harington and Sir John's mother, Isabella Markham. By 1560 Margaret had married Sir Matthew Arundel, another family friend and one of the "jurors" empanelled in *Sir John Harington's A New Discourse of a Stale Subject, Called the Metamorphosis of Ajax* (ed. Elizabeth Story Donno, 232; see also Hughey, *John Harington*, 236, 270).

tense verbs giving the statement a prophetic air. She vows to quell all efforts on behalf of "The daughter of debate," the captive Queen of Scots, who had been the focus of the Northern Rebellion. This rival, "sister" queen inspired in Elizabeth a very strong spirit of competition. In 1564 she had asked the Scottish ambassador, Sir James Melville, all about Mary's accomplishments as a dancer and player on the virginals. Afterward, Melville was conducted by Lord Hunsdon to a private chamber where he listened (unbeknownst to the queen he was to suppose), as she played on the virginals. He was then detained at the palace to watch Elizabeth dance.[12] The "unauthorized" circulation of her verses on the rebellion constitutes a ruse akin to this carefully orchestrated eavesdropping on her virginal recital. In both instances, Elizabeth could assert herself without appearing to do so. Her poem functioned as a royal proclamation:

> No foreign banished wight shall anchor in this port;
> Our realm brooks not seditious sects, let them elsewhere resort.
> My rusty sword through rest shall first his edge employ
> To poll their tops that seek such change or gape for future joy.

Patriotism was encouraged and Mary condemned in a way Elizabeth could not officially attempt without risking serious diplomatic repercussions.

A few of Harington's poems may have been written without a specific occasion at hand, and perhaps one or two of these could date from the 1560s; the same is true of Sir William Cordell's poems, but again we cannot be sure. Generally speaking, then, the eight English poems by courtiers which can be positively identified before 1571 were elicited by the same kinds of occasions which prompted courtier verse in Latin, and only the varied circumstances of their composition can account for their appearance in the vernacular. Elizabeth's celebration of her victory, with its warning against future attempts against her, would have lost much of its spontaneity and propaganda value if set forth in a studied Latin meter. Cecil rightly decided that English verses were suitable for his eleven-year-old daughter, and Ascham could not well have prefixed a Greek or Latin poem to Blundeville's translation of Demosthenes for English readers. Only Harington might have chosen to write his poems for the Seymour portrait in either Latin or English, but his long-standing commitment to English poetry obviated this choice in that Harington was writing verse in his native tongue as early as the 1540s. Even

12. Sir James Melville, *The Memoirs of Sir James Melville*, 50–51.

more important, perhaps, he did not belong to the Cambridge circle at court, as did Ascham, Cecil, Wilson, and, through adoption as it were, the queen herself, a Cantabrigian by virtue of her studies under Ascham and Cheke.

In the absence of any courtier verse undoubtedly composed for its own sake during this time, the work of another Cambridge graduate, Sir Nicholas Bacon, takes on a particular interest. Granted, a few of his poems were occasional, and they may all date from Mary's reign, yet Bacon does write in a variety of genres and forms that can only be interpreted as springing from his personal delight in poetry. The title of his collected verses, "The Recreacons of his Age," attests to this motivation, while the humorous, anecdotal nature of several of his poems stands in marked contrast to the formal compositions of Ascham and Wilson. Bacon's devotional works, his prayers and "Carroll," constitute an expression of religious feeling also strangely absent from datable courtier works until the third decade of the Elizabethan era. Furthermore, two of his poems, "Of a Lover," and "Of a Snoweballe" qualify as amorous lyrics. He also translated Horace's *Carminum* 2.10, as well as several of Sir Thomas More's epigrams. Bacon stands out, then, as perhaps the only early Elizabethan courtier who cultivated poetry for its own sake, including personal, religious, and amorous genres, both original and in translation.

Bacon's verse prayers and love poems underscore much that is puzzling about the earliest courtier verse. First, it all but ignores the important issue of religion, whether as a matter of national policy or the expression of an author's personal beliefs. Second, verse of the 1560s generally ignores the tradition of courtly love, even though the atmosphere at court would seem, on the surface of things, to have invited such expression. Elizabeth's personal life was a matter of central concern, her suitors and potential suitors the very stuff of court gossip. Love poetry might have catered to this interest, or it might just as easily have warned against it in the tradition of many of Wyatt's love complaints, particularly in light of the queen's dangerous flirtation with Lord Robert Dudley. There is no evidence, however, that poetry at court addressed itself more than tangentially to the issues of courtship and religion which dominated the courtly milieu, primarily, it would seem, for reasons of decorum. The issues were of the utmost seriousness, and only gradually did it become clear that the new regime would be able to cope with them. A courtier might appear flippant, even disloyal by injecting so frivolous a medium as verse into the crisis-ridden atmosphere of the early

Elizabethan court. Two changes must largely account for the creation of an environment that encouraged courtiers to nurture English poetry during the last two decades of the reign. First, the scornful attitude toward vernacular poetry dissipated, although it did not disappear, and second, the queen's reign moved from tentative viability to robust success. The defeat of the rebels in 1570 was a reassuring, major victory early on in the process; accordingly, the queen's poetic response to it signalled that informal means of expression were appropriate given the less urgent national circumstances. Poetry thrived as the regime gained confidence and found causes for celebration.

The diminishing tensions at court are reflected to an intermediate degree in the *Carmen Gratulatorium* which greeted Elizabeth upon her visit to Theobalds in September of 1571. Cecil's authorship of these Latin hexameters is entirely plausible considering that he had allowed Latin verse elegies to be published under his name in 1550, and that he would do so again with his eulogy for Sir Thomas Chaloner in 1579. The *Carmen*, however, is no stuffy Latin oration couched in meter, for it praises the queen and comments upon the newly created Lord Burghley's affairs in the person of the house itself. The poem is entitled a "Prosopopaea Theobaldensis," and, after Hatton's contribution to *Gismond of Salern*, it is probably the first attempt at poetic fiction by an Elizabethan courtier. Its tone harmonized with the regime's growing sense of security, for the prosopopoeia provides a light and playful touch while the Latin quantities banish any suggestion of undue frivolity. Cecil apparently viewed English rhyming as appropriate only for communicating with children.

The innovations which began filtering into courtier verse at some point in the early 1570s failed nevertheless to displace the practice of the older humanism among its courtier practitioners. Thus Lord Burghley's thirty-six-line Latin eulogy for the 1579 edition of Chaloner's *De Republica Anglorum* is more polished and ambitious than either of the epitaphs written by Wilson and Wolley for Bishop Jewel. During the 1580s, Lady Russell and her son, Sir Edward Hoby, composed formal epitaphs in Latin verse for Lord Russell, while Lady Russell was sending out poetic condolences as late as 1599 in the case of her eulogy for Egerton's son. Similarly, as the "cult of Elizabeth" reached its most extravagant pitch by identifying her with classical goddesses and heroines of courtly love, the queen herself pursued accomplishments quite foreign to the average deity or sonnet lady. In the fall of 1593 she translated Boethius's

Consolation of Philosophy into English verse, and in 1598 she did
the same for part of Horace's *Ars Poetica* and for the section on
curiosity from Plutarch's *Moralia* to a length of over five hundred
lines from the original Greek.[13] The continuity of the humanist
tradition is evidenced by Hoby's translation of a couplet from Hesiod's *Works and Days*, the same source from which Ascham took a
passage to illustrate metaphrasis in *The Scholemaster*. It is worth
noting that the *Works and Days* as well as Aratus's *Phaenomena*,
from which Hoby also translated a couplet, were primary sources of
the Virgo-Astraea myth from which was derived the glorification of
Elizabeth as Astraea, restorer of the golden age.[14] However, neither
Ascham nor Hoby drew any parallels between these tales and their
sovereign's reign—indeed, Hoby cited them to underscore the world's
degeneration since the golden age.

The shift from a strictly classics-oriented humanism to more
wide-ranging applications of humanist learning is well illustrated by
the copious output of Hoby's Eton schoolmate, Sir John Harington.
Although he translated excerpts from a host of classical authors, two
works dominate his Elizabethan writings, his translation of *Orlando
Furioso* from Ariosto's Italian, and his epigrams, which are often
modeled upon Martial's but are written in English. Where the "old"
humanism attempted to duplicate classical culture on its own terms,
Harington, among other courtiers, perpetuated the ideals of his
classical education in the vernacular, and chose as well to imitate
and translate contemporary humanists as well as the ancients. The
difference in attitude toward the classics emerges clearly in the
letter Harington wrote from court to his son's schoolmaster at Eton
just a few months before the queen's death: "trewly since I came
from Cambridge (which ys now 20 yeeres) I cannot remember that I
have written any latten verses yet by this occasion of teaching my
sonne I see I have not quite forgotten them."[15] Thus Harington's
practice of reserving Latin poetry for the instruction of children
effectively reverses Lord Burghley's views on the subject. For the

13. The Boethius, according to Camden, was undertaken in her grief over
the conversion to Catholicism of Henry IV of France (*Annals*, 475). The king
announced his conversion in July 1593, and Elizabeth is said to have completed
her entire translation between October 10 and November 5 of that year (BL,
Lansdowne MS 253, f. 200).

14. Frances A. Yates, *Astraea: The Imperial Theme in the Sixteenth Century*, 30–31.

15. Norman Egbert McClure, *The Letters and Epigrams of Sir John Harington*, 95–96.

majority of later Elizabethan courtier poets, classical learning was a means toward an end rather than an end in itself.

The New Lyricism

During the 1570s a body of courtier verse emerged that revived the emphasis upon love poetry as it had been introduced to the Tudor court by Wyatt and Surrey. Upon this revitalized foundation, amorous courtier poetics developed without interruption to the end of the reign and beyond. Unlike courtier verse of the 1560s, the new lyricism modeled itself primarily upon post-classical continental authors, from Petrarch to the Pléiade. Attention to the classics remained strong, of course, but the ancients were assimilated into the new poetics almost exclusively in the vernacular. The courtier's immediate experience is often reflected in this poetry, although the exact circumstances behind it cannot always be identified, nor does this later work necessarily mirror or grow out of actual experience. From a literary standpoint this is perhaps the most important shift away from the trends of the 1560s. Subsequent courtier verse placed a greater emphasis upon artifice in its treatment of occasional subjects, while it increasingly strayed away from real events as the most respectable inducements for writing poetry. The movement was toward fiction and the creation of poems to be valued for their own sake, not merely for their commemorative function. As courtier poets ventured anew into the realms of fiction, they made possible once again the creation of a genuine literature of the court. Progress toward a golden age of lyricism was slow, especially with regard to form and the technical aspects of composition, but the shift in direction occurred suddenly during the period between roughly 1570 and 1575.

Although Dyer has been considered the premier Elizabethan courtier poet, that is, the first to compose love lyrics there, the available evidence confers this distinction upon the earl of Oxford. His earliest datable work conforms, nevertheless, to one of the established functions for poetry practiced by Ascham and Wilson. In 1572, Oxford turned out commendatory verses for a translation of Cardano's *Comfort*, published in 1573 by his gentleman pensioner friend, Thomas Bedingfield. The poem differs from earlier efforts of the kind not so much because it appeared in English (as had Ascham's verses for Blundeville's book), but because his verses are so self-consciously poetic. The earl uses twenty-six lines to develop his formulaic exempla: Bedingfield's good efforts are enjoyed by others just as laborers, masons, bees, and so forth also work for the profit of others. Oxford flaunts a copious rhetoric in this poem in contrast with the more direct, unembellished commendatory verses of his predecessors. His greatest innovation, however, lies in his application of the same qualities of style to the eight poems assigned to him in the 1576 *Paradise of Dainty Devices*, pieces that Oxford must have composed before 1575. In January of that year he left England upon his continental tour, not to return until April of the same year in which the *Paradise* was published, and even if he had circulated his poems thereafter, it is most unlikely that they would have filtered down to the printer in the space of only a few months. Beyond reasonable doubt then, Oxford wrote these lyrics while still in his early twenties, between about 1570 and 1575, a general dating also reinforced by the echo in poem 2 of several lines from the verses for Bedingfield's book.

DeVere's eight poems in the *Paradise* create a dramatic break with everything known to have been written at the Elizabethan court up to that time. Seven of them are love lyrics, four of which are complaints set forth with variations in tone and approach that sharply differentiate them from one another (poems 2, 3, 5, 9). Poem 5 is based on Petrarch's *Rime* 102, although it could not be termed a translation, for Oxford goes far beyond his original in emphasizing the lady's disdain and lamenting his own forlorn condition. The texts of poems 3 and 9 indicate that they were meant to be sung, as were all of the *Paradise* poems according to its introduction.[16] Yet Oxford's lyrics are almost the only genuine love songs in the anthology, a book that, conservative in its beginnings, grew "more and more sedate" in later editions.[17] His poem 8 from the *Paradise* describes an allegorical encounter with Desire, while poem 4 cries out against "this losse of my good name," a defiant lyric without precedent in English Renaissance verse. The diversity of Oxford's subjects, including his varied analyses of the lover's state, were practically as unknown to contemporary out-of-court writers as they were to courtiers.

Oxford's birth and his standing at court in the 1570s made him a model of aristocratic behavior. He was, for instance, accused of introducing Italian gloves and other such fripperies at court; his example would have lent respectability even to so trivial a pursuit as

16. Winifred Maynard analyzes this anthology's connections with the five-part consort song in "*The Paradyse of Daynty Deuises* Revisited" (295–300).

17. Hyder E. Rollins, ed., *The Paradise of Dainty Devices*, lxvi.

the writing of love poetry. Thus, while it is possible that Dyer was writing poetry as early as the 1560s, his earliest datable verse, the complaint sung to the queen at Woodstock in 1575, may itself have been inspired by Oxford's work in the same vein. Dyer's first six poems in Part II are the ones he is most likely to have composed before his association with Philip Sidney. In *Old Arcadia* poem 9, Sidney implies that Dyer's "He that his mirth hath lost" was written a good while beforehand, nor for that matter is there any trace of Sidney's influence upon the first half-dozen poems attributed to Dyer in Part II. Yet even if all six of them were written by 1575, Oxford would still emerge as the chief innovator due to the range of his subject matter and the variety of its execution. By contrast, Dyer was a specialist, for eight of his twelve canonical poems are first-person amorous complaints (poems 1–7, 10), while 8, 9, and 11 are also about love. In addition, three of the four poems Dyer may have written are lovers' complaints. Dyer's output represents a great departure from courtier verse of the 1560s, and several of his poems were more widely circulated and imitated than any of Oxford's; still, the latter's experimentation provided a much broader foundation for the development of lyric poetry at court.

Oxford's poems 2–9 and Dyer's poems 1–4 reveal that the tenor and concerns of courtier verse in the 1570s differed substantially from those expressed by Henry VIII's courtiers. The sense of dread and fear for one's personal safety inspired by that often harsh and unpredictable monarch is replaced, at its most pessimistic, with an emphasis upon despair and death resulting from unrequited or lost love. The conventions of courtly love persist, but they are pursued in a far more benign atmosphere. Secrecy and the dissimulation of one's love are constant themes, reflected in such alliterative phrases as Oxford's "silent sute" and "secret sighs" or the full analysis of deceptive appearances in poem 5, "I am not as I seme to bee." Dyer writes of "one that lives in shew," or as a lover who has "secret kept my tongue" while his eyes told all. This secrecy is motivated primarily by the lover's sense of his unworthiness compared with the lady's exalted condition. No jealous husband, royal or otherwise, lurks menacingly in the background of these poems; instead there is the frequent threat of a rival, the "other man" who obtains what the lover desires in Oxford's poem 8, line 16, or those victorious others who "cam not to my faith" in Dyer's poem 2, line 40. The cast-off lover goes into exile, the "desart wonne" of Dyer's poem 1, line 5, or the zombie-like death in life of the wilderness setting in his poem 2, lines 63–72, where "wormes my feast shallbe / Wherwith my bodie shalbe fed till they doe feede on me." Oxford commits himself "an Ancre's life to leade, with nailes to scratche my grave, / Where earthly Wormes on me shall fede, is all the joyes I crave" (poem 3, lines 21–22). All this sounds rather bleak, but it is largely self-imposed and described in such hyperbolic excess as to leave no doubt that the speaker exaggerates his despair.

How well these conventions were adapted to the everyday concerns of an Elizabethan courtier can be seen through closer examination of three of these early lyrics, one of which, Dyer's poem 1, was undoubtedly written for the queen, and the other two, probably so. At worst, Dyer's poem 3 and Oxford's poem 6 could have done their authors no harm had they fallen into Elizabeth's hands. The beloved of Dyer's third complaint is described as a "Sacred presence . . . / Wherin besides Dame Venus' stayne great Majesty did shine" (lines 16, 18). His "suyte" to her never "did exceed, the Bandes of Modesty," and it has been so reduced that now "all my Sute" is only that she visit the poet's "everleastinge Grave." The mistress described and sued to in this fashion need not be the queen—any self-respecting sonnet lady might exact a similar characterization—but a courtier reading over these lines as they circulated in the Privy Chamber would surely have suspected that the "faire dame" they addressed was Elizabeth. Similarly, Oxford compares his mistress to Venus, Juno, and Pallas, then identifies her as she "alone, who yet on yearth doeth reigne" (poem 6, line 11). The gulf between poet and lady is likened to that between Vulcan and Venus or Endymion and Phoebe, comparisons suitable for any courtly love relationship, although these goddesses were repeatedly associated with Queen Elizabeth.[18]

If indeed Elizabeth ever read or heard these poems, as she undoubtedly heard Dyer's Woodstock poem, the effect must have pleased her. She has devastated her admirers, of course, both of whom are overwhelmed with passion. Dyer has gone into seclusion where "my life the shape of death must beare" (poem 1, line 17). Oxford suffers in silence, with only his sighs bearing witness to the seething passions in his heart. He cannot refrain from beholding her, while to Dyer "It was a Heaven to me to view thy face Devine" (poem 3, line 17). The object of this love has caused unspeakable suffering, but for all that she remains wholly blameless: for Dyer, Love is the culprit, "That Love I say, that luckles Love, which workes mee all this yll, /

18. The myth of Endymion and Phoebe provided an apt analogue to Elizabeth and her suitors, witness Lyly's play on the subject and Spenser's representation of the queen as Belphoebe in *The Faerie Queene*.

This ill wherof sweet Soule, thou art at all no cause" (poem 3, lines
10–11). Oxford avoids characterizing his mistress as sadistic by declaring that there's life in it yet, vowing to sail on through seas of
tears, oblivious to disdain: "Who loves alofte and setts his hart on
hie, / Deserves no paine, though he doe pine and die" (poem 6, lines
29–30).

Aside from Dyer's Woodstock poem, we do not know that any
other lyrics by Dyer or Oxford were directed to the queen, and even
if they were, we could not be sure of their intention or the circumstances in which they were composed. Sargent's belief that the
queen neglected Dyer after 1573, and that he used poem 1 to
recapture her attention, is contradicted by Lady Sidney's acknowledgment of his ability to deal with affairs at court as late as September 1574.[19] The record of Dyer's court lodgings in that same
year, coupled with the fact that Elizabeth visited him at Woodstock
in the course of her 1575 progress, all indicate that he was a courtier in good standing during the mid–1570s, in contrast to the alienated despair of his song on that occasion. Furthermore, Dyer may
have done no more than contribute these lines to the larger entertainment; we cannot be sure that he sang them in person to the
queen, or that he was identified at the time as the author of these
verses. It seems far more likely that Oxford personally directed
poem 6 to the queen to celebrate some pinnacle in their relationship such as the favoritism he enjoyed during the spring of
1573 when it was reported that Elizabeth "delitithe more in his
parsonage, and his daunsinge, and valientnes, then any other."[20]
But whatever the circumstances of composition, occasion has
become much less important as a justification for writing verse,
and poetry now serves occasions in ways quite different from its
applications during the 1560s.

In all three poems presumably addressed to Elizabeth, the courtly love tradition has been culled for those motifs best suited for
carrying on a playful flirtation with one's sovereign. The emphasis
in these poems is upon the lady's unworldly beauty, wit, and majesty, a superiority that forces the unworthy lover to hide or dissem-
ble his feelings. He stresses the joy of being with her (personal access
in the language of the court), and the morbid desolation of exile from
her presence. All this is the stock in trade of the Petrarchan son-
neteer, although the lady's innocence of all wrongdoing in the havoc

19. Ralph M. Sargent, The Life and Lyrics of Sir Edward Dyer, 29.
20. Nichols, Progresses, 1:328.

caused by her beauty is a less common theme. But with what degree
of seriousness could either poet have devised, or the queen perused, these love poems? Neither courtier was a candidate for her
hand, let alone a clandestine love affair. Oxford could not literally
hope for a relationship with Elizabeth like that of Venus with
Vulcan or Phoebe with Endymion, nor was Dyer actually languish-
ing under the torment of a living death as his song avowed. These
hyperbolic passions must have been recognized for the exaggerations they were. They may have expressed a genuine devotion to
the queen or complained of some actual slight; in either case, the
authors' intentions were distanced from the face value of their
poetry. The extravagant rhetoric and passionate stances assumed
in these complaints were more clearly intended for the amusement
of the queen and her courtiers—the direct, functional nature of
earlier courtier verse has given way here to a poetics which is to an
important degree fictional.

The same is true of other poems by Oxford and Dyer which lack
definite connections with Elizabeth. Oxford's poem 4, for example,
seemingly responds to some insult or disgrace the earl suffered, for it
is not modeled upon any recognized subgenre of lyric verse which he
might have chosen to cultivate for its own sake. If genuine rage is
expressed by these lines, however, it is partially sublimated by the
rhetoric of the poem itself. From the graphic opening metaphor of
the forlorn hope to the epic listing of entities called upon to help him
lament his loss, our attention is drawn to the artifice of the poetry
and away from the experience behind it. The excessive passions
described in Dyer's complaints are set forth in like manner; the
victim of "He that his mirth hath lost" is condemned to a life of
"raging agonies," his "prospect into hell / Wher Sisiphus, that
wretched wight, in endlesse payne doth dwell" (poem 2, lines 69,
71–72), all from unrequited love, and with all this suffering further
undercut by the punning signature toward the end of the poem, "My
song, yf any aske whose greivous case is suche, / Die er thoue lette
his name be knowen, his folie shoes to muche" (lines 77–78). The
stock attributes of mid-century verse, its exaggerated, pounding
rhythms, fixed caesuras, copious examples, and studied alliteration
furnished courtiers with a suitable vehicle for cultivated display.
These traits constituted an English equivalent to the similarly me-
chanical pleasures of quantitative verse; that is, insofar as the Elizabethan response to classical meters was at least partially an "intellectual apprehension" of the proper and intricate combinations of
syllables, "drab" poetics offered equally quantifiable, even visual

modes of appeal.[21] In either case, unfortunately, the aesthetic delight bordered upon that "peaceful province in acrostic land" that Dryden would recommend to Shadwell in *MacFlecknoe*. It was left for Sidney to argue in the *Defence* that mechanics should be subordinated to content in order to bring out the "moving" powers of poetry. The result, he realized, created a higher pleasure and one indispensable to any didactic purpose for the art.

Sidney's observation that the *energia* he aspired to in English verse was more fully practiced by "divers smally learned courtiers" than in "some professors of learning" may have concerned their style in prose and verse, yet if he was referring to poets, Oxford and Dyer were prominent among them if not the only ones he had in mind.[22] Amidst the conventionalism of their output it is nevertheless possible to find touches of authentic human emotion, dramatic lines, and apt expression. Oxford adapted the oppressively regular caesuras of poulter's measure to the lively stichomythia of his poem 11, a dialogue between the poet and Desire. The relentless anaphora of his complaint in poem 9 shifts without warning in the last line of the penultimate stanza to an attack upon the cruel mistress, and concludes, "let all those that shall her se, / Dispise her state, and pitie me" (lines 35–36). And some pangs of genuine rage shoulder their way through the stifling alliteration of his second and third stanzas in poem 10. Dyer likewise evokes a colloquial tone, as we shall see, in several passages of poem 2, and he injects this forceful simile into the sing-song banality of poem 4:

> Unrippe but that with threede is sowen
>   How lothe it dothe departe;
> Muche lother then must nedes be puld
>   The bodye from the hearte.
>
> (lines 9–12)

The life, voice, and imagination of the great Elizabethan lyricism can be detected in these poems, albeit in amounts rather too dilute to call forth Sidney's unqualified praise.

Most of the remaining works attributed to Oxford and Dyer might well have been written as poetic exercises rather than to commemorate or influence actual events, yet even the suppositional occasions underlying these poems distance them from the occasional verses of the 1560s. From a contemporary viewpoint,

21. Attridge, *Syllables*, 76–77.
22. Katherine Duncan-Jones and Jan Van Dorsten, eds., *Miscellaneous Prose of Sir Philip Sidney*, 118.

such amorous outpourings could hardly have been justified. They were precisely the kind of lyrics that gave poetry a bad name, growing as they ostensibly did out of vain love affairs. Frittering away one's time to so ungodly a purpose was indefensible, nor might the author protest that he had only written them as amusing exercises— that would be an equally unedifying pastime. It took a certain amount of audacity to circulate these verses at court, and Oxford and Dyer were apparently the only courtiers who did so until the late 1570s. Their pioneering efforts perhaps grew naturally (though by no means predictably) out of their places within the social milieu of the court. Both were royal favorites, and Oxford, a peer of the realm. His more vibrant, aggressive approach to the queen through his poetry may reflect his more exalted status as a courtier, relative to Dyer, whose despairing complaints are appropriate to a plain gentleman's unsuccessful attempts to monopolize his sovereign's favor. Leicester and Burghley may have tried to make Dyer "as great as ever was Hatton," but there is no evidence that he ever achieved so dazzling an eminence.[23] Lord Oxford, on the other hand, kept a wavering hold upon the pinnacle of Elizabeth's favoritism throughout the 1570s. Unlike the poets who had dominated courtier verse in the previous decade, neither Oxford nor Dyer held working offices in the government or household, while their lack of university training also distinguishes them from the majority of the earlier courtier poets. Their background most nearly resembles that of the elder Harington, who was also in high favor with the queen although unprovided of a significant office. And Harington's poetry, in its use of the vernacular and attention to Italian influences, strayed furthest from the norms of courtier verse in that first decade of the reign. It is as if Cecil, Ascham, Wilson, and Elizabeth took care that their dabbling in poetry did not violate their positions as state dignitaries, nor clash with the serious responsibilities left to their care. Oxford and Dyer, holding less exalted official status, were correspondingly freer to attempt something questionable, with less regard for its impact on their public image.

The Moral Strain

While the earliest courtier poets used humanist precedents, ultimately classical in origin, to legitimize their writings, and while the lyrics of Oxford and Dyer failed of any justification at all by contem-

23. Letter of May 11, 1573, reprinted in Sargent, *Life and Lyrics*, 28.

porary standards, professional poets justified their work on grounds of its didactic and moral content. The vanity of this world, the importance of moderation in all things, the uncertainty of fortune, and the profit of true friends and right living—these and a host of equally uplifting topics were explored at length in such commercial ventures as the *Paradise* or *The Mirror for Magistrates*, and in the works of George Turberville, Nicholas Breton, Thomas Howell, and dozens more. These poems could not be condemned as wanton or unthrifty when they transmitted sound moral advice or necessary wisdom. The rhyming spawned by this rationale for poetry forms a large and dreadful component of "Drab Age" verse. It is marked by a generalized, image-starved diction, alliterative phrasing, and long-line meters. Courtier poets turned out very little verse of this kind, although it would be evasive to say that the court was completely spared.

The two poems attributed to Sir William Cordell, whatever their date of composition, are good examples of poetry grounded in moral orthodoxy. Poem 307–8 in the *Arundel Harington Manuscript* was directed to an individual reader for the purpose of explaining "What lyf in courte is best for you to leade." The advice it imparts is of the kind that would set Polonius's head wagging in agreement:

> Be frend to few, but foe to none at all,
> Vse Curteis speeche to eache in their degree,
> Lead not your lyf but even with suche as shall
> by vertew wonne in league with you to be.

The first five poems attributed to Sir Thomas Heneage in Part II belong to the same tradition. The unique texts in the Harvard manuscript were transcribed before 1585, and Heneage's originals may well date back to the 1570s. Their warning against deceptive appearances might be fittingly applied to the exaggerated passions set forth in the lyrics of Oxford and Dyer. Words, we learn, can be deceptive and no one should be trusted until, as at the conclusion of a court masque, "tyme shall putt their vysardes of" (poem 2, line 6). In the vain world of the court, "faith is rare, thoe fayrest wordes be rife" (poem 4, line 4). In these works, Heneage seems to elaborate upon the sentiments he confided to Walsingham in a letter circa 1578: "Toching the Courte, our old humors growe not weake by Age, but increase by noryshment, And he ys not a Courtier .vj. dayes, but can lerne how to make hym self acceptable."[24] Malice, pride, and lust

---

24. PRO, SP 15/25/113.

are prominent among the "humors" characteristic of the court as Heneage describes it in poem 4.

Rhetorically, Heneage's muse is spare and direct in the manner of the 1560s, but there the resemblance ends. His fourth, fifth, and sixth poems are English, seven-rhyme sonnets, quite possibly the first ones written by any courtier since the death of Surrey. There is no indication that Heneage wrote his poems for such special occasions as the New Year's or Accession Day celebrations; they are instead private verse letters which impart his solemn observations on the state of affairs at court. The addressees are "My frend" (poem 2), "my Lord" (poem 4), and "Madame" (poems 3 and 6), the latter of these a response to poem 6a, the queen's verses about her oppressive sense of public responsibility. Here, Elizabeth wrote a genuinely private poem, and Heneage's response is equally confidential. All six of Sir Thomas's known poems exist in unique copies which saw little or no manuscript circulation, nor was he referred to as a poet by contemporaries. Heneage used poetry to communicate with his peers and with his sovereign, but he avoided anything so radical as the love lyrics initiated by Oxford and Dyer. By dealing with subjects of unimpeachable moral worth, Heneage endowed his poems with the same respectability found in most of the age's published, professional verse. If his output is deficient in aesthetic pleasure, it is nevertheless invaluable as a revelation of the different ways courtiers used poetry. In rank and favor with Elizabeth, Heneage held essentially the same status as Dyer, if somewhat less than Oxford. Through his office as treasurer of the chamber, however, he was assured of access to his sovereign in a way not absolutely guaranteed even to a peer of the realm. He was also a favorite of much longer standing, rewarded by Elizabeth with lands and office beyond anything Oxford or Dyer were destined to obtain. The latter two might seek to influence the queen with such flamboyant innovations as their love lyrics; the mature, settled, puritanical treasurer cultivated with greater decorum his philosophical, didactic verse. A seat on the Privy Council loomed in his future. It is a wonder that so conservative an officer as Heneage wrote poetry at all.

The liveliest example of moral didacticism in verse of the early Elizabethan court is "Sacvyles olde age," by Thomas Sackville, Lord Buckhurst. It was composed circa 1570 by a courtier and peer of the realm whose standing with Elizabeth equalled or exceeded Heneage's high favor. Sackville's verse epistle, addressed to one of the queen's physicians, Dr. Thomas Francis, is far more ambitious than Heneage's known efforts in the same vein. "Sacvyles olde age" consists of

236 lines of iambic pentameter cross rhyme (*a b a b*), their content applied to an orderly and conventional structure: since old age irresistibly debilitates both body and mind, the poet vows to renounce his youthful follies, especially poetry, and devote his remaining energies to the service of God. It is an early expression of the Elizabethan literary pattern of prodigality, repentance, and reform,[25] although Sackville's handling of the theme coupled with what is known of his youth and career as a courtier contradict much of his thesis.

Sackville bids farewell to youthful frivolities, above all his love of poetry, in fifty-nine stanzas of verse that consciously imitate Chaucer, Surrey, Wyatt, and other contemporary writers.[26] The poem's vivid descriptions resemble Sackville's style in the "Induction" to *The Mirror for Magistrates*, and thus diverge from the bulk of what was produced by the mid-century "moral" school, courtier or professional. As a renunciation of poetry, it is a remarkably ambitious, studied poem, nor is that the only irony. Thomas laments that "his chynne is whit now all his lockes are greye" (line 64), although he was writing in his late thirties, if not earlier, and well before the "twyse tewnty [*sic*] yeres" he cites as the boundary between youth's vigor and the decay of old age. He confesses his delight in Chaucer's *Troilus* and the Reeve's and Miller's tales, and in Surrey's "lofty rimes." But instead of Surrey's rhymed love lyrics, he mentions only the unrhymed translation of Virgil, the earliest blank verse in English and the very form that Sackville himself used in *Gorboduc*. Thomas bemoans his youthful devotion to love, but this too is countered by his memory of singing "wyat*es* psalmes . . . / in court amyd the heavenly ladyes bryght" (lines 92–93). It is possible that Sackville also wrote love lyrics, for Jasper Heywood praised his "Sonet*es* sweetely sauste,"[27] yet his only known earlier verses are the political, morally respectable contributions to the *Mirror* and *Gorboduc*, and his staid commendation of Hoby's *Courtier*. Then, toward the end of the poem, Thomas renounces his favorite poets with such hyperbolic praise that the rejections become an endorsement:

> my guyde my master o Chaucer alas farwell
> . . . .
> farewell Surrea iewell off englishe verse

25. For analysis of other examples of the type see Richard Helgerson, *The Elizabethan Prodigals* (23), and Rivkah Zim and M. B. Parkes, "Sacvyles Olde Age," (5–6, with other parallels noted in their commentary to the poem).
26. Zim and Parkes, "Sacvyles Olde Age," 15–20.
27. *The Seconde Tragedie of Seneca*, 1560, STC 22226, sig. *7ᵛ.

> . . . cround is thy honour wᵗ eternite
> thou syttest hyest in the house off fame
> the and thy golden verses honour I
> and on my kne fall when i here thy name
> (lines 202, 209, 213–16)

A still greater discrepancy, and one that would not have escaped Dr. Francis, is Sackville's concluding renunciation of the court, "the glisterynge palaice and the goden [*sic*] hall*es*," as he vows to devote himself to the service of "the hevenly kynge" (lines 227, 231). Instead, the career at court which began for Sackville in 1566 diverged almost at once from the largely ornamental courtiership practiced by Oxford and Dyer. Lord Buckhurst soon became, like Heneage, a working royal servant. He entertained foreign dignitaries as early as 1568, was appointed joint lieutenant of Sussex in 1569, and in 1571 undertook his first diplomatic mission abroad as Elizabeth's special envoy to France. Sackville was at least several years removed from the old age he laments in this poem, and his retirement from life at court to the service of God was an even remoter prospect. "Sacvyles olde age" is a morally orthodox work which is nevertheless compromised by its poetic style and its author's career as a royal servant. The discrepancies amount to the adoption of a conventional mask rather than genuinely imaginative fiction, yet the mask creates a playfully ironic tone. The most unfortunate irony, however, is that Thomas apparently fulfilled his promise to abandon the muses, for no later verse is known from his pen.

Oxford's poem 16 also belongs to the moral-philosophical tradition, but by far the most successful offspring of the kind, whether written by Oxford or Dyer, must be the perennial favorite, "My mind to me a kingdom is." Its composition may well date from the 1570s, although the earliest known text was transcribed in mid-1581.[28] This smug expression of a mind wholly accommodated to a simple, moderate way of life was doubly superior to most of the poems that dealt with this and similar ethical matters. First, by avoiding the fourteeners and poulter's measure which were the metrical mainstay of this tradition, its crisper tetrameters gave the work a much lighter air and faster pace. This rhythm reinforced, as well, the positive, self-satisfied tone which also makes "My mind to me" a more attractive vehicle for setting forth its commonplace ideas,

---

28. A critical text of this poem is reprinted among works possibly by Oxford in Part II. I discuss its date of composition, texts, and the claims of Oxford and Dyer in "The Authorship of 'My Mind to me a Kingdom Is'" (385–94).

whereas contemporary verse of the kind tended to be negative in tone, warning of dire consequences or expressing outrage at the excesses of fallen man.

Conclusion

It is tempting to relegate nearly all of the earliest Elizabethan courtier verse to the same aesthetic backwater that engulfs most mid-century English poetry. Certainly the classical efforts of the humanists are too undistinguished to warrant much notice; for most of them, biographical and historical interest far transcends their literary achievement. Hatton's contribution to *Gismond of Salern*, the queen's spirited reaction to the Northern Rebellion, and Sackville's verse epistle constitute the high points of English courtier verse before the 1570s, but even here it might be argued that our interest is focused primarily upon the personal and social context, nor did these works exert a discernible influence upon contemporary writers in either courtier or professional circles. From the second decade of the reign, however, several lyrics by Oxford and Dyer can claim both literary respectability and a powerful contemporary influence. "My mind to me a kingdom is" has been continuously reprinted since 1588, and it exists in at least fifteen manuscript copies dating between roughly 1581 and 1624. Both William Byrd and Orlando Gibbons set it to music, while Robert Greene and Robert Southwell are two identifiable poets among many anonymous ones who wrote imitations or continuations. Of the thousands of lines of moral and philosophical verse turned out during the first half of the Elizabethan age, only this poem seems to have captured the attention of later generations to a degree at all commensurate with its contemporary impact.

Generally, courtier verse in both the moral and amorous veins was lighter, less oppressive in rhetoric and meter, and more imaginative than the average work of the professional poets. Nevertheless, the contemporary esteem commanded by Dyer's poem 2, "He that his mirth hath lost," is not so easily explained as the on-going popularity of "My mind to me." Dyer's love-lament survives in ten contemporary manuscripts and was deemed worthy of print as late as 1660. Dyer's status as a respected courtier may help to explain such popularity, and perhaps Tudor and Stuart readers admired his ability to reproduce in this poem a tone of adamant remonstrance, the voice of love without hope:

Yet not the wished deathe . . .
Oh noe! that were to well, my death is of the mynd,

. . . .

Not that I mean henceforth this straunge will to professe,
As one that could betray suche trothe to build on ficklenes,
For yt shall never faile that my faithe bore in hand:
I gave my word, my word gave me, bothe word and gift shall
     stand.

                                        (lines 9, 11, 57–60)

In this regard it may also be significant that when Puttenham quoted two lines from a similar lament, Dyer's poem 3, he chose an equally colloquial passage:

But novv my Deere (for so my loue makes me to call you still)
That loue I say, that lucklesse loue, that vvorkes me all this ill.[29]

Dyer's rhetorical pace in poem 2 is also relatively rapid and varied; he develops, for example, metaphors of military defeat in lines 14 and 18–20, and of planting and harvesting in 25–28. He invokes the joys of successful courtship in lines 41–44. His lengthiest attention to any one facet of his plight is the ten lines devoted to his exiled life in the "solitarie wood" (lines 63–72). Contemporary poets did not always exercise a similar restraint. Oxford, as we have seen, heaped up his examples in the commendatory verses for Bedingfield, as did George Turberville in a love lament he published in 1567:

I holde the Hiue in hande and paine my selfe thereby,
While other eate the hidden foods that are not halfe so dry.
I plough the soyle with paine and cast my seede thereon:
And other come that sheare the sheaues and laugh when I am gon.
Mine is the Winters toile, and theirs the Sommers gaine.[30]

After another dozen couplets of the same Turberville asks, "what will you more I say?" Modern readers might well respond with nothing at all, but to no avail, for the poet has another half-dozen examples to deploy (signature N 3–3v). Turberville's basic rhetorical approach is identical with Dyer's, but the latter's kaleidoscopic shifts of subject are, by contrast, refreshingly swift.

For whatever reasons, the contemporary popularity and influence of "He that his mirth hath lost" is undeniable. When Sir Philip Sidney yielded the laurels of English poetry to Dyer as late as 1585,

29. Puttenham, *Arte,* 169.
30. George Turberville, *Epitaphes, Epigrams, Songs and Sonets,* sig. N 2v.

he performed a modest and gracious gesture,[31] yet he seems to have been genuinely fond of some of Dyer's poetry, and he singled out this one complaint for specific praise in the *Old Arcadia*. Sir John Harington referred in his notes after book 8 of *Orlando Furioso* to "an excellent verse" by Dyer, after which he cited line 44 of poem 2. Several of Sir Arthur Gorges's complaints borrowed from it as we shall see, while Ferdinando Stanley, Lord Strange, wrote an abbreviated version, the four sixain stanzas of his poem 1. The insistence that his grief exceeds that of all other rejected suitors, and the punning revelation of authorship ("Tell him my lines *Strange* things may well suffice"; line 21), clearly reveal the indebtedness to Dyer's model lament. Similarly, when Sir Francis Drake went about to commend Peckham's book in 1583, he turned for inspiration to Dyer's poem 2. Drake wrote in the same poulter's couplets but structured his poem rhetorically into the three quatrains and couplet of an English sonnet. The formulaic content of each line in the quatrains, "Who seeks . . . / Whose . . . / If any . . . / Lo, here," is typically illustrated by lines 5–8:

> Who seekes, by gaine and wealth, t'advaunce his house and blood:
> Whose care is great, whose toile no lesse, whose hope, is all for good.
> If anie one there bee, that covettes such a trade:
> Lo, heere the plot for common wealth, and private gaine is made.

The second and third lines of Dyer's poem, "Whose hope is vayne, whose faithe is skornd, whose trust is all betrayed, / Yf he have held them dear and can not ceasse to moan," are thus unmistakably echoed in the second and third lines of Drake's quatrains.

Fulke Greville wrote an even more elaborate imitation of the rhetoric and technical form of his friend's original, and there are other imitations by Robert Southwell and by James Murray, the compiler of Cambridge University Library Manuscript Kk.V.30. Murray also copied out a full text of Dyer's poem, converting it into Scot's dialect under the title "Inglishe Dyare." His own version is entitled "Murrayis Dyare," a phrase which may help to explain this puzzling title to a poem by King James VI, "A Dier at her Ma:ties desyer."[32] The verse which follows is in poulter's measure, an amo-

---

31. Geffrey Whitney, *A Choice of Emblemes*, 196–97.
32. Originally entitled "A Dier on her Matie" in BL, Add. MS 24195 (ff. 11–11v), and Allan F. Westcott, ed., *New Poems by James I of England* (7–9). Other contemporary texts occur in Bodl., MS 165 (f. 46, autograph); and BL, Add. MS 22601 (ff. 31v–33v, there entitled "Passionado"). Although Westcott believed that all of the king's "Amatoria," including this complaint, expressed his impa-

rous complaint bearing strong resemblance to the style and tone of Dyer's poem 2. The king's version does not follow the original wording as closely as Greville's nor does it imitate the punning signature which Stanley and Greville retained, but it repeats the same hypothetical instances (lines 49–52), the comparisons of women with angels (lines 17–22), and portrays the same desperate, forsaken lover:

> My houpe is whole transformed in blacke and colde dispaire
> Except I onlie houpe for deathe to end continuall caire:
> No, death he must not haste, my mischiefs woulde he mend
> It best becumes my miserie to dwine before I end.
>
> (lines 37–40)

Apparently, Dyer's poem was recognized as a model complaint and was termed a "Dyer" in recognition of both its authorship and the hopeless plight of its speaker, one who dies of unrequited love. King James commented upon the passionate extravagance of his imitation in the sonnet which immediately follows it in the Additional Manuscript: "My muse hath made a willfull lye I grante, / I sing of sorrows never felt by me." It is no small tribute to the popularity of Dyer's poem that it circulated at the Scottish court in the 1590s, where Queen Anne thought so highly of it as to ask her husband to compose a similar poem for her. "He that his mirth hath lost" became a prototype for this subgenre of the amorous lyric and is the earliest Elizabethan courtier verse with known international influence.

Two other poems by Oxford and Dyer enjoyed a popularity and influence denied to the vast majority of "drab" compositions. Both works may be products of the 1570s, although their earliest texts date from the 1580s; in concept and rhetoric however, both must be assigned to the tradition of mid-century poetics. Oxford's poem 13, the comparison of love to a game of tennis, occurs in six manuscripts, three of which were transcribed well into the seventeenth century, perhaps as late as mid-century. It was first printed in Cotgrave's *Wits Interpreter* of 1655, and was reprinted in the *School of Recreation* (1684), later editions of which placed Oxford's verses on the same booksellers' stalls with the more timely publications of Dryden, Pope, and Swift. Meanwhile, Dyer's "The lowest trees have tops" (poem 9) was also in print during the second half of the

---

tience as he awaited Anne's arrival from Denmark, or went to fetch her himself in the fall of 1589 (71), this title suggests a date of composition after the royal couple had reached Scotland in May of 1590.

seventeenth century, after enjoying an enormous popularity with manuscript anthologists, for at least twenty such copies are known along with various replies and continuations. Clearly, some of the most widely read of all Elizabethan lyrics were turned out by these two courtiers shortly before Sidney began his literary career, or perhaps even after his verses had begun to circulate in manuscript.

These triumphs notwithstanding, courtier poets had little enough to boast of as the 1570s drew to a close. What of lasting value had the court contributed to the overall state of English poetry as Sidney sat down to survey it along with his friends, Dyer and Greville? Those few lyrics that circulated there in manuscript could have done little to alleviate the pessimism expressed in the *Defence*. The Cambridge humanists had produced a scant handful of English verses from which fictional elements were almost totally excluded. If the sage effusions of Cordell, Heneage, and Sackville were known to Sidney and his friends, they would necessarily have been grouped with the dry lessons of the moral philosophers, for versifying alone could not well leaven them up to the realm of poetry. The most creative courtier efforts were, to be sure, the amorous lyrics of Oxford and Dyer. These poets attempted, at least, to infuse the necessary *energia* into their lines, and in doing so they produced as well an element of fiction. But to what end? Their moderate delight was connected with no discernible teaching, no positive example or ethical instruction. For Sidney and his followers, the task ahead was to combine lyric delight with sound moral instruction, and both, preferably, within a fictional context.

3

The "Blessed Trinitie"

By 1577 Philip Sidney had initiated a wholesale transformation of English poetry. The extent to which he surpassed all of his contemporaries, courtier or professional, tends to obscure the fact that he was influenced from the beginning by Dyer's earlier writings and, no doubt, by the work of other Elizabethan courtiers as well. The two friends were joined in their creative efforts by Fulke Greville, Sidney's schoolfellow, close friend, and the third member of that "blessed Trinitie" celebrated in Sidney's OP 6.[1] Initially, Sidney's muse attempted the same general kinds of poetry that Oxford and Dyer had previously explored but with so much more creativity and experimental ambition as to wholly transcend those efforts by the end of the decade.

Possible poem 1 appears to be an early effort in which Sidney's reliance upon other courtier poets may still be traced. This "Dialogue betweene two shepherds, utterd in a pastorall shew, at Wilton," was first printed in the 1613 edition of the *Arcadia;* the care with which this edition was set forth and the poem's recurrence in all later folio editions argues strongly for its authenticity.[2] Will's interrogation of Dick resembles in both form and content the interrogation of Desire (or Love personified) in Oxford's poem 11, partic-

---

1. Abbreviations and poem numbering for Sidney's poems follow William A. Ringler's designations in *The Poems of Sir Philip Sidney,* lxxi:

AS *Astrophil and Stella*
AT Wrongly Attributed Poems
CS *Certain Sonnets*
LM *The Lady of May*
OA *The Old Arcadia*
OP Other Poems
PP Poems Possibly by Sidney

2. Ringler, *Poems,* 517.

ularly in the five instances where Sidney breaks the long lines to include both question and answer:

W[ill]. . . . what food is that she gives?
D[ick]. Teares drink, sorowes meat, wherewith, not I, but in me my
    death lives.
Will. What living get you then? D[ick]. Disdayne; but just disdayne.
So have I cause my selfe to plaine, but not cause to complayne.
(lines 33–36)

Oxford's poem is also written in poulter's couplets and creates a similar effect although his questions and answers regularly break each line at the caesura:

What was thy meate and dayly foode?
    Sad syghes with great Annoy.
What hadste thow then to drinke?
    Unfayned lovers' teares.
. . . .
What findste thou most to be thy fo?
    Dysdayne of my goodwill.
(poem 11, lines 7–10, 23–24)

Dick, the tormented lover in Sidney's dialogue, likewise expresses his suffering in lines evocative of Dyer's complaints. When Will supposes that some occupational setback has caused his dejection ("is thy Bagpipe broke, or are thy lambs miswent?"), Dick replies "I would it were but thus, for thus it were too well," which sounds like a compression of Dyer's "I would yt were not as yt is," and "Oh noe! that were to well" (poem 6, line 1; poem 2, line 11). The living death he suffers also recalls Dyer's desperately morbid condition in "He that his mirth hath lost." Although conclusive evidence of Sidney's authorship is lacking, these echoes of works by Oxford and Dyer are entirely consistent for verse transitional between the founding of courtier lyricism and the multiple refinements that Sidney would shortly introduce.

The Lady of May, an early and entirely canonical dramatic entertainment, was presented before the queen in prose and verse at Wanstead, the earl of Leicester's estate, in May 1578.[3] Since the publication of Stephen Orgel's essay on the pageant in 1963, criti-

---

3. The date is established in Marie Axton's "The Tudor Mask and Elizabethan Court Drama," in Marie Axton and Raymond Williams, eds., English Drama: Forms and Development, Essays in Honour of Muriel Clara Bradbrook, 37–38, and see Edward Berry, "Sidney's May Game for the Queen," Modern Philology 86 (1989): 252–53n.

cism of the work has been virtually unanimous in supposing that, whatever Sidney's allegorical or political intentions, he meant for the queen to award the lady to Therion, the active forester (and thus a Leicester-Sidney surrogate), instead of Espilus, the passive but wealthy shepherd.[4] From Elizabeth's standpoint, however, as both primary audience and arbiter of the plot, Therion is a doubly unacceptable suitor. He would have alienated her by bragging that "Two thousand deer in wildest woods I have, / Them can I take," or, as the May Lady puts it, he "doth me many pleasures, as stealing me venison out of these forests" (p. 25). Such poaching created more than merely local problems in rural England, for the queen's personal delight in hunting necessitated an adequate stocking of both royal and private preserves. A few years later, Lord Hunsdon informed Leicester of depredations of the game near Wanstead and Havering "wherwythe she [Elizabeth] ys gretly offendyd."[5] Therion is, moreover, a "wild beast"; the meaning of his name would not have escaped Ascham's royal pupil, especially when she heard its denotation confirmed by the May Lady's complaint that "he grows to such rages, that sometimes he strikes me, sometimes he rails at me" (p. 25). The entertainment had opened with an appeal for the queen to render justice, but what justice could Elizabeth perceive in rewarding Therion's personal and social crimes by surrendering the lady to him? By contrast with this thieving ruffian, Espilus is a productive and wholly respectable citizen of the commonwealth whose devotion to the lady at least equals Therion's. Given Elizabeth's conservative approach to most decisions, the triumph of Espilus was a virtual certainty.

The Lady of May's fictional world, in which the queen's host, Leicester, is ludicrously portrayed as a "huge catholicam," was nevertheless a fiction with recognizable contours from Elizabeth's daily routine. Rombus's speech is a genuinely funny parody of the pompous orations with which she was regularly saluted on progress, and

4. Stephen Orgel, "Sidney's Experiment in Pastoral: *The Lady of May*," *Journal of the Warburg and Courtauld Institutes* 26 (1963): 198–203. The prose text cited here follows Duncan-Jones and Van Dorsten, *Miscellaneous Prose*. Subsequent references in the text to Sidney's prose follow this edition unless otherwise stated.

5. PRO, SP 12/150/14, September 13, 1581, and see Heneage's complaint to Burghley, September 1, 1590, that "foresters" such as Therion had "scattered 30 bucks gathered near where her Majesty hunted when she was with you at Theobalds and did kill xl. As great bucks as any were in Waltham forest." Heneage feared that so many deer could not again be assembled in these woodlands so convenient for her majesty's sports (BL, Lansdowne MS 65/51).

she was often called upon not only to permit but actually to promote matches between individual subjects.[6] *The Lady of May*, accordingly, presents the queen with an amusing, imaginary replica of her duties as sovereign. However she resolves its plot, it clearly affirms her royal authority in the proper exercise of justice. The poems Sidney interspersed in his text work with a singleness of purpose to praise the queen and to insist that she alone settle the conflict. Thus "The Supplication" (LM 1) is a royal encomium that makes no request of Elizabeth, and in the singing match which follows, both Therion and Espilus acknowledge the queen's beauty and magnificence. Afterward, Therion takes comfort in his defeat because the decision sprang "from fairest mind" (LM 3, line 18). The one suggestion of some deeper meaning in the piece occurs in the May Lady's comment just before the queen makes her decision, "that in judging me, you judge more than me in it" (p. 30). The most obvious reflection of the lady's circumstances upon Elizabeth in 1578 concerned, not the choice of suitors, but whether or not to marry at all. To that extent, Elizabeth's decision might be interpreted as an endorsement of marriage, which was the policy she upheld publicly when she revived the Anjou marriage negotiations a few weeks later. *The Lady of May*, however, was skillfully contrived to amuse and flatter the queen, and it was probably designed to fulfill no more ambitious a purpose.

Although Sidney's characterization of the suitors significantly favors Espilus, he apparently devised alternative verse responses to the queen's decision. LM 3 presents first a sixain which tells how the foresters' god, Silvanus, won his love, followed by a stanza recounting Hercules' humiliation of Pan, the god of shepherds. In the first four lines of the third stanza, the victor rejoices, while in the final couplet the loser consoles himself with the thought that "My foul mishap came yet from fairest mind." In fact, only these last two lines need be sung by Therion. The prose introduction to LM 3 assigns the entire piece to Espilus: "then did Espilus sing this song, tending to the greatness of his own joy, and yet to the comfort of the other side, since they were overthrown by a most worthy adversary"

6. She wrote in person to urge the widow Anne Talbot, for instance, to accept Sir Robert Stapleton's suit ("our trusty and well-beloved servant"), and she strongly encouraged a Mr. Gryffin of Dyngley to facilitate the match between his son and the daughter of Sir Thomas Gorges, in "just consideracon of the long and faythful service of the gentleman and the neerenes unto us of the ladie Marquis his wyfe, a ladye of or privy Chamber" (Nichols, *Progresses*, 2:628; PRO, SP 12/260/25).

(p. 30). Neither text of the show assigns any of these stanzas to Therion, and only the last two lines are manifestly his. Espilus apparently sang the rest, celebrating Silvanus's triumph and Pan's misadventure "to the comfort" of Therion. Moreover, a misrhyme in the first stanza suggests that Sidney had prepared an alternative song in case Elizabeth did award the lady to Therion; lines 5–6 read, " 'Nothing', sayd he, 'for most I joy in this, / That Goddesse mine, my blessed being sees.' " Sidney never rhymed *this* with long *e* but invariably with short *i*: his favorite rhymes with *this* were *bliss* and *miss*. Presumably, his alternative first stanza, to be sung by Therion, praised Pan, whose "blessed being sees" his love, while Silvanus met defeat in the second stanza. The scribe of the archetype for the 1598 and Helmingham Hall texts,[7] inadvertently copied the last line of this second song. The least likely interpretation of the poem, given Therion's multiple offensiveness to Elizabeth, is that Sidney assumed she would rule in his favor and thus wrote no backup verses for Espilus to sing.

The Wanstead pageant is Sidney's most certain occasional work, but not the only such piece connected with the canon. He probably wrote two other sets of occasional verses to entertain the court during tiltyard spectacles. The AT poems 19 and 21 are preceded in the Ottley Manuscript by a unique companion text beginning, "Waynd from the hope," and all three were almost certainly composed by Sidney. AT 19 explains that Philisides, singing in "praise of Mirrhaes hue," persuaded Menalchas to enter the Accession Day tournament. This song "was to be said by one of the Plowmen after that I had passed the Tilt with my rusticall musick."[8] Mirrhae appears to be a scribal aberration for Mira, the subject of those early lyrics in which Sidney represented himself in the fictional persona of Philisides. The story of this relationship was merged with his self-portrait in the *Old Arcadia* at some time before the completion of that work about 1580. AT 19 makes it clear that Philisides, as Mira's suitor, was to be publicly represented in the Accession Day show for which these three poems were devised. The occasion is described as "the chief of Cupides Sabaothe daies" (line 9), while AT 21 emphasizes the sabbath in lines 2–3 and also refers to the "entry" day, as does "Waynd from the hope." Between 1575 and 1586 November 17 fell twice on a Sunday, in 1577 and 1583, with the earlier date by far

7. *Lady of May* 1, in the introduction to Duncan-Jones and Van Dorsten, *Miscellaneous Prose*, 19.

8. Peter Beal, "Poems by Sir Philip Sidney," 287.

the most likely occasion, judging from the internal evidence of these poems.

The characters and allusions here all deal with Sidney's poetic concerns very early in his career as a writer, before or during his composition of the *Old Arcadia*. Thus Philisides refers to "Samos Ile" (AT 19, line 10), and he is in the *Old Arcadia* a Samothean knight.[9] In the *New Arcadia*, a revision underway no later than 1584, Philisides has become an Iberian knight, and instead of Mira he is guided by a "Star." Indeed, by 1582 at the latest, Mira had yielded to Stella as the beloved of Sidney's poetic self. Another indication of early composition is the technical form and refrain of AT 21, which closely resembles CS 30, a poem dating from about 1577–1581.[10] The reference to Menalcas as a husbandman in AT 19 might suggest that this was the work of an imitator, since Menalcas appears as a shepherd in both versions of the Arcadia, but the discrepancy could just as well argue for Sidney's authorship at a point when he had created this rustic character but had not yet cast him in the role of an Arcadian shepherd (so that Musidorus can impersonate a shepherd by exchanging clothes with him). Every element of these three poems fits in with what we know were Sidney's poetic concerns between roughly 1577 and 1580, nor are any of the details here inappropriate to a dating as early as 1577. Furthermore, in light of the first person transition between AT 19 and AT 21 in the Ottley manuscript, "after that I had passed the Tilt," it is difficult to imagine an imitator of Sidney brazen enough to present himself in the detailed trappings of Sidney's own persona at so public an occasion as the Accession Day festivities. Philisides may be translated "star lover," but its concomitant derivation from the first syllables of its author's name would, if anything, have been even more obvious to the Elizabethan court.

These three attributed poems are vestiges of a third pastoral entertainment which Sidney wrote early in his career as a poet. The tiltyard spectators were to hear (and presumably see) how "Phi-

9. Samos, as Katherine Duncan-Jones discovered ("Sidney in Samothea: A Forgotten National Myth," *Review of English Studies*, n.s., 25 [1974]: 174–77), was the legendary name for England which Sidney could have found in William Harrison's introduction to Raphael Holinshed's *The Firste Volume of the Chronicles of England, Scotlande, and Irelande* (STC 13568). W. L. Godshalk proposed that the reference to Samothea in William Lambard's *A Perambulation of Kent* (1576) was an equally likely source (letter to the editor, *Review of English Studies*, n.s., 29 [1978]: 325–26).

10. Ringler, *Poems*, 423.

lisides, the Shepherd good and true" had persuaded Menalcas the husbandman to participate in the tournament. During Elizabeth's reign, such fictional personae as black, red, green, and white knights had jousted at court as early as 1571, but there is no indication that they received further characterization.[11] Thus, if the three poems connected with Sidney belong to the tournament of 1577, they constitute the earliest Elizabethan tiltyard device in which such personae were cast in a pastoral-romantic framework. "Waynd from the hope" was addressed to the queen by a "desert knighte" who has left his wilderness retreat to celebrate "yor enitry [sic] daye." A note accompanying this poem praises Elizabeth as "Schoolemrs of Reason, / oracle of thoughts / honor of ladies & / Sainte of the saboath,"[12] flattering epithets all, but lacking in amorous innuendo. AT 21 appropriately stresses the joy that her peaceful reign has produced. AT 19, in contrast, describes Philisides singing in praise of Mira's "faire sweet lokes," which "make him loke pale and wan." The different attributes assigned to Mira and the queen indicate that they are two different women, while the knights are motivated by romantic love as well as pious devotion to their sovereign. The obscurity in these works concerns only the identities of Menalcas, Mira, and the "desert knighte," for the royal compliment is imaginative yet wholly transparent.

Sidney's only other clearly occasional verses are also works to which his claim cannot be established with absolute certainty. The two poems sung during the "Fortress of Perfect Beauty" pageant in May of 1581, PP 4 and 5, bear all the earmarks of his style and were performed at a tournament in which he played a major role. They are probably his, but they are embedded in a pageant with definite political overtones to which he may have contributed as well.[13] The show lacks any allusions to his life or works and could therefore have been more easily composed by an imitator than the Ottley poems with their detailed references to some of Sidney's most personal fictional creations.

Next to love sonnets, these semi-military pastoral entertain-

11. HMC, Rutland 1:92.

12. Beal, "Poems of Sir Philip Sidney," 288.

13. For the import of this show as a repudiation of Anjou's suit see Norman Council, "O Dea Certe: The Allegory of The Fortress of Perfect Beauty" (*Huntington Library Quarterly* 39 [1976]: 329–42). Dennis Moore (*The Politics of Spenser's "Complaints" and Sidney's "Philisides" Poems*) summarizes interpretations of the pageant's relationship to the Anjou courtship, stressing the application of the conventions of love poetry to this political crisis.

ments are considered the genre most appropriate for courtier poets, and during the reign of Elizabeth no courtier contributed more to such pageantry than Sidney. His *Lady of May*, however, is generally considered unpolished early work, and his tiltyard poems, if authentic, can hardly command an exalted place in the canon.[14] Several other courtiers are known to have written dramatic entertainments for the court: Oxford performed in a Shrovetide pageant in 1578 and is credited with writing plays which were performed at court, while Essex composed a pageant in prose and verse for the 1595 Accession Day celebration. Sir Henry Lee's "My golden locks" was sung before the queen on Accession Day in 1590, although Lee's contribution to the rest of the show on that occasion remains problematic. The only complete verse entertainment from a courtier's pen other than Sidney's is the pastoral dialogue written in preparation for a royal visit to Wilton circa 1599 by his sister, the countess of Pembroke. The remaining court pageants that have survived are of uncertain authorship or are connected with professional and court poets such as Gascoigne, Lyly, and Churchyard.

By 1580 Sidney had written most or all of the thirteen poems which recount Philisides's courtship of Mira. She is named outright in AT 19; another six were worked into the *Arcadia* (OA 9, 24, 31, 62, 73, and 74), some of them, perhaps, composed especially for Sidney's self-portrait in the romance as Philisides. An eighth lyric about Mira was adapted, rather incongruously, as song 5 of *Astrophil and Stella*,[15] while another, OP 5, was left unconnected with any of Sidney's larger collections of verse. Finally, CS 8–11, sonnets "made when his Ladie had paine in her face," also concern Mira. Sidney's conceit in CS 9 charges that a personified pain has afflicted his lady because,

> I praisde her eyes whom never chance doth move,
>   Her breath which makes a sower answer sweete,
> Her milken breasts the nurse of child-like love,
>   Her legges (O legges) her ay well stepping feete.
> (lines 5–8)

These lines apparently recall OA 62, perhaps his earliest work in the Mira series,[16] a blazon that praises in order Mira's eyes, her teeth as

---

14. A. C. Hamilton described *The Lady of May* as Sidney's "first and only work as a courtier-poet," concluding that this entertainment may be "Too slight to deserve a significant place in the canon" (*Sir Philip Sidney: A Study of his Life and Works*, 20–21, 173).

15. Ringler, *Poems*, 484.

16. Ibid., 410.

"The second sweetly-fenced warde, / Her heav'nly-dewed tongue to garde," "The lovely clusters of her brests, / Of Venus babe the wanton nests," her "brave calves," and "that round cleane foote" (lines 43–44, 53–54, 102, 105). These poems from the "Certain Sonnets" collection reveal that Mira was an actual woman whose attack of smallpox elicited these occasional verses.

It was only natural that Sidney found himself attracted to one or more "courtly nymphs" after he began attending court regularly in mid-1575, and that his romantic interests inspired these early poems. Indeed, when Languet urged him to marry in 1578, Sidney replied in the self-effacing language of Philisides, the Petrarchan poet-lover, with reference to a particular woman: "Respecting her, of whom I readily acknowledge how unworthy I am, I have written you my reasons long since." Whether or not this lady was Sidney's Mira, his poetry reveals much about his relationship with her without revealing her identity. She has been identified as Sidney's sister, Mary (an anagram for Myra); as Penelope Devereux; and as Queen Elizabeth,[17] none of whom is an entirely satisfactory candidate. Mira, we learn, has "golden locks" (OA 75, line 51) and "faire eyes" ("a faire eye," OA 74, lines 48, 27). The "blacke starres" of OA 62, line 15, mark Sidney's final adaptation of that blazon to black-eyed Stella, for all of the earliest manuscripts read simply, "As for the Starres," without reference to their color. Mira's attendance on Diana in OA 73 suggests, as Ringler noted, that the lady in question waited on the queen.[18]

The poems in this series can be readily ordered to trace the stages in a lifelike love affair, however artificial its poetic representation. Philisides describes the onset of his love for Mira in the retrospective OA 73, introduced in the *Arcadia* by a prose account of his life that parallels Sidney's own career until his return to England in 1575. The ensuing dream vision is Sidney's adaptation of the judgment of Paris, with the dreamer, Philisides, appointed to choose between Venus and Diana, while the third goddess, Juno, is replaced by Mira, a mere attendant upon Diana. When the dreamer presumptuously awards the prize to the resplendent Mira, the slighted goddesses take their revenge: Venus swears that Philisides will fall

17. Sidney to Languet, March 1, 1578, from Steuart A. Pears, *The Correspondence of Sir Philip Sidney and Hubert Languet*, 144. For the identifications of Mira see Ringler, *Poems* (418), and Moore, *Politics* (especially 92–125). Ringler suggests that Mira may have been one of the queen's attendants insofar as she belongs to Diana's train in OA 73.
18. Ringler, *Poems*, 418.

prey to Mira's beauty (as if he had not already), and Diana vows to inspire her with a regard for chastity which will drive him to despair. Philisides first, however, enjoys a period of successful courtship reflected in AT 19, his adoring commiseration with his lady's sickness in CS 8–11, and OA 62, the celebratory blazon wherein Mira is characterized in wholly positive terms. OP 5 is a lament in absence, but for Philisides this absence in unenforced in contrast with his subsequent banishment. He is separated from her by hills rather than by her despite. The allusion to the ram contesting with its rival (lines 121–23), suggests that Philisides too may have confronted a rival for Mira's affections. In the *Arcadia* Philisides explained that Mira caused all the "despairing desires" of his friend, Coredens,[19] and we recall that many of Greville's *Caelica* poems are dedicated to Mira—but this point receives no further development. Instead, Philisides looks to the west in longing anticipation of being reunited with the lady.

By the time that Philisides appears in the *Old Arcadia*'s first eclogues, the halcyon days of his pursuit of Mira are over, and the rejected suitor leads a shepherd's life in exile, in contrast with Musidorus, who takes on a degrading rustic identity in order to be near his Pamela. As a poetic dialogue, OA 9 seems to be the one work among the Philisides-Mira poems in the *Arcadia* which was necessarily composed for the purpose rather than adapted from earlier material. Dyer's influence upon Sidney's poetry at this time is here acknowledged by a graceful compliment. The old shepherd Geron employs the "no man / woman" rhyme of "He that his mirth hath lost" (lines 47–48), whereupon another shepherd interrupts the dialogue to remark that "Those woordes dyd once the Loveliest shepard use / That erst I knew, and with most plainefull muse" (lines 62–63). In OA 31, as in OA 74, a verse epistle to Mira, Philisides is banished, without hope, and expecting imminent death, the very lifeblood of forsaken Petrarchan lovers, of course, yet we know in this case that Sidney was thoroughly acquainted with Dyer's verse description of an identical crisis.

Astrophil and Stella song 5 should probably precede the other complaints in any arrangement of these thirteen poems on the basis of the relationship's temporal and psychological development. This work is spunkier in tone; "shrewd gyrles must be beat'n" is its theme, and it equates Mira with some very negative characters, including a thief, tyrant, witch, and devil. Despite Philisides' pro-

---

19. Sir Philip Sidney, *The Countess of Pembroke's Arcadia*, 341.

testations of love in the final stanza, the blunt name-calling in this poem argues that if Sidney represented the queen as Mira, he could never have shown these lines to her without risking serious royal displeasure. The desire for revenge in this poem also crops up in OA 74, before giving way to the tone of hopeless despair expressed in OA 24 and 31.

The Philisides-Mira sequence apparently grew out of Sidney's actual experience with courtship and rejection; still, the representation of this experience in verse aligns itself closely with the themes and genres of earlier lyrics composed by Oxford and Dyer. Only the "smallpox" sonnets and Sidney's sensuous blazon, OA 62, find no counterpart in their verse. This latter poem's descriptive power and emphasis upon the lady rather than the poet's reaction to her belittles the best efforts by contemporary poets in the same vein, Gascoigne's "The stately Dames of Rome" for example, or Whetstone's "Apelles, O, thou famous Greeke."[20] OP 5 is a lament in absence, as is Dyer's poem 4. OA 24, 31, 74, and AS song 5 are lover's complaints which depict Philisides in the same circumstances portrayed in Dyer's complaints 2 and 3. For Dyer, the joys of love are past: "In (was) standes my delight, in (is) and (shall) my woe" (poem 2, line 33), "Then did my Joyes take end" (poem 3, line 33). In OA 74, Philisides recalls similarly his past happiness: "What? was I then worthe such good, now worthie so muche evill? / now fled, then cherished? then so nie, now so remote?" And as in "He that his mirth hath lost," Philisides expects no other consolation than "th'approch of death" (lines 24–25).

If Sidney's desire for revenge in this poem and in AS song 5 seems rather extreme, it was anticipated in Oxford's complaint 9, which concludes, "And let all those that shall her se / Dispise her state, and pitie me." Oxford had, as well, composed an allegorical dream vision (poem 8), of which OA 73 is a full-blown narrative enlargement. The experimental elements in Sidney's treatment of his themes, his quantitative verse and pastoralism, distance his work so thoroughly from that of his courtier predecessors as to minimize any sense of indebtedness. The themes are, furthermore, hackneyed, so that Sidney need not have been familiar with the poems of Oxford and Dyer to undertake these subjects. The point is that their lyrics estab-

20. Gascoigne's blazon occurs in his "Adventures of Master F. J." (in John W. Cunliffe, ed., *The Complete Works of George Gascoigne*, 1:146). Whetstone's rather superior effort was printed in his *Rocke of Regard* (1576, STC 25348, sig. O 1v–2v).

lished a precedent that formed Sidney's immediate literary background as a courtier, and we know that he read his friend's poetry and consulted with him over a period of years as he exercised and refined his own creative abilities. Thus it may be neither a coincidence nor a function of biographical happenstance that the Philisides-Mira poems center on the plight of the lover now banished after enjoying a measure of success in his courtship of the lady.

In a poem dated January 14, 1579, Daniel Rogers praised Sidney's literary accomplishments and implied that both Dyer and Greville were writing poetry with him.[21] Spenser's letters to Gabriel Harvey also describe Sidney and Dyer collaborating to improve English verse; unfortunately, Spenser's well-publicized intimations of familiarity with the "Aereopagus" in 1579 and 1580 have probably distorted as much as they have disclosed about the "blessed Trinitie" of Sidney, Dyer, and Greville. The latter's role in the project before the 1580s has indeed been cast in doubt largely because Spenser never mentions him and because Greville himself was frequently overseas or absent from court during the late 1570s. Nevertheless, Sidney and Greville had ample opportunity before 1580 to discuss poetry and to write it together and in company with Dyer.[22]

In the course of the following decade Dyer rounded out his corpus of a dozen-odd lyrics, Greville composed the majority of his *Caelica* poems, and Sidney established his reputation as an important figure in English literature and the foremost poetic innovator of the Elizabethan age. The crossfire of theme, allusion, and direct quotation within their works reveals a significant degree of mutual influence. Poetry may have been an avocation to these three courtier friends, but it is clear that they were minutely familiar with a good many of each other's works and that the development of courtier verse under their hands was a cooperative venture however much Sidney's genius dominated their efforts. Their love lyrics evolved with ever-greater complexities of form and content in an organic process rooted in Dyer's earliest verse complaints.

21. Jan Van Dorsten, "Literary Patronage in Elizabethan England: The Early Phase," 203.

22. See Morris W. Croll, *The Works of Fulke Greville*, 5, and Ringler, *Poems*, xxx. Sidney, Greville, and Dyer visited Dr. Dee at Mortlake on January 16, 1577 (Sargent, *Life and Lyrics*, 40). Sidney and Greville were together occupied with the German embassy from February to June. In October following and in March of 1578 Sidney's letters to Languet convey Greville's regards to him. All three courtiers participated in the 1578 and 1579 New Year's gift exchanges, and early in 1579 they entertained Languet and Duke Casimir during their hastily arranged visit to England.

Under Sidney's influence, Dyer broke with the "drab" tradition to attempt such uncharacteristic forms as the English sonnet (poem 7), a narrative in trochaic heptameter couplets (poem 8), and the unrhymed lines of his elegy for Sidney (poem 12). The most striking departure from his earlier laments, however, lies in the shift from first-person to third-person speakers, particularly in poems 8, 9, and 10, while even the shepherd's lament of poem 11 is quoted within a third-person framework. In this pastoral, moreover, Dyer acknowledged Sidney's influence outright by remarking of lovers' sorrows that "as once a sheppherd sayd / Their mone [moan] nightes have no morrows," an allusion to Sidney's complaint of "my night of evils, which hath no morow" (CS 3, line 8). This and the pastoral setting of poem 11 clearly reveal Sidney's influence, albeit Dyer still clung to the fourteener couplets which Sidney's technical innovations had rendered obsolete. Thus Dyer's first-person laments, some or all of which may have been directed to the queen, gave way to love poems which are fictional in more than their exaggerated rhetoric.

His most ambitious effort is poem 8, an allegorical tale set in a pastoral landscape and culminating in dual Ovidian metamorphoses. The pastoral elements in Dyer's poem were probably inspired by Sidney and may owe something to his OP 5, especially Philisides' address to the flowers in lines 48–49: "Dresse bosome hers or hedd, / Or scatter on her bedd." This resembles Dyer's account of Amaryllis, the heroine of poem 8, after one of her suitors is transformed into the flower heartsease: "Amarillis pluckte the flowere and ware it on her heade; / Sometime she layde itt on her lapp, Somtyme upon her bedd" (lines 73–74). The narrative is otherwise akin to Philisides' first-person account of his vision of Mira (OA 73) in its personal allegory and the fact that both Mira and Amaryllis are cherished by Diana, a goddess who speaks in both poems. And as with Philisides, a goddess dooms Dyer's Coridon to despair of ever winning the lady. More than her devotion to chastity, however, Amaryllis's pursuit of fame prevents her from accepting and thus saving the lives of Coridon and Charamell, who are changed respectively into an owl and the yellow flower, heartsease. After the lovers have been metamorphosed, Dyer assures us that his characters are but shadows of the real persons who stand behind them.

Amaryllis, as Sargent suggested, is probably Dyer's name for Sidney's Mira, although his identification of this woman with the countess of Pembroke contradicts Amaryllis-Mira's devotion to Diana, goddess of chastity. The countess married in 1577, nor did she ever reject Sidney as Mira does Philisides. The identification is even less palatable if Amaryllis-Mira is also the adulterous, promiscuous Mira of Greville's lyrics. Coridon and Charamell probably represent Greville and Sidney, although which is which is unclear.[23] As protégés of Diana, both Mira and Amaryllis would have been associated by courtiers with Elizabeth's maids of honor; so Gorges refers to them as "Dianas darlinges" in the first line of poem 100. Dyer's allegory seems to treat under different pseudonyms the same unsuccessful pursuit of one of the maids recounted in some of Greville's *Caelica* lyrics and in Sidney's Philisides-Mira sequence. Unfortunately, Greville's romantic interests before the 1580s are a blank, as is the identity of the woman Sidney mentioned to Languet in 1578. Mary Burgh, a maid of honor named on the New Year's rolls from 1575 through 1577, would fit the Mira anagram (if it is one), but she is nowhere mentioned in connection with Greville or Sidney. Court gossip may have ignored the matter or the fiction may have been opaque even to courtiers, and thus safely disseminated in the Philisides-Mira poems and the four contemporary manuscripts of "Amaryllis."

From the standpoint of Dyer's poetic development the deaths of his protagonists in poem 8 create a novel situation, for his narrative then moves into the heretofore uncharted (and for a first-person speaker, the necessarily unknown) realm wherein the chaste mistress reacts to the deaths of those who have expired for her sake. To her credit, Amaryllis shows them a degree of mercy she denied them while alive by arranging for their metamorphoses through the powers of her patroness, Diana. Thus, while Sidney had probed the earlier stages of an unhappy love affair, the periods of favor and absence, Dyer moved to its termination. Under Sidney's influence, Dyer departed from his former practice in both subject and style, yet his emphasis remained firmly centered upon the misfortunes attendant upon the courtship of an unattainable, idealized mistress. What changed was not only the point of view, but, as in his remaining amorous verse as well, any reference to a period of acceptance preceding the lover's rejection and exile. The poetry continues to

---

23. Sargent, *Life and Lyrics*, 67, 69–70. Amaryllis and Coridon appear to be variants of Mira and Coredens; if so, Charamell (sweet grace) is Dyer's pastoral name for Sidney. In OA 71 (line 13ff.) Strephon describes how, through despair, he is "growne a shrich-owle to my selfe each morning." Ringler notes that Sidney may have intended some personal allegory here since Strephon, Klaius, Philisides, and Coredens are the only non-Arcadian shepherds in the Eclogues (416). Dyer's poem may be connected with this allegory, or it may only have picked up Sidney's owl-lover motif for adaptation in an entirely different context.

concentrate upon failure in love, with its concomitant pain and suffering.

Sidney, as we have seen, began his apprenticeship in love poetry with an amplification of the basic pattern set forth in Dyer's early complaints. In the Philisides-Mira series, the lady is momentarily won but she then spurns Philisides so that most of the ensuing poetry can focus upon the themes of rejection and despair. Sidney's continuing experiments in this genre were written for or subsumed into the *Arcadia*, with most of the leftovers forming the *Certain Sonnets* collection. A majority of the *Old Arcadia* love poems necessarily express frustration and suffering in love insofar as they are integrated with the plot, in which all the lovers are crossed in their desires until the resolution in book 5. Even in the third eclogues, where Sidney deals with the successful courtship and marriage of Lalus and Kala, the festive tone is disrupted by Nico's anecdote of the lout who drives his young wife to commit adultery, and Histor's anti-feminist characterization of wives in general. The *Arcadia*'s happy ending is not capped by a fifth set of eclogues in joyful celebration of love triumphant, seemingly because this denouement has been achieved at the cost of neglected duty, fornication, and intended adultery.

Sidney's early writings were motivated by his desire to improve English poetry and inspired by his private romantic concerns. In the *Arcadia* these personal interests expanded to treat more public issues, for the love stories are set in a political context where private considerations cause Basilius and Gynecia to forsake their governing responsibilities just as love keeps Musidorus and Pyrocles from their obligations beyond Arcadia. All the characters are significantly degraded as a result of these decisions. Basilius as chief abdicator is particularly held up to ridicule in his six songs about or to Cleophila-Pyrocles.[24] In the plot's resolution, far from being exonerated for their actions, these characters are measured against their reverse mirror image, Euarchus, who steadfastly upholds public over private considerations even to the point of sentencing to death his own kindred.

If his initial Arcadian fiction fell short of those elevating moral

24. OA 15, 38, 52, 55, 59, 69; in the first of these, he justifies his passion on grounds that "Old age well stayed from ranging humour lives" (lines 9–10), a grotesquely inept argument since the reader knows that he is contemplating an extramarital affair with a man disguised as a woman. Accordingly, the remaining five songs he sings to praise Cleophila or further his misdirected passion only deepen his humiliation.

ideals which he later formulated for literature in the *Defence*, Sidney was free to undertake its revision. He returned to heroic narrative in the *New Arcadia* cognizant of the fact that this was the genre most amenable to inspiring virtuous behavior. In *Astrophil and Stella* we might expect, similarly, a rewriting of the Philisides-Mira story in conformity with the same aesthetic theory, yet for all its success as love poetry, Sidney's poetic masterpiece fails to embody his highest literary ideals. The failure concerns moral rather than aesthetic idealism, of course, and it is a failure caused ultimately by the fact that his sonnet sequence, unlike his *Arcadia*, was not fictional enough.

Sidney's earliest opportunity to meet Penelope Devereux occurred during the winter of 1581 when she first came to court. He apparently did not realize that he was in love with her, however, until after her marriage in November to Lord Rich. Against the backdrop of the court, *Astrophil and Stella* recounts his relationship with her through the summer of 1582.[25] Astrophil notes that others interpret his preoccupation with Stella as concern over politics "because the Prince my service tries" (AS 23, line 7). He participates in tournaments (AS 41, 49, 53), and becomes the object of degrading taunts from "The courtly nymphs": " 'What he?' say they of me, 'now I dare sweare, / He cannot love: no, no, let him alone' " (AS 54, lines 7–8). He is embroiled in an all too conventional courtly love dilemma, the pursuit of a beautiful married woman who rejects all his advances. With the revelation of Stella's identity as Lady Rich in sonnets 24, 35, and 37, we learn also that she is a baroness and thus his social superior. Sidney explores the traditional themes of Stella's worth and Astrophil's longing in the first fifty-odd sonnets; the poetic quality and creativity are very high, but the romantic substance is more or less predictable.[26] The break with tradition occurs at sonnet 62, suddenly, and in a fashion that neither Astrophil nor the reader can thoroughly assimilate at the moment. Stella declares her love for Astrophil, but love as a commitment "Which would not let me, whome she loved, decline / From nobler course, fit for my birth and mind" (AS 62, lines 7–8). The elated Astrophil supposes that Stella's concession is but the prologue to further intimacies; song 1 expresses his sense of triumph and exaltation. Sidney's verse

25. See Ringler's commentary (*Poems*, 435–43).
26. The medieval conventions of *Astrophil and Stella* are outlined in Jean Wilson's *Entertainments for Elizabeth I* (18–21). I concur with her assessment of Stella as "a conventional medieval heroine" (18), but would argue that Sidney alters her role markedly in the course of the sequence.

concentrates at last upon the successful phase of courtship, the phase which goes largely undeveloped in the Philisides-Mira series, and is only briefly recalled in Dyer's complaints. Astrophil confirms that Stella feels a corresponding love for him (AS 66, 67, 69), he cajoles her, he steals a kiss, he presses for more, but in the crescendo of songs beginning with 4 and culminating in 8 he learns that sonnet 62 defined the exact nature of Stella's love:

> "If thou love, my love content thee,
> For all love, all faith is meant thee.
>
> "Trust me while I thee deny,
> In my selfe the smart I try,
> Tyran honour doth thus use thee,
> Stella's selfe might not refuse thee."
> (song 8, lines 90–95)

Her love for him is a true, faithful, and chaste emotion which Astrophil can interpret as rejection only by insisting that physical possession is the sine qua non of his devotion to her.

The psychological struggle between reason and passion, a struggle Sidney had explored in verse at least as early as the second eclogues of the *Old Arcadia*, concludes here with carnal desire triumphant over Astrophil. Accordingly, his plight merely duplicates the surrender to passion that afflicts all the main characters of the *Old Arcadia*, leading them to actions which deflect the plot's resolution from the ends Sidney formulated for poetry in the *Defence*. His chief innovation in the sequence as a tale of romance is Stella, a chaste mistress who is nevertheless vulnerable to love. Through this characterization, Sidney enables her to outflank the strategies upon which all earlier love laments were founded. Astrophil has gained her love, leaving him with no recourse but the rather ignoble insistence upon physical consummation. We might also expect a conventional preoccupation with impending death, but here too *Astrophil and Stella* averts the traditional pose assumed in the love laments of both Dyer and Philisides. Astrophil considers his own death in songs 4, 5, and 9, yet the overwhelming emphasis in the last third of the sequence is upon unquenchable desire, absence, and consequent sorrow. The paradoxical results of Stella's love for Astrophil leave him in a dilemma which corresponds with that of the perplexed lover described in Dyer's poem 10:

> A man in Joy, that lyveth still in woe;
> A harder hap who hath his love at liste
> And lives in love, as he all love had miste.

> Who hathe ynoughe, yet thinkes he lives withoute,
>   To lacke no love yet still to stand in doute,
> What discontent to live in suche desyre,
>   To have his will and ever to requyre.
>
> (lines 6–12)

Dyer's lines are not overtly connected with Sidney's sonnets, yet Astrophil's relationship with Stella does provide an apt solution to the riddle posed by Dyer's lyric.

Astrophil wins the lady; she is his even as the sequence concludes, yet it ends in an unsatisfactory stalemate because Astrophil cannot accommodate his passion for Stella to the honorable mandates of her love for him. The result is a powerful and compelling treatment of individual personalities coping with a love that is both requited and frustrated. It generates an intriguing if mournful delight, without fulfilling the *Defence*'s highest goals for poetry, that it move the reader to virtuous action. At best, *Astrophil and Stella* warns against illicit romances, nor does Stella's strength of character inspire the reader to emulation, for as she genuinely loves Astrophil, so she suffers from her commitment to him (AS 100, song 8).

The sequence dwindles away in sorrow, rather than building toward definitive closure, although Sidney might have availed himself of two conventional but more emphatic endings to the poem. Astrophil's misery invites on the one hand the kind of renunciation of love gratuitously provided by those critics who appended CS 31 and 32 to the sequence. Even so, the encouragement to virtuous action would remain rather a grim warning than an inspiration. As a more positive and distinctively Renaissance alternative, Astrophil could have accepted love on Stella's terms: "the Courtier by the helpe of reason must fully and wholy call backe againe the coveting of the bodie to beautie alone, and . . . beholde it in it selfe simple and pure, and frame it within his imagination sundred from all matter, and so make it friendly and loving to his soul." Possessed of such love, the suitor "shall doe no wrong to the husband," taking "this love for a stayre (as it were) to climbe up to another farre higher than it,"[27] the famous stairs of Cardinal Bembo's ascent from earthly to divine love through the ministering power of feminine beauty. Astrophil is well aware of this alternative, of course; it is succinctly outlined as early as sonnet 5 and acknowledged as late as sonnet 71. Stella both accepts and returns his love, favors not normally at-

---

27. Castiglione, *Book of the Courtier*, 317.

tained by sonnet-sequence protagonists. Astrophil's possession of so fair a prize invites him to rise above earthly passion toward virtuous, spiritual, and ultimately divine love, a resolution that could have fulfilled Sidney's insistence that poetry move its readers through delight to virtuous action. By declining this option Sidney denied his poem its fullest reconciliation with his highest aspirations for poetry. He did so, I think, because he was unable to subject his persona to a course of action he could not accept himself.

The sincerity of Philip's love for Lady Rich is witnessed by a number of biographical facts which lie outside the realm of his poetry, where they are more easily explained away as literary fictions. He may have completed *Astrophil and Stella* in 1582 but his devotion to Lady Rich continued, for Sidney characterized himself publicly as the devotee of Stella long after his marriage with Frances Walsingham in 1583. Two of the banners displayed at his funeral signify his allegiance to a star or stars, and he may have worn armor decorated with stars.[28] It would be comforting to suppose that he had transferred this symbolism to his wife after their marriage; instead, his enduring love for Penelope emerged in his deathbed confession to "a vanity wherein I had taken delight, whereof I had not rid myself. It was my Lady Rich." Duncan-Jones is no doubt correct to observe that the sentence about Lady Rich was not meant as direct quotation;[29] more likely, it was the attending minister's epitome of Sidney's fuller account of the matter. Philip professed ridding himself of this burdensome passion and experiencing a subsequent feeling of relief shortly before he died. This resolution of his love for Lady Rich toward the end of his life took the place of the neo-Platonic apotheosis that his critical ideals demanded for *Astrophil and Stella*.

In contrast with the treatment of love in Sidney's sequence, Greville's *Caelica* makes the transition from earthly to heavenly

28. Katherine Duncan-Jones, "Sidney's Personal Imprese," *Journal of the Warburg and Courtauld Institutes* 33 (1970): 322. Astrophil mentions bearing "stars upon mine armour" in AS 104, line 10.

29. Duncan-Jones and Van Dorsten, *Miscellaneous Prose*, 169, 164, and see Jean Robertson's "Sir Philip Sidney and Lady Penelope Rich," *Review of English Studies*, n.s., 15 (1964): 296–97. Thomas P. Roche, Jr., argues that the vanity Sidney referred to was his poetry about a wholly fictitious passion for Lady Rich ("Autobiographical Elements in Sidney's Astrophil and Stella," *Spenser Studies* 5 [1985]: 209–29). This does not explain, it seems to me, Philip's preservation of the sonnets in a single, uncirculated manuscript or how he could "rid" himself of a sonnet sequence. The twice-repeated "rid myself" is more appropriate to the suppression of vain love for a married woman.

love, but without the slightest use of the Platonic pathway that Bembo advocated and Sidney declined. Greville's exact intentions in his lyric sequence, however, are difficult to assess for several reasons. Neither the 1633 folio edition of his works (F), nor the Warwick Manuscript (E) preserves the Elizabethan ordering of the poems, their order of composition, or the Elizabethan state of the text. In 1619, when Greville's scribe copied the *Caelica* poems into E, he inadvertently copied poems 77–82 before poem 83, an error acknowledged by the note in Greville's hand on folio 56, "this to com after with the rest."[30] The six-poem intrusion totally disrupts the series of amorous lyrics which precedes it, for it includes a poem in praise of Queen Elizabeth, an epitaph, and three poems on wholly political subjects. Thereafter, *Caelica* poems 83–87 form a fitting conclusion to the love poems with graceful transitions to the themes of morality and religion which dominate the remainder of the sequence. The disruption probably occurred because the immediate ancestor of E was a looseleaf collection of Greville's poems, six of which were out of place. The omission of sonnets 6 and 32 from E, with their inclusion at those two points in the F ordering of the poems is further evidence of *Caelica*'s previous looseleaf format, modeled perhaps on that of Sidney's "Certain Sonnets."[31] Greville's note on folio 56 could of course mean that only poem 82 on that page was misplaced, yet it seems more likely that he referred to the entire six-poem intrusion which, coming "after with the rest," would divide *Caelica* into an amatory section, poems 1–76, 83–87, and a miscellaneous section on religious, political, and philosophical subjects, poems 77–82 and 88–109.

Geoffrey Bullough speculated that Sidney's death caused Greville to abandon love poetry, and critics have attempted to explain the received order of the poems as a chronological reflection of the author's intellectual and artistic development.[32] But if we consider

30. BL, Add. MS 54570 (E). Folio 56v is blank, the only such gap in the transcription. W. Hilton Kelliher suggests that Greville may have left room to expand the sixth poem or to insert another one here ("The Warwick Manuscripts of Fulke Greville," 112), but the blank may simply mark the point at which his scribe realized that he had left out part of his copy and returned to insert it. Although he revised the E transcript on at least three different occasions (113), Greville apparently made no effort to restore its poems to the order indicated by his note on folio 56.

31. Ringler, *Poems*, 425.

32. Geoffrey Bullough, *The Poems and Dramas of Fulke Greville, First Lord Brooke*, 1:52. Ronald A. Rebholz (*The Life of Fulke Greville, First Lord Brooke*, 59) interprets the increasing frequency of six-line stanzas in *Caelica* as a sign of

Caelica as a product of Greville's interaction with his fellow courtiers Sidney and Dyer, it appears that by 1619 Greville had altered its
chronological sequence, organizing the poems by subject and further rearranging the love lyrics into a pattern determined by both his
experiences as a courtier and his views of poetry's restricted potential to influence human affairs.

It is inherently improbable, I think, that Greville wrote nothing
but love poetry in his first seventy-odd encounters with the muse,
then abruptly turned away from love in 1587 to write on a variety of
other themes. Not only were Greville's religious and political interests well-developed beforehand, his adherence to Sidney's example
argues against such a practice. Sidney had explored a number of
philosophical, religious, and political issues in verse: he treated
amorous subjects far more often, of course, yet these other themes
may have held a special importance for him if, as A. C. Hamilton
argues, he fulfilled in his writings virtues he could not practice in
the service of his country.[33] As we shall see, Greville was undoubtedly familiar with OA 30, a verse dialogue that offers consolation for
human misery in an imperfect world. In *Caelica* the increasing
emphasis upon the woeful imperfection of this world culminates in
poems 94 and 102. Similarly, Philisides' fable of mankind's creation
(OA 66), deals allegorically with the fragile political power of the
aristocracy, a theme which Greville treats ironically in his sonnets
on nobility, 91 and 92. It seems unlikely that Greville would have
waited until after Sidney's death to deal with these and the other
non-amorous subjects that do find expression in his verse.

Individual *Caelica* poems also suggest that their present order is
not that of their composition. Not only did Greville have ample
opportunity to discuss and write poetry with Sidney and Dyer dur-

---

Greville's gradual progress toward the form he found most suitable for his later
writings. Alternatively, this stanza is generally more suitable for discursive
poems, while sonnets are traditionally associated with love poetry. Thus the
increasing number of sixains may simply reflect *Caelica*'s movement from amorous to non-amorous subjects. Gary L. Litt ("'Images of Life': A Study of Narrative and Structure in Fulke Greville's *Caelica*," 219–21) argues for the unity
of the sequence in its received order, but builds as well upon Croll's remarks
(*Works of Greville*) that some of the sonnets may be out of order or rewritten by
an older and wiser Greville.

33. *Sir Philip Sidney*, 173. Robert E. Stillman provides thoughtful analysis of
the political dimensions of the Phagonian revolt in the *Old Arcadia* and of OA
66, along with a summary of recent scholarship in "The Politics of Sidney's
Pastoral: Mystification and Mythology in The Old Arcadia" (*English Literary
History* 52 [1985]: 795–814).

ing the late 1570s, fully a dozen of his lyrics echo works which his friends composed by about 1580. Bullough, in his *Poems and Dramas of Fulke Greville*, notes the specific echoes of Dyer's poem 7 in *Caelica* 96, and the full-dress imitation of "He that his mirth hath lost" in *Caelica* 83. Greville's question in sonnet 18, "I say, where is the sawce should make that sweet?" (line 12), derives from Dyer's similar question, "Then love wher is the sawce that makes thie tormentes sweete?" (poem 2, line 41), and Dyer's lament is also paraphrased in *Caelica* 95, lines 13–14, and in 6, Greville's only poem in quantitative meter, a type of experimentation which Sidney and Dyer had largely abandoned by the early 1580s.[34] The description of the naked Cynthia in *Caelica* 56 (line 20ff. in E) owes a number of its details to what was originally Philisides' description of Mira in OA 62. From the *Old Arcadia* Greville also borrowed the striking image of Caelica "Washing the water with her beauties white" (22, line 26; OA 29, line 107). Sidney's Eronae, whose breasts were "made pale with minde's disease" (OA 30, line 48), may have inspired Greville's "They must looke pale without that feele disease" (57, line 4). A simile from OA 30, line 33, comparing grief to "a toppe which nought but whipping moves" appears as a metaphor emphasizing the same sort of compulsion in *Caelica* 86, line 10, "Life is a top which whipping Sorrow driveth," and in 96, line 49, "Flesh but the top, which only whips make go."[35] The first line of the unique text from the Ottley Manuscript, "Waynd from the hope which made affection glad," is more than slightly reminiscent of Greville's assertion in *Caelica* 59 that "beawties skye . . . / Weans not the heart from his sweet god, affection" (lines 9, 14). Finally, the third poem in Greville's series concerns a motif which Sidney and Dyer had explored in some detail by 1580. Greville's "heavenly fire / Kindled above to show the Makers glory" (poem 3, lines 1–2) invokes the same creation myth cited by Geron at OA 9, line 100, "man, who sprong of heav'nly fire." Sidney also used the phrase at OA 73, line 43, and in OA 66, the poem recited by Philisides wherein Jove lends the beasts a fragment of his "heav'nly fire" from which Man is created. After 1580, Sidney mentioned it only once in describing Stella as a "starre of heavenly fier" (AS song 8, line 31). Dyer does not refer to heavenly fire in his extant poetry, but he founded

34. Bullough, *Poems and Dramas*, also connects CS 3 with *Caelica* 7, lines 9–12. See also his commentary to poems 6, 22, 83, and 96.

35. Greville might have derived this figure from a similar one in *The Aeneid*, book 7, line 383 (cited by Ringler, *Poems*, 401), yet he habitually echoed Sidney rather than Virgil.

poem 7 upon the related myth of "Prometheus when first from heaven hie, / He brought downe fire, ere then on earth not seene." Spenser's *Amoretti* 8, a well-defined companion poem with *Caelica* 3, is no doubt a relic of Spenser's involvement with the Sidney circle in 1579–1580 and further evidence of their concentration on the heavenly fire motif at that time.

Aside from these early works by Sidney and Dyer, the only extensive traceable influence upon *Caelica* is *Astrophil and Stella*, which Greville would not have known before 1582. The many correspondences between these two collections have been carefully noted by previous scholars, yet their findings call into question the theory of *Caelica*'s chronological order when considered along with Greville's borrowings from his friends' earlier works. *Caelica* 11, 12, and 13, for instance, are Anacreontic sonnets modeled on AS 8 and 17.[36] If the poems are in roughly chronological order, this would mean that Greville had composed fewer than a dozen poems by the time he began drawing upon *Astrophil and Stella* in 1582 or thereafter. Moreover, when he wrote *Caelica* 83, perhaps four to five years later, he supposedly chose to imitate at length Dyer's old-fashioned long-line complaint, and Greville's poem would have had to filter down almost at once to the out-of-court poet Matthew Gwinne, who cites its pun on Greville's name in his Latin contribution to a 1587 Sidney memorial volume. In that same volume, Greville is referred to as Myraphill, a pseudonym he used in *Caelica* 73. Again, another of Greville's lyrics not known to have circulated in print or manuscript must precipitously find its way into the hands of a commercial poet if we are to accept the chronological theory of the *Caelica* sequence.[37]

The borrowings from *Astrophil and Stella*, furthermore, are not only distributed more or less evenly within the amorous section of Greville's collection, they are interspersed with poems that borrow from earlier works by Sidney and Dyer which crop up throughout the entire sequence, in poems 3, 6, 7, 18, 22, 56, 57, 59, 83, 95, and 96. Greville could have regularly worked these echoes of his friends' earliest poetry into his later verse, yet it seems far more probable

36. Bullough, *Poems and Dramas*, 1:236, and see his commentary, passim, for correspondences between the two sequences. The parallels are also studied by Croll (*Works of Greville*, 8–10). J. M. Purcell argued for a very close alignment of these works in "Sidney's *Astrophel and Stella* and Greville's *Caelica*" (*PMLA* 50 [1935]: 413–22).

37. *Exequiae Illustrissimi Equitis, D. Philippi Sidnaei*, cited by Rebholz, *Life of Greville*, 327.

that he dealt with most of these themes and phrases while they were of immediate concern to the group, and that their present distribution within *Caelica* resulted from his subsequent division of his poems into two parts according to their content. This is not to say that Greville never alluded to Sidney's or Dyer's early works in his later writings. At some time between 1599 and 1620, for instance, OA 66 provided him with the simile of the beasts who desired a king and "gave him every thinge," for his *Treatise of Monarchy*. In the "Letter to an Honorable Lady," which probably dates from the 1590s, Greville writes of spirits "whose senses are but spies of conscience," and of "our flesh beinge like a Toppe, which onlie goes upright with whippinge." The distribution of influences from these early works and from *Astrophil and Stella* within *Caelica* considered as chronological sequence would suggest, however, that Greville drew alternately upon both groups of poems over a period of twenty-odd years. This distribution is more readily explained, I contend, as resulting from Greville's purposeful reorganization of his collected lyrics.[38]

In addition to the two-part grouping of his poems, Greville apparently further disrupted the order of his love lyrics to create the bewildering conglomeration of mistresses in this part of the sequence. With Sidney, he probably dedicated his earliest poems to Mira, then added Caelica and perhaps Cynthia, as Sidney shifted his attentions to Stella. As it stands, the sequence follows no narrative thread and develops no consistent internal movement beyond a growing condemnation of women as objects of male devotion. The Mira of sonnet 29 for example, a "Saint . . . Faire and true," cannot be reconciled with the Mira of the following poem who is both promiscuous and a married woman. Caelica's promiscuity in sonnets 38 and 39 likewise jars with her positive characterization as an angel in 47.

All of the elements are nevertheless present in the amatory section of *Caelica* for the representation of one or more fully developed courtships, that is, courtships moving in the Dyer-Sidney pattern from initial worship through unsuccessful pursuit to acceptance, absence, and ultimate rejection and despair. Indeed, the eight lyrics bearing the strongest ties to Dyer and Sidney's early work follow precisely this pattern: *Caelica* 3 and 6 introduce the mistress as a heavenly creature who has subdued all the poet's powers. In 18 his "beloved saint" treats him with contempt and cruelty; by 22 he can

---

38. Fulke Greville, *The Remains, Being Poems of Monarchy and Religion,* stanza 122; John Gouws, ed., *Prose Works of Fulke Greville,* 140, 162.

only recall past happiness while waiting for her to return to him. Poem 56 is the moonlight escapade in which he blazons her naked beauty only to have her flee from him. In 57 she ridicules his inability to endure absence from her, and in 59 he describes the sufferings one must risk to win her "chaste heart." Poem 83, the Dyer imitation, finds the lover pitched from favor into the depths of morbid despair. Perhaps in these eight poems, wherein Mira, Caelica, and Cynthia all figure, we glimpse the skeleton of an original sequence written in emulation of Sidney's Philisides-Mira poems. If so, their redistribution throughout the amorous part of the collection marks Greville's deliberate effort to obscure any trace of temporal, narrative development, an effort much enhanced in the sequence at large by the equating of Mira with Caelica in 37 and with Cynthia in 46, Caelica with Cynthia in 48, and all three together in poem 74.

Although Richard Waswo believed that Greville wrote about his three mistresses as the name fit the theme or meter of his poems,[39] in fact only Mira is consistently adapted to the rhythm of Greville's lines. He uses Caelica to produce regular trochaic feet in poems 74 and 75; elsewhere, Caelica produces rhythmically perfect feet in only eight places (9, 37, 39, 42[2], 51, 58, and 59). Caelica is always a substitute dactylic foot when it is the first word in the line (twenty-three instances), as is true for Cynthia (four instances), a name which forms a substitute foot every time Greville uses it. Some of these lines are awkwardly ametrical as a result (poem 18, line 14; poem 44, line 14; and poem 66, line 1; for example), yet Greville was quite capable of treating the third syllable of Caelica as stressed to create such pleasingly rhythmic lines as poem 9, line 19; poem 39, line 10; and poem 42, line 7. Where the name jars, the rhythm would invariably be restored by replacing Caelica with Mira. It is tempting to conclude that Greville imposed the later Caelica upon some earlier poems he had written about Mira; perhaps he did, yet one of the eight instances of his metrical use of Caelica occurs in poem 59 with its echo of Sidney's early Accession Day poem from the Ottley Manuscript.

Whether Greville altered the original names in some of his lyrics, or simply scrambled the names as he wrote, he clearly went out of his way to thwart any identification of actual ladies or love affairs represented in his poems. Something besides a desire for confidentiality, however, may have motivated this intentional confusion.

---

39. Richard Waswo, *The Fatal Mirror*, 66.

Philosophically, Greville's disrupted sequence accords with the negative conclusions he reached concerning the moral efficacy of poetry. Sidney's belief in its moral power encouraged his attention to the aesthetic coherence of all his works; even the miscellaneous "Certain Sonnets" were reorganized from their order of composition into a sequence which announced the subject of love, viewed it from many angles, and bid it farewell.[40] In contrast, Greville found himself stripped of this motivation by the twin discoveries that he could not find happiness with a woman and that poetry could not improve or reform mankind's futile, self-deceptive struggle with earthly passions.[41] What reason then to fashion a well-articulated structure for the *Caelica* lyrics and thereby risk revealing any actual events that might underlie them? Their fragmented, inconsistent presentation reflects their author's final views about love and the moral inefficacy of poetic representation.

Unity within the amorous section of *Caelica* is achieved, if at all, by an increasing darkness of tone and concentration upon the shortcomings of Mira-Caelica-Cynthia. The poet's assurances that "Myra never varies" (poem 7, line 17), that Caelica is synonymous with worthiness (poem 9), and that the beloved is associated with heavenly verities above the realm of change—all are naively sanguine interpretations that Greville begins to contradict as early as *Caelica* 5.[42] He acknowledges the existence of the neo-Platonic stairway before barricading it with the lumber of his own disastrous encounters with earthly women whose beauty should have encouraged him to the ascent. Adultery and cuckoldry are obliquely introduced in the Merlin anecdote (23), then fully developed with regard to Mira and Caelica in 30–31, 33, and 38–39. After poem 29, fully one-third of the remaining amorous lyrics deal explicitly with feminine inconstancy and promiscuity. Greville's treatment of the Petrarchan conventions is more than ironic, it wholly undercuts the traditional stances that Sidney explored in good faith in his sequence. Its lack of narrative progression keeps *Caelica* from paralleling *Astrophil and Stella*, yet Greville's inversions and subversions of his friend's romantic idealism create a significant degree of coordination between the two sequences.

Caelica 56 for example, singled out by Waswo as "Greville's most

40. Ringler, *Poems*, 425.

41. Rebholz, *Life of Greville*, 51–56, 66–67; Waswo, *Fatal Mirror*, 37–38.

42. Waswo notes the implications of *Caelica* 5, that no earthly love is exempt from change so that the worship of women as saints of constant love is self-deception (*Fatal Mirror*, 49).

penetrating criticism of the Petrarchan pose,"[43] dramatizes the idea that rhapsodic adoration of one's mistress can prove a hindrance to love when love moves toward sexual fulfillment. Greville's trochaic tetrameter quatrains and the situation he describes resemble AS song 1, where Astrophil finds Stella asleep, notes that her hands and tongue, guardians of "the fort," are at rest, vacillates, steals a kiss, then flees the chamber as she awakens. Greville by contrast finds Cynthia naked in bed, but this inspires a poetic reverie of sexual fantasizing during which the lady awakens and, like Astrophil, flees the chamber. Greville is left behind, an inept and comic poet-lover who gains neither a kiss nor further gratification, but is left to conclude that "Wonder hinders love and hate." The inversions of Sidney's stance are multiple, but the primary rebuke is leveled at elaborate poetic contemplation where the goal is sexual union. Here is an odd twist indeed to Greville's distrust of the power of poetry to move one to virtuous action, for in this poem he asserts its failure to facilitate lust as well.

The brunt of Greville's assault upon the Petrarchan tradition and its embodiment in the works of both Dyer and Sidney is reserved for his treatment of the sonnet lady. His heroines remain altogether alluring even as the scope of his praise diminishes after poem 29. Neither Mira nor Caelica harbors a fairer guest within their beauteous forms; thus Caelica rejects his love while to others she "is prov'd a common field" (poem 38, line 14). Mira assures him that her fickleness is governed by consistency: "I found desert and to desert am true / Still dealing by it as I dealt by you" (poem 73, lines 13–14).[44] The climactic moments of both *Astrophil and Stella* and *Caelica* occur in trochaic songs (AS song 8, *Caelica* 75), whose many parallels have received careful critical attention. Greville's innovations as a courtier poet are here defined by his reversals of Sidney's approach. In contrast with Stella's profession of love for Astrophil, Caelica no longer loves Philocell, and that is all that matters. She will not risk exposing herself to slanderous gossip, "At least for one I

43. Ibid., 70, and see Charles A. Bergman's " 'Alarums to Desire': Fulke Greville's Poetic and Sonnet LVI" (*Style* 15 [1981]: 373–78) for analysis of the poem's speaker as a victim of hubris and one who repents his failure as a lover without rejecting love or "the sinfulness of the attempt" on Cynthia.

44. Litt argues that the speaker of 73 must be Caelica in light of her prominence in sonnets 63–72 with their themes of exile and her changing affections ("Images of Life," 228–29). Elsewhere, however, Greville's speaker is consistently Philocell in the poems which involve Caelica. Caelica and Mira may also be names for a single woman, nor can we be sure of so consistent a narrative development as Litt finds in this part of the sequence.

do not love"; "My delight is all my care / All laws else despised are."
Her concern for honor amounts only to a hypocritical regard for
appearances. No higher principles govern Caelica's will; she is a
devotee of sexual hedonism for whom Philocell has become an
inadequate partner. He is as thoroughly rejected as any lover who
laments his case in the poetry of Dyer or Sidney, and Greville's
persona also falls from a state of former happiness (as in 46 and 73).
The difference here is that the fall results from the lady's enthusiastic promiscuity rather than her regard for his honor or her chastity.
The *Caelica* lyrics turn to religious themes not conducted there by
beauty but in full retreat from the disappointing ugliness of earthly
love; of the flesh, Greville writes, "forsake thyself, to heaven turn
thee / Her flames enlighten nature, never burn thee" (poem 86,
lines 13–14).

The negative portrayals of women in *Caelica* have been attributed to Greville's unsuccessful relationships with women, a plausible hypothesis in light of his failure to marry. At the same time,
something beyond his own disappointments probably influenced
the darker natures of his sonnet ladies. Within a few years of Sidney's death, Greville was acquainted perforce with the scandal that
Sir Philip's Stella had become Sir Charles Blount's mistress. By 1590
their affair was so notorious that even George Peele could pun on
Blount's "rich" aspirations in his account of the 1590 Accession Day
tilt, a contest in which Greville also participated.[45] Penelope's
brother, the earl of Essex, headed the court faction with which
Greville had aligned himself by the mid–1590s, and Greville frequently must have associated with Blount and Lady Rich both at
court and at Essex House, where he often resided during the last few
years of the reign. By dismissing the notion of *Caelica*'s chronological order, we leave open the possibility that some of its more ironic,
anti-feminist, and anti-Petrarchan lyrics grew out of Greville's sul-
len awareness that his dearest friend had worshiped a tarnished and
now fallen star, that the anguish Sidney had endured for her was
mocked by her subsequent behavior. To be sure, Greville's poetic
mistresses are far more promiscuous and brazen than Lady Rich,
who merely turned from an unsuitable husband to a man whom she
loved and eventually married. Yet her adultery, ironically reversing
Sidney's idealized portrait of Stella, probably helped to sour Greville's attitude toward romantic love and feminine chastity as he

---

45. *Polyhymnia*, in Horne, *Works of George Peele*, 236: "Rich in his colours,
richer in his thoughts."

completed the *Caelica* poems and arranged their amorous component along an increasingly anti-feminist scale.

The style of *Caelica* adheres to Elizabethan norms more closely than does its treatment of love and the sonnet lady. Greville retained more high Renaissance ornamentation in many of these lyrics than in his later works. His frequent use of the correlative pattern (as in poems 8, 14, 21, 62), the addresses to Cupid, and the positing of examples, especially classical or mythological ones with which to compare facets of the lover's state (as in poems 11, 30, 34, 42, 44, 47), all are the stock in trade of Elizabethan "golden" poets. At the same time, Greville's approach to his comparisons anticipates, and at times duplicates, the reconciliation of bold incongruities so characteristic of the metaphysical conceit.[46] Moreover, his love poetry moves, as we have seen, toward a cynical, negative portrayal of women; Mira-Caelica turns out to be even darker than the mistress of Shakespeare's sonnets. Greville expresses a flippant, cavalier attitude toward women in *Caelica* 52, but this alleviates only momentarily his dominant tone in the last half of the amatory sequence. He endures a Petrarchan lover's suffering to a degree from which seventeenth-century poets were generally exempt, while his heroines are quite as self-willed, faithless, and lascivious as any who appear in the verses of Donne, Carew, Suckling, or Rochester.

In the amorous works of Sidney, Dyer, and Greville, courtier verse receded from its normal function during the first two decades of the reign. Composition in direct pursuit of royal favor or to memorialize public occasions at court all but disappears. None of Dyer's poems after poem 3 were addressed to Elizabeth nor were they otherwise certainly occasional until poem 12, his elegy for Sidney. Similarly, only Greville's *Caelica* 81, and perhaps 17, were intended as royal flattery, with none of the rest dedicated to a particular person or tied to an identifiable event. Sidney's *Lady of May* and the tiltyard poems fulfill traditional, public functions by praising the queen and entertaining the court, but only in the case of PP 4 and 5 is an overt political purpose discernible. In these works, moreover, Sidney used poetry to create events at court rather than merely to celebrate or commemorate them. His verse grew out of his experi-

---

46. The resemblances are investigated by Croll (*Works of Greville*, 28–30), and Waswo (*Fatal Mirror*, with a number of examples in chapter 2). Bullough, however, characterized Greville's wit as "gnomic compression rather than . . . analytic association" (*Poems and Dramas*, 1:223). It seems to me that in such poems as *Caelica* 39 and 59 Greville's style requires even stricter compression in order to achieve a genuine "metaphysical" effect.

ence as a courtier yet subordinated that experience to the art it inspired. The transfer of OA 62 and AS song 5 from Mira to Stella show the extent to which he could grant priority to art over his personal feelings. Where Dyer and Oxford adapted Petrarchan conventions to their courtship of the queen, Sidney applied them directly neither to Elizabeth nor in his pursuit of other women at court. Dyer, for example, addressed poem 3 to his mistress, while Sidney asks in OA 62 what tongue can her (not your) perfections tell? Sidney's verse demonstrated less his virtuosity in courtship than in the questionable undertaking of poetic composition.

His final work on the *Old Arcadia* at Wilton during 1580 was simply another aspect of his career as a courtier, not a product of banishment from the court. He maintained his access to Elizabeth and exchanged New Year's gifts with her in 1580 and 1581 despite the tennis-court quarrel with Oxford and royal uneasiness over the "Anjou" letter, nor did he retreat to Wilton early in 1580 out of frustration with the queen's protracted marriage negotiations or her refusal to form a Protestant league. Rather, Sidney invoked "necessity," the want of money, as his official excuse to the queen for his absence from court.[47] His stay at Wilton was no doubt motivated as well by personal, family concerns, for in April the countess of Pembroke gave birth to her first son, William, heir to the earldom and godson to the queen. If Philip drafted most of the *Old Arcadia* from March through August of that year, the pages he read or sent to Mary as he finished them must have provided a welcome diversion during her lying-in and thereafter.[48] Given Philip's devotion to his sister it is only natural that he joined her and her family at Wilton at this time of crisis and subsequent celebration. Most of the Arcadian poetry was probably composed under these circumstances for the immediate delight of another courtier. Moreover, the direct addresses to "fair ladies" throughout the book indicate that Philip also assumed a wider audience, presumably the lady friends with whom Mary would share this "trifle, triflingly handled," and within the year he was promising to send a copy of this "toy" to his brother Robert.[49] It was nevertheless a far more private work than his court

47. Albert Feuillerat, *The Prose Works of Sir Philip Sidney*, 3:129.
48. Sidney, *Arcadia*, xvi. Simon Bowyer, gentleman usher of the Black Rod, attended at Wilton for ten days in May in order to arrange for the queen's sponsorship at the christening in absentia (PRO, E 351/542, f. 11v). Sidney's dedicatory letter to his sister calls the *Arcadia* "this child which I am loath to father," and deals throughout with the metaphor of childbirth as it applies to his writing of the book.
49. Feuillerat, *Prose Works*, 3:132.

entertainments, and it was followed by the even more secretive *Astrophil and Stella*.

Although Astrophil claims that he turned to poetry in hopes that it would help him win Stella, and even that she sang some of his complaints (AS 1, line 57), I doubt that Sidney actually wooed Lady Rich with any of these lyrics. His fictional representation of the subject is clearest in songs 8 and 11, which record interviews between the lovers as narrated from a third-person standpoint. How else to introduce Stella's immediate presence into the sequence? Her dramatized appearances, meaningless as seduction ploys, facilitate Sidney's complete account of his relationship with Lady Rich. Sidney's creative practice, especially in *Astrophil and Stella*, mirrored the role of poetry as he had portrayed it in the *Old Arcadia*. The Arcadians' world was a golden one in its elegance if not in its moral tenor, for aristocrats and shepherds alike communicated with one another in verse, using it as well in private meditation to vent their most intimate thoughts and passions. When Philip found himself overwhelmed by a desire fully as hopeless as Basilius's or Gynecia's for Cleophila, he sublimated his emotions into private, poetic creativity the results of which are intrinsically worthwhile verse. Here Sidney's artistry completely reversed the rationale of courtier verse of the 1560s, where ceremonial events at court elicited and excused the writing of poems for which our knowledge of the social context comprises their chief interest.

The artistic value of *Astrophil and Stella* cannot disguise the fact that both its substance and privacy contradicted poetry's highest mission as formulated in the *Defence*. It conveys no "delightful teaching which is the end of poesy" in order to move us to virtuous action.[50] Sidney's secondary goal, the improvement of English verse, was likewise defeated by the necessity of keeping the work secret. Five of its songs turn up in manuscript anthologies, but the sonnets, which clearly identify the principals in the affair, were kept close. Whereas the Arcadian poems about Mira circulated widely during the 1580s, none of the sonnets can be shown to have done so during Sidney's lifetime.[51] *Astrophil and Stella* was Sidney's creative response to an obsession in his life that was otherwise denied meaningful outlet.

50. Duncan-Jones and Van Dorsten, *Miscellaneous Prose*, 116.
51. Ringler posits a single holograph original, "never subsequently revised," from which all other texts descend through another unique lost copy (*Poems*, 447–55).

As Sidney allowed the majority of his poems to circulate in manuscript even after he had written the *Defence*, it is difficult to discern any further motivation beyond entertaining his readers by showing them the delightful potentialities of English verse. If individual characters and episodes in the *Arcadia* inspire courage and other kinds of virtuous action, the overall handling of the plot fails of this purpose. His individual poems, furthermore, are primarily love lyrics which Sidney could not explicitly justify in the *Defence*, where he maintained instead that they were an abuse of the art of poetry. Subsequently he criticized English love poetry for its lack of fervor: "truly many of such writings as come under the banner of unresistible love, if I were a mistress, would never persuade me they were in love: so coldly they apply fiery speeches."[52] From an orthodox Elizabethan moral perspective this was tantamount to saying that such poetry was not abusive enough. Fortunately, Sidney's concern for aesthetic delight won out over the age's almost unanimous strictures against delight in any form. The *Defence* was obliged, nonetheless, to accommodate itself in the main to the ethical norm for want of any equally respectable alternative standard. English humanism, inhibited by the onslaught of the Reformation and its chaotic aftermath, was still struggling toward the unabashed secularism that had prevailed on the continent generations ago. When Sidney handed Edward Bannister a copy of CS 30, an out-and-out love lyric void of ethically redeeming substance, he demonstrated his commitment to art above moral exigency. For this discrepancy between his theory as set forth in the *Defence* and his practice of publicly disseminating his poems, English poetry is much the richer.

Sidney's poetic theories had only a moderate impact upon Dyer, whose muse was born into the golden world trailing clouds of drabness, for he adapted Sidney's pastoralism and even his trochaics to the long-line rhythms of mid-century. Dyer's output was the least ambitious of the participants in the "blessed Trinitie" to judge from what has survived, a handful of discrete lyrics which he composed over the span of a dozen-odd years. Unlike Sidney, he seemingly made no effort to preserve his works, but he must have allowed them to circulate freely since all but four have survived in multiple copies.[53] Dyer attempted increasingly complicated poetry in both

52. Duncan-Jones and Van Dorsten, *Miscellaneous Prose*, 103–5, 116–17.
53. These four are: poem 3, apparently addressed to the queen, but known as well to Puttenham, who quoted two lines in the *Arte*; poems 4, 11, and 12, his

form and content without producing anything which positively illustrates Sidney's argument that poesy moves the reader to virtuous
action. For Dyer, writing poetry with Sidney and Greville was a
stimulating pastime conducive to a modest degree of social display
as a poet, rather than directed toward any identifiable didactic
purpose.

Greville, in contrast with his two friends, followed Castiglione's
advice that a courtier's poetry should be kept close and shown at
most to someone the poet could trust. Sir John Harington was a
close friend of both Greville and Dyer, and a keen collector of elite
courtier verse, but only two of Greville's poems appear in his family
papers. *Caelica* 1, 5, 29, and 52 likewise reached print, anonymously, before the end of the reign; beyond these instances, however, his lyrics are not known to have circulated. Greville avoided
personal display as a poet or any other public function for his verse.
With a few exceptions, he also declined to follow Sidney's cultivation of pastoralism, for his artificial personae, although modeled
upon Sidney's practice, seldom appear in pastoral settings. He rejected Sidney's belief in poetry's moral value, and he may have
decided that his own lyrics would contribute little to the improvement of English poetics by comparison with Philip's more ambitious and polished efforts.[54] Greville was the most reclusive member of Sidney's circle, a courtier for whom poetry was largely a
private matter throughout his life.

By 1587, Sidney, Greville, and Dyer had greatly expanded the
possibilities for both courtier verse and English poetry in general.
Sidney wrote the first English sonnet sequence, introduced a multiplicity of new forms, and among his many fictions popularized a
genteel pastoralism that merged with Spenser's humbler strain to
foster a rich progeny in the decades ahead. He fully explored the
adaptation of quantitative verse in English, thus carrying out a well-
defined but essentially unfulfilled ambition of the first generation of
courtier poets. Above all he dignified poetry as a respectable aristocratic pastime. The accessibility of Sidney's works, coupled with his
position as model courtier and national hero, gave maximum impetus to a new and positive recognition of poetry as a worthwhile art
form. At the same time, he had created in *Astrophil and Stella* an

---

final tribute to Sidney which Byrd set to music without the reference to authorship found in the last line of the Christ Church College text.

54. Rebholz summarizes Greville's expressions of humility and deference to
Sidney (*Life of Greville*, 66).

intensely personal work devoid of any external or overriding moral purpose. Greville's much fuller regard for privacy kept his works from exerting a known contemporary influence, yet he produced a series of mature and original lyrics, coordinated with those of Sidney and Dyer but so radically different in tone and conception as to earn him an independently honored standing as an Elizabethan poet. And Dyer too produced a few lyrics of enduring popularity and influence. Within Sidney's lifetime, however, neither he nor his friends carried out the morally idealistic task which he had prescribed for poetry in the *Defence*.

4

Utilitarian Poetics

Gorges, Ralegh, and Essex

As Sidney, Dyer, and Greville continued to influence each other's poetry during the early 1580s, substantial lyric verse was being composed by other courtiers with little or no discernible influence from the Sidney circle. Before the 1590s, the wide circulation of works by Sidney and Dyer appears to have had little impact upon the output of their fellow courtiers, particularly with regard to such important innovations as the adaptation of pastoral fictions to life at court, quantitative verse, or the use of new forms and meters. Where similar experimentation occurs during the 1580s, it can seldom be traced to the influence of "the blessed Trinitie"; meanwhile, other courtiers used poetry for purposes of individual advancement and display largely unexplored by Sidney and his friends.

Sir Arthur Gorges composed a greater number of love lyrics than any other courtier poet except Sir Philip Sidney. About 1585 or 1586 Gorges employed a scribe to copy fair his "Vannetyes and Toyes," the first ninety-five entries in BL, Egerton Manuscript 3165.[1] The scribe then copied poems 96, 97, and 98, the first two of which are elegies for Sidney that Gorges had no doubt composed in late 1586 or 1587. Poem 98 is a pastoral love lyric revised by Gorges. Poem 99 is a lover's lament entirely in Gorges's handwriting, and poem 100, also holograph, was apparently entered at a later time. The total of one hundred Elizabethan poems in this collection is rounded out by poem 109, which was sung by a mermaid to honor the queen as she

---

1. Helen Estabrook Sandison, ed., *The Poems of Sir Arthur Gorges.* This total excludes an intrusive text on folio 59v by Thomas Churchyard, and it comprises only ninety-four different lyrics in that poems 28 and 55 are identical. Poem 24 may not be by Gorges either, since it was copied in an unidentified hand as a response to poem 23.

passed Gorges's house on the Thames in November 1599. All but the two elegies and poems 54 and 78 are amorous in subject or approach, including several poems in praise of Elizabeth.

Among the first ninety-five poems in the manuscript, at least fifty are translations or adaptations from contemporary French poets, primarily Desportes and DuBellay.[2] Gorges's knowledge of the language may have led to his being sent to France in 1576 and 1578 with letters for the English ambassador. Elizabeth considered him for the ambassadorship in 1595, and his knowledge of French was put to good use entertaining the Duke de Biron and his party upon their arrival in London in 1601.[3] Gorges introduced more French lyric verse into English than did any other Elizabethan translator. His ties with France and its poetry supplement the steady Italian influence on courtier verse, traceable from Wyatt and Surrey through several of Oxford's poems to Sidney, whose literary models were almost exclusively Italian, classical, or Spanish.

Critical enthusiasm for Gorges's innovation has been tempered, however, by the style in which he adapted his French originals; as Prescott remarks of his treatment of Desportes, Gorges's borrowings sound rather old-fashioned. Much of the translation changes French poetry into the jog-trot rhythms, alliterative phrasing, and neo-Petrarchan figures of speech that typify the worst components of "drab" verse. For this style, in turn, Gorges owed much to the work of George Turberville, a "textbook" practitioner of drab poetics.[4] Excerpts from Turberville's poems are adapted, even grafted word for word to five of Gorges's lyrics (for which see Helen Estabrook Sandison's commentary to poems 25, 26, 40, 89, and 90). The mid-century flavor of much of Gorges's verse, original or translation, is often indistinguishable from that of love lyrics written by Oxford

2. Anne Lake Prescott (*French Poets and the English Renaissance*) concludes that at least twenty-three of Gorges' lyrics were based on poems by DuBellay (52), twenty from Desportes (138), two from Ronsard (108), one from Marot (13), and four from French songbooks. Sandison identifies and analyzes the influence of these poets in the commentary to her edition.

3. Ralegh, Sir Arthur's cousin, informed Sir Robert Cecil that Gorges and Sir Arthur Savage had toured London with the visitors and should continue to accompany them because "they speak French well and are familiar with them" (HMC, Salisbury, 11:382).

4. Prescott, *French Poets*, 141. Sandison speculates that Gorges may have known Turberville personally as a west-country neighbor (*Poems*, xlv-xlvi). As late as the 1590s, Sir John Harington praised Turberville's pioneering work in English verse; see Harington's epigram 43 (McClure, *Letters and Epigrams*, 164), and the reference in Harington's translation of Ariosto's *Orlando Furioso* (69).

and Dyer during the 1570s, and it seems reasonably certain that several of Gorges's poulter's measure complaints are indebted to Dyer's "He that his mirth hath lost." Poem 25, for example, owes more to Dyer's lament than it does to Turberville's "Dido to Aeneas" from which it borrows three couplets outright. When Puttenham quoted four excerpts from Gorges's poem in the *Arte*, he attributed only one of them correctly. He ascribed one to "a lover," but two others to Dyer, probably because he confused these very similar complaints. The tone of hopeless despair is the same in both, and both poets exempt their mistresses from blame in similar terms.[5] Gorges's poems 12 and 26 also resemble Dyer's work; the former announces the poet's "wished welcome death" (line 17), which is more alliterative and emphatic than Dyer's "wished deathe" (poem 2, line 9), before turning to an inventory of his thoughts, sighs, hope, tears, and so forth in a manner corresponding with Dyer's list of his knowledge, heart, fancies, and arguments. The continuity of style in courtier verse is illustrated as well by poem 76, which Gorges probably adapted from works by Ronsard and Desportes, yet is couched in ideas and phrasing that follow mid-century conventions approximated in an otherwise unrelated poem by the Earl of Oxford:

> To lyke in harte, yett feare to shewe the same
> To seeke releefe from whence I reape my woes
> To cloake my inwarde greyfe with outewarde game
> To fayne dislik yett languyshe in Desyre
> (Gorges, poem 76, lines 8–11)

> I lyke in harte, yet dare not saye I love,
>   And lookes alone do lend me cheefe releife.
> I dwelt sometymes at rest yet must remove,
>   With fayngned joye I hyde my secret greefe
>   (Oxford, poem 12, lines 13–16)

The rhetoric of Gorges's verse is often predictable, made up of standard formulas as typical of the poetry in Tottel or the *Paradise* as of works by Turberville, Dyer, and Oxford. But it would be unfair to dismiss Gorges as a courtier poet who merely attired the Pléiade in worn-out English trappings. At its best, his muse is capable of light-

---

5. Gorges wrote of his suffering, "Yett cursse I nott the wighte / the causer off the same / Nor never will, butt with regarde / and honor use the name" (lines 45–48), with which compare Dyer's "Yet hate I but the fault and not the faultie one, / Nor can I rid from me the bonds in which I lie alone" (poem 2, lines 49–50). Perhaps Gorges intended a pun in poem 92 at line 3, where he refers to "a deyr complainte off loves to[o] cruell lawes" in this poulter's measure remonstrance against just such poetic laments as Dyer's poem 2.

er, less rhetorically self-conscious lyrics, whether original or translated. His rendering of Desportes in "The gentell Season of the yeare" is fresh, vivid, and almost devoid of conventional rhetoric until its last two stanzas. In the *Phoenix Nest* of 1593, it blends in gracefully with the other "golden" poetry of that anthology, as does Gorges's poem 46, "Woolde I were changde into that golden Showre," a translation from Ronsard. Among Gorges's better original lyrics is sonnet 58, which compares favorably with similar Anacreontic efforts by Sidney and Greville. Poem 72 is a respectable blazon with an epigrammatic last line fit for a sonnet, and in poem 39 we witness the evolution of mid-century wordplay into true poetry. The work is essentially a long-line complaint which the lover sings to his lute; its organization is governed by a repetitive formula, "Wittness with me my _____," typical of so many "drab" rhetorical structures. Gorges transcends this tradition, however, by providing a narrative introduction to the lament, plus this concluding couplet after the lover breaks his lute strings and throws the instrument to the ground: "And dyscontent he lyves / and vowes soo to remayne / Till Shee vouchsaffe with her faire hande / to tune his lute againe" (lines 57–60). The symbolism of these lines deftly evokes a restoration of harmony to the relationship, where a drab poet would only belabor the point directly and at length.

A number of Gorges's lyrics are skillful enough to warrant the charge that they have been unfairly neglected by modern anthologists. On the other hand, the collection as a whole is amorphous to a degree surpassing that of Greville's *Caelica*. As with *Caelica*, clusters of poems on the same theme crop up here and there, yet the "Vannetyes and Toyes" form a miscellaneous collection rather than a sequence. Their entry in BL, Egerton MS 3165, does not follow the order of their composition, and their connection with Gorges's courtship of his first wife, Lady Douglas Howard, has been somewhat exaggerated.[6] Gorges's poems often reflect his immediate circumstances as a courtier, including his courtship of Lady Howard,

---

6. Although Sandison thought it likely that poems 1–95, at least, were transcribed in the order of their composition (*Poems*, xxx), this seems not to have been the case insofar as Churchyard's intrusive elegy for Anjou (d. 1584) occurs well beyond the midpoint of the series yet precedes poem 87, written from prison and thus datable to Gorges's commitment to the Marshalsea in March of 1580 (J. R. Dasent, *Acts of the Privy Council of England*, 11:422). Sandison (*Poems*) assigns this episode to 1582, apparently by mistake, nor have I found any mention of another imprisonment until that of 1597 when the queen sent Gorges to the Tower for marrying Lady Clinton.

while they also reveal his interest in poetic experimentation and translation ostensibly as a pastime and for its own sake.

Among the first ninety-five poems in the series, eleven were apparently addressed to Douglas or concerned with their relationship. She is identified as of "the lyons kinde" in poem 26, a reference to the Howard arms, while poems 29, 44, 48, 52, 53, 57, 63, 66, and 69 were marked by Gorges with a capital D. Sandison argued, persuasively, that these initials stood for Douglas or for Daphne, the pastoral name by which Spenser immortalized Gorges's wife in his elegiac *Daphnaida*, and she may also be referred to as the Daphne of poems 94 and 98. It seems less probable however that these lyrics provide a coherent record of Gorges's wooing of his first wife, that he consistently wrote about her as Daphne, or that he devised for himself a fictional identity as Alcyon.

The ten lyrics most closely associated with Douglas Howard (poem 26 and the nine "D" poems) begin with the lover's lament at the point of death. Poem 29 praises her through the well-worn ploy of submitting her charms to the judgment of Paris. Poem 44 is a third-person lament, while 48, an original English sonnet, appears to be a sincere address to "My deare." It encourages her to endure "this fortune badde," and argues that hardships have certain positive effects; they help us discern our true friends from our foes, "And which is more, our selves wee learne to know" (line 14). His otherwise trite commentary on inconstant fortune ends on a note of sincere and original insight suggesting that the poem was no pat exercise but was designed genuinely to comfort Lady Howard in the midst of adversity. Poem 52, although translated from Desportes, pledges a constant love in keeping with the intimate tone of poem 48. Yet the remaining five poems, three of them from French sources, are despairing complaints quite incompatible with Gorges's successful wooing of twelve-year-old Douglas during the summer of 1584, a courtship which culminated in a mid-October wedding. Only poem 48 conveys genuine, rhetorically unadorned or exaggerated, sentiments. The laments are standard fare, as are most of the remaining unmarked poems which Sandison connects with young Lady Howard. Perhaps Douglas asked her husband to compose these lover's complaints for her just as Queen Anne made a similar request of King James. Either way, the result would be a fictitious representation in the "Vannetyes and Toyes" from which no actual love affair, real or imaginary, could be pieced together. Furthermore, the lyrics concerned with Douglas produce a fragmented impression because they project no well-defined and consistent image of the lady as Daphne, nor does the name Alcyon occur in Gorges's verse. He fails to develop, in short, any sustained personae in the manner of Philisides, Mira, or Caelica. Daphne is referred to in three poems, but the name identifies the mistress in only two of them, while if Gorges ever represented himself by means of a persona, he apparently did so under the name of Phylander, not Alcyon.

In poem 44, Gorges alludes to Daphne as he recounts the myth of the laurel tree. Here, however, the allusion applies not to the lady but to a lovelorn shepherd's desire to escape the pangs of love through a similar metamorphosis. The French song upon which Gorges based his poem treats the myth in like fashion, although Gorges altered it by providing his lament with a four-line introduction that identifies the disconsolate shepherd as Phylander. Thus in poem 44 Gorges may have assumed this pastoral name to complain of his love for "D" (Douglas or Daphne), who is in no way associated with the reference to Daphne in the poem. The only lyric Gorges wrote before 1587 which might refer to Douglas as Daphne is poem 94, a pastoral from the French in which Gorges goes beyond his source by giving that name to the beloved shepherdess. In poem 98, the pastoral dialogue which Gorges copied into the manuscript at some time after 1587, the shepherd declares that he will continue to love Daphne however far above him she may be, and into this dialogue Gorges transferred some half-dozen lines from poem 94, including references to flowers which are there associated with Daphne: the woodbyne, primrose, and violet. Neither poem 94 nor poem 98 is marked with a D or otherwise clearly connected with Douglas, an equation that first appeared in Spenser's 1591 *Daphnaida*. As Ralegh's protégé, Spenser had no doubt met Gorges when he attended court with Ralegh during the winter of 1589–1590. Furthermore, Spenser worked into *Daphnaida* a number of motifs and phrases from the "Vannetyes and Toyes," indicating that he had read at least some of Gorges's lyrics by the time he wrote his elegy for Douglas.[7] Spenser probably took his cue from the Daphne of poem 94 and perhaps poem 98. He dubbed Gorges Alcyon instead of Phylander in deference to the Ceys and Alcyone story in Chaucer's *Book of the*

---

7. Thus William A. Oram in his "Daphnaida and Spenser's Later Poetry" (*Spenser Studies* 2 [1981]: 141–58) notes Alcyon's extreme melancholy, black dress, and long, uncombed locks, and suggests a connection with the "self-destructive melancholy" of Despair in *The Faerie Queene* (1.9.143). These details of appearance, however, no doubt derived from Gorges's poem 53 with its "D" heading and first-person description of the lover dressed in mourning black whose "feltred lockes doo overshade my face" (lines 9–10).

Duchess, a primary source for the elegiac strategy of *Daphnaida*.[8] Thus Spenser expanded the fictional personae of Gorges's lyrics beyond anything which can be reasonably inferred about the author's own intentions for the characterization of either himself or his wife.

Gorges's poems for or about Douglas Howard probably constitute a relatively minor part of the "Vannetyes and Toyes," while a number of its poems reflect other facets of his service at court as a gentleman pensioner. Poem 8, for example, describes a lady dressed in white, with carnation hose bound by a blue garter. As a gentleman pensioner, Gorges served in the Presence Chamber with the maids of honor, who were traditionally attired in white gowns; moreover, this lady's "desire a virgins stepps to treade" (line 5) suggests that she intended to follow in the queen's footsteps. Ironically, the white and carnation colors of her costume symbolized desire, thus leading Gorges to address the lady directly at line 15 with an offer to mend "that faulte" if the chaste symbolism of her garter does not reflect her true intentions.[9]

Poem 78, a decidedly non-amorous lyric, describes a fierce but unsuccessful attack on the poet by some underling "Whose spighte at others better Estate / bewrayes his want off gentell blood" (lines 9–10). In 1582 Gorges was threatened by just such a social inferior. He was apparently on duty in the Presence Chamber when he was insulted and challenged to a duel by one Gilbert, the servant of a fellow pensioner, Sir John Scudamour. Gorges declined to cross swords with such a rascal, whereupon Gilbert searched the streets for him with twenty armed men according to Gorges's letter of protest to Sir John, which concludes with the observation that Arthur serves "A Mistres asmuch to be respected as any mans Master."[10] Gorges may also refer to his chamber office when he compares his opponent to "the Dogg that howles by nighte / agaynste bryghte synthyas face in vayne" (lines 13–14). The poem is not a translation but seems to record a firsthand situation, as does poem 8.

Several other poems in the collection were written for identifi-

---

8. See Edmund Spenser, *The Works of Edmund Spenser: A Variorum Edition* (commentary, 7:438), citing Nadal's article in *PMLA* 23:658–59.

9. Goldwell's account of the "Fortress of Perfect Beauty" pageant of May 1581 includes a description of a lady dressed in white and carnation as the colors of desire (Nichols, *Progresses*, 2:327).

10. Gorges's observation that "crafte lurkes moste in clowted shooes" indicates the lowly status of his adversary; the letter to Scudamour is preserved in PRO, C 115 (Box M 18, letter 7430, June 7, 1582).

able occasions. Poem 87 stemmed from a court-related incident, Gorges's imprisonment in the Marshalsea in March of 1580 "for giving the lye and other speaches passed betwen him and the Lord Windesour in the Chamber of Presence."[11] Gorges based his poem on a neo-Petrarchan conceit, the analogy between his physical confinement and his otherwise complete captivation by his mistress. Gorges wrote poem 109 in 1599 as part of his ceremonial presentation of a "fair jewell" to the queen.[12] The gift may have been meant as a conciliatory gesture in the wake of his marriage in 1597 to Lady Elizabeth Clinton, a match that aroused royal indignation and led to another term of imprisonment for Sir Arthur.

Poems 96 and 97, the epitaphs for Sidney, are of interest not only as marks of his admiration for this fellow courtier but for what they reveal about his literary tastes. He mentions those who "In pryase of the[e] have cloathed with theyr quyll / the papers whyte in lynes of moornynge blacke," presumably with reference to the poetic memorial volumes published shortly after Sidney's death. To Gorges, these are poets "whose love surmounts theyr skill," whose creative abilities fall short of Sidney's talents (poem 96, lines 5–8). Gorges here implies that he has read both Sidney's poetry, as is also indicated by his reference to the *Arcadia* in poem 97, and the collections of verse dedicated to Sidney's memory. At the same time, Gorges expressed his relatively meager esteem for English verse by ascribing Sidney's eternal fame to his brief military career rather than to his muse.

Four poems in the manuscript seem to delineate a single, unsuccessful romance with a consistency and specificity of detail suggesting that they grew out of Gorges's pursuit of a noble lady other than Douglas Howard. Poems 38 and 40 deal with some "false Cresseid" who deserted the poet for a rival. These lyrics are too bitter in tone to apply to Daphne, nor was there quite time enough to crowd so many romantic upheavals into Gorges's courtship of his wife. His point of view in both poems is that his mistress, who scorned him as Cressida did Troilus, may find that her new love is a Diomede who will serve her in the same way.[13] Poems 93 and 94 probably deal with the same failure in love. In the first of them Gorges rebukes a woman who, as in poem 40, turned to another man during the poet's

11. Dasent, *Acts of the Privy Council*, 11:422.
12. Nichols, *Progresses*, 3:422.
13. Gorges's supposition that he would then pity her forlorn condition may derive from Robert Henryson's *Testament of Cresseid*, although Turberville treated the same episode in his *Epitaphs, Epigrams, Songs and Sonets* (sig. T2–3v).

absence: "Whilste hope high Honnors place to have / estraungde from me thy parson brave" (lines 1–2). These lines suggest that he was engaged in some official mission at the time of his displacement by a wealthy rival. His mistress, herself of "noble kinde," has rejected him "Onely for clownishe muckes desyre" (poem 93, lines 42, 46). Poem 94 emphasizes the lady's high estate by referring to "the glory of thy name," yet the poet rejects such court ladies, "attyred all in crafte and guile," for a simple country lass—and here Gorges first names Daphne as the object of his love. Accordingly, Gorges may have pursued another heiress before courting Lady Howard, who caught him "on the rebound" from a woman who was herself a fortune hunter.

Of Gorges's four certain poems about the queen, those from the first section of "Vannetyes and Toyes" (poems 47, 49, and 61) derive from French originals by Desportes and DuBellay. While none can be traced to a particular suit, Gorges's characterization of Elizabeth adopts specific strategies for flattering her which are not indebted to his sources nor to works in a like vein by earlier courtiers. Sonnet 47 for instance follows DuBellay's *Regrets* 168 very closely through the first six lines, whereas the last eight develop ideas not found in his source. Gorges apparently translated this lyric as a birthday present for Elizabeth since its opening lines, "Prodigall was nature fruitfull and devyne / Att hir birth day to yelde her best and moste," point to such an occasion, while his original version of line 2, "yr birth day," follows his source and suggests firsthand presentation to the queen. Elizabeth, he affirms, is "The worldes belovde, whom love cannott surpryse" (line 8). The suggestion that she is immune to love puts a graceful, reassuring interpretation upon the collapse of all her marriage negotiations including, no doubt, the Anjou proposal of 1579–1581. She is likewise invulnerable to fortune because she possesses "Wysedome by fortune not to bee controlde" (lines 8–9). Here, Gorges may have intended fortune in the restricted sense of high or good fortune, the happy status of favored, noble courtiers. This was, as we shall see, Ralegh's meaning of the word in the verses he directed to Elizabeth in 1587. Finally, the queen's "skill that refynes our Baser age to golde" summarizes a conventional pastoral image of the queen as the restorer of the Golden Age, a convention that had not yet been applied by other courtiers, however, in their praises of Elizabeth.[14]

Poem 49, also adapted from DuBellay, once more exalts the queen

14. For the relationship to pastoral see Wilson, *Entertainments*, 23.

above the goddesses Paris judged, and it addresses her throughout in the second person. In comparing her with Alexander the Great in poem 61, Gorges repeats the praises developed in his earlier sonnets: she is beloved of all the world, "hyr woundynge eyes hath slayne" the hearts of those who pursued her, while her beauty is protected for all time by "Devyne chastytie." These lyrics attribute to Elizabeth the qualities of the typical sonnet lady; she is irresistibly attractive but chaste, even cruel in her ability to repulse the demands of her admirers. Gorges adapts not only his French sources to the praise of the queen but often surpasses them by infusing his praise with the language of Petrarchan love poetry. The resulting lyrics are not mere outgrowths of the earlier laments by Oxford and Dyer, for there is nothing of their complaining tone in Gorges's work. His tone is instead admiring and celebratory. Perhaps Greville achieved a similar effect in *Caelica* 17, yet his only definite verses in praise of Elizabeth, *Caelica* 81, are formal, distanced, and quite devoid of amorous flattery by comparison with Gorges's offerings.

Gorges's "A Pastorall unfynyshed," poem 100, is the "sweet Eglantine of Meriflure" that Spenser encouraged him to complete in *Colin Clouts Come Home Againe* (line 389ff). Although Sandison argued that this is a hybrid poem originally drafted in praise of Daphne and then altered into a tribute both to Douglas and Elizabeth,[15] it was more likely dedicated to the queen from the start. The "sober Ladd" who bemoans his lost love amidst "Dianas darlinges" is the pastoral equivalent of Gorges on duty in the Presence Chamber among the maids of honor. His songs in praise of various flowers are carefully differentiated between the listing in stanza three, which includes "the Prymrose and sweet woodbynds," variants of the eglantine, and the eglantine itself of stanza 4.

Sandison noted Daphne's association with the primrose, woodbine, and violet in poems 94 and 99 and connected them with the Howard family's right to impale the red and white roses of the royal arms.[16] Thus Gorges's praise of the eglantine might do double duty as praise of both the queen and Douglas Howard, yet the only connection between Douglas and the eglantine occurs, supposedly, in poem 82. Here Gorges adapted lines by DuBellay in order to pledge his abiding faith to a lady who gave him her garter embroidered with "eglantynes and lyllyes for your name" (line 7). These flowers, precisely appropriate to the queen, do not appear in the Howard

15. Sandison, *Poems*, 225.
16. Ibid., 212–13.

arms, nor is poem 82 in any other way connected with Douglas. A more likely explanation is that Gorges received this royal token from Elizabeth, a sign of particular but not unprecedented favor. She bestowed similar tokens on a number of other courtiers: Essex and Cumberland received gloves, and it was Charles Blount's flaunting of a chess queen Elizabeth gave him that caused Essex to challenge him to a duel. Heneage, Hatton, and Sir Humphrey Gilbert received symbolic jewelry from the queen, all in keeping with the amorous, medieval style of courtiership that she cultivated as woman and monarch.[17] Gorges may have received a royal garter in the course of some conventional flirtation with Elizabeth and addressed poem 82 to her afterward to commemorate the gift. The sixth and last stanza of poem 100 points unequivocally to Elizabeth, tracing her lineage from "Dardane kynges" (that is, through the mythical founding of Britain by a descendant of Aeneas), to the "Conqueringe lyne," to the strife between the red and white roses which is "apeasde in thys brave Eglantyne."

Gorges may have modeled his pastoral upon Ralegh's lost "Ocean to Cynthia"; at least the surviving fragments of this ambitious work in praise of Elizabeth likewise employ pastoral conventions. And both courtiers drew on *The Faerie Queene* as they worked on these unfinished projects after 1589. Thus Gorges represented himself "As on[e] for loste love much dismayde" because of his wife's death in August of 1590. His songs of the primrose and related flowers in the third stanza refer to the verses he had written for Douglas, but this pastoral is not about her nor in her memory. Spenser was aware of the distinction, for in *Daphnaida* he made Gorges/Alcyon describe Queen Elizabeth as "the Rose, the glory of the day," in contrast with Daphne, "the Primrose in the lowly shade" (lines 232–33). And when Spenser encouraged him to continue his unfinished tribute to Elizabeth he characterized it not as an elegy but as a poem "That may thy Muse and mates to mirth allure."[18] Gorges's familiarity with Spenser's work at this time is revealed by his adaptation in his poem's fifth stanza of lines from *The Faerie Queene*, 3.5.52ff., a

---

17. Naunton, *Fragmenta Regalia*, 119–20; Roy Strong and V. J. Murrell, *Artists of the Tudor Court*, 134–35. For Heneage see the account in Part II; for Hatton, my "Companion Poems in the Ralegh Canon." Ralegh wrote Gilbert on March 17, 1583, "Brother I have sent you a token from her Majesty, an ancor guided by a lady," signifying her regard for his safety as he embarked upon what was, ironically, his last voyage (Edward Edwards, *The Life of Sir Walter Ralegh*, 2:19).

18. *Colin Clouts Come Home Againe*, in Spenser, *Works*, 7:391.

passage which traces the queen's lineage as Belphoebe, the huntress who rescues the wounded Timias and heals him with the aid of tobacco. The allegorical parallels with Elizabeth, Ralegh, and his promotion of tobacco in England are obvious, and it was thus only natural that Gorges found this episode of particular interest and that he worked a few of its lines into his own verses for the queen.[19]

Gorges's use of poetry differs from Sidney's in several respects. He addressed at least a half-dozen of his poems, including translations from the French, directly to the praise of both his wife and the queen. With the bulk of his poetry, however, he was far more secretive than Philip—only eight of his lyrics saw contemporary circulation. His works reflect various aspects of his life as a courtier yet reveal as well his dedication to poetry as an end in itself. For example, his longest poem in the Egerton Manuscript, the 576-line lament written in the person of Dido (poem 90), is a close translation of DuBellay garnished with excerpts from Turberville's translation of the same original. It is hard to imagine how this undertaking could have reflected his own circumstances or promoted his personal ambitions at court. Instead, he wrote for his own satisfaction or for a quite restricted audience. In this as in the miscellaneous nature of his collected poems, Gorges's concept of the value and uses of poetry comes closest to Greville's, whose *Caelica* more nearly resembles the "Vannetyes and Toyes" than any other courtier's collected verses.

Gorges's experimentation is further evidence of his interest in verse for its own sake. In addition to his twenty-two sonnets with English rhyme schemes, he wrote two poems in iambic octameter couplets (19 and 35), plus an unrhymed long-line poem of various hexameter, heptameter, and octameter rhythms, along with lighter tetrameter and trimeter lyrics which follow such demanding stanza forms as poem 42's *a a a b c c c b*. Yet he did not attempt Sidney's trochaics nor his quantitative verse. In five poems (56, 60, 61, 77, and 81), Gorges undertook metrical experiments which Sandison interpreted as quantitative, yet their effect is totally unlike either Sidney's or Greville's, and all five are written in rhyme. Although poem 56 bears some resemblance to the English quantitative manner, these poems seem instead to be Gorges's efforts to reproduce the non-accentual rhythms of French verse in English. Syllable count is quite regular in these poems: poem 60 is in ten-syllable lines except

---

19. James P. Bednarz offers a detailed explication of this passage in "Ralegh in Spenser's Historical Allegory" (58–62).

for line 9 which has eleven; poems 61 and 81 are in twelve syllables with but three exceptions, and poem 77 is composed of eleven-syllable lines.[20] Such regularity would be difficult to manage as well as irrelevant to almost any system of quantitative scansion applied to English verse, but it is regular enough to approximate the effect of French decasyllables and Alexandrines.

The minority of Gorges's poems which reflect his career at court stand in sharp contrast with the output of his cousin and lifelong friend, Walter Ralegh. Ralegh and Gorges may have attended Oxford University together in 1574–1575, and by 1576 both were in London with an eye toward advancement at court. Ralegh's interest in poetry at this point in his career is evidenced by his commendatory verses for Gascoigne's *The Steele Glas* (1576), and he may also have written verses in company with George Whetstone before being promoted in 1582 from army captain and esquire for the body extraordinary to courtier and royal favorite.[21] The works of these popular poets, combined with that of Gorges, constitute the identifiable influences on Ralegh's verse as he began his career as a courtier. With Gorges, he may also have studied French verse, for a rough text in BL, Additional Manuscript 5956, folios 25–25v, which begins "Repentinge folly that myn eye had soe deceived me," appears to be translated from the same unknown source he used for poem 5, "Calling to mind, mine eye went long about."

The genres of three of Ralegh's subsequent poems conform to traditionally respectable subjects for courtier verse, the Sidney elegy and the two commendatory poems for *The Faerie Queene*. An anonymous verse epitaph upon Sidney's tomb in St. Paul's influenced lines 45–48 of Ralegh's poem 3,[22] and some degree of mutual influence is likely between his work and Gorges's poem 97, both of which parcel out Sidney's virtues to eternity. Sorrow is an active agent in Ralegh's poem: "In worthy harts sorow hath made thy tombe, / Thy soule and spright enrich the heavens above" (lines 51–52), while Gorges concludes that "worthy fame . . . Entombes his harte in wyde worlds love and prayse / And of his mynde a newe heavensman doth rayse." The emphasis upon martial prowess in Gorges's poem

20. Poem 60, line 9, has eleven syllables after eliding "Even" to "e'en." A trisyllabic "praetious" at poem 61, line 12, gives the line twelve syllables, but "Quaylde" must be disyllabic to bring line 14 to equal length. At poem 77, line 12, "persevereth" must be pronounced "persevreth" to achieve twelve syllables.
    21. For the possible ties with Whetstone, see my "Companion Poems."
    22. Thomas Zouch, *Memoirs of the Life and Writings of Sir Philip Sidney*, 288, acknowledged in Michael Rudick's, "The Poems of Sir Walter Ralegh," 27.

96 is likewise treated in three of the fifteen stanzas of Ralegh's poem, but Sidney's literary achievements are explicitly acknowledged in only one line, and shared even so with his military acclaim as the "Scipio, Cicero, and Petrarch of our time." Sidney's literary influence, moreover, becomes no more apparent in Ralegh's verse than in Gorges's. Ralegh admits that his love for Sidney was suppressed by envy (line 7), yet this hardly seems sufficient motive for shunning Sir Philip's example as a poet. Rather, it appears that Walter had developed a genuine if dilettante interest in poetry before becoming a courtier, only to have the competitive experience of royal favoritism divert that interest away from the essentially contemplative, creative purposes it had assumed for Sidney and his friends. Above all, Ralegh used his poetic talents to defend and promote his status as a courtier, for of the fifteen canonical poems he composed by the end of the reign, twelve directly reflected his circumstances at court and at least six of these were about or addressed to the queen.

In addition to the Sidney elegy, several of his early lyrics bear direct ties to fellow courtiers. "The word of denial" is a poetic rebus upon the name of his friend Henry Noel, who responded in kind.[23] The two men had probably known each other since 1578 so that the exchange of mildly insulting couplets was probably carried out in a spirit of playful camaraderie. By contrast, Sir Thomas Heneage's poem 1, a response to Ralegh's "Farewell false love," grew out of a genuine rivalry during the early 1580s in which Heneage and Hatton cooperated to offset Ralegh's astonishing ascent in the queen's favor. The different perceptions of poetry's role in courtiership are revealed by the different textual histories of the Ralegh-Heneage companion poems. Heneage's response survives in a unique text; he may well have shown it to Elizabeth, but he did not allow it to circulate. This was confidential, literally in-house, anti-Ralegh propaganda, designed to counter what must have been the notorious circulation of Ralegh's poem at court, for it is Heneage's only known amorous verse. "Farewell false love," on the other hand, circulated widely in the manuscript anthologies and had found its way into print by 1588 when it was set to music in Byrd's *Psalmes, Sonets and Songs*.

Ralegh's claim to possible poem 2, "Lady farewell, whome I in Sylence serve," is made plausible by both its appearance in BL, Harleian Manuscript 7392, which preserves elite courtier verse of the 1580s, and by the very specific title in an early seventeenth-

23. Rudick, "Poems," poem 4.

century anthology, "A poem put into my Lady Laitons Pocket by Sir W. Rawleigh." This was probably Elizabeth Knollys, daughter of Sir Francis Knollys, treasurer of the household; she received a wedding gift from the queen upon her marriage to Sir Thomas Leighton circa 1578, and Elizabeth also stood godmother to her daughter, who was christened March 8, 1582. She served as lady of the Privy Chamber to the end of the reign.[24] Ralegh would have been foolhardy to profess love in earnest to a married woman so closely connected with the queen. Although the verses Lady Leighton supposedly received from him conclude, "I thynke I Love thee Beste," they are standard Petrarchan fare replete with "scorchyng fyre" and a "wynde of woe" that "hath torne my Tree of Truste." If Ralegh delivered them as the Chetham Manuscript affirms, they were no doubt presented in a spirit of playful socializing.

Ralegh allowed most of his poems to circulate freely either in manuscript or print. By the early 1580s, after all, Oxford, Dyer, and Sidney were well known as courtier poets, while Heneage, Greville, Gorges, and Elizabeth herself had composed a significant number of less widely dispersed poems. At court the stigma of poetry eroded as its potential for enhancing one's image as a courtier was explored, in public display by Sidney, with moral decorum by Heneage, and with amorous abandon by Oxford and Dyer. For Ralegh, these tentative steps toward a truly utilitarian poetics were but crude prototypes. By the end of the decade he had amplified their potential beyond all earlier attempts, and in so doing he set the course for the development of this type of courtier verse to the end of the reign.

It was above all in his manner of addressing Elizabeth that Ralegh adapted poetry to courtiership, devising a multitude of styles and fictions richer in their variety and concentration than anything undertaken by previous courtiers. Not that Elizabeth was a stranger to the extravagant and imaginative praises called forth by her beauty and wisdom. Hatton showed himself a master of the lofty, despairing style in prose as early as 1573 in the letters he sent to her during an absence from court: "to serve you is a heaven, but to lack you is more than hell's torment. . . . My heart is full of woe. . . . Would God I were with you but for one hour. My wits are overwrought with thoughts. I find myself amazed. Bear with me, my most dear sweet Lady. Passion overcometh me. . . . Love me; for I love you." He continued in the same vein a few days later, "This is the twelfth day

24. BL, Add. MS 38857, f. 63; Harleian MS 1644, f. 90. Lady Leighton is named on every New Year's roll from 1582 to 1603 and in the funeral accounts.

since I saw the brightness of that Sun that giveth light unto my sense and soul."[25] Although the moon's associations with chaste beauty made it the most popular symbol for the queen, the queen-sun metaphor was also consistently exploited by courtiers. Sidney characterized her as the defender of Protestantism "and the only sun that dazzleth" Catholic eyes, and he probably wrote the "Fortress of Perfect Beauty" pageant in which Elizabeth is described as the sun besieged by desire and as the "most renowned and divine Beautie, whose beames shine like the sun."[26] Still more impassioned effusions on the same theme occur in letters sent to the queen by Robert, second earl of Essex:

> For the 2 windowes of your privy chamber shallbe the poles of my sphere wher, as long as your Majestie will please to have me, I am fixed and unmoveable: when you thinke thatt heaven to good for me, I will nott fall like a starr, butt be consumed like a vapor by the sun thatt drew me up to such a heyght. While your Majestie geves me leave to say I love you my fortune is as my affection unmatchable. yf ever you deny me thatt liberty, you may end my lyfe, butt never shake my constancy. for weare the sweetnes of your nature turned into the greatest bitternes thatt cold be yt is nott in your power, (as greatt a Queen as you are) to make me love you lesse.[27]

Elizabeth was assured by her courtiers that she commanded their groveling adoration and steadfast love regardless of how she treated them in return. Heneage expressed his unwavering loyalty during a period of displeasure in the following terms: "For I will never shoote but to serve your Majesty alone, leavyng divers markes for conynger archers. . . . And thus will I conclude: whatsoever be the cause that the dogge must be strycken, I can best assure your Majesty he will nether breake cheyn nor coller but byde at your feete."[28] The lively imagination behind these comparisons is little in evidence in the prosaic verse letter Heneage addressed to the queen (poem 6). Similarly, Hatton's most emotional communications with Elizabeth are expressed in prose, although he acknowledged her sensitivity to

25. Sir Harris Nicolas, *Memoirs of the Life and Times of Sir Christopher Hatton*, 26–27. Hatton once emerged from an audience with the queen to warn the younger Harington that it would be unwise to press a suit because "The Sunne dothe not shine" (*Nugae Antiquae* [1779], 2:221). Neville Williams examines the "Sun Queen" motif in "The Tudors" (162).

26. "A Letter to Queen Elizabeth," in Duncan-Jones and Van Dorsten, *Miscellaneous Prose*, 52; Nichols, *Progresses*, 2:320–22.

27. Letter of October 18, 1591, Hulton Papers, BL, Loan MS 23, ff. 37–37v. The italics are my expansion of abbreviations in the original manuscript.

28. HMC, Salisbury, 23:5–6, circa 1585.

verse when he wrote that "The life (as you well remember), is too long that loathsomely lasteth," paraphrasing the first line of a poem that the elder Harington may have composed in the Tower while Elizabeth was also confined there in 1554.[29]

Among the queen's favorites of the first magnitude before Ralegh, only Oxford had wooed her in verse. Dyer's complaints from the same era expressed an intensity of emotion that surpassed even Hatton's letters, yet Dyer apparently abandoned this form of royal address after the 1570s. Royal flattery in the *Lady of May* songs and Greville's poem 81 are impersonal, public displays of courtier devotion. Accordingly the three poems that Gorges addressed to Elizabeth by 1587 mark a revival of personal courtier communication through poetry, although it is possible that in so doing Gorges was following Ralegh's lead. Certainly Ralegh's "Farewell false love" circulated at court under his name during the early 1580s, along with poem 3, "Calling to mind," and Ralegh may well have used both poems to promote and maintain his rapport with Elizabeth. The earliest datable lines he addressed to her, however, belong to 1587 and the first serious crisis in their relationship. Despite occasional conflicts with Hatton and Leicester, Ralegh solidified his status at court and in the queen's favor without interruption between 1582 and 1586. He avoided or overcame serious challenges to his position until November of 1586 when Robert Devereux, second earl of Essex, returned from campaigning in the Low Countries. This young nobleman, who had just come of age, participated in the annual Accession Day tilt and in the 1587 New Year's gift exchange; he spent increasing amounts of time with Elizabeth. Ralegh expressed his fear of abandonment in the poem, which is edited before the queen's response in Part II. Both the content and context of Ralegh's "Fortune hath taken thee away my Love" argue that he composed it during the first half of 1587 in an effort to counteract Elizabeth's growing partiality for Essex.[30] Ralegh may have associated himself with fortune as a personal motif well before 1587.

29. Nicolas, *Memoirs*, 26, letter of June 5, 1573. Hatton's allusion strengthens the attribution of this poem to Harington found in *Nugae Antiquae* (1779, 3:269), for the queen would have had good reason to remember these verses had he addressed them to her during the crisis of 1554. Ruth Hughey classifies the poem as doubtful in her edition (*John Harington*, 124–25).

30. The text in BL, Add. MS 63742, occurs among entries that date from 1586 to the end of 1587, and while this anthology does not seem to have been compiled in strict chronological order, the position of this text associates it with those years.

Naunton described him as "one that it seems fortune had picked out of purpose to make an example," and added that early in his career as favorite the opposition of other courtiers "made him shortly after to sing 'Fortune my foe.'"[31] The poems exchanged between Ralegh and the queen were combined, moreover, with an existing ballad to produce the popular "Fortune my foe, why doest thou frowne on me." Ralegh's identification with fortune is also revealed by his description as "Fortune's child, nature's defiler" in a verse libel possibly written by Essex in the mid–1590s (possible poem I). In dealing with the threat posed by Essex in 1587 however, Ralegh shifted the identification with fortune from himself to his opponent.

Ralegh's dilemma corresponded with that described in Dyer's poem 3, where the poet likewise complained of losing his mistress to a rival. Dyer had exempted his lady from blame not by implicating his rival, but through mourning that

> . . . Fortune framde it so,
> As neyther I, nor you nor Hee but did endure some wo,
> Then did my Joyes take end, suche force hathe Jelousy.
> (lines 31–33)

But where Dyer portrayed himself as a victim of fate and his own immoderate passion, Ralegh adopts a more aggressive strategy, exonerating the queen by blaming his loss on "Fortune," which as Leonard Tennenhouse observes, refers in context to a person of superior social standing, undoubtedly Essex.[32]

Ralegh's intentions, what he wanted the poem to "do," however, concerned no economic reward nor a specific suit to the queen. Rather, his lines dealt with the very essence of courtiership, his social relationship with his sovereign. He played on the ambiguous meaning of "Fortune" in this poem to attack Essex by implying that this nobleman's superiority was merely an accident of fate and by then attributing to him the goddess Fortuna's shortcomings: she only "rules on earth and earthlie things," and she is blind to the distinction between true worth and the undeserving. He also portrays Fortune as a thief who victimizes Elizabeth herself, through the fourfold repetition of "Fortune hath taken" in the first six lines of the poem. Moreover, Essex-Fortune holds the queen captive in "worthlesse bands." Her passive helplessness (and thus her lack of any active role in the estrangement from Ralegh) is expressed in his

31. *Fragmenta*, 71–72.
32. "Sir Walter Ralegh and the Literature of Clientage," 240.

plaintive conclusion: "But Love farewell, though fortune conquer thee, / No fortune base shall ever alter me."

If the amorous sentiments expressed in this complaint are generally akin to the earlier, neo-Petrarchan laments of Dyer and Oxford, Ralegh's persuasive strategy far outdistances his predecessors' efforts. He does employ a few scraps of mid-century phrasing, the "fancy's foe" of line 8 or perhaps the personified Sorrow of line 16, yet the veiled association of Essex with fortune is no Petrarchan conceit, nor does he commit himself to a lingering death in the wake of his rejection. Ralegh mutes the emotionalism of earlier complaints by consigning himself merely to a life of sorrow, and his rhetoric supports this more realistic pose. The use of anaphora and repetitive phrasing creates an emphatic, mournful chant rather than merely redundant listings. The feminine rhyme in lines 3–4 and the frequent substitute feet (with seven of his twenty-four iambic lines beginning with trochees) remove his rhythms from any suggestion of "drab" singsong. Ralegh's lament is calculated to persuade Elizabeth into siding with her elder favorite against the predatory invasion of an upstart nobleman. His rhetorical approach was probably influenced by the poem beginning "Fortune, thy restless, wavering state," Elizabeth's own remonstrance against fortune which she had inscribed on a wall at Woodstock Palace while imprisoned there by Queen Mary in 1555. Her verses were widely known, their existence at Woodstock a popular tourist attraction.[33] By attacking fortune, Ralegh could remind the queen that his plight as the victim of a social superior owed as much to mere fortune as did hers as a victim of her elder half-sister Mary. Ralegh's poem was carefully fashioned for its recipient, yet Elizabeth's policy of entertaining multiple favorites had been established long before 1587, and it should be kept in mind that Heneage, Hatton, and Leicester were alive and in favor while Ralegh and Essex competed as if they were the only rivals for her affection. What Ralegh faced was the poignant but relatively slight demotion from favorite *précieux* to elder favorite, a transition that Leicester, Hatton, Heneage, and Oxford all had weathered before him.

Elizabeth had no intention of discarding her "pug"; indeed, she

---

33. Leicester Bradner prints the queen's poem from a restored text originally copied by Paul Hentzner in 1597 (*Poems*, 3, 71). A more accurate transcription was made by Thomas Platter (see Clare Williams, *Thomas Platter's Travels in England, 1599*, 220–21). The poem was also copied in 1600 by Baron Waldstein, as printed in G. W. Groos, trans. and ed., *The Diary of Baron Waldstein* (117, 119).

was sufficiently moved by Ralegh's lament to respond to it in kind. Her companion verses, while they avoid the amorous language of Ralegh's poem, do not actually revert to the mundane language of client-patron transactions as Tennenhouse argues.[34] Instead her response, carefully coordinated with Ralegh's lines, develops its own remarkably tender, coaxing tone. She denies that fortune can turn her heart against him, that she chose him "by foolish fortune's reede," or that "Thie Love, thie Joy" is bound by fortune's bands. The diction is too intimate for patron-client discourse, yet the impression is less that of a mistress encouraging her beloved than of a mother reassuring her fearful child. And just as she declines to acknowledge the seriousness of Ralegh's despair, so her reassurance ignores the ambiguous significations of fortune in his poem, for Elizabeth consistently treats fortune as the blind goddess, equivalent to fate and able only on occasion ("sometimes") to conquer kings. The message imparted to Ralegh indicates that while she will not disparage his adversary, his own position as a favorite remains secure.

The resolution of this first phase of the Ralegh-Essex rivalry occurred in July of 1587 in a showdown between Devereux and Elizabeth which can be reconstructed as the conversational equivalent of her exchange of poems with Ralegh. As Sir Walter stood within earshot at the chamber door, Essex told the queen what "that knave Raleigh . . . had been, and what he was; and then I did let her see, whether I had cause to disdain his competition of Love; or whether I could have Comfort to give myself over to the Service of a Mistress, that was in Aw of such a Man."[35] Essex too used the language of courtly love, and Elizabeth again refused to countenance the attack on a rival, insisting that he had no cause to disdain Ralegh. In the face of this repulse, the earl complained to Dyer that he would return to the wars in Holland. The status of both courtiers, and Lord Robert's flight from the court, were described a few days later in the following terms: "Mr. Rale standes emongste othares undare the clothe of a state; My Lord of Essekes is all in alle bute

<hr />

34. Tennenhouse ("Sir Walter Ralegh") notes the queen's more colloquial style but construes her final words, "the better shalt thou speed," as having explicitly commercial overtones. "Speed" was however routinely applied to courtship as well; thus Julia to Proteus in *The Two Gentlemen of Verona*, "Yet will I woo for him, but yet so coldly / As, heaven it knows, I would not have him speed" (4.4.106–7), and see *The Taming of the Shrew* (2.1.244–25) and *The Merry Wives of Windsor* (3.5.63–66).

35. Bodl., Tanner MS 76, f. 84v.

apone thorsda laste my Lord of Essekes was gone in a feume frome the courte as fare as Margete . . . I fere it was seyche a toye as wole done heme no good." Dyer probably informed the queen of the earl's impulsive plans, for she sent Robert Carey to intercept him at Sandwich. No lasting displeasure ensued, however, for Essex, with the earl of Cumberland, was among the foremost performers in the Accession Day tournament that November.[36]

With the advent of Essex as principal favorite, Ralegh's star had dimmed but not suffered eclipse. His subsequent sense of rejection was probably set forth in his "Farewell to the Court" (poem 8), where references to "My love misled," "my life in fortunes hand," and hastening "to find my fortunes folde" are of a piece with his language and approach to the Essex rivalry in "Fortune hath taken thee away." By the winter of 1589–1590 however, Ralegh turned from complaint to praise of his sovereign and a more vigorous offensive against the earl when he brought Edmund Spenser to court to present Elizabeth with *The Faerie Queene*. There is no evidence that Ralegh was in fact out of favor in 1589 nor that by introducing Spenser to the queen he might somehow placate her; rather, it was his retention of royal favor, and that "never better" as he himself affirmed, which made Spenser's successful debut at court practical.[37] In the event, it also provided Ralegh with a good opportunity to set forth some very public royal flattery. His English sonnet in commendation of his friend's book is an extraordinarily efficient piece of verse communication. It is cast in the form of an abbreviated dream vision, appropriate to the gothic nature of Spenser's poem, but anticipated by such earlier courtier works as Oxford's poem 8 and Sidney's OA 73. Ralegh's rhetorical strategy resembles that of "Fortune hath taken thee away," in that his ambiguous praise of "the Faery Queene" simultaneously describes the literary displacement of Petrarch by Spenser while affirming that in the process the graces formerly attendant upon Laura, "faire love, and fairer vertue," now wait upon Elizabeth as the Fairy Queen. His reference in the couplet to Homer trembling with grief acknowledges the

36. HMC, 17th report, 49, Martin Frobisher to Lord Willoughby, July 30, 1587. According to Frobisher, Essex fled to Margate on July 27. The earl's letter to Dyer, in which he vows to be at Margate "this night," is transcribed in the Tanner Manuscript under the date "2ith of July," apparently an error for the 27th. For Essex at tilt see Philip Gawdy's letter to his father of November 24, 1587 (in HMC, 7th report, Appendix, 520).

37. Edwards, *Life of Sir Walter Ralegh*, 2:42, and see the analysis of Ralegh's status at this time by Tennenhouse ("Sir Walter Ralegh," 243–44).

heroic superiority of Spenser's verse, as the triumph over Petrarch symbolizes its superiority as romance. Ralegh's concise, dramatic fiction with its efficient incorporation of two levels of praise produces an unusually successful poem within the confines of the normally prosaic commendatory genre.

Far less successful as poetry is Ralegh's second set of commendatory verses, the disparagement in poulter's measure of even favorable critics of Spenser's work, beginning, "The prayse of meaner wits this work like profit brings / As doth the Cuckoes song delight when Philumena sings." Although addressed to Spenser himself, its personifications of the queen as virtue and beauty maintain the level of royal flattery achieved in the first poem. Conceivably, Essex was one of the courtier "Cuckoes" who praised Spenser's verse, and who, in short, tried to appropriate Ralegh's protégé to his own credit. The earl knew Ralegh's lines at any rate, for he picked up their imagery in poem 1, which he apparently composed during the disgrace he suffered in 1590 after Elizabeth found out about his secret marriage to Sidney's widow, Frances Walsingham.[38] In particular, his references to the queen as beauty and virtue, to his opponent as a cursed cuckoo who "hath crost sweete Philomela's note," and to fortune treading under foot the Muses' concord, reveal a consistent language of poetic competition at court. Essex inverts Ralegh's symbolism by identifying himself with Philomela, and Ralegh ("puddle water") with the cuckoo and fortune. As a result of his opponent's machinations, he wrote, "Beauty must seeme to goe against her kinde, / In crossinge nature in her sweetest Joyes" (poem 1, lines 33–34). Ralegh may have exacerbated the queen's displeasure over Essex's marriage, or he may even have been the first to inform her of it. He performed a similar office in 1591 when it was learned that Essex was bestowing inordinate numbers of knighthoods in France: "yt was told her the last day in the Afternoone by Sr W: Rawleigh . . . since which time her highness hath not forgotten yt."[39] The Ralegh-Essex rivalry was among the reign's bitterest struggles for power as measured by a courtier's place in the hierarchy of Elizabeth's immediate personal favor. By 1590 Essex had learned to use poetry along with letters and speeches to the queen as a means of defending his own position and degrading his adversary.

38. I discuss the symbolism of Essex's poem and its probable context in the commentary to my edition ("The Poems of Edward DeVere, Seventeenth Earl of Oxford, and of Robert Devereux, Second Earl of Essex," 85–88).

39. University College, London, Ogden MS 7 (41), f. 24, letter of October 27, 1591.

Not only is this aggressive use of poetry to promote immediate concerns at court new but as a propaganda medium it borrows almost nothing from earlier courtier verse. The self-representations and use of personae, for example, rely either upon abstractions (fortune, beauty, honor) or established, often mythical entities (Philomela, Mars, and Venus); the technique is fluid, symbolic, and quite unlike the development of fictional personae practiced by the Sidney circle.

In Devereux's remaining Elizabethan poetry, as in Ralegh's, there is little evidence of composition for its own sake or as a function of passive retirement from courtiership. For these rivals, the muse had become an ally in their campaigns of self-promotion at court. The earl's remaining canonical poems show him following Ralegh's lead by adapting his poetry to self-serving, political ends. Poem 3 was embedded in his part of the elaborate Accession Day show which he sponsored in 1595 both in the tiltyard and in an after-dinner continuation. The address in poem 5 to "her whom all the world admird, . . . / . . . her that can love none" (lines 5–6) shows that it was meant for the queen, as was sonnet 8, a similar complaint wherein the poet suffers because his beloved "useth the advantage tyme and fortune gave, / Of worth and power to gett the libertie." Poem 7 is a lament from "Your Majesty's Exiled Servant, Rob: Essex," in which the poet foresees his own death, but unlike his other verses for the queen it is set forth without recourse to the language of courtly love or indeed any outright attribution of his death to unrequited love. The internal evidence of the earl's remaining poems, 4, 6, 9, and 10, is ambiguous with regard to the contexts and purposes for which they were written, although the first two are amorous complaints and all four might have been directed to Elizabeth with advantage as Robert attempted to maneuver and control his royal mistress through the quarrels and reconciliations of the 1590s that led to Ireland, disgrace, and a traitor's death.

The hallmark of Devereux's poetic addresses to Elizabeth is their straightforward, unembellished expression of personal sentiment. Rhetorical display had constituted a primary effect of the love poetry written by Oxford and Dyer, including the lyrics they wrote for the queen. Essex subordinates rhetoric to the expository representation of himself and his mistress. She is not a goddess or May Lady for him even within the fictional context of the Accession Day pageant; she is instead a queen endowed with virtue, majesty, and "pollicie" (poem 3). The themes are those that she often found in his letters and those of other courtiers. Thus she is told to "Forget my name since you have scornd by love, / And woman-like doe not to late lamente" (poem 5, lines 9–10), yet simultaneously he assures her that "I none accuse nor nothinge doe repent," and that "All strength of love is infinite in mee" (poem 5, line 12; poem 8, line 10). The style is direct, its sincerity and concise, graceful language making up for its lack of ornament, as in the couplet to sonnet 5, "I was as fond as ever shee was faire, / Yet lovd I not more then I now despaire."

Essex may have learned from Ralegh how to use poetry in his dealings with Elizabeth, yet his plain style is very different from the increasingly ornamental verses that Ralegh composed for the queen. Before 1592, and probably before 1590, Ralegh wrote poem 9, "Now we have present made," to accompany some special but unidentified gift for Elizabeth. Here the mode of address is typical of the "cult of Elizabeth," yet no courtier had bedecked her in verse with these attributes prior to Ralegh. She is all but submerged in a crowd of fictional personae: "Cynthia, phaebe, flora, / Diana and Aurora." Her servants, "Love, nature, and perfection" anticipate the personified love and virtue attendant upon the Fairy Queen in Ralegh's first commendatory poem for Spenser's masterpiece.[40] This poetic celebration is rhetorically and imaginatively far more elaborate than the relatively straightforward complaint about "Fortune" of 1587. The tendency toward ornament and fiction gained momentum in 1592, as Ralegh subsided into a five-year period of disgrace and exile from the court, for in seeking to regain Elizabeth's favor he wrote the fullest expression in courtier verse of her "cult," the four poems of his "Ocean to Cynthia" (poems 10–13).

With Rudick I concur in assigning these fragments to the summer and fall of 1592 when it was Ralegh's turn to endure the queen's ire over his secret marriage to Elizabeth Throckmorton, a gentlewoman of the Privy Chamber.[41] After his arrest, his cousin Gorges collaborated with him in a variety of melodramatic efforts to regain royal favor. Wording from the longest of the "Cynthia" fragments, poem 12, lines 413 and 415, shows up in Gorges's sonnet 110, which

40. If Ralegh systematically changed his designation of the queen as Phoebe to Belphoebe (as in poem 12, lines 271, 327) after reading Spenser's work in 1589, then poem 9 must precede their meeting. Rudick ("Poems") transposed "affection" and "perfection" as the rhyme words of poem 9, lines 22–23, by conjecture and in contradiction of all three substantive texts, one of them in Ralegh's holograph. But Elizabeth as "princess of worlds affection" agrees with Gorges's characterization of her as one who possesses "the worldes love" and is "The worldes belovde" (poem 61, line 7; poem 47, line 8).

41. Elizabeth Throckmorton appears among the gentlewomen on the extant New Year's gift rolls, 1585–1589, but is never listed with the maids of honor.

was probably composed at the time of Ralegh's imprisonment although not entered into the Egerton Manuscript until 1599 or thereafter. Gorges's poem 87, a love lyric inspired by his imprisonment in 1580, may have helped Ralegh develop his own complaint from prison, poem 11. Both works contrast the body's captive state with the mind's delightful subjection to a beloved mistress, and both base their comparisons specifically upon differences in diet, keeper, and access to light. Gorges and Ralegh also wrote impassioned letters to Sir Robert Cecil in July 1592, describing at length the desperate, even deranged frame of mind induced in Sir Walter by his confinement. The consistency of approach is striking: Ralegh "wyll shortely growe [to be] Orlando furioso; If the bryght Angelyca perseuer agaynst [hyme]" wrote Gorges; the newlywed has been driven to the brink of madness by his separation from Elizabeth Regina, not Elizabeth Ralegh.[42] The prisoner remembered the queen "riding like *Alexander*, hunting like *Diana*, walking like *Venus*, the gentle wind blowing her fair hair about her pure cheeks, like a nymph."[43] These letters, and no doubt the "Cynthia" poems as well were delivered to Cecil that he might convey them to their intended audience, the queen, for all six documents are clearly designed to influence her. The choice of Cecil was a desperate one given the boldness with which Ralegh had lied to him about his marriage, but he was apparently Ralegh's best remaining hope. The only living nobleman in any way indebted to Ralegh was Oxford, who had long since lost Elizabeth's ear. Heneage and Greville were rivals of long standing. Lord Admiral Howard had apparently moved the queen to relent, yet Ralegh channeled his principal efforts toward Cecil.[44] Sir Robert was probably closer to Elizabeth than any other Privy Councillor both in personal esteem and in the day-by-day transaction of official business. Ralegh may have supposed that Cecil and Lord Burghley would prefer to rescue him rather than leave the queen subject to but one dashing favorite, Essex.

The "Cynthia" that Ralegh may have begun even before he met Spenser in Ireland in 1589 and that is thrice referred to in the first installment of *The Faerie Queene* must have been devoted to

---

42. Helen Estabrook Sandison, "Arthur Gorges: Spenser's Alcyon and Ralegh's Friend," 658.

43. Edwards, *Life of Sir Walter Ralegh*, 2:51. The allusion to Alexander may owe something to Gorges's poem 61, an extended comparison of Elizabeth to "the great Macedon."

44. Ibid., 2:52–54. Ralegh urged Howard "not to offend Her Majestye any farther by sewing for mee."

elaborate praise of the queen, although it may have been little more developed than Gorges's "Eglantine."[45] Part of Ralegh's early work on this theme apparently survives in recension as lines 348–50 of poem 12 where Ralegh reminds himself, "such didsst thow her longe since discribe." His desperate plight in 1592 caused him to return to the idea of this poem, now transformed from praise to complaint, a transformation noted in Spenser's entirely different characterization of it in *Colin Clouts Come Home Againe* as "a lamentable lay, / Of great vnkindnesse, and of vsage hard, / Of *Cynthia.*"[46] The "Ocean to Cynthia's" indebtedness to Spenser concerns its scope (with fragments 12 and 13 labeled the twenty-first and twenty-second books), although it seems quite unlikely that Ralegh had in fact written twenty earlier books of a length similar to poem 12's more than five hundred lines.[47] Ralegh's diction resembles Spenser's here and there, as in the description of a stream that

> douth than all unawares in sunder teare
> the forsed bounds and raginge runn att large
> in th'auncient channells as they wounted weare
> (poem 12, lines 225–27)

Furthermore, the ten well-defined epic similes and two references to the queen as Belphoebe were no doubt directly influenced by *The Faerie Queene*. But Ralegh's "Cynthia" is an ambitious poem written by a courtier to regain his sovereign's grace, and it therefore diverges from Spenser's example in its personal tone and persuasive strategy. Narrative is replaced by lyric expression, and allegory by an abbreviated symbolic fiction. Ralegh's approach essentially duplicates that of "Fortune hath taken thee away," in that both assert the

45. Spenser, *Works*, 1:168, 3:2, 196.

46. Lines 164–66. The belief of some critics that this describes the original or earlier "Cynthia" overlooks Spenser's revisions of *Colin Clouts Come Home Againe* to make it fit the circumstances of publication in 1595. This suggests as well that Spenser was in touch with Ralegh even after his disgrace and sufficiently concerned about his patron's fall to work its story into the allegory of the second installment of *The Faerie Queene*.

47. Stephen Jay Greenblatt presents the case against Ralegh's composition of so lengthy a work (*Sir Walter Ralegh, The Renaissance Man and his Roles*, 61–62). For the numbering of the books as "21th" and "22" see Stacy M. Clanton, "The 'Number' of Sir Walter Ralegh's *Booke of the Ocean to Scinthia*" (*Studies in Philology* 82 [1985]: 200–211). Ralegh may well have composed more of the "Cynthia" than survives in the Hatfield House Manuscript. In "Une Nouvelle Version de la 'Petition to Queen Anne' de Sir Walter Ralegh" (57–67), Pierre Lefranc argues plausibly that a newly discovered text of Ralegh's "Petition" incorporates a dozen stanzas from the original state of poem 13.

poet's constant, irrepressible love for her worth and beauty, a love now unjustly excluded from Elizabeth's wavering affections.

Ralegh's rhapsodic language revives the melodramatic style of Dyer's poem 3, but it is set forth in pentameter cross rhyme and a comparatively conversational language in which similes of all kinds are the primary ornamental device. Ralegh fully exploits the correspondences between his fall and the sonnet lady's rejection of a suitor: he recalls "the joyes her grace begate" as he "in sylence served, and obayed / with secret hart, and hydden loyaltye" (poem 12, lines 387, 398–99), an outrageously truthless description of Ralegh's flamboyant style of courtiership. Incurably afflicted with "loves dart," he foresees his approaching death through the scorn of a mistress whose eternal beauty signifies her perfection in all virtues except mercy. As Cynthia and Belphoebe she is endowed with supernatural attributes: as one "whom love hath chose for his devinnitye / A vestall fier that burnes, but never wasteth" (poem 12, lines 188–89). Ralegh creates the image but he also threatens its dissolution, for in rejecting him Elizabeth has jeopardized her own divine identity:

> But love was gonn, So would I, my life weare.
> a Queen shee was to mee, no more Belphebe
> a Lion then, no more a milke white Dove.
> (poem 12, lines 326–28)

This metamorphosis concerns not only the "Cynthia" poems; by hardening her heart to his complaint she will deprive herself of celebratory songs in the future.

Ralegh's despairing mood is expressed as intensely as in any of Dyer's laments, but unlike Dyer, Ralegh presumes to blame his mistress for rejecting him. He touches very lightly upon his "error," the "frayle effect of mortall livinge" (line 445), and weighs it against his twelve years of obedient service.[48] In addition to the Petrarchan overtones of "Cynthia," the "fludds of sorrow and whole seas of wo" that afflict the poet, a plentiful strain of nature imagery and pastoralism create a fresh, image-laden texture that may derive from both Spenser's and Sidney's influence and that wholly distances the

---

48. Counting back from mid–1592 when Elizabeth became aware of Ralegh's indiscretion, the "Twelve yeares intire I wasted in this warr" for the queen's affections would have begun in mid–1580 when Ralegh was sent as a captain to Ireland but more than a year before he is known to have caught the queen's eye as a royal favorite. The slight exaggeration maximizes his sacrifice of "my most happy younger dayes" to Elizabeth's service.

poem from royal encomia in the mid-century style. The gothic and pastoral traditions merge in Ralegh's identification of the queen with the sun, an amalgamation of the sonnet lady's eyes, those enticing beams, and the all-powerful beams of the sun as an analogue of royal authority, a power which accounts for Elizabeth's indifference to

> levinge each withered boddy to be torne
> by fortune, and by tymes tempestious,
> which by her vertu, once faire frute have borne,
> knowinge shee cann renew, and cann create
> green from the grounde, and floures, yeven out of stonn.
>   (poem 13, lines 13–17)

Ralegh's metaphor brings out the full implications of the queen's ability to create courtiers (such as Ralegh himself) out of nothing and to reduce them to nothing again, a figurative but vivid acknowledgment of the courtier's ultimately abject dependence upon the sovereign's favor.

Pastoralism in the "Ocean to Cynthia" emphasizes not only the poet's humble status, it specifically acknowledges the court as the center of bounty. Ralegh describes himself as a gatherer of "withred leves," one who gleans "the broken eares with misers hands," where formerly he "did injoy the waighty sheves" (poem 12, lines 21–23). Elizabeth's hands as immediate dispensers of royal largesse are described in pastoral terms:

> I love the bearinge and not bearinge sprayes
> which now to others do ther sweetnes send
> th'incarnat, snow driven white, and purest asure,
> Who from high heaven douth on their feilds dissend
> fillinge their barnes with grayne, and towres with treasure
>   (poem 12, lines 306–10)

And Ralegh uses the idea of pastoral exile to announce the end of his songs in praise of Elizabeth as well as his impending death:

> falce hope, my shepherds staff, now age hath brast,
> My pipe, which loves own hand, gave my desire
> to singe her prayses, and my wo uppon,
> Dispaire hath often threatned to the fier
> as vayne to keipe now all the rest ar gonn.
> Thus home I draw, as deaths longe night drawes onn
>   (poem 12, lines 504–9)

The courtier who offended his queen through marriage and starting a family depicts himself as an aged shepherd in solitary retreat to his cottage toward the end of his life. The role was aptly chosen for its appeal to Elizabeth's well-known loyalty to servants of long standing. In keeping with this pose Ralegh falls into the moralizing tone of the sadder but wiser, older man. How difficult it is to maintain a woman's affections:

> onn houre deverts, onn instant overthrowes
> for which our lives, for which our fortunes thrale
> so many yeares thos joyes have deerely bought.
>   (poem 12, lines 231–33, and compare
>   the tone of lines 417–20, 253–68)

The emphasis upon fleeting joys coupled with the all-embracing plural pronouns duplicate both the content and style of Heneage's sober reflections in poems 5 and 6. Ralegh casts himself in multiple and somewhat inconsistent roles in the Cynthia poems as passionate lover, elderly shepherd-servant, and sage philosopher.

The Cynthia fragments, particularly poems 12 and 13, bring the lover's lament as a means of regaining lost favor to a point of refinement that incorporates an unprecedented number of literary and rhetorical devices in the service of the "cult of Elizabeth." Her fictional identity as goddess contrasts with his self-representation as banished shepherd, while this hierarchical discrepancy facilitates the interweaving of courtly love motifs with pastoral conventions. Within his figurative constructs, moreover, Ralegh reminds the queen of the very tangible and positive aspects of more than a decade of high favor in her sight such as "the tokens hunge onn brest, and kyndly worne" (poem 12, line 263), or his many songs in her praise, including his allusion to the refrain of "Like truthless dreams" (poem 8) at poem 12, line 123. This poem was also a complaint rather than a hymn of praise, but Ralegh's quotation from it here suggests that he had written it for the queen and could expect her to remember it as the forerunner of his current lament.

There is no reason to suppose, however, that Elizabeth read the four "Ocean to Cynthia" fragments. Ralegh's poetic skills and personal knowledge of his sovereign enabled him to compose elaborate complaints well-calculated to please and placate her. The sentiments strike us now as extravagantly artificial, but placed in the context of the passionate outbursts which other favorites addressed to her in prose, Ralegh's lines appear less hyperbolic. What he lacked was the means of delivering his complaints to their principal audience, for the fallen courtier was above all deprived of royal access. That was, apparently, the sum of his punishment. He retained Sherborne and Durham House, his office as warden of the stannaries, and even his position as captain of the guard. He could not attend court, however, nor would Elizabeth receive him personally for the space of some five years. His exile from the source of royal power and bounty is glanced at outright in several passages of "Cynthia" and repeatedly symbolized by his deprivation of the light which emanates from "her life gevinge soonn" (poem 12, line 78; poem 12, lines 55–56, 200). How then was his elaborate verse tribute to be brought to Elizabeth's eyes? In all likelihood it never was. The existence of the unique text among the Cecil Papers at Hatfield House suggests that Ralegh sent his draft to Sir Robert Cecil to dispose of as he saw fit. Similarly, Gorges had described to Cecil Ralegh's melodramatic reaction at being denied a glimpse of his sovereign and then urged him to use his own discretion with regard to showing his account to the queen. Again there is no evidence that she ever saw it. Cecil may have held fast to Ralegh's poem because he considered Elizabeth susceptible to such an ostensibly spontaneous overflow of loving emotions. The house of Cecil had no interest in rescuing Ralegh, for now that he had eliminated himself from the competition, Burghley and his son could devote their full energies to controlling a single favorite, Essex.

Previously, while he still enjoyed access to Elizabeth, Ralegh may have altered the way poetic messages were delivered to her. If Dyer's "Song in the Oak" (poem 1) was indeed performed as a personal complaint or on behalf of its author it would mark the first time that courtier verse was presented to the queen with musical accompaniment. The practice was common, of course, in the public shows that honored her. Sidney's verses in *The Lady of May* and those for the "Fortress of Perfect Beauty" tilt were sung in her praise as was the case in the pageants of out-of-court authors. It is possible that, in addition to his vigorous use of poetry in the service of courtiership, Ralegh combined it with music, particularly in the verses he addressed to Elizabeth personally. Naunton's assertion that he was led "to sing 'Fortune my foe'" may well be a literal statement, for both "Fortune hath taken thee away" and Elizabeth's response to it "exactly fit the tune of 'Fortune,'"[49] suggesting that the ballad on this theme was already well known by 1587 when Ralegh fitted his lament to its tune. Elizabeth might even have sung her reply, for Ralegh recalled from the Tower how he "was wont to behold her . . .

49. Gerald Abraham, letter to *Times Literary Supplement*, May 30, 1968, 558.

sometime singing like an angell."[50] Poem 9 was clearly addressed to the queen, and its use of the plural pronoun along with the part-song setting in the St. Michael's, Tenbury, manuscripts indicate that he arranged for this lyric to be sung before her to accompany the delivery of a special gift.

Whether Ralegh revived or initiated the singing of courtier verses directly to Elizabeth, the practice became fairly common during the last dozen years of the reign. The mixture of first- and third-person pronouns in the texts of Sir Henry Lee's "His/My golden locks time hath to silver turned" probably reflects the adaptation of Lee's work for singing by Robert Hales during the Accession Day pageantry of 1590. Hales also performed Essex's poem 2 before Elizabeth in an effort to offset the encroachment into her favor of the earl of Southampton.[51] Thus Devereux may have appropriated the same technique for influencing the queen that Ralegh had used to complain of his displacement by Essex in 1587. Moreover, among Essex's first six poems, the ones he wrote before the disgrace of 1599, only poem 1 lacks a contemporary musical setting or indication that it was in fact sung before Elizabeth. The fullest description of music and poetry in the service of courtiership, however, concerns some flirtatious cavorting in September of 1602 when the queen discovered that the countess of Derby wore a bejeweled locket enclosing a portrait of her uncle, Sir Robert Cecil. Her Majesty then

> snatcht it away, and, tyed itt upon her shoe, and walked long with it there; then took it thence and pinned itt on her elbow, and wore it there some time also; which Mr. Secretary being told of, made these verses, and had Hales to sing them in his [Cecil's] chamber. It was told her Majesty, that Mr. Secretary had rare musick, and song; she would needes hear them; and so this ditty was soung which you see first written. More verses there be lykewise, whereof som, or all, were lyke-wyse soung.[52]

This incident allows us a rare glimpse of Elizabeth (who had just turned sixty-nine) playfully teasing her courtiers. Cecil found it appropriate to respond with poetry set to music, and this in turn elicited more poetry and song. His lost lyric apparently took the form of an amorous complaint, for it was described as arguing "that he repynes not, thoughe her Majesty please to grace others, and

---

50. Edwards, *Life of Sir Walter Ralegh*, 2:51.
51. See the commentary to my edition of Essex's poems ("Poems," 88).
52. Nichols, *Progresses*, 3:596–97.

contents himself with the favour he hath."[53] Thus Cecil, through a verse lament that sounds similar to those written by Ralegh and Essex, transformed the queen's seizure of his portrait, a manifest sign of her fondness for him, into an occasion for poetical complaint. And lest the dour little secretary seem an unlikely participant in such light-hearted frivolity, it should be noted that he is a "lost" courtier poet with known literary interests. Less than a month after Hales sang for Cecil at court, John Chamberlain reported giving him pictures and verses which he had received from his friend, Dudley Carleton. From Harington Cecil acquired a copy of an amusing verse narrative by Greville. Sir Robert is credited with writing the prose "Hermit's Oration at Theobalds," and Gabriel Harvey mused, "when shall we tast the preserved dainties of Sir Edward Dyer, Sir Walter Raleigh, M. secretarie Cecill . . . ?"[54]

Elizabeth's flippant behavior in 1602 warranted a rather full contemporary account because it deviated from her normally reserved manner. She did not usually interact with her courtiers at the same rhapsodic pitch found in so many of their communications with her, as her verses to Ralegh in 1587 and her letters to Essex in 1591 testify. The queen's regard for poetry and the manner of self-portrayal in her own verses are generally at odds with the fanciful literary outpourings of her courtiers.

In addition to responding to Ralegh's verse lament, she had beyond reasonable doubt replied in Latin verse to an epigram dedicated to her by the eminent German humanist, Melissus (Paul Schede).[55] Her lines include the candid acknowledgment of how poets operate in the service of monarchy by transforming rulers "from demigods to be gods." She thoroughly appreciated the power-enhancing benefits of poetic praise and all forms of literary and symbolic adulation.

53. Ibid., 3:597.
54. McClure, *Letters of John Chamberlain*, 1:163. The oration, printed in Nichols, *Progresses* (3:241–45), was recited at Theobalds before the queen, probably upon her arrival in June of 1594 (Chambers, *Elizabethan Stage*, 4:108; G. C. Moore Smith, *Gabriel Harvey's Marginalia*, 231). Greville's poem is number 69 in Ruth Hughey's edition of *The Arundel Harington Manuscript*; the Hatfield text descends from this version or a near intermediary. It is transcribed and printed in facsimile in Norman K. Farmer's "A Newly Discovered Poem by Fulke Greville" (*English Literary Renaissance* 9 [1979]: 64–68).
55. See James E. Phillips, "Elizabeth I as a Latin Poet: An Epigram on Paul Melissus," 289–98. My references to the queen's verses follow Phillips's English rendering on page 290n. Bradner (*Poems*) questioned the attribution on grounds that no other Latin verse by the queen was known, but her poem in the book once belonging to Heneage demonstrates that she was quite capable of composing as well as translating Latin meters.

She was known, too, for her skill in capitalizing upon public opportunities to identify herself with poetic, fictional entities.[56] The self-representation that emerges in her own poetry, however, is often at odds with the roles that her courtiers devised for her, yet it reveals both her respect for poetry and her adaptation of art to ends as utilitarian if different in kind from those of Ralegh and Essex.

Elizabeth's interest in poetry led her to translate the first 178 lines of Horace's *Ars Poetica*. It is ironic however that this excerpt dealing with poetic language and the decorum of its parts found little room for application in her own verses, original or translated. Elizabeth was seldom involved with fictional representation of the kind analyzed by Horace, and certainly aesthetic pleasure was of small concern in her translations of Boethius and Plutarch. Her English versions are cast in irregular accentual lines with their syntax so closely bound to the originals' that it must often be retranslated into idiomatic English as it is read. These works were not prepared for readers however; in contrast with the wide circulation of "The doubt of future foes," these poems are preserved in unique, partially holograph copies now in the Public Record Office. Their function as royal propaganda concerned intellectual rather than artistic accomplishment, with the message explicitly created instead of being intrinsic to the texts themselves. The queen did not publish these poems, but it became well known that she had written them and, above all, in a very short time at that: the Plutarch in one week, the entire Boethius in just twenty-odd hours.[57] These humanist wind sprints demonstrated to her courtiers that she indeed possessed the learning which they attributed to her in their own verses.

Elizabeth apparently intended no further public role for her poetry, original or translated, although in both kinds there is a consistency of themes that shows her turning to verse much as had Sidney

---

56. Sidney, along with many other royal pageant writers, knew that he could depend on the queen's theatrical acumen when he prepared a decisive role for her in *The Lady of May*. Her participation in her coronation shows is examined in David M. Bergeron's *English Civic Pageantry, 1558–1642* (15–20). Her identification with the pelican as a symbol of sacrificial love and self-denial received public dissemination in her official "Pelican portrait."

57. The accounts in the PRO documents vary from between twenty-four to twenty-seven hours (see Caroline Pemberton, ed., *Queen Elizabeth's Englishings*, ix–x). BL, Lansdowne MS 253, f. 200, preserves notes to a similar effect. John Clapham referred to her translations of Boethius, and Plutarch, "with diverse others" in *Elizabeth of England: Certain Observations Concerning the Life and Reign of Queen Elizabeth* (88–89). Essex praised the queen's translations in a letter to Francis Bacon, August 24, 1593 (cited by Pemberton, *Englishings*, vii).

and Greville as a reflective medium and a creative escape from her public concerns. A recurrent motif in her work is cogently symbolized by her identification with the self-sacrificing pelican. In the Latin quatrain which she translated into English in Heneage's book (as reprinted in Part II), she portrays herself as a thrall to the will of others: "I serve the route, and all their follies beare," to the neglect of her own contentment. The verses she allegedly wrote upon Anjou's departure in 1582 also express the constraints of public duty in conflict with private emotions: "I grieve and dare not show my discontent, / I love and yet am forced to seem to hate." Both poems are complaints, yet even the latter, amorous one protests in context the deprivation required by official necessity rather than unrequited or unattainable love.[58]

Several of the works she chose to translate repeat and amplify this idea while also dealing with the problem of unjust fortune, the theme of her "Woodstock" verses. The likelihood that she did translate the second chorus from Seneca's *Hercules Oetaeus* increases when we consider not only her other undisputed translations from this author but also the emphasis in this passage upon pitting faith against the "harming hurl of fortune's arm," and its observations that rulers must endure "the vulgar crew [who] fill full thy gates."[59] Boethius makes the goddess Fortuna an interlocutor in the prose portion of his dialogue, while the verse too deals with the injustice of blind fate by describing how the

> wicked stamps on holy necks
> With uniust turne,
> And cleare uertu dimmed
> With thick blackenis lurketh.
> (1.5.31–34)

---

58. Bradner, *Poems*, 5. The three seventeenth-century manuscript texts of this poem show that Elizabeth did not allow it to circulate as a propaganda piece as she had with "The doubt of future foes." The delay in circulation may indicate that this was a genuinely private expression of feeling which did not "get out" until after her death.

59. In 1567 she sent the elder Harington a translation from Seneca which urges resolution in the face of uncontrollable fate (*Nugae Antiquae* [1779], 2:304–10). Heneage quoted a few words from another, lost translation from Seneca's *Epistola* 79 in a letter to Hatton of August 12, 1579 (Nicolas, *Memoirs*, 127). The subject is, again, the power of adverse fortune: "*illustravit Fortuna, dum vexat,*" as translated by the queen, "it graces whom it grates." Sir John Harington recalled that "she did much admire Seneca's wholesome advisinges, . . . and I saw muche of hir translating thereof" (McClure, *Letters and Epigrams*, 123).

The Senecan chorus applies fortune's arbitrary vacillations specifically to the downfall of kings, who are

> made in an instant short, and marred;
> So icy is their joy and hopeless woe.
> The love of kingdom's rule observed with care,
> But for himself a king but few regard.
> The court's luster a stale guest made for me,
> Delighted with the shine no woe forthought.
> (lines 25–30)

And the Phaeton and Icarus myths are invoked to the same allegorical end, implying that political elevation is hazardous.

Elizabeth's interest in the passage she translated from Plutarch's
Moralia is explicable once we understand that its somewhat misleading title, "Of Curiosity," refers to the vice of prying busybodies
who seek out scandals which they both savor and disseminate. This
character type lacks any corresponding interest in virtue: "Suche
one as hedes not to behold a chast and wel ruuld hous, / No thogh a
man in treating sort wold cal him to that sight," but he is rather
"Euen suche as in the night to Dianes temple dedicate were, / With
hedy yea [eye] espies what faultz he may find ther."[60] Plutarch's
treatise provides an anatomy of one way to undermine the monarch's already perilous position. It was also a type of assault to which
queens were particularly vulnerable, for Diana's Temple and the
royal household were, after all, one and the same under Elizabeth.
During the first two decades of her reign, as she played off the
attractive prize of her hand in marriage against Catholic Europe's
ambition to seize the kingdom by force, reports of unbecoming
sexual behavior jeopardized vital foreign policy, and with it, her
subjects' loyalty. Now in her latter years, such tales threatened her
personal hold upon the hearts of her people, the crucial bond in her
long, successful reign.[61] The queen's poetry consistently expresses
her awareness of the threatening, uncontrollable power of destiny
and the vulnerability of rulers. Within this context, Elizabeth portrayed herself in constrained and overburdened roles that compelled
her to sacrifice her personal desires and welfare for that of her peo-

60. Bradner, *Poems*, 55, lines 23–24, 33–34.
61. Carole Levin surveys the kinds of sexual slanders the queen and her government contended with in "Power, Politics, and Sexuality: Images of Elizabeth
I" (in *The Politics of Gender in Early Modern Europe*, ed. Jean R. Brink, Allison
P. Coudert, and Maryanne C. Horowitz, Sixteenth Century Essays and Studies,
vol. 13 [1989]: 100–108).

ple. Through poetry she found an outlet for dealing with these feelings as well as for displaying the mental agility that permitted her to carry out her responsibilities so effectively.

Between Sidney's death and the end of Elizabeth's reign, courtier lyrics as represented preeminently by the poets discussed in this chapter are remarkable for their independence from the advances in English verse made by Sidney and his friends. This is not surprising of course in Elizabeth's case, for her background in humanist and mid-century poetics left her little inclined to study or imitate the works of even so model a courtier as Sir Philip. Nor would we expect that Drake the sea dog would labor to provide an Arcadian air for his commendatory lines before Peckham's book in 1583—his workmanlike poulter's couplets are quite fitting under the circumstances. It is a good deal less understandable to recall, however, that as late as 1590 Ralegh composed similar long-line verses to commend *The Faerie Queene*, and that both Ralegh and Gorges, as Sidney's associates at court, were familiar with at least some of his work besides being themselves active proponents of courtier verse. Yet the discernible influences upon their work include such out-of-court models as George Turberville and Spenser.

Even more surprising is Essex's failure to follow Sidney's example, for young Devereux was in many ways Sir Philip's heir. This was literally true with respect to the sword that his dying friend bequeathed him, and it took on a further reality when Essex married Sidney's widow and pursued at court those active ideals that Sidney had espoused. Essex, in fact, lived to fulfill the dreams of state service which Philip had longed for, including the command of English forces abroad, major official duties as a Privy Councillor, and considerable influence at court as a royal favorite. Essex entertained serious intellectual interests, literary ones included, yet there is no evidence that he read or valued Sidney's writings. Their literary careers are exact opposites, with Sidney's muse withdrawing gradually from public display in *The Lady of May* and tiltyard shows to such private endeavors as *Astrophil and Stella* and his translations of the psalms. In contrast, Essex, taking his cue from Ralegh instead of Sidney, devised purposeful lyrics for influencing the queen, and these he deployed on both public and private occasions at the very center of court activity. The distribution of Ralegh's verse follows the same pattern except that it gained a much wider circulation than most of the earl's works and was thus obviously parceled out to a much wider audience at court. At the same time, the neglect of Sidney did not condemn succeeding courtier verse to mid-century stagnation. The works of Gorges and Ralegh evolved out of that tradition, while Essex, despite the limitations of his muse, never succumbed to the drab manner. These three poets turned out respectable sonnets and elaborate poetic fictions in which rhetoric was generally subordinated to their larger aesthetic goals. For Ralegh and Essex in particular, poetry developed a specialized function in the repertoire of their behavior as courtiers; the contrasting ways in which they developed their talents with respect either to Sidney or to each other indicate with what caution we should approach generalizations about the style, language, or tastes of the Elizabethan court.

5

Satire and Narrative Verse

Sir John Harington

Poetry was a more absorbing interest in Sir John Harington's life than it was even for Sidney and a more salient feature of his style as a courtier than it became for Ralegh, Essex, or any other Elizabethan. Yet Harington did not contribute to the dominant mode of courtier verse practiced by his generation, the love poetry introduced by Oxford and Dyer, refined by Sidney, Greville, and Gorges, and exploited as an instrument of social and political advancement by Ralegh and Essex. Harington was apparently inspired to write at least one such lyric to celebrate an incident at court after Elizabeth rose and rested on his arm: "Oh, what swete burden to my nexte songe—Petrarke shall eke out good Matter for this businesse."[1] But no such song seems to have been forthcoming. Instead, Sir John's attitude toward conventional love poetry is summed up in his satiric analysis of the lover who compared his mistress to the three goddesses:

> *Pallas* was fowle and grim was out of measure,
> That neither gods nor men in her tooke pleasure,
> *Iuno* so proud, and curst was of her tongue,
> All men misliked her both old and yong.
> *Venus* vnchaste, that she strong *Mars* entices,
> With yong *Adonis*, and with old *Anchises*.
>   How thinke you, are these praises few or meane,
>   Compared to a shrow, a slut, or queane?[2]

This mocking rejection is all the more unexpected in light of Harington's close ties with most of the practitioners of romantic poetry

---

1. *Nugae Antiquae* (1779), 2:211.
2. McClure, *Letters and Epigrams*, epigram 333, with variants from BL, Add. MS 12049.

at court, his familiarity with their work, and his appreciation of it. As early as 1580, he was writing to Dyer as to an old friend of the family. He cited excerpts from two of Dyer's poems in the notes to his translation of *Orlando Furioso* (1591), and he referred to him years later as one "that can wryte very well" before quoting a couplet from Dyer's classic lover's lament, poem 2.[3] At Cambridge Harington also became acquainted with Robert, earl of Essex, whose faction at court he sided with throughout the 1590s. He wrote two of his epigrams for the earl and it is possible that the "I poor I" of epigram 210 consciously echoes the last line of Essex's poem 8.[4] Greville also belonged to the Essex circle. Two of his closely kept poems found their way into the *Arundel Harington Manuscript*, an anthology that preserves a good deal of amatory verse by such courtiers as Wyatt, Surrey, Oxford, and Ralegh as well as by Greville and Dyer. Harington also had access to Sidney's most important works before they were published, including the *Old Arcadia*, *Astrophil and Stella*, and the *Defence*. He was well-acquainted too with Sir Robert Sidney, although there is no evidence that he knew of his poetry.

As an enthusiastic devotee of all kinds of literature, Harington was also well acquainted with courtier poets of a very different stamp. He was respectfully attentive to the elder Harington's verse, incorporating a stanza of his father's translation from Ariosto into his own translation of the *Orlando*. Sir John's output built upon but greatly expanded his father's interest in Italian literature, complicated rhyme schemes, and the writing of occasional poems in the vernacular. Harington knew and praised Lady Russell's funeral verses, read most of his *Metamorphosis of Ajax* to her, and claimed her son, Edward Hoby, as a friend from their school days at Eton. He read and admired the countess of Pembroke's translations of the Psalms, and we would not know that Sir Walter Mildmay or Gilbert,

---

3. McClure prints John's letter to Dyer (*Letters and Epigrams*, 61–62). In the notes to canto 16 of his translation of Ariosto's *Orlando Furioso*, Harington quotes line 27 of poem 6, and he alludes to line 44 of poem 2 in the notes to canto 8. In epigram 416, moreover, he used the "no man/woman" rhyme which Sidney had previously employed with acknowledgment to Dyer in *Old Arcadia* (OA) poem 9. About 1606 he sent Prince Henry his translation of book 6 of the *Aeneid* along with an original interpretive essay; the reference to Dyer occurs in section 7, "Of reeding poetry" (Trumbull, Add. MS 23, Berkshire Record Office).

4. Epigrams 77 and 373 are addressed to Essex. Epigram 13 concerns a lecture at Oxford during the progress of 1592 that both the earl and Harington attended. Epigram 264 is an elegy for Essex, Sir Christopher Blount, and Sir Henry Danvers.

earl of Shrewsbury, were poets at all had not brief excerpts from their works been preserved by Harington.[5] Harington's muse aligned itself with the more serious, non-amatory works of these poets as witnessed by his emphasis upon translation, the writing of occasional verse, and above all the concentration upon nonfictional poetics. These traits are well represented by his 432 Elizabethan epigrams in BL, Additional Manuscript 12409.

Harington prepared this collection in 1602 as a mock-up for the New Year's gift he sent to King James in 1603. The poems were probably written between about 1585 and 1602, although most of them seem to belong to the 1590s.[6] Their order of composition has been considerably disrupted in the Additional Manuscript as in the other manuscripts and prints. Harington referred to these poems as epigrams, yet nothing in their technical form or structure would lead us toward a meaningful generic definition. Puttenham, for example, declared that "ditties, Odes & Epigrammes" should not exceed twelve verses, and that epigrammatists customarily used such short poems for "taunting and scoffing at vndecent things."[7] More than a quarter of Harington's epigrams, however, run to more than twelve lines, and he shows his disregard for length as a standard for judging them in his rebukes of Faustus, who accuses him of writing epigrams that are both too short (55), and too long (220). There is a good deal of taunting and scoffing in the collection, yet this is only one of the diverse purposes Harington undertook with them. The forty-six epigrams he addressed to his wife and mother-in-law, for instance, are for the most part complimentary, coaxing, or defensive. Others fall within such traditionally sociable uses of courtier verse as the commendation of Lewkenor's book (224), and the elegies for Lady Rogers, his mother-in-law, and for John Astley,

5. See the notes to the *Orlando*, canto 37, and Harington's letter to Lady Russell in McClure, *Letters and Epigrams* (65). He praised the countess's psalms in epigram 396 and in his "Treatise of Play" (*Nugae Antiquae* [1779], 2:159). He sent three of these psalms to Lucy, countess of Bedford, in December of 1600 (McClure, *Letters and Epigrams*, 87) and quoted two lines from Psalm 137 in Donno, *Metamorphosis* (151).

6. Of the epigrams I have been able to date, I would assign only seven to the period before 1591 (5, 22, 29, 189, 214, 317, and 336), while over fifty others were rather certainly written between 1591 and late 1602.

7. *Arte of English Poesie*, 101, 26. In *Martial and the English Epigram*, T. K. Whipple argues that the essence of this genre is its form, a two-part structure consisting of exposition leading up to an emphatic conclusion (282). Harington's practice would often fit this definition, yet his tendency toward multiple conclusions, extended exposition, and outright narrative reveals that such a structure was not vital to his concept of the epigram.

master of the Jewel House (348, 387). At least fifty-three of the epigrams are translated or adapted out of Martial, while epigram 48 renders a Latin epigram by Sir Thomas More and epigram 181 translates Ovid's *Amores* 2, elegy 4, "for Generall Norreys. 1593."[8] The collection includes two brief epithalamia, one for his kinswoman, Sara Hastings (421), and the other for the dowager countess of Derby who married Lord Keeper Egerton in 1600 (248). Harington also used his poetry to promote his interests at court. The magistrate addressed in epigram 325, from whom he begged "not a reward," but "lesse by a sillable, a Ward," must have been Lord Burghley, master of the court of wards. He sent epigrams to the queen to placate her after the publication of the *Metamorphosis* (44), and to thank her for pardoning him (53), to flatter her with an implied comparison to King David (188), and to press a suit with her (267).

Neither length, purpose, nor structure adequately define Harington's widely diversified epigrams. What he meant by the term may be more easily apprehended by considering their content and the manner of its treatment. In the poems he addressed to Elizabeth, for example, she is his "Dread Soueraigne," "deare Liege," his "For euer deare, for euer dreaded Prince." There are no suns, Cynthias, or Belphoebes, no fictitious or hyperbolic praises even here where he would most wish to flatter and cajole. The style is a measure both of his integrity and of the well-defined if expansive domain that he claimed for the epigram. The title to the second poem in the series explains "That his Poetrie shall be no fictions, but truthes," a claim repeated in the last Elizabethan entry in the collection: "Occasion oft my penn doth entertayne / With trew discourse; let others Muses fayn" (424). Most of Harington's epigrams are in fact occasional, and while they often put witty, humorous, or satiric interpretations upon their subjects, they impose outright fictions seldom and sparingly. The style is also objectively oriented, concentrating on what the poem is about rather than upon the poet's subjective thoughts and feelings, the primary focus of so many Renaissance love lyrics. This formulation of poetic range and style defined the epigram for Harington, including most of those he translated. The genre deals with real, not imaginary subjects, and it treats them in

8. At about this same time Marlowe's translation of Ovid's poem appeared in the *Epigrammes and Elegies by I. D. and C. M.* (STC 18931). I. D. was Harington's friend, Sir John Davies. Sir John Norris, general of the English forces in the Low Countries, was in England from early 1592 until September 1593, a furlough that must have given Harington the opportunity to prepare this translation for him.

an essentially nonfictional manner. Thus Harington's failure to compose conventional love poetry may be explained as his adherence to poetic theory insofar as amatory verse ordinarily reveled in creative, hyperbolic disregard for the truth. Yet Harington's theory did not prevent him from writing love poetry altogether; what he wrote in this vein was literal love poetry, his forthright expressions of love for Mall, his wife, comforting her on the loss of a child (222), frankly declaring his attraction to her (26, 390), or urging her to "be as wanton, toying as an Ape" when they are in bed (299).

Harington was the most prolific writer of the various kinds of nonfictional verse that characterize his epigrams, but he was not the first Elizabethan courtier to write in this fashion. Sir Walter Mildmay's "little volume" may have contained a number of similar epigrams in Latin verse, and Hatton's Latin quatrain expressing his gratitude to Elizabeth serves an equally straightforward purpose. In English verse, Sir Nicholas Bacon's poems comment directly upon a variety of moral and philosophical issues, although they may date from before 1558 and they apparently saw little circulation at court. Sidney's *Certain Sonnets* 12, 13, and 14 translate respectively verses by Horace, Catullus, and Seneca from the same tradition of wisdom literature which marks so many of Harington's epigrams. CS 12, for example, renders the same commendation of a simple life previously translated by Bacon; its message is repeated in Harington's collection not by his own verses but by Surrey's translation of Martial's epigram which Sir John included on page 150 of the Additional Manuscript. For the most part, these works convey their meanings in the same earnest tones of Sir Thomas Heneage's sedentary verse epistles. One of Harington's signal achievements in the epigrams, however, was to supply nonfictional courtier poetry with a witty, humorous vitality, a style that emerges with particular freshness in his satirical epigrams.

Harington was quite capable of using his poetry for purposes of attack and ridicule. He once threatened to "write a damnable storie, and put it in goodlie verse aboute Lorde A——; he hathe done me some ill turnes."[9] Many of Sir John's epigrams about his contemporaries, particularly those which ridicule his fellow courtiers, are necessarily less than straightforward. Although it is often assumed

---

9. *Nugae Antiquae* (1779), 2:210. The most likely "Lord A" for Harington to have had in mind was George Tuchet, eleventh Baron Audley. He may be the unidentified lord attacked in epigram 228 for charging Harington interest in a sale of land.

that those in the know at court readily identified the objects of his satire, in epigram 423 he apologized to a lord for not revealing to him those "who are meant / By Cinna, Lynus, Lesbia, and the rest." His attacks are often sufficiently personal and biting to require a degree of protective disguise; thus the information he supplies about his victims is often ambiguous or inadequate for sure identification, although Harington seldom fictionalizes beyond the Latin pseudonyms he gives his protagonists. Galla, for instance, may well be Lady Mary Baker, sister of the gentleman pensioner Sir George Gifford. She was accused of sexual misconduct during her first husband's lifetime, while her remarriage in 1595 to Richard Fletcher, bishop of London, caused a scandal that was recorded in a number of satiric poems.[10] Harington's Galla is accused of cuckolding her husband (250), and of an indiscreet marriage to a prelate (366). The portrait fits Lady Baker as far as it goes but without identifying her unmistakably.

In one of Harington's cleverest examples of wordplay, Galla, pursued by Paulus, "sweares that fayne she would of him bee rid." But Faustus reports that Galla and Paulus have slept together, leaving Harington to lament, "God forbid, / chaste dames of wanton guests should so be rid." The liaison between Galla and Paulus, frequent victims of Sir John's satire, is of particular interest because of the likely identification of Paulus as Sir Walter Ralegh.[11] The two have much in common. Both were accused of atheism (122), and Harington's assertion that Paulus has a wife yet was never married (410) aptly satirizes Ralegh's evasiveness about his marriage with Elizabeth Throckmorton. Paulus constantly smokes tobacco, sells it, and promotes it as a panacea (134), as did Ralegh. In epigram 126 Paulus is said to acquire his wealth through a "writ of Mart" which allows him to "spoile the Spaniards," an apparent allusion to the royal commission granted Ralegh in December of 1594 which authorized him to plunder the king of Spain. "Mart" is a variant of marque, letters of marque being royal warrants to seek reprisals on the ship-

10. Robert Krueger attributes five of these to Sir John Davies in *The Poems of Sir John Davies* (177–79). Norman McClure suggested that Galla might be the London widow who married Thomas Godwin, bishop of Bath and Wells ("Harington's Epigrams," *Times Literary Supplement*, May 19, 1927, 355).

11. This was first suggested in G. C. Moore-Smith's "Sir Walter Raleigh as Seen by Sir John Harington" (*Times Literary Supplement*, March 10, 1927, 160). V. T. Harlow presented the case in more detail and pronounced the identification "conclusive" ("Harington's Epigrams," *Times Literary Supplement*, July 14, 1927, 488).

ping of a hostile foreign power. Ralegh's commission of 1594 had precisely that intent whether or not it was formally issued as a letter or writ of mart.[12] The description of Paulus's servile devotion to Elizabeth in epigram 315 is also appropriate for Ralegh, as we have seen, albeit his adoring attitude was certainly not unique among her courtiers; however, the reference here to Paulus "singing this old song, re mi fa sol" may again connect Ralegh with singing, perhaps the singing of his poetry to the queen. If the identification with Ralegh is correct, then Paulus's promotion "to high degree" in epigram 22 probably refers to Ralegh's appointment as captain of the guard about 1585. In epigram 15, Paulus is Harington's friend, but in 60 he is one "who I haue thought my friend sometimes," and he is under attack in every epigram in which he figures after 15. This may well reflect both a vestige of the collection's original, chronological sequence and the likelihood that Harington was on good terms with Ralegh and sought his favor before Essex arrived at court in 1586. Thereafter the epigrams attack Ralegh as Paulus in consequence of Harington's adherence to the earl's circle at court.

Another likely identification of a Harington pseudonym with court connections is the Lelia of epigram 300, she who "hapt to be deflowred by an Earle." This must refer to Ann Vavasour, who gave birth to the earl of Oxford's illegitimate son at court in March of 1581. Harington preserved in the *Arundel Harington Manuscript* a copy of Oxford's possible poem I which concerns this affair. Ann's compromising dilemma was not unique during Elizabeth's reign, so it is Harington's pseudonym itself that identifies her beyond question. By 1590, Ann had become the mistress of Sir Henry Lee, the Lelius of Sidney's tournament in book 2 of the *New Arcadia*.[13] Lee made no secret of his attachment to Ann, even appearing at tilt in armor etched over with the initials A V. Lelia is the obvious feminine

12. In "Raleigh Satirized by Harington and Davies" (*Review of English Studies*, n. s., 22 [1972]: 52–56), Carolyn J. Bishop accepts the identification of Harington's Paulus and Davies's Paulum as Ralegh, but suggests that the "lawfull mart" by which Davies's persona derived so much wealth referred to Ralegh's Sherborne estate. It is, however, wealth specifically taken "out of the Ocean" (Krueger, *Poems*, 148), just as Paulus's money clearly comes from the sea in Harington's epigram. For Ralegh's commission see CSPD, 250/46, and the description of similar letters of marque in CSPD, 238/64.

13. Harington's text of the Oxford-Vavasour poem is number 179 in Ruth Hughey's edition. The representation of Lee as Lelius was established by James Hanford and Sara Ruth Watson in "Personal Allegory in the *Arcadia:* Philisides and Lelius" (*Modern Philology* 32 [1934]: 1–10). For Sir Henry's liaison with Ann see E. K. Chambers, *Sir Henry Lee* (155–62).

counterpart of the pseudonym that Sidney had conferred on Ann's benefactor.

Epigram 368 may have even more direct connections with Sidney although its protagonists cannot be so confidently identified as is the case with Lelia. Harington's title designates them as Romans, while the source of the lady's "Heroicall Awnswer" was probably Rabelais. Nevertheless, we learn that this "great ritch Lady" is "Soch as perhaps in theis dayes found thear may be." The suggestion that this rich lady may be Penelope, Lady Rich, becomes more emphatic as Harington relates her marital infidelity and her husband's acquiescence to it. Indeed, the epigram centers upon the husband's wonderment that despite his wife's promiscuity, her children resemble him. The situation fits both Lord Rich's tolerance of his wife's affair with Sir Charles Blount and the fact that she had been Blount's mistress for perhaps nine years before bearing the first of her five children by him in 1597.[14]

Many of Harington's epigrams were written about or for easily identifiable persons; they reveal the scope of his social contacts, his tastes, and the pervasive role of poetry in his life. He addressed four epigrams to his Somersetshire neighbor, Sir Hugh Portman, who preceded Harington as sheriff of the county in 1590. Sir John also impaneled Portman on the mock jury he assembled in the *Metamorphosis*.[15] The "vertuous Dame" of epigram 94, whose name is synonymous with "the chiefest instrument in writing," is obviously Juliana Penne, an old family friend whose son by her first marriage, Michael Hickes, was Lord Burghley's patronage secretary. Harington had written to her as a schoolboy at Eton in 1571. Her unwanted guest in the epigram may be the Justice Randall described in Harington's "Apologie" as "a man passing impotent in body but much more in mind," who took many meals "of his franke neighbour the widdow Penne."[16] Two other epigrams were addressed to young men who had joined the Essex circle. Epigram 207 was directed to Sir Maurice Berkeley whom Essex had knighted during the

14. Cyril Falls, *Mountjoy: Elizabethan General*, 66. Upon this circumstance Harington apparently superimposed Rabelais's advice to women that "once the pregnancy is public they may push boldly on, full sail ahead, since the hold is full, . . . after the manner of a ship, which does not take on her pilot until she is caulked and loaded" (*The Histories of Gargantua and Pantagruel*, 47).

15. Donno, *Metamorphosis*, 236–37, and see McClure, *Letters and Epigrams*, 382.

16. I refer throughout to Harington's critical treatise prefixed to the *Orlando* as his "Apologie" (Ariosto, 8). The "Apology" within his *Metamorphosis of Ajax* is cited by the title to that work. For widow Penne's career see Alan G. R. Smith, *Servant of the Cecils: The Life of Sir Michael Hickes* (especially 87ff.).

Cadiz voyage of 1596. Harington had received a warrant dormant from Sir Maurice's father, Henry, and his sole purpose in the epigram was to prod the son into honoring this document. The doughty heroine of epigram 237, who saves her jewelry from thieves who attempt to rob her on the stairs of a playhouse, was perhaps Lady Elizabeth Leigh, wife of the poem's addressee, Sir John Leigh. He too had been knighted by Essex at Cadiz and served under him in Ireland as a fellow captain of horse with Harington.[17] Harington also addressed epigrams to Samuel Daniel (126) and Sir John Davies (163, 388), both of whom he counted as friends and whose poetry he clearly admired. He praised Thomas Bastard's epigrams (160) and the poetry of Sidney, Constable, and Spenser (196); on the other hand, the poet Lynus, who may represent Barnaby Barnes, is attacked more often than any of the other pseudonymous figures, and it is also clear from epigram 196 that Harington held Thomas Churchyard's work in rather low esteem. Despite these expressions of interest in contemporary poetry, and the publication of his *Orlando* in 1591 and the *Metamorphosis* in 1596, Harington was not sought out as a literary patron. He received no book dedications during Elizabeth's reign, although epigram 393 accompanied his reward to Charles Fitzgeffrey, who presented him with a copy of his *Affaniae* (1601), which included an epigram addressed to Sir John.

Many of Harington's epigrams were specifically used to entertain and communicate with his fellow courtiers. His verses apparently circulated widely among the most aristocratic habitués of the chamber. He observes in epigram 200 that "the great Ladies of the Court" commend some of his epigrams but dislike others. His epigram of the preacher who could find no biblical reference to a certain woman led Lady Mary Cheke, who is not otherwise known as a poet, to write answering verses (both of these epigrams are included in Part II). A Privy Chamber attendant throughout the reign, Mary seems to have enjoyed a full measure of royal confidence and favor. It is fitting that, as the widow of the Protestant scholar and exile Sir John Cheke, she should demonstrate in her verses a more detailed knowledge of the scriptures than Harington's hapless minister. The object of Sir John's satire is, of course, clerical ignorance; the preacher confuses the meaning of *certain* as a demonstrative with its meaning of "definite," or "unerring." Lady Cheke subverts this wordplay by refuting the cleric on his own ground. She cites four instances of

17. For Berkeley and Leigh see P. W. Hasler, *The House of Commons, 1558–1603* (1:432 and 2:455).

certain women in the Bible and concludes that he was correct only in saying that there is now no certain man. Harington had carefully acquiesced to this charge in his first line, "There was (not certain when) a certaine preacher." The poet admits to his own uncertainty from the beginning, leaving Lady Cheke to attack the anti-feminist assertions of his strawman persona. These companion poems amount to little more than some friendly sparring in the war between the sexes. Invidious maneuvering for political advantage at court was not at issue here, as it was in the exchange between Ralegh and the queen or in Essex's "Muses no more" with its aspersions on Ralegh. The Harington-Cheke companion poems resemble instead those lost works by Cecil and other courtiers that were occasioned by Elizabeth's appropriation of Lady Derby's locket. They provide further evidence that by the 1590s a number of courtiers wrote vernacular poetry without embarrassment as a means of carrying on polite social discourse as well as to influence the queen and promote their own status as courtiers.

While many of Harington's epigrams serve this benign social function, a number of them were too satiric, personal, or otherwise offensive to commit to unregulated circulation. Among the verses he sent to Lady Rogers in 1600 were some "that were showd to our Soveraigne Lady, and some, that I durst never show any Ladie, but you two."[18] Presumably Sir John exercised considerable restraint in circulating the epigrams that characterize recognizable contemporaries in such unflattering roles as drunks, lechers, scolds, fools, and hypocrites. Those who could identify themselves in these poems, or merely supposed that they could, might seek revenge, as Harington writes of Don Pedro who

> thinkes I scorne him in my Rime,
> And vowes, if he can proue I vse detraction,
> Of the great scandall he will haue his action.
>   (155)

Other poems would have offended by their content alone, particularly the more risqué ventures, of which there are quite a number: the friar cured of priapism (339), the maid who falls into a melancholy upon hearing a sermon on the prick of conscience (354), and Cayus, who first enjoyed his mistress in a privy (109). Lesbia, we are told, criticized his verse when it strayed from these wanton subjects to deal with virtue (412), but the queen remarked after he read some

18. McClure, *Letters and Epigrams*, 86, letter of December 19, 1600.

of his poetry to her that when he grew older "these fooleries will please thee lesse."[19] It was, furthermore, his translation of Ariosto's tale of Jocundo, with its implication that all women are faithless nymphomaniacs, that caused Elizabeth to banish Harington from court until he had translated the entire *Orlando*. It may well have been the anti-feminism rather than the explicit sexuality of this tale that angered Elizabeth, for there is a harsh discrepancy between the Petrarchan idealization of women in the mainstream of courtier verse and Harington's often irreverent, earthy characterizations of the sex in both his translation of Ariosto and in the epigrams.[20] Throughout his poetry, however, he avoids the contemptuous misogyny of his much-admired Rabelais, as well as the explicit pornography found in both Rabelais and Martial.

Harington's satire frequently turns from individuals to more generalized aspects of life at court. His most scathing attack on the court is epigram 130, which begins, "Misacmos hath long time a suter beene, / To serue in some neere place about the Queen." A remnant of this suit is his attempt to obtain the position of "reader" to the queen which fell vacant early in 1601 upon the death of Dr. John James, one of the royal physicians.[21] The poem stresses Harington's proficiency in "humane studyes" and "stories read," his industry, memory, and pursuit of truth, all of which are the reasons, he concludes, for the failure of his suit. He thus condemns not only the quality of the highest royal servants but also the queen's judgment in appointing and retaining them. A number of individual courtiers might also have taken offense at this disparaging line from epigram 84: "When Monopolies are giu'n of toyes and trashes." Several prominent favorites may be glanced at here. John Spillman, the royal jeweler, held the patent to buy linen rags for the making of paper. Edward Darcy, groom of the Privy Chamber, was licensed to make, import, and sell playing cards; and the gentleman pensioner Thomas Cornwallis was the sole licenser of gaming houses.[22] The same epigram ridicules courtiers who "mar good clothes, with cuts & slashes," a somewhat ironic gibe since Sir John was not above play-

---

19. Ibid., 97.

20. Townsend Rich contends that the aspersions on virginity in the Jocundo passage amounted to a political offence that Elizabeth could not overlook, while the wantonness itself was not offensive to court society (*Harington and Ariosto: A Study in Elizabethan Verse Translation*, 123–24).

21. McClure, *Letters and Epigrams*, 88. James exchanged New Year's gifts with Elizabeth in 1598, 1599, and 1600.

22. Price, *English Patents*, 142, 147, 149.

ing up to Elizabeth's delight in appearances, noting in his "Remembrauncer" that "the Queene loveth to see me in my laste frize jerkin, and saithe tis well enoughe cutt."23 His concern for fashion also comes out in epigram 156 where he complains "That oft in Court Knaues goe as braue as Kings," and he attacks women who violate the sumptuary laws in epigram 364.

Even more ironic are Harington's attacks on the distribution of church lands among royal favorites, since his own family's fortune was literally grounded in church lands obtained from the crown during the dissolution of the monasteries. This did not deter Sir John, however, from satirizing the ongoing process in epigrams 92, 103, 281, and 290. The latter verses, by lamenting the alienation of lands from the see of Salisbury, may have been directed at Ralegh in particular, who obtained Sherborne from that bishopric. The earl of Oxford's annuity was paid out of revenues from the bishopric of Ely, and Harington intervened personally to prevent another courtier poet, Heneage, a "zealous Puritan," from depriving the bishopric of Bath and Wells of Banwell Manor and Park.24 More than a dozen epigrams attack radical reformers in the established church under such epithets as "pure," "precise," and Brownist. Numbers 374 and 413 ridicule the Family of Love, an extreme Protestant sect imported from the Low Countries. The absence in the epigrams of any similar degree of contempt for Catholics is quite noticeable; anti-Catholic satire is restricted to criticism of the Pope, who excommunicated Queen Elizabeth (317), and a rather mild attack on "Women recusants" (401). Harington was probably not an outright Roman Catholic, as Lynus charges in epigram 365, yet epigrams 263, 394, and 400 clearly indicate that he entertained nostalgic ideals of a national church as wealthy, prosperous, and doctrinally united as he supposed the pre-Reformation church to have been. And Sir John's sympathies no doubt inclined toward the son's advice to his father on the relative merits of the Catholic and reformed churches in epigram 376, "Live in the new, dy yf you can in th'olde."

The epigrams are primarily verse communications directed to family members and fellow courtiers; from this perspective they more closely resemble Heneage's poems than the works of any earlier courtier poet. Harington at times delivers satiric judgments in tones as solemn as those used by Sir Thomas; in epigram 31 for

23. *Nugae Antiquae* (1779), 2:211.
24. For Harington's account of this incident see his *Supplie or Addicion to the Catalogue of Bishops to the Yeare 1608* (122).

instance, he attributes the dearth caused by heavy rains to the heavens weeping "to see our wickednesse." Usually however, and even as he deplores unethical practices that offended him deeply, such as simony (223, 293–94, 405) or usury (214, 228), his wordplay and sarcasm raise his emphasis above the dour expressions of outright condemnation that typify the moral style at its most self-righteous. Thus Sir John's wit tempers without blurring the ethical foundation of his attacks on the greed, deceit, lust, and hypocrisy that beset late Tudor England. He may not have captured the sardonic tone, the jarring impact of Martial's epigrams, but he nevertheless adapted them to his satiric needs, conveying moral judgments in a sprightly, entertaining fashion.[25]

A number of Harington's epigrams illustrate life at court in ways that are subordinate to his satiric intentions or neutral to mildly disapproving in tone. Thus when Titus produces a plank so heavy that "Two of the Gard might scantly well it lift" (170), and when he boasts that he "would haue ouer-lifted all the Gard, / Out-throwne them at the barre, the sledge, the stone" (174), Harington simply alludes to the fact that the queen's yeomen of the guard were exceptionally tall, strong men.[26] Harington's criticism of "Old Guillam" in epigram 173 likewise treats a familiar class of court personnel. Guillam is an alien resident who argues that English writers produce "barren" works except for what they take from foreign authors—the charge no doubt struck a sensitive nerve in the translator of Ariosto. Harington responds that Guillam prefers nonetheless to live in England and collect his royal pension. A number of aliens who served at court held such annuities throughout the reign: Sir John's victim may well have been Petruccio Ubaldini for instance, although many royal musicians, "artificers," and employees of the stable were foreigners with similar grants.[27]

Harington deals with gambling and card games in several epi-

---

25. Whipple judged his translations of the classical epigram "not quite incompetent" (*Martial and the English Epigram*, 346).

26. Foreign visitors often remarked on the guard's splendid appearance; the duke of Stettin-Pomerania described them as "fine big fellows" (Gottfried Von Bülow, ed., "Diary of the Journey of Philip Julius, Duke of Stettin-Pomerania, Through England in the Year 1602," *Transactions of the Royal Historical Society*, n.s., 6 [1892]:53; and see William Brenchley Rye, *England as Seen by Foreigners in the Days of Elizabeth and James the First*, 87).

27. Annuities paid through the treasurer of the chamber during Sir John Mason's tenure (1558–1566) included, for example, Alphonso Ferrabosco "Italyon" and Lucretia de Tedesche as well as Ubaldini (BL, Cotton MS Vespasian C.xiv, ff. 73–73v).

grams. He laughs at wastral Marcus's "life at Primero," which leads
him from the card table to debtors prison (195), but epigram 266 is
simply a witty catalog of the changing fashions in card games at
court, and epigram 387 urges as "A rule to Play" that gamblers
should be patient and good humored. Gambling was, after all, a
significant pastime at court. When Rowland Whyte informed Sir
Robert Sidney in 1595 that "nothing is so much thought upon" at
court "as Dancing and Playing," the playing he referred to was
gambling. Lord North and Sir Henry Lee, he continued, attended
court in hopes of preferment; both played "at Cards with the Queen,
and it is like to be all the Honor that will fall unto them this year."
During the "great golden play" of January 1603, Secretary Cecil
allegedly lost more than "800 pounds in one night, and as much
more at other times." Courtiers' account books are sprinkled with
entries concerning their losses "at play." Besides cards, dice, chess,
and tennis games, courtiers placed bets on contests of their own
devising. Robert Carey won two thousand pounds, a sum which
enabled him "to live at court a good while after," by wagering with
other courtiers that he could walk from London to Berwick in
twelve days.[28] Harington's own treatise "Of Playe" asserts that gambling is an honorable aristocratic pastime when the stakes are moderate, and he contends that "many noble mynded cowrtiers frequent
often such vertuous exercyses, and, if they would more often by my
perswasyon, I would bee not a little glad of yt."[29]

In both the "Apologie" and his essay "of reeding poetry," Harington emphasized the ornamental and thus pleasurable qualities of
verse. Accordingly, one of his motives in writing the epigrams was to
entertain his audience by clothing everyday matters in the more
pleasing garb of poetry. This theory is itself the subject of epigram
149 in which Sextus takes credit for one of Harington's epigrams
about Sir John Rainsford: "That Epigram was mine, who euer made
it. / I told him that conceit, from me, he had it." Harington counters
by charging that Sextus's original anecdote "Was like a ragged stone,

---

28. Arthur Collins, *Letters and Memorials of State*, 1:385; McClure, *Letters of John Chamberlain*, 1:180. Gambling expenses were listed among such significant "line item" expenditures by the earl of Essex as court diet, apparel, and
servants' wages (Longleat House, Devereux Papers 2, ff. 82–83 and 90v, preserve
detailed accounts of the earl's losses at "plaie"). For Carey's wager see F. H. Mares,
The Memoirs of Robert Carey (12). Sir Robert Sidney's formal covenant with
Carey for one hundred pounds of the total is preserved in BL, Lansdowne MS
56/46.
29. *Nugae Antiquae* (1779), 2:159.

dig'd from thy foolish head, / Now 'tis a Statue caru'd by vs, and polished." That Harington's efforts did not go unappreciated is shown, for example, by a flattering letter from Sir Robert Sidney who insists that "I do read Ariosto, and commend the translator to all friends," and he asks Sir John to "send me verses when you can."[30] Lady Kildare even commissioned Harington to write an epigram on the occasion of her wearing a straw hat to court. The poet obliged with fifty-four lines of verse "In commendation of a straw" (345). This poem includes what is probably Harington's closest approach to serious Petrarchism, his blazon of the lady as

> An yuory house, dores Rubies, windows tuch,
> A gilded roofe, with straw all ouerthatcht.
> Where shall perls bide, when grace of straw is such?

He no doubt genuinely admired Lady Kildare who was, furthermore, someone to reckon with at court. She was a Howard by birth, a countess by marriage, and a confidante of the queen, who provided her with a seven-hundred-pound annuity to compensate for the loss of her jointure in Ireland.[31] The countess was pleased with the epigram, for, according to a second one that Harington addressed to her, she responded to it by praising his "memory" to Elizabeth. Sir John took this opportunity to ask that she commend instead his forgetfulness, that is, his ability to forget a wrong, for he was apparently in some disgrace with the queen, and wished that she might do the same. In these epigrams we see Harington using his poetic talents to ingratiate himself with a fellow courtier, then moving her to help him regain royal favor.

At the same time that the epigrams amplified established uses for nonfictional verse at court and explored new ones, particularly of a satiric nature, they contributed substantially to the variety of technical forms attempted by courtier poets. Harington tried out dozens of new stanzas in this collection, many of which he used only once. He necessarily became skilled at devising stanzas of ottava rima in English while translating over four thousand of them from Ariosto, yet only eight of the epigrams are cast in this form (17, 26, 43, 52, 74, 165, 275). Four poems employ rhyme royal (3, 91, 169, 296), and the heroic couplet appears frequently. Otherwise, Sir John's technique expresses his deliberate independence from the most popular

---

30. Ibid., 2:255.
31. This lady's career is summarized in Robert W. Kenny's *Elizabeth's Admiral: The Political Career of Charles Howard, Earl of Nottingham, 1536–1624* (94, 252); the annuity is recorded in McClure, *Letters of John Chamberlain* (1:52).

verse forms of the day, whether new or traditional. He conscientiously limited his use of the popular "sixain" stanza, the form chosen by Shakespeare for *Venus and Adonis* and *Lucrece* and the stanza which Greville adopted as the mainstay of his mature poetry. Harington used it in fourteen epigrams, but he elsewhere went out of his way to avoid it, for many more of his six-line poems are in couplets: the *a a a a b b* rhyme scheme of epigrams 81, 204, and 383; the *a b b a c c* form of 75, 137, 153, 253, and 378; or the *a b a b a a* pattern of epigram 207. Similarly, thirty-two of the epigrams have fourteen lines, but only one Petrarchan sonnet (77) and four English ones are among them (158, 214, 321, and 373). In the remainder, Harington distanced his epigrams in form as well as content from the sonnet's amorous associations. Thus epigram 84 is an old-fashioned satire set forth in fourteen lines on a single rhyme; epigram 159 employs only three different rhyme sounds and epigram 116 only four. Epigram 118 consists of three triplets plus a repetition of the *b* rhyme in the couplet. Most of the remaining fourteen-line epigrams are in couplets, as if their length were a coincidence rather than intentional. Harington's remaining forms include experiments that defy classification. Several poems use five, six, seven, or even nine successive *a* rhymes before changing rhyme in the couplet. Epigram 209 uses only the seven different rhymes of the English sonnet while more than doubling the sonnet's scope in its thirty-one lines.

Among the courtier poets, only Sir Philip Sidney and the countess of Pembroke made efforts comparable to Harington's toward introducing a variety of new forms into their poetry. A few of Harington's unique stanzas are identical with those used by Sidney, such as the monorhyme sonnet (epigram 84 and *Old Arcadia* poem 42) and epigram 387, which has the same complicated ten-line form as *Certain Sonnets* poem 22. Yet there is very little overlap in the more exotic forms devised by these poets, and no reason to suppose that Sir John relied on the Sidneys for either the forms or content of his poetry. Given his familiarity with their works, however, it is unfortunate that he did not develop a better ear for the rhythmic subtleties of their lines. He shows no interest, for example, in Sir Philip's trochaics or his frequent interweaving of varied meters within the same poem. Harington wrote one epigram in ballad stanza (328), and another in accentual verse (327); a handful of "odd" meters crop up in his miscellaneous lyrics and translations. Yet his mainstay was the iambic pentameter. Substitute feet occur often enough to keep most of his epigrams from reverting to doggerel, yet the rhythms are regular enough for all that, and the preponderance of end-stopped lines conspires with this regularity to make Harington far less versatile as a metrist than as a deviser of new forms.

In the course of entertaining his peers with poetic commentary on whatever he saw or heard around him, Harington's epigrams ranged from witty observations to anecdotes to outright narratives, the latter a genre that had been previously attempted among the courtier poets only by Sidney, Dyer, and Greville. Indeed, Sidney's longest poem, *Other Poems* 4, is an unfinished, rather tedious account of rustic lovers playing a game of barley-break. Earlier in his poetic career, Sidney had composed Philisides' beast fable (OA 66) and dream vision (OA 73), as well as Nico's tale of an unfit, jealous husband who harasses his young wife into cuckolding him (OA 64). Dyer's "Amaryllis" (poem 8) preceded Harington's narrative epigrams as did, presumably, Greville's tale of Scoggin's wife (*Caelica* 50.)[32] All of these works differ from Harington's, however, in their fictional basis. His seven narratives (17, 93, 141, 195, 209, 237, and 239) adhere to the nonfictional criterion that governed his concept of the epigram generally. There is no reason to doubt, for example, that Sir John's versified accounts of the husband and wife who resolved a quarrel when she threatened to cuckold him (17), the lady who avenged herself on a double-dealing peddler (239), or the lady who saved her jewelry from thieves at a playhouse (237) derive from actual occurrences. Moreover, the minimal characterization Harington supplied allowed him to preserve the tone of aloof objectivity that marks the rest of the epigrams. The effects of these stories, whether satirical or merely amusing, depends largely upon the novelty of incident in each case, upon what happens rather than upon the persons involved, their thoughts, or feelings. Harington treats his stories with an economy reminiscent of Chaucer's fabliaux; indeed, epigrams 93 and 239 may be rightly considered Renaissance fabliaux without meaningful generic similarity to the epigram.

The originality of Harington's brief narratives inspired at least one imitator, Fulke Greville, whose versified tale in the *Arundel Harington Manuscript* (poem 69) is exactly the kind of real-life anecdote that Harington seized upon for his narratives. Greville's

---

32. *Caelica* 56, the moonlight escapade, and 74–75, the lovers' interviews, might also be considered narrative along with the poems by Sidney which inspired them, *Astrophil and Stella* songs 2, 4, and 8. They lack the complexity of incident found in Harington's narratives, however, and are further differentiated from his manner by their personal, subjective points of view.

tale is a "true reporte" recounted by the "Mr of the Rolles that nowe is and his ladye," either Sir Gilbert Gerrard, who held the office from 1581 to 1593, or his successor, Thomas Egerton. The first line, "A tale I once did heare a true man tell," resembles the opening of Harington's epigram 93, "I heard a pleasant tale at Cammington" (which turns out to be the story of a bailiff and tenant who cuckold each other). Greville's poem concerns a wench who lies on her back in the fields one evening until a man falls upon her and, meeting with no significant resistance, takes full advantage of her prone passivity. The master of the rolls and his wife witness these intimacies, and at the wife's insistence the pair is summoned before a magistrate where they confess that they are total strangers who "had no lawe to warrant copulacyone." Greville's characterization and commentary lead to a ninety-line account of the incident, one which Harington would have treated at half the length. Greville scorns both of his protagonists, but in keeping with the tenor of his *Caelica* sequence, the woman fares much the worse. As she lies on her back her thoughts mount up to the skies because "all lighte thinges by nature vpward ryse" (line 10), and her idle speculations are termed "suche Conceytes as ar in women founde" (line 18). Her reactions to the assault are just so many foolish contradictions:

> she clyppes him fast and would hav this a rape
> A rape bycause she neuer gave consent
> vnlesse you make consent in lying styll.
>   (lines 30–32)

Her plea before her accusers is especially idiotic: she "would have cryed for helpe when we weare theare / but that she was afrayde least we should heare" (lines 71–72). Greville's ironic wit injects life and humor into his poetic account of an essentially prosaic incident. The anecdotal narratives written by Harington and Greville constitute a subgenre of courtier verse well suited to entertaining a courtly audience, although there is no evidence that other Elizabethan courtiers or their Jacobean counterparts followed their lead.

The longest narrative verse undertaken by any Elizabethan courtier is Harington's translation of *Orlando Furioso*. Out of this formidable act of penance which Elizabeth had imposed on him Harington created and dedicated to her a literary and bibliographic landmark. It reaches to almost thirty-three thousand lines of ottava rima, plus numerous marginal notes, the "Apologie" as its preface, an elaborate commentary for each canto, a biography of Ariosto, and an index. With its full-page copper plates before each canto, a first for English printing, it became "the most elaborate work" attempted in Richard Field's printshop, a publishing as well as a literary event.[33] That Harington chose to publish so grandiose a project is not really surprising; Sir John Wolley, Lord Burghley, the earl of Oxford, and Sir Francis Drake were courtiers who had published verses before him under their own names, while in 1584 King James of Scotland had set forth his own poetry in *The Essayes of a Prentise*, to be followed by *His Majesties Poeticall Exercises* which appeared in the same year as Harington's *Orlando*. By the 1590s, the unwritten strictures forbidding aristocrats to publish their poetry met with increasingly frequent violations, and this process was accelerated by the publication of most of Sir Philip Sidney's poetry during the decade as a memorial to this national hero. Accordingly, Sir John makes no coy protestations about losing control over his work or finding it published against his will; he not only saw his translation through the press but circulated "advance" copies to various courtier friends. One of these, dedicated to a gentleman pensioner and member of Essex's circle, is inscribed "To Sir Thomas Coningsby by the frendly guift of the autor."[34]

Its publication aside, Harington's magnum opus may well have offended at least some widely held Elizabethan ethical norms, albeit his violations were as intentional as they are surreptitious. The first generation of university-educated humanist courtiers, the generation of Ascham, Wilson, and Wolley, was followed only by Hoby, Harington, and the earl of Cumberland among courtier poets who pursued their formal education through the master's degree. Hoby deviated from conservative humanist precedents insofar as he translated two contemporary tracts from French and Spanish, but Harington represents a far more radical shift in the focus of English humanism at court. Earlier humanists vigorously denounced medieval romances in general and Ariosto in particular. Ascham inveighed specifically against "the schole of *Petrarke* and *Ariostus*," while his attacks on the translating of Italian books and on the bloodshed and lechery in the *Morte d'Arthur* would apply in full measure as well to the *Orlando*. Nevertheless, when we consider Sir John's overall

---

33. Ariosto, *Orlando*, xlii.

34. For an outline of this gradual change see my "Tudor Aristocrats and the Mythical 'Stigma of Print'" (*Renaissance Papers* [1980]: 11–18). Rich (*Harington and Ariosto*, 180) cites Coningsby's autographed copy of the *Orlando* in the Rosenbach collection. Sir Thomas had performed in the tiltyard at court as early as 1571 and had traveled on the continent with Sir Philip Sidney in 1573. He was knighted by Essex before Rouen in September 1591.

literary career, his translations of the Psalms, Virgil, and excerpts from a dozen other classical poets, his appreciation of Ariosto appears less as a rejection of the older humanism than an expansion of its tenets to embrace contemporary vernacular works along with the classics. Still, the translation of such a work was in itself offensive to conservative Elizabethans and made more so by the way Harington handled his source, for as he embraces, he renders the *Orlando* partially but undeniably his own. He fully exploits the wanton aspects of the story but couples this tendency with a rather inconsistent emphasis upon moral didacticism and Christian piety.

Harington's amplification of the risqué and anti-feminist elements in Ariosto's work was revealed by Townsend Rich's comparison of the translation with the original. Sir John's interpolations are of a kind with the humorous, droll, and erotic passages he apparently devised for his personal copy of the *Arcadia*.[35] Rich found that, whereas Harington condensed or deleted fully 728 of Ariosto's stanzas, he retained or added to most of the passages that dealt with sexuality and anti-feminism. Moreover, he used the notes he appended to each canto to focus attention upon immoral and above all lascivious acts committed by women in the narrative. He likewise undercut Ariosto's apologetic efforts to defend women.[36] The spirit with which Harington pursued his task is epitomized by his alterations of the plate depicting the events of canto 28, which include the Host's tale of Jocundo that aroused Elizabeth's indignation in the first place. Sir John caused his engraver to alter the innocuous Italian plate he used as a model to include three scenes of copulation illustrative of the Host's story.

Here as in the translation itself, Harington seems bent on magnifying his original indiscretion, yet by enjoining him to translate the entire romance Elizabeth had in effect invited just such a result. And lest Harington be labeled either a misogynist or pornographer, two qualifications of Rich's thesis should be noted. First, the translation maintains an equitable emphasis upon the abilities and virtues of women. He expands by two stanzas the tale of Isabella, who preserves her chastity by tricking Rodomonte into beheading her (canto 29). It might be argued that Sir John dwelt upon her self-sacrifice out of respect for his mother, Isabella Harington, whose exemplary life

35. P. J. Croft, "Sir John Harington's Manuscript of Sir Philip Sidney's *Arcadia*," 61–62.

36. Rich, *Harington and Ariosto*, 71, 108–9, and see chapter 7 for a detailed analysis of Sir John's method.

he compares in his "Morall" with that of the heroine of this book. The result all the same tends to heighten rather than diminish one of Ariosto's most vivid accounts of feminine strength of character and wit. Similarly, Harington does full justice to Ariosto's commendations of women in canto 37, where he elaborates in the "Morall" on their practical abilities, above all their capacity for "rule and government," while in the "Historie" he summarizes the careers of prominent women who are only mentioned in the Italian. He refers approvingly to a pro-feminist tract by Lord Henry Howard (undoubtedly his "Dutifull Defence of the Lawful Regiment of Women"),[37] and in the "Allusion" he ranks the four learned Cooke sisters (among them Lady Burghley and Lady Elizabeth Russell) as intellectual equals of the Italian ladies celebrated by Ariosto. Thus Harington amplified the varied tributes to women which he found in his original and applied Ariosto's praises to specific English women, including the queen.

In the second place, Harington's additions to the racier passages of the story are for the most part less explicit than Ariosto himself at his most erotic. To Astolpho's description of Alcina, for instance, Sir John adds the reference to her "corrall lippes to kisse," yet almost every sonnet-lady was similarly endowed so that this extra detail could hardly have raised many contemporary eyebrows. Harington expands and savors the account of Mandricardo and Doralice spending the night together in the peasant's cottage (canto 14, stanza 53), even urging his reader in the marginal note to imagine their activities; yet everything is in fact left to the imagination, as it is in the original. There are no lurid details, nor even a suggestive summary of the incident. Harington's most controversial addition to the original wording concerns an episode of interracial homosexuality in canto 43; Sir John equates the "Gipsen's" proposition to Anselmo with that which the "Sodomits did make for guests of Lot,"[38] and he introduces the Elizabethan term for the act, "bugger," a word that occurs in the manuscript and is indicated by the rhyme with "mugger," although its place in the printed stanza is left blank. Ariosto, of course, had left no doubt as to the nature of this encounter, the intentions of *"il brutto Moro,"* or *"suo voler maluagio"*; Harington named the practice, but again without any further account of what

37. The DNB states that Howard completed his treatise in 1589 and cites copies in BL, Harleian MS 7021 and an unnamed Bodleian manuscript (s.v. "Howard, Henry, earl of Northampton"). It is also preserved in Harvard, f MS Eng. 826.
38. Ariosto, *Orlando*, 507.

happened. Here as elsewhere he enhanced as well as preserved the risqué flavor of his original. He did not, however, contribute erotic or pornographic detail to Ariosto's story, and he balanced his expansions and highlighting of Ariosto's anti-feminism with an equal regard for his author's commendations of women.

Along with the themes of feminine licentiousness and infidelity, both well represented in the epigrams, Sir John's handling of the *Orlando* also shares with the epigrams a concern for piety and the rebuke of vice. At canto 7, stanza 63, for example, he inserts a stanza disparaging the use of wigs and cosmetics, vanities that are also under attack in epigrams 40, 162, and 201. In this same canto, Rogero's orgy at Alcina's palace leads Harington to three stanzas of somber warning indistinguishable from the standard poetic moralizing of the age:

> O poysond hooke that lurks in sugred bait,
> O pleasures vaine that in this world are found
> Which like a subtile theefe do lye in waite
> To swallow man in sinke of sinne profound.

Harington's moral sensitivity leads him to several specifically Christian interpolations, just as in the manuscript of his epigrams he included the Lord's Prayer in verse and a poetic summary of the fifteen Christian devotions, as well as his epigrams in defense of the church.[39] Thus Ariosto mentions Isabella's prayers, which become specifically directed to the Virgin Mary and her Son in the translation. Sir John adds a five-stanza account of Astolpho, Gryphon, and Aquilant at Christ's tomb in Jerusalem, a passage that includes a penitential lament and the introduction of a priest who absolves these characters of their sins (canto 15, stanzas 73–77). Similarly, Harington's commentaries on the story after most of the cantos extol wisdom and virtue and deplore "lewd Doctrine" and vice. Overall, then, his translation allowed him a vicarious indulgence in the fleshly pleasures he condemned in Rogero, but at the same time he could honestly protest that on a page-by-page basis, his *Orlando* and its commentaries provided far more good and godly instruction than he had found in the Italian.

In addition to changing certain aspects of Ariosto's eroticism, anti-feminism, and moral emphasis, Harington altered some details of the *Orlando* to reflect his own experiences and standing as a courtier. His description of Irish soldiers in the two stanzas he

39. R. H. Miller, "Unpublished Poems by Sir John Harington," 157–58.

inserted in canto 10 (74–75) was based on a knowledge of that country derived from his travels there in 1586. In stanza 74, he replaced the earl of Desmond, representing a house that bred many rebels during Elizabeth's reign, with the earl of Ormond. Thomas Butler, the tenth earl, was a prominent figure at the English court whom Sir John refers to as "A most honorable Earle, and true friend" in the *Metamorphosis*. In the *Tract on the Succession*, he recalls how Ormond teased him in the earl of Leicester's presence because he had read excerpts from the scandalous "Leicester's Commonwealth" to his fellow courtiers.[40] Rich supposed that Harington added the earl of Cumberland to the list of English peers in book 10 for the sake of a rhyme with Northumberland. In the context of his other changes here, however, a different explanation seems more likely. He correctly assigned the dragon insignia to Cumberland and he corrected the earl of Essex's heraldry from Ariosto's two snakes to a hound, derived, as Rich noted, from the talbot in the Devereux crest.[41] He likewise substituted "The bay tree . . . that doth flourish still" for the earl of Derby's badge, "*Il can,*" the dog. Although the bay seems unrelated to the Stanley family's arms, as a symbol of victory it was perhaps intended to compliment both Henry, the fourth earl, and his son and heir Ferdinando, whom Harington compares with Sir Charles Brandon as "likest to him for armes and cavallarie" in the "Allusion" to canto 32.[42] These are the only substantive changes in the catalog, yet Sir John's marginal notes draw attention to Ariosto's historical inaccuracies, and Harington might easily have rectified the errors had he wished to; the earl of Oxford's device, for instance, could have been corrected with the change of a single letter, from "Beare" to "Boare." Harington's attention to the earl of Essex signified, no doubt, his allegiance to the Essex circle at court, and the earl furthermore, read and approved of the *Orlando*, according to epigram 77. Sir John probably added the earl of Cumberland to Ariosto's list of warlike Englishmen because he and Essex were friends and leaders of military expeditions as well as the court's foremost participants in chivalric entertainments. Each rode in all but one of the Accession Day tilts from 1586 through 1591, they were the chief combatants in 1587, and in 1590 Clifford succeeded Sir Henry Lee as the queen's champion.[43] Cumberland, however, set

40. Donno, *Metamorphosis*, 253; *A Tract on the Succession to the Crown (A.D. 1602)*, 44.
41. Rich, *Harington and Ariosto*, 86.
42. Ariosto, *Orlando*, 369.
43. In the fall of 1592 these noblemen delivered their joint challenge in the

certain limits to his regard for *Orlando Furioso*, for on one of his privateering voyages he found a gallant reading from it during morning prayers and threatened to throw the book overboard.[44] He had perhaps forgotten that he and Essex were the only noblemen in the English version whose family arms were correct, thanks to Harington's revisions, and that neither Cumberland nor Ormond had a place in Ariosto's great work until Harington slipped them in as a token of his personal regard.

By the time he completed the *Orlando*, Harington had turned out a greater number of verses than any other Elizabethan courtier poet. His English renderings of Martial and Ovid, and to a lesser degree, Horace, Dante, and Tasso, add to his stature as a translator, while his attention to these authors reveals a considerable liberalizing expansion of the ideals and tastes of earlier courtier humanists. In his original epigrams Harington created an extremely diverse collection of nonfictional poems that were nevertheless lively and entertaining. A number of the genres he attempted—the elegy, commendatory verse, and congratulatory poems—had previously been tried by other courtiers, yet a number of others, particularly satire and satiric narrative, were apparently first cultivated by Harington.

The only other courtiers who wrote nonfictional satiric verse were Ralegh and perhaps Essex, who are connected with a cluster of related poems centered upon Ralegh's "The Lie" (14). None of Sir John's epigrams touch on this quarrel, nor do his satiric techniques influence its conduct. Ralegh levels heavy-handed charges against a long list of contemporary institutions and offices, including the court, church, lawyers and "potentates," instead of illustrating in detail a single instance of folly as Harington usually does. Ralegh's anaphoristic accusations take on a chant-like quality which is intensified in Essex's possible poem I, an ad hominem refutation of Ralegh's charges. The earl's possible poem II is an equally direct rebuttal; its moderate tone more nearly resembles Harington's manner, although its long-line rhythms are completely unlike the pentameter epigrams. Above all, the Ralegh-Essex satires lack the ironic humor and wordplay so characteristic of Harington's style. It was this type of satire, modeled upon Martial and often accompanied with his Latinate pseudonyms, that Harington began to deploy at court by the late 1580s. Davies may have been writing similar

---

Privy Chamber to meet all comers at a tournament the following February (HMC, 7th report, appendix, 520, 524).

44. G. C. Williamson, *George, Third Earl of Cumberland (1558–1605)*, 281.

epigrams at about the same time, but he is at most a co-founder of the vogue for satiric classical epigrams which, if they attracted no other courtier proponents, were tremendously popular among out-of-court poets during the 1590s and well into the next century. Meanwhile, Harington's anecdotal narratives provided the court with a verse equivalent of the Renaissance jestbook. Indeed, of Greville's two similar ventures of the kind, *Caelica* 50 apparently relates in verse the story of Scoggin's wife taken from one of the most popular of the printed jestbooks. Aside from Greville, however, neither courtiers nor professional poets followed Harington's lead in this subgenre of narrative verse.

Harington adapted a number of epigrams to his immediate concerns as a courtier, such as those he addressed to the queen, Essex, Burghley, and Lady Kildare, or his attacks on a factional opponent in the poems that deride Ralegh as Paulus. He wrote individual epigrams praising James VI and his claim to the succession, and late in 1602 he sent him the bulk of his collection with a special dedicatory poem as a New Year's gift. The poet-king graciously acknowledged this gift and even discussed poetry with Sir John in a private audience after gaining the English throne, yet no meaningful patronage was forthcoming. Along with Ralegh, among other superfluous Elizabethan courtiers, Harington was left to dedicate his pen and wits to the service of Prince Henry, whose death in 1612 dashed their hopes for court preferment based upon literary accomplishment.

Most of Sir John's Elizabethan poetry adheres to a consistent theory for which he has received little recognition despite its forward-looking implications for the development of English verse. He was aware that he could not claim "the glorious name of Poet" either for his original works, which were largely nonfictional and therefore not poetic by Sidney's definition, or for his translations, which were deemed mere versifications by contemporary critics such as Puttenham. By declining the title of true poet, Sir John must have been tempted as well to decline the accusations leveled against poets. Thus in the "Apologie," where he so often depends upon Sidney's *Defence* for both style and content, Harington concurs that poets do not lie because they do not affirm. The obvious corollary for the writer of nonfictional epigrams is that such authors are innocent because they deal only with the truth from the outset, yet this was not to be Harington's excuse. He confessed from the beginning that all profane studies are to a degree irrelevant to the Christian, and he commended satiric verse because it reproves vice. He was no more able than Sidney, however, to justify love poetry within this moral context. Instead, he lists epigrams with pastorals and sonnets as genres that often "savour of wantonnes" even "into plaine scurrilitie." It is a bold concession. Among such pastorals he must have included, preeminently, the works of Sidney and Dyer. By sonnets he undoubtedly meant love poems in general, as in epigram 38, a "Comparison of the Sonnet, and the Epigram," where Faustus declares sonnets to be superior because "Their sugred taste best likes his likresse senses."[45]

Pastorals and sonnets are products of Sidney's "right Poet"; by yoking them with his own genre, the epigram, Harington left his occasional, nonfictional trifles subject to the same moral condemnation directed at creative writing. But after granting all this, he counters with an audaciously independent justification of wanton, scurrilous, secular works: "even the worst of them may be not ill applied and are, I must confesse, too delightfull." He then appeals to Martial's dictum, "*Laudant illa, sed ista legunt*": we praise holy and instructive works, but we read the naughty ones. This Sir John illustrates with another epigram from Martial: "*Lucrecia* (by which he signifies any chast matron) will blush and be ashamed to read a lascivious booke, but how? not except *Brutus* be by, that is if any grave man should see her read it, but if *Brutus* turne his backe, she will to it agayne and read it all."[46] Literature must be reckoned with, indeed tolerated, because it is delightful and will be read. Harington's blunt honesty opposes Elizabethan ethical norms as neither Sidney nor any other theorist of the age dared to do outright. Sir John's iconoclastic observation is in fact undercut by the gothic levels of interpretation he imposed on the *Orlando*, and as late as his essay "Of reeding" he advised Prince Henry to "moralyce" unedifying poetry. Meanwhile, Harington continued to write epigrams for the delight of his readers and with frequent disregard for their moral value. In both theory and practice then, one courtier confronted head on the hypocrisy that centered on the cultivation of the arts at court, where patronage of all that was merely delightful clashed with official opposition to anything that did not promote spiritual and moral enlightenment.

45. Ariosto, *Orlando*, 5, 3, 9. In the essay "Of reeding," Harington also lumps together all amorous verse as "love sonnets."
46. Ariosto, *Orlando*, 9.

6

The Sidney Legacy

During the 1590s Sir Philip Sidney's literary innovations attracted numerous out-of-court practitioners, most notably Shakespeare and Spenser in the sonnet sequence, and Robert Greene and Thomas Lodge with their romances in prose and verse modeled upon the *Arcadia*. A number of courtier poets, including Ralegh, Gorges, and Harington, acknowledged Sidney's achievement without permitting it to influence their own poetic careers, at least with respect to the genres and forms they employed. Presumably, Sir Philip's example lent increased respectability to the open cultivation of poetry at court, and this may account in part for the handful of minor lyric poets who can be identified there during the last two decades of the reign. Yet only his sister, the countess of Pembroke, his brother Robert, and his close friend Fulke Greville can be rightfully considered his literary heirs, and even their writings tend less toward imitation than toward the extension and fulfillment of Sidney's ideals for English verse.

Verse Drama

The countess of Pembroke finished her translation of Robert Garnier's *Antonie* in November of 1590. It was published in 1592 by William Ponsonby, the undisputed if unofficial printer to the Sidney-Herbert circle,[1] along with her translation of Philippe de Mornay's

---

1. Every authorized Elizabethan edition of Sidney's works, including the 1590 *Arcadia* which Greville supervised through the press, was issued under Ponsonby's auspices. The printer John Charlewood had enjoyed similar patronage from another courtier family, that branch of the Howards headed by Philip, earl of Arundel, for on the title page of Lord Henry Howard's *A Defensative Against the Poyson of Supposed Prophecies* (1583), Charlewood styled himself "Printer to the right Honourable Earle of Arundell."

Discourse of Life and Death. Subsequent Elizabethan editions of the play alone appeared in 1595 and 1600. Between about 1595 and 1601 Greville composed three similar Senecan plays only the first two of which, *Mustapha* and *Alaham*, have survived. The dating of his plays and their similarities to *Antonie* indicate that Greville was following Lady Pembroke's lead, although it is possible that both courtiers were influenced as well by Samuel Daniel, whose *Tragedie of Cleopatra* effectively rounds out the Antony and Cleopatra story as dramatized by the countess.[2] These closet dramas represent a genre unexplored by Sidney, who ventured no further into dramatic poetry than the pastoral dialogue attributed to him as possible poem 1, and his comic pageant *The Lady of May.* In the *Defence*, however, Sir Philip explained his criteria for a successful tragedy. He praised *Gorboduc* because it approximated the Senecan style, and he argued that a good tragedy's didactic purpose was to represent "tyrannical humours" in order that "kings [might] fear to be tyrants."[3] This was not a particularly relevant message for Elizabeth's courtiers to convey to her in the 1590s,[4] nor is there evidence that the court feared that her most likely successor, James of Scotland, displayed tyrannical leanings. Yet the subject of just and successful rule remained a topic of immediate courtier concern, and tragedy was the only literary form specifically designated by Sidney as a means of communicating with one's sovereign. All three neo-Senecan plays lead their readers to condemn tyranny while they imply in various ways their approval of Elizabeth's benevolent regime.

The countess probably authorized the publication of *Antonie* because it illustrated the precepts of dramatic tragedy formulated in the *Defence*, treated subjects which Sir Philip had dealt with in his own poetry, and asserted that a good ruler seeks to be loved rather than feared by his subjects. Garnier's imitation of Seneca preserved

2. Daniel was patronized by both Greville and the countess. He served as a tutor in the Pembroke household, and in 1595 received a parsonage on the Isle of Wight as a result of Greville's intervention on his behalf (Rebholz, *Life of Greville*, 143). For the suggestion that Daniel's *Cleopatra* is a companion to Lady Pembroke's play, and that she chose to translate Garnier because of his adherence to Sidney's dramatic precepts see Virginia Walcott Beauchamp's "Sidney's Sister as Translator of Garnier" (12–13).

3. Duncan-Jones and Van Dorsten, *Miscellaneous Prose*, 96.

4. Greville's eulogy of Elizabeth in the *Dedication to Sir Philip Sidney* (*Life of Sidney*), for example, praises her for such qualities as her refusal to take revenge on those who persecuted her during Mary's reign and her "steady hand in the government of sovereignty," as opposed to a policy of "Imperious forcing" (Gouws, *Prose Works*, 98, 105).

the classical unities as Sidney advised by coming "to the principal point of that one action," in this case, the final hours of Antony's life.[5] The French original, translated virtually line for line in *Antonie*, also emphasized the themes of passion versus reason and private interest in conflict with public responsibility so vital to both of Sidney's *Arcadias* as well as to *Astrophil and Stella*. The play diverges however from Sidney's customary focus upon the preliminary stages of courtship leading either to acceptance or rejection of the lover. Antony and Cleopatra are veteran lovers who are nevertheless subject to the same reason-effacing debilitations that afflict love's neophytes. The nature of their commitment to one another has been established before the opening scene so that its exposition through testing can become the substance of the plot and the primary source of suspense. This process is accordingly dramatized without further interaction between the main characters—in contrast with such romantic treatments of the story as Shakespeare's play, Mary's Antony and Cleopatra do not even converse directly with one another.

The dramatic representation is centered upon parallel conflicts in which the protagonists are tempted by the well-intentioned but faulty advice of their closest associates. Cleopatra's ladies-in-waiting encourage her to blame Antony's defeat upon the irresistible will of the gods, and to forsake him in order to accommodate herself to Caesar's hegemony. In response she insists that lapses of human reason, not the gods are to blame for mortal disasters:

> If we therein sometimes some faults commit,
> We may them not to their high majesties,
> But to our selves impute; whose passions
> Plunge us each day in all afflictions.
> (act 2, lines 475–78)

She likewise takes full responsibility for the defeat at Actium: "I am sole cause: I did it, only I" (act 2, line 448). She refuses to desert Antony but dedicates herself instead to the mandates of duty grounded on virtue that compel her to follow him to the grave (act 2, lines 642ff.). Antony is equally positive that his fall resulted not from destiny but from his irrational surrender to pleasure: "Falne from a souldior to a chamberer, / Careles of vertue, careles of all praise" (act 3, lines 1153–54). He likewise rejects Lucilius's plea that he seek

---

5. Duncan-Jones and Van Dorsten, *Miscellaneous Prose*, 114. References to *Antonie* follow the text in Geoffrey Bullough, ed., *Narrative and Dramatic Sources of Shakespeare*, vol. 5.

mercy from Caesar and exits at the end of act 3 to commit suicide. The play endorses adherence to principle and full acceptance of moral responsibility, while neither glorifying nor denigrating romantic love. Both protagonists view their circumstances more accurately than do their attendants, and both command the steadfast strength of character needed to face the crisis with dignity and integrity. Thus *Antonie* dramatizes the triumph of rulers who make correct decisions despite the flattering but ultimately degrading advice of their courtiers. Antony and Cleopatra's decisions, which necessarily lead them to suicide, grow out of a resolve that strikes us as correct and noble when judged as due compensation for their past mistakes, and without regard to anachronistic Christian standards of conduct.

In order to increase our admiration for Antony and Cleopatra, the character of Caesar Augustus is considerably degraded. He is pompous, proud, and above all, the new-fledged tyrant bent upon stamping out any potential challenge to his rule, whatever the cost in human bloodshed:

> Then to the end none, while my daies endure,
> Seeking to raise himselfe may succours find,
> We must with bloud marke this our victory,
> For just example to all memorie
> Murther we must, until not one we leave,
> Which may hereafter us of rest bereave.
>   (act 4, lines 1495–1500)

After this pronouncement a scene unfolds between Caesar and Agrippa which is a reverse image of the scenes between Antony, Cleopatra, and their counselors, for Agrippa tenders sound advice which his master summarily rejects. "Marke it with murther? Who of that can like?" (act 4, line 1501), asks Agrippa, who discourages Caesar from terrorizing his subjects and urges him to endear himself to them instead: "No guard so sure, no forte so strong doth prove, / No such defence, as is the peoples love" (act 4, lines 1513–14). Sir John Harington had simply sidestepped Machiavelli's question as to whether a prince should be loved or feared when he declared that he both feared and loved Queen Elizabeth. In light of her style as a ruler, however, Agrippa's advice provides an equally valid response as well as a complete rejection of Machiavelli's conclusion that it is better for princes to be feared. Caesar serves as a negative contrast to Elizabeth, just as Antony and Cleopatra's emotional excesses contrast with the queen's deliberate suppression of her personal desires for the sake of royal duty. On the other hand, Garnier's choice of subject precluded the creation of a tragedy that would cause rulers to fear becoming tyrants, for neither the lovers' fall nor the triumph of Caesar Augustus inspires such fear. Yet the example of Caesar might well make rulers disdain to be tyrants, and the story is deployed within a thematic and aesthetic context otherwise in harmony with Sidney's ideas about the nature of tragedy.

Greville's plays, although they treat many of the same themes dealt with in *Antonie*, differ from Lady Mary's practice regarding Sidney's literary ideals and as responses to the environment at court that led Greville to dramatize these episodes from oriental history. In his *Dedication to Sir Philip Sidney* (*Life of Sidney*), Greville explained his intention in the plays "to trace out the highways of ambitious governors, and to show in the practice of life that the more audacity, advantage and good success such sovereignties have, the more they hasten to their own desolation and ruin."[6] Thus Greville devised a dramatic formula for implementing Sidney's general purpose for tragedy, that it make kings fear to be tyrants. As a result, both of Greville's plays adhere more closely to Sir Philip's precepts than does *Antonie*. At the same time, Greville works variations upon the theme of reason versus passion with the same creative independence that kept *Caelica* from becoming a mere imitation of *Astrophil and Stella*.

The protagonist of *Mustapha*, the Emperor Soliman, is a ruler subjected to the good and bad advice of his courtiers; as in *Antonie*, the consideration of alternative courses of action dominates the plot. Soliman's wife, Rossa, along with his leading courtiers, urge him to kill his son and heir, Mustapha, while the righteous basha, Achmet, and Soliman's daughter, Camena, dissuade him from the murder. Unlike the countess's protagonists, however, Soliman is at length persuaded to reject his true counsellors and succumb to the advice of those who would have him destroy his son in order to promote their own ambitions. The conflict between reason and passion surfaces in act 1, scene 2, as Soliman recounts the creation of man by a personified nature goddess. Here, the equation of human and animal passions is no doubt indebted to Sidney's creation myth in *Old Arcadia* poem 66:

> When man shee made, and his same sparke devine,
> reason infused in him, that only hee,

6. Gouws, *Prose Works*, 133.

> in tyme might diverse to the Angells bee,
> . . . .
> Shee doth within the bodye where it lives,
> affections place, and hence drawne from the beasts
> to warr with reason, still refineinge itt.[7]

For Soliman, the conflict between his higher and baser powers is unusually complicated, for his reason impels him both to secure his throne by cutting off his supposedly ambitious son and to save him:

> Truth methincks speakes both with him, and against hime,
> and as for reason, that should rule theis passions,
> I finde her so effeminate a powre,
> as shee bidds kill to save, bidds save, and doubt not,
> keeping my love and feare in equall ballaunce
>
> (folio 4)

Unlike the majority of instances in Sidney's works, Soliman's correct course of action is dictated by emotion, his instinctive love for his son, but this love is short-circuited by the evil advice of his wife, Rossa, who seeks the throne for her own son, Zanger.

Mustapha is linked with *Antonie* in two ways that are more specific than their common emphasis upon reason and passion or the centrality in their plots of rulers who must accept or reject their courtiers' advice. Mustapha resembles both Antony and Cleopatra in his dedication to principle, for despite the explicit warnings of his peril he insists upon coming before his father unaccompanied by his guard, and instead of resisting his death by strangulation he puts the cord around his neck, thus becoming an accomplice to his own murder. The prince is controlled by other-worldly religious and ethical precepts that cause him to welcome martyrdom; his steadfastness resembles the Roman virtue practiced by Antony in Lady Pembroke's play. Furthermore, the choruses after acts 2 and 4 underscore Mustapha's determination to die by emphasizing the futility of mortal existence and the benefit of escaping it through death, just as the chorus of Egyptians after act 3 of *Antonie* expresses precisely the same attitude toward death.

In addition to these similarities between the two plays, the careers of Antony, Cleopatra, and Mustapha, insofar as they depict characters who knowingly follow their highest convictions even to the point of self-destruction, no doubt held a particular interest for these courtiers as examples, in quite different circumstances, of the

---

7. Folger, MS V.b.223, f. 4. Subsequent references to *Mustapha* follow this text.

same devotion to principle that led Sidney to the ill-fated hazarding of his life at Zutphen. Although critics have noted the parallels between Mustapha and the earl of Essex, Greville's characterization of the prince minimizes their most obvious similarities, military service to the crown and popularity with the common people. Mustapha more nearly resembles Sidney, whom Greville described as one who "made the religion he professed the firm basis of his life, . . . his chief ends being not friends, wife, children or himself, but above all things, the honour of his maker and service of his prince or country."[8]

In *Mustapha* Greville successfully applied Sidney's criteria for good tragedy, yet he allowed his fascination with the story's political dimensions to sabotage the play's larger aesthetic impact. *Mustapha* adheres to the unity of place, does not mix comic with serious action, and preserves the unity of time if we assume that Achmet and Mustapha arrived at court on the same day that Rossa killed her daughter. Rossa justified her crime on the bogus charge that Camena's warning to Mustapha revealed her complicity in a plot against their father, and this murder constitutes the turning point of the play because it persuades Soliman that his son must also die. The subsequent assassination, by which means Soliman intended to preserve his reign, leads instead to a general rebellion in which he and his wicked counselors are rendered helpless and threatened with death. To this point the action is unified and fulfills Sidney's requirement for tragic didacticism. Through Achmet, Greville enunciates the moral of Soliman's corrupt decision and its aftermath: "for kinges when least you for your people Care / You subject to your meanest Subjectes are" (folio 26v). Greville did not, however, let the catastrophic reversal speak for itself; instead, he disrupted the play's unity at this point by adding a fifth act concerned with Achmet's response to Soliman's overthrow. Achmet now becomes the protagonist since he alone can make significant decisions because he commands enough popular respect to end the rebellion. In doing so, he may save his country from anarchy and prolonged civil war at the price of leaving the government in the hands of the tyrant Soliman, and his ruthless, decidedly powerful wife, Rossa. In the end, Achmet resists the temptation to let Soliman's regime pay for its crimes:

> States trespasse not indeed, though Princes swerve,
> Kinges are the rodds or blessinges of the skie

8. Gouws, *Prose Works*, 22, 25.

God only Judge. and knowes what they deserve.
Solyman shall still bee safe, or I will dye.
(folio 28)

So ends the play, its imperfect structure the result of Greville's portrayal through Achmet of the triumph of rational political understanding over largely emotional desires for justice and revenge.[9]

In *Alaham*, Greville dealt with the same themes of reason overcoming passion and the self-destructive force of tyrannical rule, but in doing so he created a play that is aesthetically more successful than *Mustapha. Alaham* is the story of a king's younger son who has long manipulated his father, the royal counselors, and favorites, but cannot finally prevent the confirmation of his elder brother as rightful heir to the throne. The plot centers upon Alaham's efforts to seize power by destroying the royal family and suppressing two powerful courtiers, Mohamet and Caine. The conflicts between personal and political morality are akin to those explored by Sidney in the *Old Arcadia* and, increasingly, in the proliferating episodes of the *New Arcadia*. In fact, Greville may have chosen to dramatize the Alaham story because of its similarity to the tale of the old Paphlagonian king in the *New Arcadia*, book 2, chapter 10, although it is conceivable that both Sidney's story and his friend's play derive from a common reading of the sources during their "youth and familiar exercise."[10] In both plots, an ambitious son deposes and blinds his royal father. The king is succored by loyal offspring who become themselves objects of the usurper's murderous intentions. Variations upon this basic story by Sidney and Greville make it impossible to be sure that their accounts are related, just as it is impossible to be sure that Shakespeare drew upon the *Arcadia* episode for the Gloucester subplot of *King Lear*.[11]

The first of Greville's two significant departures from his source is his creation of Celica, the old king's loyal daughter, whom Greville seems to have created out of the more admirable representa-

9. Joan Rees notes Greville's effort to repair this structural flaw in his revision of the play by concentrating the climactic action of the plot between Mustapha's death and Achmet's decision to intervene into the final act *(Fulke Greville, Lord Brooke, 1554–1628: A Critical Biography,* 166).

10. References to *Alaham* follow the text in Bullough, *Poems and Dramas,* vol. 2. Bullough cites accounts of Alaham's coup d'état in Ludovico di Varthema's *Itinerary* (1510), with derivative versions in Bandello, Belleforest, and R. S[mythe]'s *Straunge, lamentable and tragicall hystories* (1577, STC 13524).

11. See Fitzroy Pyle, "*Twelfth Night, King Lear,* and *Arcadia,*" *Modern Language Review* 43 (1948): 449–55, and the analysis by Bullough, *Narrative and Dramatic Sources,* 7:284.

tions of her namesake among his *Caelica* lyrics. She defies Alaham, comforts and tries to rescue her father and elder brother, and is burned at the stake with them. Through this character Greville adds a virtuous if impotent woman to the story, although Celica's role is quite overshadowed by his conception of Alaham's wife, Hala, just as in *Mustapha*, Camena's moral actions are wholly overshadowed by Rossa's villainy.

Greville's second departure from his source concerns his substitution of Hala for Mohamet as the revenging antagonist to Alaham. The usurper readily enlists his wife's aid in setting her current, adulterous lover, Caine, against her former lover, Mohamet, both of whom are potential threats to Alaham's political ambitions. By act 3 he is powerful enough to order Caine's execution, and does so without ever considering that Hala might have formed some genuine attachment to her lover. Caine's murder is the turning point of the play as well as the point at which Greville devised a curious variation upon the reason-passion conflict as ordinarily formulated by Sidney. In the wake of Caine's murder, Hala dedicates herself to her husband's destruction, but for her revenge to succeed she must conceal her fury in order not to arouse Alaham's suspicions. Accordingly, she advises him to bury Caine with an elaborate show of grief and to secure his grip on the throne by destroying his father (act 3, scene 3, lines 57–67). Only after Alaham leaves the room does she give way to her rage, vowing to kill her husband and her children by him so that her illegitimate children by Caine may inherit the throne. Greville here manages, again, an imaginative inversion of Sidney's approach to such conflicts. Astrophil, for example, succumbs to his emotions and necessarily strays from the path of virtue, just as Stella upholds virtue by insisting that reason govern her passions. In contrast, Hala's emotional control enables her to poison her husband and kill her son (albeit Greville devised an appropriately self-defeating twist to the infanticide by having her murder Caine's child by mistake).

Hala is a formidably rational woman whose talents are unrestrained by moral sensitivity. She is quite as ambitious as Alaham, whom she originally planned to overthrow after he had gained the crown so that she and Caine could rule. With Rossa, she insures the ascendancy of scheming, vicious women in Greville's plays, an impression which is but partially offset by his portrayals of the virtuous women, Camena and Celica. The ratio of admirable to immoral women is approximately the same as it is in *Caelica*, with negative characterization predominating in all three works. Greville recognized that the plays might leave him open to charges of anti-feminism, and in the *Dedication* he justified the imbalance with the somewhat lame excuse that, since poets ordinarily gave virtues feminine attributes, he might use women to represent vices with equal propriety.[12]

Alaham is one of Greville's most ambitious and successful literary undertakings, a work truly poetic in Sidney's sense of the word because it transforms the historical incident into a work of fiction. Greville's additions to the story include not only Celica and Hala's critical role in the plot, but also the adaptation of Deianira's poisoned robe and Medea's slaughter of her children as the specific means of Hala's revenge. The play moves toward a single well-motivated catastrophe wherein malice and ruthless ambition work a mutual overthrow. Hala's accidental murder of the wrong child is a slight improbability, yet necessary to Greville's conception of the story as an exemplum against tyranny. Despite its ambivalence with regard to the unity of time, it conforms in purpose and effect to Sidney's criteria for tragedy to a degree unattained by either *Antonie* or *Mustapha*.

The political context of Queen Elizabeth's final years has a bearing upon all three of these courtier plays, although they do not relate to the succession question in quite the allegorical fashion that has often been posited for them. Greville claimed to have destroyed his own play about Antony and Cleopatra due to "many members in that creature (by the opinion of those few eyes which saw it) having some childish wantonness in them apt enough to be construed or strained to a personating of vices in the present governors and government."[13] This statement has spawned an essentially futile search for court allegory in the two surviving plays. *Mustapha* and *Alaham* are, however, domestic tragedies which take place within royal households, and while their catastrophes lead to abrupt transitions of rule, they do so in ways that apply to the Elizabethan context of the 1590s only in a very general fashion. Were it otherwise, Greville would no doubt have destroyed these plays as well.

By the early 1590s, the two major factions at court, those headed by Cecil and Essex, had swung firmly behind the claim of James Stuart to become the next English monarch. Both leaders, along with several fellow courtiers, maintained a secret correspondence with the Scottish king, the inevitability of whose accession became

12. Gouws, *Prose Works*, 133.
13. Ibid., 93.

ever clearer during the very years that Greville was writing his plays. In 1595 the earl of Hertford petitioned once more for the legitimization of his marriage to Lady Catherine Grey. Had he prevailed, his sons by Catherine might have laid claim to the throne after Elizabeth's death, but Hertford was instead briefly consigned to the Tower for his impudence and in 1603 he dutifully proclaimed James's accession at Salisbury despite "his son's pretended title."[14] Potential royal claimants in the houses of Stanley, earl of Derby, and Hastings, earl of Huntingdon, displayed a discreet lack of interest in the throne, while the Essex rebellion of 1601 proved that even an extremely popular nobleman could not hope to break the aging queen's hold upon the hearts and loyalty of her people. The matter of succession had long ceased to be a real issue in terms of who would take the throne or by what means; the only remaining question was when.

Accordingly, the relevance of the succession to the plays of Pembroke and Greville will not be found in the various transfers of power they dramatize. No meaningful Elizabethan implications derive from Caesar's exploitation of Antony's surrender to passion, or Soliman's murder of his son and rightful heir, or from Alaham's brutal usurpation. Instead, these plays allowed their courtier authors to dramatize their awareness of the invaluable moderation of Elizabeth's rule, and their anxieties as to what might happen under the new regime. Agrippa's arguments that Caesar would be better off to bind his new subjects to him with love are echoed in the fourth chorus of *Alaham*, where kings are urged to cherish rather than oppress their subjects: "Your safest racke to winde vs vp is Loue" (line 34). The examples of inept or tyrannical rule central to each of the three plays represent not prophecies of what these courtiers expected when James took the throne but their apprehension about the dangerous potentialities of any change in governance after Elizabeth's temperate reign. The expansion of his domain might tempt James, like Caesar, into a more autocratic style of governance. With Soliman, he might be swayed by selfish and unethical counselors to reject the advice of loyal courtiers, or he might allow himself to be controlled by such favorites as Greville represented in Mohamet, Caine, and Alaham himself. Thus the countess and Greville expressed through their plays their approval of Elizabeth's rule and, with far greater emphasis, their misgivings about how her death might affect the benign rule they had so long enjoyed.

14. DNB, s.v. "Seymour, Sir Edward, Earl of Hertford"; Clapham, *Certain Observations*, 106.

In addition to these neo-Senecan tragedies, a much lighter example of courtier verse drama survives from the 1590s, for in 1599 the countess of Pembroke made elaborate literary preparations for the queen's visit to Wilton. Mary intended to present Elizabeth with a fair copy of the Psalter which she and Sir Philip had translated, and this volume was to be prefaced by her dedicatory poem to the queen and a verse elegy for her brother. She also devised a poetic entertainment, a "Dialogve betweene two shepheards," that was apparently modeled on the pastoral dialogue attributed to Sidney (possible poem 1), which had also been performed at Wilton as part of a larger "pastoral shew."[15] As we have seen, this dialogue's style is consistent with what we would expect of Sidney's early poetry. The countess adapted its superlative praise of a shepherdess to her own praise of the queen, but she wisely replaced its old-fashioned poulter's measure with a six-line stanza rhyming $a\ a\ b\ c\ c\ b$, where the a and c lines are tetrameters and the b lines, trimeters with consistently feminine endings. This change clearly reflects Sidney's influence, for of his seven uses of the same rhyme scheme, six occur in his translation of the Psalms, with his only exact duplication of the "Dialogve's" form, including its alternation of masculine and feminine rhymes, in Psalm 32. Sidney cast each of his forty-three Psalms in a different form, and the countess was quite attentive to these technical matters as she completed the translation and then revised her work for presentation to the queen. Among the diversity of forms she used in these poems are three close variations on the "Dialogve's" stanza; thus she may have chosen this form as one which Sidney had used but which she had not employed in her own Psalm translations.[16]

The countess's verse entertainment may be a trifle, yet it is also one of the most enjoyable and clever instances of dramatic praise offered to the queen. In place of the question-and-answer format that dominated the earlier dialogue, she gives Piers the last three lines of each stanza with which to contradict and correct what

---

15. John Davies of Hereford was her calligrapher for this project, but the resulting manuscript, according to Ringler, was too defaced by corrections to serve as a gift for royalty (*Poems*, 547). References to Mary's dedicatory poem, elegy, and the "Dialogve" follow the texts in Gary F. Waller's *The Triumph of Death and Other Unpublished and Uncollected Poems by Mary Sidney, Countess of Pembroke (1561–1621)* (88–95, 181–83).

16. Ringler, *Poems*, 501. Waller adduces "164 distinct stanzaic patterns . . . and 94 quite distinct metrical patterns" in her translation (*Triumph of Death*, 37).

Thenot has said about the queen in the first three lines. As a result
Thenot finds himself repeatedly accused of lying because his hyperbolic flattery falls short of Elizabeth's actual worth. It is an amusing
and lively dramatic encounter, gracefully resolved. The earlier dialogue had closed rather arbitrarily after Will's abrupt suggestion,
"Then Dick let us go hence lest wee great fokes annoy" (line 45). By
contrast, Thenot at last begs Piers to tell him

> . . . why,
> My meaning true, my words should ly,
> And striue in uaine to raise her?

The answer, which brings the dialogue to a witty and logical ending,
is that

> Words from conceit do only rise,
> Aboue conceit her honour flies;
> But silence, nought can praise her.
> (lines 55–60)

The identification of Elizabeth with the goddess Astraea throughout the dialogue enhances the difficulty of yielding her due praise.
While Ascham and Sir Edward Hoby had translated excerpts from
the Astraea story into English, the countess is the only courtier who
applied this myth to the queen. The "Dialogve" moreover, probably
influenced Sir John Davies's *Hymnes to Astraea*, a series of twenty-
six lyrics in praise of Elizabeth which appeared in the same year as
her intended visit to Wilton. Davies's choice of the Astraea myth by
itself need not imply indebtedness, for its resemblance to Elizabeth's career had been celebrated by other poets since at least
1588.[17] But it can hardly be coincidental as well that in all twenty-
six stanzas based on the acrostic "REGINA," Davies used the "Dialogve's" six-line stanza with the same pattern of tetrameter lines
and trimeter lines with feminine endings. Davies seems not to have
been a Pembroke protégé, but the Wilton entertainment was not
kept secret either, for its text appeared in the 1602 *Poetical Rhapsody*. Presumably, Davies had access to it soon enough after its

---

17. Yates, *Astraea*, 62–64. By contrast with such popular associations of the
queen with Diana, Cynthia, or the more homespun Fairy Queen, it took Professor Yates's scholarship to demonstrate that Elizabeth's subjects did in fact think
of her in terms of the Astraea myth, and even so, explicit examples of this correspondence are limited to a bare handful, with the works of Davies and the countess of Pembroke prominent among them.

composition to prepare his own poems for entry in the Stationers'
Register on November 17.

Lyric Poetry

Sidney exerted a varied influence upon the lyric verse written by
courtiers, although there is no evidence aside from his sister's translation of the Psalms that they tried, as she and Greville had with
respect to the drama, to fulfill his literary program. Sir Philip could
not well have foreseen, for example, that the nationwide mourning
after his death would elicit the most significant outpouring of funeral verse written by courtiers in English. The genre itself had
acquired aristocratic respectability by virtue of the Latin elegies
composed by Burghley, Wolley, Wilson, Lady Russell, and her son,
Sir Edward Hoby. The only prior contributions by Elizabethan courtiers in their native tongue, however, were the elder Harington's
poem on Lord Admiral Seymour (circa 1567), and Lady Russell's
epitaph for her daughter. These were followed by epigrams about
George Turberville, John Astley, and Lady Jane Rogers which Sir John
Harington termed epitaphs.[18] Meanwhile, the elegies for Sidney by
Dyer (poem 12) and the countess of Pembroke sounded sincere notes
of personal grief quite as poignant as any of the Latin funerary verses
and far superior as poetry and as expressions of sentiment to the
earlier efforts in English. Dyer's lines convey a sense of pathos that
transcends the emotional reserve characterizing so much Elizabethan lyric poetry; the intensity peaks as he contemplates suicide in
reaction to Sidney's death:

> The dolefull debt due to thy herse I paie,
> Teares from the Sowle that ay thy want shall moan,
> And by my Will my life it self wolde yelde
> If heathen blame ne might my faith distein;
> O heavie tyme!
>
> (lines 9–13)

Lady Pembroke's lines generate a similarly personal tone by addressing Sidney's "Angell spirit" directly, by dedicating the Psalms to him
as "theise dearest offrings of my hart," and with her wish, like
Dyer's, to join her brother in the afterlife:

18. These are epigrams 43, 387, and 348. Epigram 336 laments the execution
of Mary, Queen of Scots, and could be rightly considered elegiac, while epigram
210 honors Sidney but is primarily a commentary upon Harington's reputation
as a poet relative to Philip's.

> Sorrowe still striues, would mount thy highest sphere
> presuming so iust cause might meet thee there,
> Oh happie chaunge! could I so take my leaue.
>
> (lines 89–91)

Hers is the only courtier elegy to place any considerable emphasis upon Sidney's literary achievements or to observe (granted, from a retrospective distance some dozen years after his death) that his writings are now "worthilie embrac't / By all of worth, where never Envie bites" (lines 62–63). She in turn "embraces" his poetry by echoing a number of his lines in her lament for him.[19]

These very personal elegies by Dyer and the countess join the two by Gorges and Ralegh's sixty-line lament to create a spectrum of elegiac expression ranging from the rather formal praise and condolence of his fellow courtiers to the personal, emotional language of his sister and close friend.[20] Yet despite their diversity in tone and emphasis, the courtier elegies differ in several respects from the published memorial volumes that began to appear shortly after Sir Philip's death. Both universities were quick to bring out such anthologies, made up primarily of testimonials in Latin and Greek verse. During the reign of King James, Greville planned and may have composed an epitaph for Sidney in Latin verse, but otherwise Sidney's courtier friends paid tribute to him in the native English verse he had so arduously cultivated.[21] Ironically, however, the formal, printed volumes stress throughout his qualities as poet and patron even as they couch their praises in various foreign tongues,[22] while the courtier elegies deal for the most part with his virtues and his achievements as soldier and statesman.

Mary's elegy for her brother was probably the last of a variety of literary tasks she undertook in an effort to cope with his premature

---

19. "Reason's audite" of *Astrophil and Stella* 18, for instance, is converted by Mary Herbert to "this Audit of my woe." Her "thoughts, whence so strange passions flowe" (line 45), recalls *Arcadia* 41, "Like those sicke folkes, in whome strange humors flowe," and her inquiry, "such losse hath this world ought / can equall it?" (lines 75–76), echoes *Astrophil and Stella* 21, "Hath this world ought so faire as Stella is?"

20. Sandison, *Poems of Sir Arthur Gorges*, nos. 96–97; Michael Rudick, "The Poems of Sir Walter Ralegh: An Edition," no. III.

21. Rebholz, *Life of Greville*, 66n, 78. It is possible that Dyer's unrhymed elegy, poem 12, was meant to reproduce the rhythmic effects of English quantitative verse. John Shawcross informs me, however, that if Dyer actually attempted quantities in this poem, his form was arcane, perhaps logaoedic verse using the Pherecratic.

22. John Buxton, *Sir Philip Sidney and the English Renaissance*, 175–77.

death. Her prose translation of Mornay's *A Discourse of Life and Death* was a doubly appropriate response to Philip's death because first, it rendered into English an author whom Sidney admired and whose treatise, *De la Vérité de la Religion Chrétienne*, he had partially translated, although not as part of the full English version published in 1587 by Arthur Golding.[23] *The Discourse* also offered consolation for an early death by emphasizing the uncertainties and frustrations of earthly life, particularly for persons "great about Princes," and for those who are "commanders of Armies" (signature B2).

Among her poetic endeavors at about the same time, the countess translated Petrarch's "Triumph of Death," undoubtedly as another consolatory literary exercise.[24] As with Garnier's play she adhered closely to her original, including its terza rima form. Petrarch's medieval vision and dialogue offered her a reassuring deflation of the horrors of death along with meaningful analogues to her grief for Philip and her memories of him. Petrarch too bewails the loss of a superlative individual: "Vertue is dead; and dead is beawtie too, / And Dead is curtesie" (chapter 1, lines 145–46). In the second chapter, Laura's spirit converses with the poet, assuring him that her own death was a painless experience: "An unrepented syghe, not els, is death" (chapter 2, line 51); her attitude approximates the description of Sidney's last moments as recounted by George Gifford, who quoted Philip as saying, " 'I would not change my joy for the empire of the world.' For the nearer he saw death approach, the more his comfort seemed to increase."[25] The emotional crest of the "Triumph" concerns Laura's revelation of her lifelong and continuing compassion for Petrarch: "Neuer were / Our hearts but one, nor neuer two shall be" (chapter 2, lines 88–89). Her professed devotion to him, tempered by virtue, no doubt reflects the countess's passionate love for her brother as Waller suggests,[26] just as it expresses sentiments she may have longingly imagined that Philip's spirit might have addressed to her. Moreover, one section of Laura's address graphically parallels Sidney's own life and work in that it explicitly summarizes the nature of Stella's love for Astrophil and by extension, Lady Rich's love for Philip:

23. Duncan-Jones and Van Dorsten, *Miscellaneous Prose*, 155–57.
24. References to the "Triumph" follow Waller's edition in *Triumph of Death* (66–79). Waller dates this translation to circa 1593 (18).
25. Duncan-Jones and Van Dorsten, *Miscellaneous Prose*, 170.
26. *Triumph of Death*, 12.

A thousand times wrath in my face did flame
My heart meane-while with loue did inlie burne,
But neuer will, my reason ouercame:
For, if woe-vanquisht once, I sawe thee mourne;
Thy life, or honor, ioyntlie to preserve
Myne eyes to thee sweetelie did I turne.
But if thy passion did from reason swarue,
Feare in my words, and sorrowe in my face
Did then to thee for salutation serue.

(chapter 2, lines 100–108)

After borrowing from Petrarch this many-faceted analogue to her grief for her brother, Mary composed her original verse elegy to accompany the presentation copy of the Psalms which she intended to give to the queen.

To accompany her gift of the Psalms, Lady Pembroke also composed verses for Elizabeth in twelve octaves, beginning "Even now that Care. . . ." The poem acknowledges Philip's dominant role in the project but is primarily devised as a carefully structured, complimentary tribute to Elizabeth's successful reign. It at first enunciates the conflict of the gift as a distraction from the queen's "Care," her governing duties which might render offensive even the presentation of so trivial a gift, let alone its perusal. Mary then offers a twofold resolution to this conflict. First, the gift will be acceptable by virtue of Elizabeth's "grace," intellect, and goodness. Her personal qualities allow her to perform her duties with becoming *sprezzatura*, so that what "To others [were] toile, is Exercise to thee" (line 16). Second, the countess reconciles the gift with its recipient; these Psalms, as with all things English, belong by right to the English sovereign (lines 41–42). A queen, furthermore, deserves a kingly gift, and in King David's reign she may see a just (if slightly diminished) image of the glories of her own reign, for like David, she was oppressed, then enthroned by God, and then triumphant over her own and God's enemies (lines 65–72).

This rhetoric of praise through comparison with a biblical figure was of course wholly conventional; the parallel between Elizabeth and Deborah, for instance, had been vividly drawn during the queen's coronation pageantry. Sir John Harington summarized David's career in epigram 188 and dedicated it to the queen without drawing explicit parallels between the two rulers. Mary Herbert's poem, however, emphasizes the comparable royal achievements that were especially amenable to the aggressive overseas policies espoused by Leicester and Sir Philip, and which the Essex faction pursued throughout the

1590s. Thus the countess evoked the Armada defeat ("The very windes did on thy partie blowe") and celebrated England's tentative probings in the new world: "Of thee two hemispheres on honor talke, / and hands and seas thy Trophees iointly showe" (lines 77, 75–76). Foreign kings obey and depend on her: "one moving all, herselfe unmou'd the while." Latent within this praise we may detect admonition, as Margaret Hannay argues, but there is no overt warning or even mild exhortation in the text itself.[27] Instead, Philip's interest in English colonialism and a Protestant League are invoked as faits accomplis. This celebration of Elizabeth's triumph is confirmed, moreover, by its sincere and personal tone, including the frequent and consistent address to the queen with the familiar pronoun: "Thy brest the Cabinet, thy seat the shrine, / Where Muses hang their vowed memories" (lines 45–46).

By 1599, the approximate year in which Mary wrote these verses to Elizabeth and her elegy for Philip, she had completed her literary efforts in his honor. With the translation of Garnier she had produced English verse drama as specified in the *Defence*. She had completed his translation of the Psalms, and had written or translated three elegiac works in the process of mourning his loss. Meanwhile, the printed editions of his works had become universally recognized monuments to his name. The countess had sponsored the most important of these publications, culminating in the 1598 *Arcadia* which was, in effect, Sidney's collected literary works in verse and prose. The widespread circulation of most of his writings in manuscript, coupled with the surreptitious editions of *Astrophil and Stella*, legitimized as well as popularized aristocratic cultivation of poetry. The efficacy of Sidney's example is impossible to measure, of course, in isolation from simultaneous assaults against the "stigma" of poetry by other authors, including preeminently the countess's publication of *Antonie* and King James's publication of his own poetry in 1584 and 1591. The works of several courtier poets who wrote during the 1590s are nevertheless sufficiently aligned with genres and styles that Philip introduced to be considered his followers, however much they lag behind the ambitious efforts of Greville and the countess in fulfilling his literary ideals.

Although the four poems attributed to Ferdinando Stanley, Lord Strange, cannot be placed in a definite order of composition, they seem to reflect the shift in poetic style at court that was influenced

27. Margaret P. Hannay, " 'Doo What Men May Sing'; Mary Sidney and the Tradition of Admonitory Dedication," in *Silent But for the Word*, 149–65.

to at least some degree by Sidney's example. Stanley first attended court during his teens in the 1570s when the love lyrics of Oxford and Dyer were just beginning to circulate there. He emerged as a prominent courtier during the late 1580s, by which time the shift in taste was well underway. Accordingly his first and second poems in Part II are despairing lover's complaints, the latter obviously indebted to Dyer's "He that his mirth hath lost" for its diction, tone, and punning signature in the last stanza. The reliance upon alliteration in both poems, and their expression of a static, near-death despair, are the hallmarks of early Elizabethan love poetry which, as Sidney affirmed in the *Defence*, "If I were a Mistress, would never persuade me they were in love."[28]

Stanley's poem 3 is so completely different as to suggest both a greater maturity and a heightened exposure or sensitivity to the verse of Sidney and his followers. Through its first ten lines, however, this lyric closely follows a twelve-line poem from Timothe Kendall's *Flowers of Epigrammes* (1577).[29] Kendall's title affirms that his verses were "Translated out of an Italian writer," but this may be only a ploy to help justify the inclusion of this slightly risqué poem in his book. In any event, Lord Strange's dozen-odd verbal variants from Kendall's text are couched in his meter, rhymes, and rhyme scheme, making it highly unlikely that he worked independently from the alleged Italian original. Rather, the adaptation extends the poem to thirty-two lines and completely transforms its purpose and effect.

Kendall's lyric praised the mistress by recounting Cupid's discovery that her breasts were more desirable than those of his mother, Venus: "My mothers brests with milke do strowt, / but these with Nectar swell." Stanley adds vitality and conflict to Kendall's basic situation first by making himself a witness to Cupid's encounter with the lady, and then by criticizing her in direct address for permitting such intimacies. The poem's central section, lines 17–27, defines love by playing upon the word's dual meaning as both an emotional state and a name for the god of love. The negative illustrative examples are similar to Ralegh's in "Farewell false love," yet Stanley's use of enjambment and lack of alliteration mark the break with mid-century style. He turns the poem to his own seductive purposes by asking the lady to distinguish "betwyxte a man / And

28. Duncan-Jones and Van Dorsten, *Miscellaneous Prose*, 117.
29. Timothe Kendall, *Flowers of Epigrammes*, 292–93. Kendall's poem begins, "Lycoris in her bosome beares, / two Aples faire that shine."

suche a chyllde as love" (lines 31–32). The poem is neither a static blazon nor an Anacreontic incident; its argument, developed with fanciful chop-logic, imparts a light and witty tone in contrast with the hyperbolic seriousness of his previous laments.

Stanley's pastoral narrative, poem 4, is also indebted to Sidney, albeit the influence may have been transmitted through one of Dyer's poems. The prototype for this kind of pastoral is Sidney's *Other Poems* 4, an unfinished narrative written circa 1581–1583. Its opening stanzas announce a low subject and simple style. The subsequent account of rural amours derives its texture not from archaic diction but through parenthetical asides and redundant, qualifying antitheses that characterize the narrator as simple in more than just style. Sidney's "Ther was (o seldome blessed word of was!) / A paire of frends, or rather one cal'd two," and his account of Klaius as one who "Among the wisest was accounted wise, / Yet not so wise, as of unstained harte,"[30] illustrate the belabored hesitancy and backtracking that are even more fully developed in Stanley's narrative. His poem 4 may have taken its cue from a manuscript text of Sidney's narrative, or from that in the 1593 *Arcadia*, but it is more likely that he knew Dyer's poem 11, a pastoral complaint couched in a similarly naive rhetoric: "One day (I neede not name the daye)," "And all a lone (if he remayne alone that is in loue)" (lines 9, 13). All three poems thus cross the boundary between idealized pastoralism and a distanced, comic portrayal of lowlife love-mooning. Sidney's Strephon and Klaius allow their passion for Urania to disrupt the game of barley-break, with the game itself recounted at such length as to generate its own parodic force. The nameless shepherd-protagonists of the pastorals by Dyer and Stanley abandon their flocks, so powerful is their love-longing, and although both poems are set forth as narratives, neither shepherd actually finds or confronts the nymph for whom he pines. The mock-pastoral tone is most fully exploited in Stanley's work as when, for example, his shepherd deserts his flock to wander in vague pursuit of Phillis:

> Leaving the playnes, the playnes whereon
> They playd and hourelye fed,
> The plaines to them, they to the plaines,
> From plaines and them he fledd.
> Yet fledd he not, but went awaye
> As one that had free scope,

30. Ringler, *Poems*, 242–43, lines 17–18, 34–35.

> Oft loath to leave and yet would leave
> His quiet for his hope.
>
> (lines 41–48)

Throughout, Stanley nurtures the comic potential of both the shepherd's futile behavior and the narrator's tediously inept efforts to describe it.

Nicholas Breton's "Fair in a morn" closely resembles the belabored narrative style of Lord Strange's pastoral and might possibly have inspired it, although it is more likely that the influence ran the other way. Breton's poem was printed in *Englands Helicon* (1600), but it exists in two manuscripts that may have been transcribed a decade or so earlier. On the other hand, Breton's approach to his lowly subject is condescending without being derisive; his Coridon and Phillis are a well-matched pair and the poem concludes hopefully.[31] The mockery of the courtier pastorals harmonizes with the fundamental aristocratic attitude toward ordinary folk who work with their hands—they are inferior persons and thus deserving objects of scorn and laughter. As we consider the cultivation of pastoral art at Elizabeth's court, we should remember Musidorus's humiliating self-degradation as the shepherd-servant of Dametas and the pitiless humor with which Sidney describes the way his two noblemen hack to pieces the common tradesmen who attack the royal party in the *New Arcadia* (poem 2, lines 25–26).

A handful of lyrics can be assigned to courtiers who, like Stanley, were highly visible in the showier aspects of personal display at court during the late 1580s and early 1590s. Henry Noel; George, third earl of Cumberland; and Sir Henry Lee were prominent participants in chivalric entertainments at court, although only Lee's poetry can be dated with certainty and assigned to a known episode of his courtiership. The pastoral lament attributed to Noel in *Englands Helicon* (poem 2) shows Sidney's influence in its avoidance of archaic diction and its descriptive, idealized evocation of country life, short-line form, and feminine rhyme. At the same time, its anapestic and dactylic dimeters attempt rhythms unpracticed by Sidney. The earl of Cumberland's only extant poem is a lover's complaint tinged with alliteration and a few prefabricated phrases such as "sorrowe's might," and "silent grones and hart's teares." Its pentameter rhythms, on the other hand, are sufficiently supple and

31. See my "Spenser's 'Amyntas': Three Poems by Ferdinando Stanley, Lord Strange, Fifth Earl of Derby" (49–50) for the textual sources and a brief comparison of Breton's style with Stanley's.

varied to avoid any charge of mid-century doggerel, while the sincere tone and the question injected in line 5 are marks of lyric maturity unknown in Elizabethan amorous verse before Sidney.

Both of the poems attributed to Sir Henry Lee concern his retirement from participation in the tiltyard on Accession Day 1590, when Cumberland took his place as Elizabeth's champion. These poems contrast his former prowess as the queen's "man-at-arms" with his future as her "beadsman," offering up prayers to his saint from his "homely cell." The pose is "poetic" in several respects, from its invocations of Elizabeth as saint and goddess to its assurance that her knight will now retire "from court to cottage"—he was actively seeking household office as late as 1595. As Clayton concluded with regard to Lee's most certain verse, "His golden locks," it constitutes "an affecting poem and a graceful song."[32] It should be noted as well that Lee had tilted with Sidney on at least one occasion, as commemorated in the *New Arcadia* in the description of Lelius jousting with Philisides, and that Philip was the earliest known courtier to devise such poetic fictions for presentation in the tiltyard.

It is difficult to pinpoint the indebtedness to Sidney in the lyrics by Stanley, Noel, Cumberland, and Lee even in those cases where the influence of a specific Sidnean model seems likely. The impetus of these poets away from mere imitation toward variation and extension of received styles and themes also characterizes the output of Sir Robert Sidney, and next to Greville, Robert is the most ambitious follower of his brother's example as a lyric poet.

About 1596, Sir Robert Sidney began transcribing his poems into the unique manuscript which preserves them, now BL, Additional Manuscript 58435. Although many of these entries were subsequently revised by the author, all were derived from prior copies so that it is impossible to say how long before the mid–1590s Robert was writing verse, or how long he continued to make entries in the manuscript.[33] It is probably safe to conclude that the collection dates from the last decade of Elizabeth's reign, with the provision that some poems and many revisions may be Jacobean. Robert's

32. Thomas Clayton, "'Sir Henry Lee's Farewell to the Court': The Texts and Authorship of 'His Golden Locks Time Hath to Silver Turned,'" 275.

33. Hilton Kelliher and Katherine Duncan-Jones suggest 1596 "as the terminus a quo" for the transcription, primarily from their analysis of the manuscript's watermarks ("A Manuscript of Poems by Robert Sidney: Some Early Impressions," 113). For the transcription from previous drafts see Katherine Duncan-Jones, "'Rosis and Lysa': Selections from the Poems of Sir Robert Sidney" (241).

sixty-six complete poems and one fragment show many signs of indebtedness to Sir Philip's work: a dozen-odd verbal parallels reveal the younger Sidney's close attention to his brother's major writings, as do his use of trochaic meters in seven poems, cultivation of pastoralism, and his fondness for correlative patterns.[34] Robert's debt to other courtier poets, noticeably Greville, Dyer, and Ralegh, is limited to minor turns of phrase or the adaptation of an occasional motif from their verse.[35]

In contrast with Greville and the countess of Pembroke, Robert did not use poetry to express his political philosophy, nor did he dedicate his verse to any significant extension of Philip's program for English poetry. The make-up of his collection most closely resembles Gorges's "toyes and vannatyes" in its mixture of occasional works, translations, and lyrics which appear to be largely or wholly fictional. As with *Caelica*, certain themes are repeated and expanded, yet it would be difficult to show that Robert's emphasis upon absence, betrayal, or any other aspect of love gives his poetry a sense of direction as does the increasing condemnation of women in Greville's sequence. On the other hand, Robert's systematic numbering and renumbering of all but eight of his poems has prompted critical expectations that they are (or were going to be) organized into a meaningful sequence.[36] Sidney numbered his thirty-five sonnets in order, 1 through 34, with both the thirty-second and thirty-third being headed "Son: 32." Interspersed among the sonnets are another thirty-one complete poems, also numbered sequentially 1 through

34. Kelliher and Duncan-Jones, in "A Manuscript," cite a number of parallels in the commentary to the poems they transcribed (138–42); and see the commentary passim to P. J. Croft's *The Poems of Robert Sidney.* Subsequent citations of Sidney's verse follow Croft's edition.

35. Kelliher and Duncan-Jones, in "A Manuscript," argue for Ralegh's influence on sonnet 22 and song 19 (118, 139, 142), while Croft notes the echo of Ralegh's "Calling to mind" in sonnet 3. Sonnet 32/33 (Croft, *Poems,* 258) parallels the ideas and in part the diction of Greville's *Caelica* 3. The first lines of sonnet 12, "Who gives himself, may ill his words deny; / My words gaue me to you, my word I gaue," recall *Arcadia* 47.13–14 as Croft notes (312), but are equally close to Dyer's poem 2, line 60, "I gave my word, my word gave me, bothe word and gift shall stand."

36. Duncan-Jones believes that the manuscript "is more than just a collection of 'loose' lyrics" ("Rosis and Lysa," 242). Croft argues for an overall thematic and metrical design in the collection while assuming that "the Elizabethan sonnet sequence . . . exists not to tell a story but to portray the perennial experience of the lover in a series of sometimes meditative, sometimes dramatic monologues" (*Poems,* 106). He concludes his section on "The Sequence as a Form" (104–14) with the observation that it is probably not in an order that the author considered final.

23, with the last entry in this series unnumbered. These lyrics are designated as pastorals or songs, except for the sixteenth item in the series which is entitled "Elegy. 16." Of the remaining, unnumbered poems, four occur after sonnet 34/35, and three after elegy 16. In addition, Sidney assigned a different set of numerals to sixteen of the first eighteen poems in the manuscript, beginning with sonnet 4 which he annotated, "This showld bee first."[37] What all these numbers may mean and what design, if any, Robert intended for the entire collection begins to emerge with an examination of the individual poems.

Although no other copies of any of Sidney's poems have come to light, at least a few of them must have been seen by others. The collection is inscribed on folio 1 "For the Countess of Pembroke," yet it seems unlikely that Robert submitted this much revised working notebook for her perusal. Sonnet 24, with its references to "bitter storms, that beate thee from the shore," and forsaking "the mine whose golden store / must make thee ritch," may well have been addressed to Ralegh after his return from the "Guiana" voyage of 1595. Ralegh's kinship with Sidney's wife, Barbara, helps to make this identification plausible, while the topical allusion accords with a date of composition and transcription in the mid–1590s or thereafter. A copy of the poem entitled "Vpon a Snufkin" was clearly presented with a gift to an unidentified lady.[38] Sidney's most intriguing occasional poems are sonnets 11–14 and the first quatrain of another which comprise his "Crown of sonnets unfinished." The lady whose charms are celebrated in this series of poems also commissioned them, for the poet explains that he would not presume to praise her in verse except that "yowr wil the charge on mee doth lay" (sonnet 11, line 9). Efforts to identify her necessarily become entangled with identifying the other women who are specifically designated in the larger sequence: the lady interlocutor of song 6, Lysa of pastoral 7 and sonnet 28, and Charys, whose name replaces Lysa through authorial revision in the latter poem, and who is the subject as well of elegy 16, song 20, and song 21. These biographical questions are in turn critical to our understanding of the role of poetry in Robert's life and the exact nature of his collected verse as a sequence.

Sonnet 12, the second in the "Crown," is pivotal to any attempt

---

37. Croft, *Poems*, 122.

38. Kelliher and Duncan-Jones suggest that "For the Countess of Pembroke" might amount to a delivery direction rather than a dedication; they also argue for the connections between Ralegh and sonnet 24 ("A Manuscript," 114, 118).

at identifying the lady for whom it was composed because of this significant clue:

> For ere on earthe in yow trew beauty kame
> my first breath I had drawn, vpon the day
> Sacred to yow, blessed in yowr faire name
> (lines 9–11)

Kelliher and Duncan-Jones were first to establish that Robert's birthday on November 19 was sacred to St. Elizabeth of Hungary, and they proceeded, on the assumption that Lysa, Charys, and Elizabeth of the "Crown" represent a single woman, to identify her tentatively with Elizabeth Carey, daughter of the second Baron Hunsdon. Her name may be shadowed in the Lysa and Charys pseudonyms just as Rosis in pastoral 7 is an obvious pseudonym for Robert Sidney by analogy with Philip's Philisides.[39] Croft noted however, that during the 1590s Sidney had no known connections, official or social, with Mistress Carey, but rather than offering an alternative identification, Croft denied that any real woman is meant either here or in Sidney's lyrics generally. Robert's assertion in sonnet 12 that he was destined to love the lady is expanded by Croft into a comprehensive neoplatonic reading whereby the poet's birthday is sacred not to the obscure St. Elizabeth, but to the mistress herself for the very reason that she and the poet were predestined to love one another. For Croft, this ideal love, a passion that "transcends the body," is the pervasive subject of Sidney's amorous lyrics and a source of their collective unity, yet this view overlooks both the celebrations of St. Elizabeth's day at court and Sidney's focus upon standard amatory conventions which are anything but platonic.[40]

St. Elizabeth's Day may have been an obscure feast in the Catholic Church calendar as Croft argued, but it had been revived and enthusiastically observed by courtiers of Robert's generation. Essex was probably the first to seize on this heavenly saint's day as an apt occasion for worshiping that earthly saint to whom he dedicated his hyperbolic praise. In 1588, apparently for the first time, the Accession Day tilting was resumed on November 19, as it was in 1589, 1590, 1594, 1596, 1598, 1599, and 1600. Indeed, a court correspondent specified that the tournament of 1590 was held on St. Elizabeth's Day, with Essex, Cumberland, and Lord Burgh the challengers. Thus, by the mid–1590s when Sidney was composing his

---

39. Ibid., 122–23.
40. Croft, *Poems*, 94, 92–93, 105ff.

lyrics, his birthday was an established day of celebration in the court calendar and he could be sure that any courtier who read his sonnet 12 would inevitably connect the date with a woman named Elizabeth.[41]

Croft's neoplatonic interpretation of Sidney's verse fares well enough in such poems as sonnet 24, where Robert is content "if loue doe liue, thogh liue in cares and feares," or song 4, which affirms that "True pleasure is in loue / onely to loue / and not seeke to obtaine." The difficulties arise when we compare this approach to love with that in pastoral 7, where shepherd Rosis attempts to shield "Lysa fayr Nymph" from the cold air:

> and wth glad arms her body sweet did fold
> where whyle into his brest
> thowsand contentments sancke
> and wth broad eyes hee thowsand beauties dranck
>
> ·
>
> in his close brest, a hot fyre soon did make
> w[ch] when hee felt to ryse
> wth eys where sparcks did swarme
> and wth hot sighs hee sowght the Nymph to warme.
>   (lines 15–18, 21–24)

Neither this piece nor the desire for a kiss in sonnet 28 ("and of her lips the Nectar someway tast"), nor the poet's "boyling hart" in "Once to my lips,"[42] wherein he begs and receives a kiss, fits the neoplatonic interpretation imposed on the collection by Croft. Sidney's amorous verse does not consistently presuppose any philosophical system. In the context of the "Crown," for example, destiny is a general term quite as compatible with Calvinism as with Platonism. Robert's verse belongs to an essentially medieval, Petrarchan tradition of love poetry, its philosophical underpinnings based upon the system of courtly love insofar as anything systematic can be posited for so wide-ranging a literary corpus. Sidney portrays himself in the majority of his poems as a victim of unrequited love, a man scorned and at times betrayed by a superior mistress, his heart ablaze with fires ignited by the suns of her eyes, his hopes drowned by the floods of her disdain. Song 4, sonnet 22, and elegy 16 offer good examples of his conventional stances, stances utterly contrary to the suggestion that the poet's birthday or any-

41. Alan Young, *Tudor and Jacobean Tournaments*, 203–5. Richard Brakenbury to Lord Talbot, November 20, 1590, in Lodge, *Illustrations of British History*, 2:419–20.
42. Croft, *Poems*, 282.

thing else about him is sacred to the mistress. In sonnet 1, as a further example, the lady holds him in no special regard; she acknowledges him "but wth the rest," and even this represents something of a high point in the beloved's esteem for him since he is otherwise rejected outright by the lady or ladies who figure in his lyrics.

Among the original love poems, song 6 is the only exception to the dominant mood of rejection and longing. Sidney here adapted the pilgrim-lover dialogue of the popular "Walsingham" ballad to his personal circumstances by imagining how news of his death in the Low Countries might be received by his wife.[43] The lady dwells "neer ritch Tons sandy bed," which was corrected by Robert to "Medwayes sandy bed." Both Tonbridge and the Medway River are located near the Sidneys' family seat at Penshurst, Barbara's favorite residence. The lady learns from the pilgrim that her knight died near the sea, and that "absent ioies did him kil," suggesting that the poem was occasioned by one of Robert's five tours of duty at Flushing during the 1590s.[44] The absence which caused his death extrapolates upon Sidney's own frequent complaints of lengthy, enforced absences from home and family. As a love poem, the song's strategy for praising the lady resembles the despairing laments of Oxford and Dyer in which their impending deaths will likewise result from their longing for unobtainable mistresses. By dealing with the post-mortem experience, however, Sidney's lyric more nearly approximates Dyer's "Amaryllis" (poem 8), but with this noticeable variation in the lady's favor. Unlike Amaryllis, the heroine of song 6 has not caused her lover's death by rejecting him, for unlike the mistresses of Robert's other poems (or the typical sonnet lady), the lady of song 6 is devoted to him; she berates the pilgrim for the bad news he brings and vows that

> In my brest his tombe shall stand
> . . . .
> where loue wth truthes stedfast hand
> this Epitaf shall wryte
> (lines 129, 131–32)

43. A text of the ballad is attributed to Ralegh in Bodl., Rawl. poet. MS 85, but his claim to the poem is rejected in C. S. Lewis's *English Literature in the Sixteenth Century Excluding Drama* (519–20), and by Rudick ("Poems," 69–70).

44. Croft, *Poems*, 79. The bridge at Tonbridge crosses the Medway; no river Ton flows near Penshurst, and Sidney apparently revised Song 12 to compensate for this error. Aside from the knight's death, the details of this verse are well-suited to Robert and Barbara's circumstances during most of the 1590s. The dates of Sidney's service at Flushing are conveniently charted in Millicent V. Hay's *The Life of Robert Sidney, Earl of Leicester (1563–1626)* (138).

The characterizations of both knight and lady agree with the external evidence that Robert and Barbara shared a particularly loving and happy marriage,[45] with this poem a tribute above all to Barbara's sincere commitment to the relationship.

In song 6, as in the lyrics that deal with parting and separation, Robert's poetry seems to grow naturally out of his actual experience. The majority of his works that complain of unrequited love, however, are clearly at odds with his enjoyment of a successful marriage. They may, of course, be nothing more than creative exercises, yet despite Robert's devotion to Barbara, she was not the only woman in his life, for his attraction to other ladies of the court was an ill-kept secret. Early in 1597 the queen qualified her praise of Sidney by noting that his "mynd was to much addicted to the presence chamber" (that is, the household chamber where the maids of honor ordinarily waited), and Sidney's agent at court, postmaster Rowland Whyte, also warned him that "Two letters of yours sealed with gold and the broad arrow head, directed to two of the maydes," were known to have been delivered at court. Scarcely a year later, Whyte informed Sidney that he was reputed unfit for the office of Vice-Chamberlain of the household because "you are too young and too amourous to be conversant among the ladies," an assessment substantiated by this notice of his efforts to initiate a newly sworn maid of honor during the Christmas festivities of 1601: "Mrs. Nevill . . . is sworn maid of honour; Sir Robert Sydney is in chase to make her foreswear both maid and honour."[46] Accordingly, if Lysa, Charys, and the Elizabeth for whom Sidney wrote his crown of sonnets are not poetic fictions but women who actually figured in his life, they should be sought among the women who waited on the queen.

Although Robert is not known to have pursued Elizabeth Carey, he was assuredly concerned with the fortunes of another woman of this name, Elizabeth Brydges, as Whyte's account of her difficulties in April of 1597 makes clear: "The Queen hath of late used the faire Mrs. Bridges with words and blowes of anger, and she with Mrs. Russel were put out of the Coffer Chamber. They lay 3 nights at my Lady Staffords, but are now returned againe to their wonted wayting."[47] The maids of honor ordinarily lodged at court in the Coffer Chamber, although a list of court lodgings for 1601–1602 places

45. Hay, *Life*, 173–77; Croft, *Poems*, 72–74.
46. Croft (*Poems*, 85–87) and Kelliher and Duncan-Jones ("A Manuscript," 124) have assembled these references from HMC, De L'Isle and Dudley, vol. 2, and CSPD, 282/48, for the incident involving Mary Neville.
47. HMC, De L'Isle and Dudley, 2:265.

Mistress Brydges there along with three other ladies of the Privy Chamber. "Mrs. Russel" was one of the dowager Elizabeth Russell's daughters, either Anne, the maid of honor, or Elizabeth, who served in the Privy Chamber. Whyte reports the incident not as a mere matter of court gossip, for it is clearly "faire Mrs. Bridges" who makes it newsworthy while Mistress Russell is a secondary figure. Elizabeth, the daughter of Giles Brydges, third Baron Chandos, served as a gentlewoman of the Privy Chamber from at least 1596, for she is listed on the New Year's rolls in that capacity in 1597, 1598, 1599, and 1603.[48] Her connections with Robert's immediate circle of friends at court are also revealed by her liaison with the earl of Essex, for in February of 1598 Whyte wrote, "Yt is spied out by envye, that 1000 [Essex] is againe fallen in love with his fairest B. Yt cannot chuse but come to 1500 [the queen's] eares; then is he undonne, and all they that depend upon his favor."[49] The "fairest B." is again Elizabeth Brydges, while Sidney himself was prominent among the earl's associates who might suffer should the queen punish him insofar as Essex faithfully pressed suits at court for Robert in absentia. However, neither the earl nor Mistress Brydges seems to have incurred significant royal displeasure from the resumption of their romance. Elizabeth's place in the Essex-Sidney circle is also confirmed by the Welsh poet and pamphleteer Thomas Powell, who dedicated his *Loves Leprosie* to Robert in 1598. In 1603 he dedicated *A Welch Bayte* to Essex's close friend the earl of Southampton, and concluded it with verses addressed to Sir Edward Dyer and to "the vnparaleld blesst disposition The Lady Elizabeth Bridges" (signature E 1v).

In addition to her name and social connections, Elizabeth's romantic intrigues at court argue as well that she was the Elizabeth of

48. BL, Egerton MS 2026, f. 23. In 1603 she not only exchanged New Year's gifts with the queen as gentlewoman of the Privy Chamber, but apparently received a "Free Gift" as mother of the maids (Mrs. Jones likewise appears twice on the rolls in 1589 as holder of the same two offices, Nichols, *Progresses*, 3:20). Brydges appears as a maid of honor in the funeral accounts, with a later reference in this document apparently owing to her office as mother of the maids (PRO, LC 2/4 (4), ff. 19, 45v).

49. HMC, De L'Isle and Dudley, 2:322. For the lady's identification as Elizabeth Brydges see Thomas Birch, *Memoirs of the Reign of Queen Elizabeth* (2:380), and George Edward Cokayne, *The Complete Peerage* (3:127). The anagram on "Lady Elisabeth Bridget [*sic*]," "Bright Lady Bes" which John Manningham recorded in his diary in November of 1602 was probably written to commend the Earl's "fairest B" (Robert Parker Sorlien, ed., *The Diary of John Manningham of the Middle Temple, 1602–1603*, 141).

Robert's "Crown," the Lysa of two later poems, and the enticing but faithless lady who figures in a number of his other lyrics. Sidney presumably accosted her shortly after she came to court in the mid–1590s, just as he was prompt in pursuit of the new maid Mary Neville in 1601. Perhaps Elizabeth asked him to write poetry for her in emulation of Lady Rich, for whom, it was by then well known, Robert's brother had written *Astrophil and Stella.* Following the "Crown," in pastorals 8 and 9, song 10, and sonnet 27, the poet is the victim of a mistress who has broken her vows and deserted him for another man, all of which was entirely in character for Mistress Brydges. She presumably dropped Sir Robert for the earl of Essex well before 1598, while in December of that year another suitor, Charles Lister, charged her with wheedling large sums of money and expensive gifts from him in return for her promise of marriage.[50] The equally transient nature of Robert's romances at court is indicated by sonnet 14, the fourth one of the "Crown," in which he defends himself from the lady's accusation that he abandoned another woman for her: "Ah let not mee, for changing blame indure / whoe onely changd, by chang to finde the best." Thereafter, Sidney revised sonnet 28 to adapt at least this one poem to the praise of a new mistress.

The substitution of Charys for Lysa in sonnet 28 serves no discernible poetic function, and is most easily explained as an indication that Lysa and Charys are two different women. The pastoral pseudonym Charys, meaning grace, finds a precedent in Sidney-circle poetry in Dyer's Charamell (sweet grace), one of the rival lovers of his poem 8. Robert's Charys may refer to Mary Neville, but if Kelliher and Duncan-Jones are correct in suggesting that the name is an apt poetic pseudonym for Carey, then the mistress of sonnet 28, elegy 16, and songs 20 and 21 was most likely Anne Carey, who served as a maid of honor from about 1598 to the end of the reign. She was the daughter of Lady Catherine Paget-Carey and Sir Edward Carey, who succeeded John Astley as master of the Jewel House. Anne performed in the masque honoring the Russell-Worcester mar-

---

50. CSPD, 269/10, December 11, 1598, and see Hasler, *House of Commons* (2:479), where Brydges is described as a widow of Lambeth Marsh. Lister was appointed gentleman usher extraordinary during Queen Mary's reign but did not hold office at court under Elizabeth. That Lister's intended bride was Elizabeth Brydges of the court is suggested by his assertion that he gave her ten pounds in Lady Stafford's chamber, where Elizabeth and Anne Russell had taken refuge in 1597. Lister affirmed that she also borrowed 150 pounds "to venture with my Lord of Essex," presumably on the "Islands Voyage" of 1597.

riage in June of 1600; Whyte names her in a letter to Sidney in which he describes the masque, albeit he lists Anne without further comment as the third among eight participants.[51] Still, her name and her arrival at court as a maid in the late 1590s make her a plausible successor to Elizabeth Brydges as the subject of Robert's verse, while both identifications mesh with a transcription of the poems into the notebook in the general order of their composition.

If Charys in fact represents a new love, the dissolution of Robert's affair with Lysa is chronicled in the three poems which lead up to sonnet 28 and the three that follow it. These are the last poems in the notebook which deal with betrayal, and it is worth noting that betrayal implies prior acceptance, although, as in the Philisides-Mira poems, the successful aspects of courtship receive no poetic representation. Robert's poems, in their received order, thus constitute a sequence only in the sense that they relate in chronological order his poetic responses to a random succession of aulic amours extending over a period of years. The underlying circumstances would presumably form a disjointed narrative of sorts: his desertion of an unnamed mistress for Elizabeth of the Crown; his anguish at enforced separation from his wife as expressed in song 6; his acceptance by Elizabeth-Lysa, and her betrayal of him for another man; their rapprochement and a second betrayal, followed by his infatuation with Charys. From an aesthetic standpoint, this hypothetical chronology is formless in itself, while its component events are obscured by Robert's adherence to poetic convention whereby love's failures receive most of the attention.

The numbering of the poems represents, accordingly, neither parallel sequences nor any particular order for the sonnets and songs at all. It reflects in part the concern for technical form which both Robert and the countess of Pembroke inherited from Philip, as well as the younger Sidney's identification of the items out of which a genuine sequence of poems was to be fashioned. He presumably meant to number the last entry in the notebook as song 24, but regarded the seven other unnumbered poems as unfit for his larger design. The three unnumbered octaves after elegy 16 might well have qualified as "Songs," or more likely as a "Pastoral" in the case of "From fayrest brest, a shepheard tooke a knott." Sidney may have viewed them, however, as experiments rather than products of his emotional experience. They are shorter than any of the numbered poems except for the eight lines of song 17, and it would not be

51. Collins, *Letters and Memorials*, 2:201.

surprising to find that he translated them from originals in ottava rima. The two translations from Seneca and one from Montemayor were disqualified by their subjects and inspiration, as were, no doubt, the "Snufkin" verses.

A snuffkin (variously snoskyn, skimskyn, snufekyn) was a muff, an article of clothing frequently embroidered, bejeweled, and presented to the queen as a New Year's gift.[52] Robert's poem probably accompanied a snuffkin that he sent to Elizabeth from Holland as a New Year's present in 1597. The list for that year records under knights who received gifts from the queen, "To my skuvskyne for my Pantaples." Sidney's name does not appear in this part of the roll, but he is listed among the knights who gave presents to Elizabeth. Strangely, however, his gift went unrecorded—the line after his name was left blank. And Sidney is the only knight without a corresponding entry in the roster of those who received gifts from Elizabeth, although the last entry among the knights reads, "By my Skimskine for my pantable, one skimskyn of black veluet imbroidered all ouer like bee hives and bees of seede pearles." Pantables (pantofles) probably refer here to a kind of indoor slipper, whether a part of Sidney's gift or the queen's gift to him it seems impossible to tell. The most likely solution to these mysterious and unprecedented entries in the 1597 New Year's list is that Elizabeth was so taken with Robert's gift and its accompanying verses that she playfully nicknamed him her snuffkin (skimskine), and had their exchange of presents enrolled accordingly, leaving the Sidney entry incomplete. If the "Snufkin" poem was in fact written for the queen on this occasion, it was not sufficiently enthralling to procure for him the leave from his post that he had been requesting for months. It does support however, the hypothesis that Robert numbered only the poems that concerned his romantic interests.

As amorous verse, Sidney's numbered poems resemble the earliest courtier efforts by Oxford and Dyer in which actual courtship of the queen's favor was transmitted through hyperbolic fictions. In the wake of Sir Philip's intervening contributions to courtier verse, however, Robert set forth his traditional motifs in a straightforward style and in pentameter or shorter measures far removed from the alliterative phrasing and long-line forms that dominated courtier love poems of the 1570s. In a further departure from the earliest

52. See Nichols, *Progresses*, 3:8–9 (skimskyn), 3:452, and gifts from Mrs. Elizabeth Howard in the 1581 list and from gentlewomen Sackford and Raynsford in that of 1603.

models, and again under his brother's influence, Robert began the reorganization of his lyrics into a legitimate sequence, the initial phase of which appears in what Croft terms the "Alternative Sequence."[53] Sixteen of the first eighteen poems in the manuscript are assigned different numbers, beginning with sonnet 4 which is now to come first. Robert's intentions are signalled by his omission of sonnets 7 and 8. In the first of these he describes himself as "scornd, repulst, hartbroken," and in the second he has lost the lady beyond recovery. The poems which received the alternative numbering are appropriate, on the other hand, to the initial stages of a standard poetic love affair. Sonnet 9, the second in the revised sequence, explains that he had often "past the ioies and greefes in loue," and had renounced desire until he met her, thus establishing the background of the affair just as *Astrophil and Stella* 2 explains the gradual development of Astrophil's love for Stella. The remaining lyrics are concerned primarily with celebration of the lady's worth and professions of the poet's love for her. Although Croft interprets sonnet 6 as "the one thoroughly despondent sonnet in the alternative sequence," the dejection is mitigated by the fact that only night and not necessarily the lady's disdain has separated them, leaving him to dwell upon her "crueltee" in a state of absence which tends to magnify his sense of failure.[54] This is not to say that Sidney meant to reorder his poems into a narrative account of a single love affair. He had scarcely enough variety in his collection to complete such a task. From this beginning however, it appears that he was attempting a coherent organization of his poems along thematic lines, perhaps in the manner of Greville's *Caelica*. If so, his emphasis in the remaining lyrics upon absence, betrayal, and the ultimate renunciation of love would have provided ample material for devising an aesthetically unified sequence.

Robert's documented "chamber" romances, coupled with plausible identifications of Lysa and Charys, indicate that most of his poems grew out of his extramarital romantic interests, just as *Astrophil and Stella* was elicited by Philip's passion for Lady Rich. Robert's muse, however, was not oppressed by the struggle between reason and passion or the guilt induced by an illicit, perhaps adulterous affair. Indeed, he defends his love for Charys by arguing that

> Reason in mee neuer tyred
> to consider her, doth say

53. Croft, *Poems*, 124.
54. Ibid., 113.

> that of sens not ledd astray
> onely shee showld bee desyred
> (song 20, lines 39–42)

The essence of Robert's collected verse concerns the hopelessness of the chase, given the aloof perfection of an often faithless mistress. Convention dictated that love poetry emphasize longing and failure. In adhering to this tradition, Sidney blurred the extent to which actual events spawned his poems so that we cannot determine where genuine emotion gives way to the exaggerations of amorous rhetoric.

It is tempting to explain Robert's somewhat cavalier approach to his love poems as evidence that he wrote them in grudging emulation of Philip's dedication to the muse, almost as an obligation of his place as brother and heir. His letter to Harington, however, in which he speaks of praising the *Orlando* at court, and asks Sir John to send him verses, testifies to a lively and sincere interest in poetry. His divergence from Philip's style and earnest intensity of approach shows the same creative independence that marks Greville's rejection of idealized love in *Caelica*. The traces of Sidney's influence in the lyrics by Lord Strange, Noel, Cumberland, and Lee are even less distinct, although it is difficult to believe that Philip's example had no bearing at all upon their creation. Artistic independence, however, is here commensurate with the independent status of these poets as courtiers: both are matters of degree. Greville and Robert Sidney, with many others, were subordinate to the earl of Essex but nevertheless his courtier peers. They were not his dependents in the same sense as were such clients as his secretary, William Jones, or his chaplain, William Alabaster. Unless they were out of favor, courtiers remained aloof from admissions of servile subordination to anyone but the queen herself. Accordingly, their assertion of social independence through personal display at court would necessarily be compromised by blatant mimicry of their courtier peers. As a result, Sir Philip's closest imitators were professional, out-of-court writers, while the courtiers who followed his example in the writing of poetry consistently differentiated their work from his.

7

Devotional Verse

A disaffected courtier, the former esquire for the body Sir Nicholas Poyntz, excused his absence from court by asking, "how wyllingly, tell me, wold you go into hell, to salute the devills their, though you weare standing upon the brink thereoff?"[1] The Elizabethan court was occasionally described as a godless place, as in Donne's Fourth Satire, yet such criticism ordinarily came from outsiders and is akin to the same popular mythology of the court which affirms that courtiers routinely wrote love sonnets, never published their works, and generally fell victim to arranged marriages. It is true that denizens of the court often acknowledged its shortcomings, but they almost always did so with a resigned ambivalence that sidestepped explicitly religious issues. Ascham, for example, warned that great courtiers might by their example lead others to "be made cold in Religion," but he couched his warning in prudently hypothetical terms.[2] Sir George Carey reminded a gentleman pensioner friend that "you in court [are] daily in hazard to be daungerously poisoned with the secrette stinges of smilinge Enemies," yet there is little of Poyntz's bitterness and much of the commonplace in Carey's subsequent comparison of the advantages of country life to that of the court.[3] A similar conventionalism and skirting of religious issues typifies most of the references to the court in courtier verse. Sidney's poetry never characterizes the religious climate there although he designates envy as its peculiar vice in both his translation of Horace (*Certain Sonnets* 12), and in his reference to "clime-fall Court, the envy-hatching place" (*Other Poems* 4, line 61). The

1. Poyntz to his sister, Lady Anne Heneage, May 19, 1575, HMC, Finch, 1:21.
2. *The Scholemaster*, in Wright, *Ascham*, 220.
3. Carey to John Scudamour, June 15, 1585, PRO, C 115, box M 15, letter 7364.

"Atheists" of Greville's *Caelica* 29 reject Cupid rather than the Christian godhead in their adherence to the faction and fortune that "ever dwells / in court, where wit excels." Accordingly, they banish true love to the forests, as it is banished to the countryside in Sidney's *Other Poems* 7. And Ralegh, himself banished from court in the mid–1590s, attacked both church and court in "Go soul, the body's guest," but stopped short of attributing impiety to the royal household.

The competition for royal favor, efforts to appease or quell rivals, and attempts to enlist the support of courtier allies invited envy, deceit, backbiting, and flattery as well as the vanity of courtly display in its myriad forms. Yet it would be unfair as well as imprudent to assume from these failings that the queen's household, the residence of the head of the Church of England, was a godless institution. If Elizabeth's personal concern with religion was rather less intense than it had been for her sister Mary, religious services were nevertheless a regular and prominent part of life at court. The queen's processions to chapel, and the services themselves, were well-attended semipublic displays of the sovereign's piety. A "great plenty of ladies" were said to be gathered at court in March of 1574 to hear sermons, and with good cause, for the queen's chaplains included some of the best and most learned preachers of the age, men such as Henry Parry, Thomas Blague, and William Barlow. Sir John Harington recalled hearing one sermon at court which was so powerful that "though Courtiers eares are commonly so open as it goes in at one ear and out at the other," yet this one impressed them all.[4] The efficacy of these services was also invoked as evidence that the earl of Essex had abandoned his philandering ways and was now attending all the public prayers and sermons at court. Preaching might occur on a daily basis, as was the case after Easter in 1600 when Dudley Carleton observed that he "came too short for Dr. Andrews who preached on Monday morning: on Tuesday we had Dr. Parrie."[5]

The ready availability of religious instruction at court is reflected in Heneage's maxim, "Heare learne we vice, and look one vertues bookes" (poem 4, line 5). And when we consider that Heneage, Mildmay, William Cecil, and Sir Philip Sidney were among the more devout courtier poets, it is surprising that they produced little or no divine poetry before the 1580s. They had, after all, ample precedent

4. HMC, Rutland, 1:101; Harington, *Supplie*, 140–41.
5. Birch, *Memoirs*, 2:122, letter of September 7, 1596; PRO, SP 274/86.

for doing so. Both Sir Thomas Smith, who became principal secretary in 1572, and Robert, earl of Leicester, had made verse translations of selected Psalms before the queen's reign, although they are not known to have written verse thereafter. Substantial verse paraphrases of the Bible by Wyatt and Surrey circulated in manuscript and were also in print as early as the 1550s. The earlier Elizabethan courtiers, however, failed to perpetuate this tradition. Granted, their private devotional poetry may simply have been lost, yet the only evidence that it might have been written at all consists in Sir Nicholas Bacon's hymns and prayers, none of which is necessarily Elizabethan.

It is, in fact, doubly unlikely that much in the way of early divine poetry by Elizabethan courtiers has been lost. First, between 1558 and 1570, as we have seen, the dominant mode of courtier verse was humanist in inspiration and set forth in Latin quantities. To render the Bible into Latin verse, however, would have contradicted a central tenet of the Reformation, the accessibility of Scripture in the vernacular. Indeed, any treatment of religious subjects in classical meters would necessarily have savored of Catholicism. The pervasive distrust of vernacular poetry, meanwhile, prevented devout courtiers from treating spiritual matters in so trivial a fashion. Poetry itself had first to be raised up within the court through the wholly secular efforts of Oxford, Dyer, Sidney, and the queen herself before it could evolve into a suitable medium for religious expression.

During the last two decades of the reign this process was sufficiently complete that some half-dozen courtier poets turned out various types of divine poetry. Elizabeth's meditation in French verse, of which 270 lines survive in the queen's hand at Hatfield House, may be the earliest significant work in this vein. The poem's context is obscure; it is perhaps a relic of the Anjou marriage negotiations which ended in 1582. Philip Sidney, his sister, Mary, and Sir John Harington wrote metrical Psalms, while the earl of Arundel translated several devotional poems while he was imprisoned in the Tower. There, Arundel also composed his lengthy meditation upon the four last things, and Essex likewise wrote his penitential "Passion" in the Tower a few days before his execution in February of 1601. Finally, it is probable, if beyond demonstration, that at least some of Greville's religious lyrics in the *Caelica* series were written before James took the throne.

Sidney's metrical versions of Psalms 1–43 far surpass most previous efforts of the kind, yet his translations have been rightly criticized as inferior to his best work and significantly inferior to his sister's skillful completion of the project. Philip's relatively halting poetry has convinced a number of scholars that the Psalms are early work,[6] although their faults are probably rooted in causes other than artistic immaturity. A coherent picture of his major concerns as a courtier poet in 1584–1585 would envision him at work revising the *Arcadia*, translating the Psalms, and composing his lost version of DuBartas's *Première Semaine*. In the *New Arcadia* he was transforming his Mediterranean romance into a heroic story consistent with the theory set forth in the *Defence* that poetry should move the reader to virtuous action. Thus, his essentially simultaneous attention to divine poetry should not be construed as middle-aged renunciation of secular vanity, but, rather, his mature cultivation of an art form whose vanity Philip had never conceded in the first place.

Sidney viewed the poetic books of the Bible as right imitations of "the unconceivable excellencies of God," excellencies he hesitated even to associate with poetry lest he "profane that holy name, applying it to poetry, which is among us thrown down to so ridiculous an estimation."[7] He obviously meant for his translation of the Psalms to be an intricate tribute to God as well as a poetic representation of Divine majesty. The appropriate vehicle for this task was, of course, lyric verse, in that the Psalms were simply songs, both of which he classified as "that lyrical kind of songs and sonnets: which, Lord, if He gave us so good minds, how well it might be employed, and with how heavenly fruit, both private and public, in singing the praises of the immortal beauty."[8] From so deferential a treatment of divine poetry he turned immediately in the *Defence* to analyze the failure of English love poetry. It was thus predictable that Sidney confined his muse primarily to the less serious subgenre of the amorous lyric before graduating to the translation of biblical lyrics. He took extraordinary pains with the technical forms of his Psalms precisely because he deemed himself sufficiently beyond his apprenticeship to accomplish this solemn task. In contriving a dif-

6. J. C. A. Rathmell places them before *Astrophil and Stella* (*The Psalms of Sir Philip Sidney and the Countess of Pembroke*, xxvi). In "The Poetry of Sir Philip Sidney" (*English Literary History* 12 [1945]: 254), Theodore Spencer termed them his earliest efforts at writing poetry. William A. Ringler (*Poems*, 500, li) opted for circa 1585, noting that Sidney used forms and "rhetorical structures that he had already mastered." Citations of Sidney's metrical psalms follow Ringler's edition; references to the countess of Pembroke's psalms follow Rathmell.

7. *The Defence*, in Duncan-Jones and Van Dorsten, *Miscellaneous Prose*, 80, 77.

8. Ibid., 77, 116.

ferent form for each Psalm, he made full but innovative use of the varied meters, complex stanzas, and combinations of masculine with feminine rhymes that he had already developed and perfected.[9] As further evidence that this was not early work, moreover, the quantitative measures which he had esteemed so highly as he finished the *Old Arcadia* are lacking here, just as they were demoted to a single line given to Dametas in the *New Arcadia*.

In part, the inferiority of Sidney's Psalms result from the demands he imposed on his technical virtuosity from the beginning of the project. Their complex rhyme schemes were frequently compounded in difficulty by his choice of meters, for twenty-five of his forty-three Psalms are dominated by tetrameter or shorter lines. His longest lines are the hexameters of Psalm 18, yet his only other uses of this meter alternate it with trimeter lines in Psalm 2 and tetrameters in Psalm 24. His performance was further encumbered by his respect for the original text, as signalled by his enumeration of the corresponding biblical verse numbers in the left margins of his translation. He was far less prone than was Mary to rearrange the order of subjects treated in the Psalms or to amplify, let alone revise their content.

Given these restrictions it is not quite fair to suppose that Sidney failed to apply all of his creative powers to the translation, or that he was unimaginative in the conceptual formulation or phrasing of these poems. Rather, his muse was torn between his allegiance to Scripture and the demands of poetic form. In meeting these demands he necessarily sacrificed syntax, and with it that felicitous, compelling expression denoted in the *Defence* by the word *energia*. Thus Philip worked an excellent metaphor into Psalm 25, "But Lord remember not / Sins brew'd in youthfull glass" (lines 25–26), where the Geneva text has only "Remember not the sinnes of my youth." The metaphor is flawed, nonetheless, by over-compression to accommodate the trimeter line. An extra word or two ("The sins I brewed," perhaps), would give the line a more idiomatic ring. Too often, meter forces similar omissions, usually modifiers required for the natural expression of thought: "Let name of Jacob's God," "If I have been unkynd for friendly part," or, "That Name of God a fable is" (Psalms 20:3, 7:10, 10:16).

An even more common problem is the wrenched and inverted syntax: "Thou under his Dominion plac't / Both sheep and Oxen wholy hast"; "He rests me in green pasture his" (Psalms 8:25–26,

9. Ringler notes that he employed only two of the stanza forms he had used in his previous writings (*Poems*, 581).

23:4). Granted, the demanding Petrarchan sonnets of *Astrophil and Stella*, with their octaves ordinarily rhyming on just two sounds, elicited similar inversions and omissions, as was the case in a number of Sidney's other poems. The difference here is a matter of both degree and frequency. Such faults are simply too awkward and too characteristic of his style as a psalmist. Nouns followed by possessive pronouns, for example "in Tabernacle Thine," "let mercy thine" (Psalms 15:1, 30:31), are particularly affected expressions altogether avoided in *Astrophil and Stella*. Such anomalies in the Psalms too often confound whole lines and stanzas. Where the Geneva text records that God "setteth me upon mine high places. He teacheth mine hands to fight" (Psalm 18:33–34), Sidney wrote that "I Climb'd highest hill, he me warr points did show." And despite their enjambment, these lines from Psalm 27 fall short of an appropriate lyric dignity and grace:

> One thing in deed I did and will
> For ever crave, that dwell I may
> In house of High Jehova still,
> On beauty His my eyes to stay
> And look into
> His Temple too.
> (lines 19–24)

Ironically, in both their rhetoric and the tendency of short-line stanzas toward a sing-song rhythm, the effect of Sidney's Psalms often harkens back to the "drab" verse which his advances in technique had largely rendered passé. In the final analysis, these forty-three Psalms, however ingeniously contrived, are only competent in execution. We cannot know, however, what he might have made of this unrevised fragment, nor to what use beyond private devotions he might have put this, the first important work of divine poetry by an Elizabethan courtier.

His sister's translation, and frequent retranslation of the Psalms apparently began as a private devotional task in memory of Philip, but the final results were disseminated in at least sixteen contemporary manuscript copies, while individual Psalms also circulated in manuscript. Sir John Harington owned two copies of the Sidney-Pembroke Psalter, one of them by 1595, apparently, when he quoted two lines from Mary's Psalm 137 in his *Metamorphosis of Ajax*. And late in 1600 he sent three Psalms of Mary's translation to Lucy, countess of Bedford.[10] Lady Pembroke had John Davies of Hereford produce

10. Ringler, *Poems*, 552; McClure, *Letters and Epigrams*, 87, Sir John to the countess of Bedford, December 19, 1600.

the Penshurst copy as a gift for the queen in 1599, with the elegy for Philip and her dedicatory verses to Elizabeth serving as the preliminaries to this volume. Robert Southwell aside, these Psalms probably constitute the finest substantial collection of Elizabethan divine poetry and possibly, as Waller contends, the best "post-Reformation religious verse in English before Herbert's *The Temple.*"[11]

Lady Pembroke's muse was nevertheless subject to many of the same shortcomings that diminished the success of her brother's portion of the work. A pronounced mid-century ring is imparted to her version of Psalm 91, for example, with its inversions, missing adjectives, and the alternation of trimeter and tetrameter lines rendering its rhythm equivalent to internally rhymed poulter's measure:

> To him the highest keepes
>   In closet of his care,
> Who in th'allmighties shadow sleepes,
>   For one affirme I dare.
>
>   (lines 1–4)

Her tendency toward alliteration and end-stopped lines occasionally produces similarly old-fashioned effects as in Psalm 107:

> How many wantonly missled,
> While, fooles, they follow Follies traine,
> For sinne confined to their bed,
> This guerdon of their folly gaine!
>   (lines 41–44)

Still, these traits of the "drab" style and of contorted, unnatural phrasing are less prevalent, less virulent, than in Philip's Psalms. Mary's revisions of his Psalms 22 and 26 are notable for their correction of his awkward syntax, although it does not appear that she consciously labored to avoid the particular rhetorical flaws of her brother's verse. Her greater facility grew naturally out of her overall development as a poet and from her willingness to meditate upon the Psalms and then set forth their essential meaning with some independence from the precise ordering and diction of her Scriptural sources.[12] In so doing she deviated admirably from the

11. Waller, *Triumph of Death,* 36.

12. Rathmell explores the results of her meditative practice in his introduction (*Psalms,* xx–xxv). The development of her creative powers, as revealed in the revisions she made between the Rawlinson and the Penshurst manuscripts is well treated by Waller (*Triumph of Death,* 28–34). The best analysis of her originality and craftsmanship in the translation is Waller's *Mary Sidney, Countess of Pembroke: A Critical Study of Her Writings and Literary Milieu* (chapters 7 and 8),

compulsive literalism with which she had rendered Garnier's
Antonie.

The countess's Psalms achieve their superior phrasing within the
confines of a technical complexity little short of her brother's most
intricate work: Psalm 49 is a sestina, Psalm 55 extends to seventy-
two lines on only three rhymes, Psalm 104 consists of fourteen
octaves, each rhyming *a b a b b a b a.* Intermingled with these are a
number of established forms such as rhyme royal, ottava rima,
heroic couplets, and a final Petrarchan sonnet, Psalm 150. She demonstrates a full mastery of Philip's metrical experiments as well,
including a total of ten Psalms in quantitative meters. The original
version of Psalm 89, according to Derek Attridge, "can probably be
considered as the most successful Elizabethan attempt to naturalise
the hexameter." In contrast with Greville's fitful control of trochaic
rhythms in *Caelica* 56, Lady Pembroke writes consistent trochaics
in more than a half-dozen Psalms and is able to alternate trochaic
and iambic lines purposefully (if not to brilliant effect), in such
Psalms as 81 and 119, sections K and P. She devised different forms
for all but four of the Psalms,[13] not counting the unique forms in
which she originally cast some of them, only to abandon them upon
revision in the Penshurst Manuscript.

Where Philip's translations were primarily influenced by the
Marot-Beza Psalter, his sister's completion of the project was significantly inspired by Sidney's own accomplishments as a poet. The
countess incorporated into her Psalms particular and striking effects
from his works such as the trochaic tetrameter couplets of her
Psalm 99, with its alternating masculine and feminine rhymes exactly duplicating the rhythmic effect of *Astrophil and Stella* song 8.
Similarly, the last four lines of all six stanzas of Psalm 143 echo the
rhythm and rhymes of the refrain to *Certain Sonnets* 30. Her emphatic repetitions, "heere O heere" (Psalms 132:25) and "so shall, so
shall it be" (108:40), reveal her sensitivity to a rhetorical device
Philip often used to lend a personal, emotional tone to his verse.[14]

---

and see Beth Wynne Fisken's "Mary Sidney's *Psalmes:* Education and Wi[sd]om"
(166–83) for a thoughtful appreciation of the countess's achievement as psalmist.

13. Derek Attridge, *Well-Weighed Syllables,* 203, 205. Rathmell counts four
pairs of repeats (*Psalms,* xvii), but I read predominately iambic rhythms and
regularly recurring trimeter lines in Psalm 32, unlike the trochaic tetrameters of
Psalm 71, while the rhyme scheme of Psalm 70 differs from that of Psalm 144.

14. Cf. "Too long, too long asleepe thou hast me brought" (*Certain Sonnets*
31.7); "I, I, o I may say, that she is mine" (*Astrophil and Stella* 69.11); "Yet sighs,
deere sighs" (*Astrophil and Stella* 95.1). Waller notes other parallels (*Mary Sidney,* 199).

Attentive as she was to Philip's emphasis on form and even to his rhetorical patterning, Mary's greater willingness to venture beyond the strictly literal boundaries of Scripture is well-illustrated by her representation of the heavenly court in terms of the Tudor court. Both Philip and Mary rendered God's token or sign as "livery" (Psalms 34:78, 106:10), or a "Cognisance" (86:43), the heraldic badge worn by retainers of nobility or royalty. In two Psalms Mary enunciates the central principle of courtiership, access to the sovereign, in the plea that God will "Admitt to presence what I crave" (88:7), and that God's favor will bring its recipients "In nearer place their happie daies to spend" (55:6). In Psalm 65 she envisions those who are admitted to the heavenly court as being added to the divine "checkrole," just as Elizabethan court attendance in such offices as the guard and band of gentleman pensioners was recorded in checkrolls kept by clerks of the cheque. The queen's attendants in Psalm 45 become "maides of honor," while in Psalm 84, God's court is equated with a household where one may serve as a "household-man," a term that designated a member of the king's retinue until it gave way to "courtier" toward the end of the fifteenth century. Similarly, the Geneva Bible's "dore keper" (Psalms 84:10) becomes for Mary "a porter at thy gates" who would rather serve in that lowly post "Than dwell a lord with wicked mates" (39–40).[15] Perhaps Mary's dedicatory verses to Elizabeth imply admonition, even criticism, as Hannay argues,[16] yet in Psalm 47 she extenuates the praises of royalty in keeping with the interpretation of this Psalm provided in the Geneva gloss. There, "great princes" are termed "shields to the feloship of his Church," while in Psalm 47 Mary describes them as "Princes, the shields that earth defend" (line 20). Her emphasis here may be interpreted as favoring the institution of kingship rather than Elizabeth's reign specifically, although it is more difficult to see in Psalm 72 anything less than an outright and gratuitous allusion to Cynthia-Diana as the "many-formed queene" who waxes and wanes while the "kings sonne" is groomed for eventual succession to the throne. Thus the queen and her court had noticeably influenced the countess's translation of the Psalms well before she employed Davies of Hereford to prepare it in fair copy for Elizabeth.

It is possible that at least the first canto of Spenser's *Faerie*

15. The sentiment is closely echoed by Sir William Cornwallis's suit to become groom porter: "So I may be about her majesty, I care not to be a Grome of the Schoulerye" (PRO, SP 12/263/75). For "household-man" see David Starkey's "Introduction," 3.
16. Margaret P. Hannay, "Doo What Men May Sing," 151–52.

Queene also influenced Mary's work. Psalm 78 is a narrative account of the exodus from Egypt and wandering in the wilderness which Mary casts in ottava rima. She expands the Geneva reference to Egyptian "riuers" (verse 44) into the graphic description of "All that rich land, where over Nilus trailes / Of his wett robe the slymy seedy train" (lines 153–54), evocative of Spenser's epic simile in *Faerie Queene* 1.1.21 where "old father Nilus" floods Egypt and "his fattie waves doe fertile slime outwell" from which "fruitful seed" hordes of disgusting creatures are spawned. And just as Spenser follows up this simile with that in stanza 23 of the shepherd engulfed by a swarm of "cumbrous gnattes," so Mary works into lines 161–64 her own epic simile of a shepherd who wisely houses his flock as a storm approaches. Spenser's wording may also be reflected in the "watry Nilus" of Psalms 105:59 and in the "fertile Nilus" of 106:58.

It is tempting but ultimately misleading to attribute several of the countess's stanza forms to Spenser's influence as well. Psalm 100 is, after all, cast in the same rhyme scheme as most of the *Amoretti* sonnets, while in another ten Psalms plus the dozen stanzas of "Even now that Care," her dedicatory poem to the queen, she writes Monk's Tale octaves that lack only the final *c* rhyme of the Spenserian stanza. In Psalms 94, 98, 104, 108, and 146 moreover, she plays near variations on this form; every stanza in these Psalms begins with the *a b a b b* rhyme scheme and exceeds the final couplet of rhyme royal. It is possible that she was merely extending the rhyme royal scheme she used in four of the Psalms, and it is certainly difficult to see how she could have copied Spenser's *Amoretti* forms, first published in 1595, given Michael Brennan's discovery that she had finished translating the psalter by 1594.[17] If she revised Psalm 100 to copy Spenser's sonnets after their publication, no trace of her earlier version has survived, and since neither the sonnet nor octave form occurs among Philip's works, the most likely inspiration was neither his work nor Chaucer's but King James's *Essayes of a Prentise*, published in 1584. This little volume included twelve sonnets in the "Spenserian" form plus a translation of Lucan in five Monk's Tale stanzas, the exact rhyme scheme for ten of the countess's Psalms and her verses addressed to the queen. Thus, while major aspects of her skill as a technician can be traced to her brother's example, King James was an important secondary influence upon the forms in which she cast her translation of the Psalms.

17. Michael Brennan, "The Date of the Countess of Pembroke's Translation of the Psalms," 434–36.

The Psalms are Lady Pembroke's foremost poetic accomplishment and a notable one at that. In contrast with her timidly literal
translation of Garnier, she here took control of both her scriptural
sources and Philip's rendering of the first forty-three Psalms. The
creative independence with which she carried out the task is well
illustrated by the epic simile she added to Psalm 78, her reordering
of subjects within her translations, and even her wholesale departures at times from all but the most basic devotional impetus of her
originals. Waller found, for example, no "connection except in the
most general sense" between the biblical versions of Psalm 117 and
her treatment of it beyond the fact that "both are hymns of praise."[18]
The aspects of style isolated in Beth Wayne Fisken's study, "a complicated, conversational syntax, studded with questions, exclama-
tions, interruptions, and parenthetical interjections," elevate Mary's
best Psalms to that vibrant plane of poetic energy that Philip aspired
to in the *Defence* and achieved in many of his other verses. In the
abrupt utterances so characteristic of this style, and particularly in
the dramatic openings of Psalms 52, 115, and 119, Waller argues for
the germ of the metaphysical style.[19] It seems safe to conclude that
her meditative approach to the Psalms, with its emphasis upon their
devotional force rather than line-by-line recreation, allowed her to
write metrical versions superior to her brother's in their grace and
expressiveness and yet little short of his efforts in their technical
intricacy.

The Sidney-Pembroke Psalms no doubt reflect quite personal
religious commitments, and ones set forth intentionally to display
what English poetry might do in the service of religion. By contrast,
the religious verses of Harington, Greville, and the earl of Arundel
show the degree to which the writing of poetry had become a natural
and well-established mode of expression for Elizabethan courtiers
by the end of the reign. Harington, the most public of courtier
authors, apparently chose not to send his devotional works into
general circulation. In Greville's case, the privacy is less surprising
than the fact that he found verse a fit vehicle for the serious investigation of moral and divine issues. As a prominent courtier during
the 1570s and 1580s, the earl of Arundel apparently wrote no poetry,
yet he composed over one thousand lines of devotional verse, original and translated, while imprisoned in the Tower between 1585 and
1595. The half-dozen late Elizabethan courtiers who wrote religious

18. *Mary Sidney*, 196.
19. Fisken, "Mary Sidney's *Psalmes*," 171ff.; Waller, *Mary Sidney*, 200.

verse testify to the final triumph of this long-denigrated art form as an accepted component of their innermost personal lives.

The luster of Lady Pembroke's accomplishment as a psalmist was fully appreciated and celebrated by Harington, although he made little effort to emulate, much less surpass her work. Beyond his quotation from her Psalms in the *Metamorphosis* and the Psalms he sent to Lady Bedford, he praised Mary's entire translation in epigram 398, quoted from Psalm 104 in his marginal notes to the *Aeneid*, and in his notes at the end of that volume he set forth the third stanza of her fifty-first Psalm. He lamented, moreover, in his "Treatise of Play" (circa 1594), that "those precious leaves . . . are unpublyshed, but lye still inclosed within Wilton's walls lyke prisoners, though many have made great suyt for theyr liberty."[20]

Two aspects of Harington's response as a courtier poet to the Sidney-Pembroke Psalter stand out at once. First, he seems not to have been aware that Philip was at all involved with the project. Sir John referred to both his manuscripts of the work as the countess of Pembroke's Psalms, and after noting in the *Supplie* that "it was more then a womans skill, to expresse the sence so right as she hath done in her verse," he suggested that her collaborator had been not her brother, but the household chaplain, Gervase Babington.[21] Accordingly, he must have obtained his copies of the Psalms at second hand from a member of the Pembroke circle other than the countess herself, perhaps from Dyer or Sir Robert Sidney, with both of whom he was good friends. The doubts he expressed in the *Supplie*, which were set down during Mary's lifetime, are that much less surprising, however astonishing in their smug antifeminism.

Rather more unexpected is Harington's enthusiasm for these Psalms despite their decidedly Calvinistic flavor. The extent of this coloring has been surveyed by Waller; it emerges clearly in Psalm 80, for instance, where Israel is characterized as God's "ellected one," a metaphorical vineyard "ordained not to wither."[22] Sir John's religious sympathies tended in quite the opposite direction. His epigrams, as we have seen, favor the Catholic viewpoint, and in epigram 365 he denied the charge that he was himself a papist. Meanwhile, his frequent expressions of contempt for Puritans clearly indicate that it

20. *Nugae Antiquae* (1779), 2:159.
21. Harington, *Supplie*, 129. See Ringler for Harington's reference to his manuscripts and refutation of the charge that Babington could have materially influenced the translation (*Poems*, 452, 501).
22. Waller, *Mary Sidney*, 215–18, and see his " 'This Matching of Contraries': Calvinism and Courtly Philosophy in the Sidney *Psalms*," 22–31.

was not the doctrine of these Psalms that he admired nor Sir Philip's part in them, but simply their poetic excellence.

When Harington turned to his own translation of the Psalms, beginning with the seven Penitentials, he made no effort to devise new stanza forms nor otherwise to follow the demanding technical and rhetorical standards set for him by Philip and Mary. The variety of complicated forms that Harington employed in his epigrams is missing here, as if he consciously declined to compete with or emulate a fellow courtier so openly. His first four Psalms are written in the common "sixain" stanza, 102 is in rhyme royal, and 130 and 143 are in variants of ottava rima. As Karl E. Schmutzler suggests, he probably referred to the prose Psalter appended to the *Book of Common Prayer* as he composed these Psalms,[23] yet his phrasing owes almost nothing to this source, being much closer to the Geneva text and to the Sidney-Pembroke Psalter he so much admired. Harington's use of both sources is tellingly illustrated in the last stanza of his sixth Psalm, where the first line probably borrows from Sidney, while the Geneva text largely accounts for the wording of both the metrical versions thereafter:

> But gett yee hence from mee yee wicked ones
> For god hath heard the voice of all my weepinge
> . . . .
> Now yow my foes that made my greife your game
> Confounded are, put back, and vext with shame.
> (Harington)

> Gett hence you evill, who in my ill rejoice,
> . . . .
> For God hath heard the weeping sobbing voice
> Of my complayning.
> . . . .
> They shall be sham'd and vext, that breed my dyeng:
> And turn their backs, and straight on backs appeare
> Their shamfull flyeng.
> (Sidney, Psalms 6:25, 27–28, 30–31)

Awaie from me all ye workers of iniquitie: for the Lord hathe heard the voyce of my weping. . . . All mine enemies shalbe confunded & sore vexed: thei shal be turned backe, and put to shame suddenly. (Geneva, Psalms 6:8, 10)

Sir John's reliance on feminine rhyme in the Psalms denotes his ordinary practice, as in the epigrams, a carryover from his extensive

---

23. Karl E. Schmutzler, "Harington's Metrical Paraphrases of the Seven Penitential Psalms: Three Manuscript Versions," 248.

translation of Italian rather than in imitation of Sidney's style. His inverted syntax and derivative wording render these Penitentials a competent but uninspired beginning to his subsequent translation of the rest of the Psalter.

Nothing prevented Harington from circulating both his metrical versions of these Psalms and his rather wooden translation of the Lord's Prayer, and indeed he did prepare his complete Psalter for the press about 1612. His third devotional work, however, a translation of verses on the "Fifteen Devotions," with the emblems that were meant to accompany them, was far too Catholic a work to have been prudently disseminated during Elizabeth's reign. He explained his attitude toward pictorial aids to worship in epigram 338 where he condoned his wife's habit of praying before saints' pictures or the crucifix with only the caveat that "though I do allow thow kneele before it, / Yet would I in no wise you showld adore it." These sentiments are Protestant enough, yet aside from the emblems, the "Fifteen Devotions" were themselves too closely associated with the rosary to be accepted by Protestant courtiers.

The themes of the religious lyrics in Greville's *Caelica* sequence contrast sharply with Harington's affinity for Catholic worship and are indeed more emphatically Calvinistic than anything suggested by the Sidney-Pembroke Psalms. Idols, for example, are repeatedly attacked by Greville: in the Manicheans, who worshiped no idols, "yet idols did in their ideas take" (poem 89, line 3), or Nature "like an idol" luring us in our youth (poem 96, line 5), and the "earthly idols" of poem 109, line 20.[24] The tone, however, rarely resembles that of Harington's flippant, derisive satires in those epigrams dealing with moral failures of man and the Church. Instead, Greville laments human depravity and prays for salvation. He may well have been the first Elizabethan courtier since Sir Nicholas Bacon to compose original meditative verses. Echoes of poems by Sidney and Dyer in *Caelica* 86, 95, and 96 suggest early dates of composition, just as allusions to "The exchequer man" in 94 and the prince's "few dark friends" in 101 and 102 connect those poems with Greville's disillusionment under King James.

Greville does not otherwise glance at the court nor attack its immorality in his religious lyrics, yet the court is reflected here in the style of these poems. He uses such standard elements of courtier love lyrics as the sonnets of *Caelica* 86, 100, and 103; refrains in 98, 99, and 109; the familiar correlative pattern in 86; and the stanza of metaphors that concludes *Caelica* 96, their listing, one per line,

24. References to Greville's poems follow Bullough, *Poems and Dramas*.

producing an effect identical to the opening stanzas of Ralegh's "Farewell false love." In condemning the emptiness of worldly pleasure, Greville even borrows a figure from Dyer's earlier lament in the "satyr-like" man of *Caelica* 96 who kisses the deceptive flame as does the satyr of Dyer's poem 7.

Through these religious lyrics, with their adaptations of amatory forms and rhetoric, Greville made his overall sequence place poetry in the service of virtue. *Caelica* traces an essentially medieval pattern from the exploration of earthly temptations through their rejection to a steadfast repentance and longing for salvation. The title thus aptly names first the apparently heavenly woman who inspires Greville's love poems, and finally the eternal goal and true heaven to which he aspires as the sequence closes. In its final ordering, *Caelica* moves from the rejection of love to the rejection of all sensual pleasures in 86–87, countered by the denial in 88 that man can understand divine mysteries. These themes are varied and repeated in *Caelica* 89, 93, 94, 96, and 97, leading up to 98 where the poet's first-person voice, last heard in the farewell to Cupid of *Caelica* 84, returns in the prayerful refrain, "Lord, I have synn'd, and my iniquitie, / Deserves this hell; yet Lord deliver mee." *Caelica* 99 continues with an equally personal but more hopeful refrain, "Even there appeares this saving God of myne," and the sequence ends with the plea that Zion and its Church will be delivered from their sinful folly. Compared to the uncompromising rejection of women and love earlier in the work, *Caelica* ends on a guardedly optimistic note.

In contrast with Greville's works, the religious poetry of Philip Howard, earl of Arundel, borrowed nothing at all from the lyric language and forms developed by courtiers, although his longest poem glances at the queen and some of her courtiers as Greville's religious verse does not.

Arundel's high favor with Elizabeth had continued from about 1575 until 1583, when his religious sympathies began to gravitate toward the old faith. Thereafter, his complicity or suspected association with Catholic agitators such as Charles Paget and Thomas Morgan led to increasingly strained relations with the crown. In December of 1583 Elizabeth and the French ambassadors feasted with him at Arundel House in London, but he was confined to house arrest on the spot for a period of over three months while the Privy Council probed his Catholic connections.[25] After his formal conver-

25. John Hungerford Pollen and William MacMahon, "The Ven. Philip Howard, Earl of Arundel, 1557–1595," 41, 56, 351.

sion to Catholicism in September of 1584, he allowed his nonconformity to become a matter of open defiance at court. In November he broke ranks from the elaborately hierarchical ceremonies marking the opening of Parliament, and while the queen and her court heard a sermon in Westminster Abbey, Arundel loitered by himself in the aisles. During the winter of 1585 he escorted Elizabeth to Chapel, but then returned to the Presence Chamber or Privy Chamber in order to avoid actual participation in the Protestant services.[26]

So public a display of religious deviation by a man of Arundel's stature in the realm could not long be tolerated. These were the years when the conspiracies on behalf of the Queen of Scots forced the government to undertake increasingly oppressive measures. The earl's house arrest had undoubtedly been triggered by the state of general alarm in the wake of the Throckmorton plot. At about the same time late in 1583 Lord Thomas Paget had fled to the continent, and there was every appearance of a general dissolution of nobility and courtiers away from their allegiance to the queen. The Bond of Association, which pledged its subscribers to assassinate anyone who attained Elizabeth's throne through violence, began circulating in 1584. The discovery of William Parry's plan to kill the queen in February of 1585 further heightened the state of official anxiety, insofar as that was possible. Arundel knew that his blatantly Catholic stance was untenable, and he secretly took shipping for the continent in April, only to be captured at sea and returned to England. That it was the queen's dignity and image as head of the Church that was at stake is shown by her offer to release Philip on condition that he "bear the sword as usual before" her in procession to Chapel and wait upon her during divine service and evensong.[27] Upon his refusal, he was convicted in 1587 of intriguing with Catholics and attempting to fly the country without license. He was subsequently tried in 1589 on charges of high treason and attainted, although the warrant for his execution was never signed and he was left instead in close confinement in the Tower, where he died in 1595.

26. Ibid., 105–6.
27. Ibid., 319. Why Arundel would have ordinarily borne the sword of state on these occasions is unclear, although he was in a position to claim two major offices of state. Henry VIII had created his grandfather, the earl of Surrey, earl marshal, with provision that the office would descend to his heirs male. Also, Philip's maternal grandfather, the last Fitzalan earl of Arundel, had served as Lord High Constable at the time of Elizabeth's coronation. See William J. Thoms, *The Book of the Court*, 243, 239.

For this nobleman, the end of his career as a successful courtier marked the beginning of his career as a poet and man of letters. During his imprisonment he studied the inspirational works of many Catholic authors, translated Lanspergius's book, and wrote three treatises on the "Excellency and Utility of Vertue."[28] The poetry he translated for the Lanspergius volume suggests that he had paid scant attention to the poetry of his courtier peers; there is no hint, for example, that he was personally present to hear the verses from the "Four Foster Children of Desire" show of 1581, yet he rode as a co-challenger with Sidney on that occasion. Arundel's muse dredges up the old-fashioned, long-line forms and the rhetoric associated with them. His style is exactly what we might expect of a courtier of the 1560s or early 1570s who had decided, rather suddenly, to try his hand at poetry. The "Hymne of the Life and Passion of our Saviour Christ" is set forth in iambic octameter couplets, as are the couplet beginning "Use ever silence in thy tongue," and the similar quatrain which begins, "Have special care to rule thy tong." "O Christ the glorious crown" is in poulter's measure, while both the dialogue translated from Marulus and the prayer from the Sydenham Manuscript are in fourteener couplets. These verses are plagued by awkward inversions of syntax despite the distances between rhymes, by heavy caesuras, end-stopped lines, and the unalleviated sharp contrasts between alternating stressed and unstressed syllables. The Marulus dialogue between Christ on the cross and a Christian (poem 1) has some merit as an imaginative catechism in reverse, with the neophyte asking his superior to explain his earthly mission. Unfortunately, the wooden style of Arundel's couplet-by-couplet interchange minimizes the dramatic force inherent in the situation:

> Christian.
> What forced thee, who alway wert,
>   From every sinne so pure,
> Such grievous paines, and death with all,
>   So gladly to endure?
>
> Christ.
> The love I bare to man that him,
>   Whom sinne had clogged so:
> Our blood (by clearing well) might make
>   Above the stars to goe.
>   (lines 11–20)

28. Duke of Norfolk, ed., *The Lives of Philip Howard, Earl of Arundel, and of Anne Dacres, His Wife*, 106–7.

And Christ's extended warning about the inconveniences of spending eternity in hell often revives the effects of mid-century alliterative doggerel:

> The quenchelesse fire, the uglie darke,
>   Which never shall abate,
> The gnawing worme for aye, for aye,
>   The bitter, wretched state.
> The griesly groanes, the sorrowes sharpe,
>   The woefull weal-aday;
> The endles plaints, the cursed ill,
>   Which never will away.
>
> (lines 79–86)

For all their antiquated technique, the earl's translations in verse are at least appropriate to his plight as a victim of religious persecution and, after 1589, as a man facing apparently imminent death. The ninety-two couplets of "Almightie Lord whose love to us" is both a hymn to God and prayer for mercy and forgiveness. "O Christ the glorious crown" likewise praises the Son and begs forgiveness, while the Marulus dialogue explains the nature of Christ's sacrificial mission and the necessity of rejecting earthly pleasure for dedication to God and salvation. All are, in short, spiritual exercises well suited to strengthening the convert's resolve and helping him to cope with his imprisonment and the threat to his life. They were also appropriate for dissemination to his coreligionists, and the author of the *Lives* asserts that Philip arranged for his translation of Lanspergius, with its accompanying verses, "to be printed for the furtherance of Devotion."[29] The Sydenham prayer, with its emphasis upon attaining God's grace and cultivating Christian virtues likewise fits the circumstances of Arundel's imprisonment, but the 756 lines of his "Fourefold Meditation" are not wholly in keeping with his need for spiritual strength in anticipation of a traitor's death.

The title of Arundel's long and apparently original composition in Folger, MS. Z.e.28, affirms that it was "written against Christmas: 1587," more than a year after he had been found guilty in Star Chamber on the original charges. His punishment in that case had been a ten-thousand-pound fine and imprisonment during pleasure but not the threat of a death sentence. According to two other manuscripts of the "Meditation," he had composed it after his attainder for high treason in 1589, a verdict which did carry the death penalty. This latter dating would be preferred were the poem itself a

29. Ibid., 106.

more satisfactory means of preparation for death, yet the Folger title is both more specific and more in keeping with the nature of the "Fourefold Meditation" as a devotional poem.

The treatises that Philip might have consulted to prepare for impending execution, such as Gaspar Loarte's *Exercise of a Christian Life* (translated by Stephen Brinkley in 1584) or Robert Parsons's *First Booke of the Christian Exercise* (1582) urged their readers to imagine that the hour of their death was at hand. They were then to concentrate upon the agony of dying, the grief of leaving family and friends, and the fear of an unknown afterlife throughout all eternity.[30] Now, the earl's poem dwells upon all these miseries as well as the Last Judgment, the torments of hell, and joys of heaven, but not from the standpoint of his personal apprehension about such matters. Nor does his meditation dwell upon his past sins, penitence for them, or his hope of salvation. Rather, the poem is addressed throughout to a sinner for whom all hope has vanished. The addressee is a man who is reminded that, in anticipation of his demise, "Thy wife doth howle, hir shrikes do pearse the skies" (signature B 1v). On the day of Judgment Christ speaks in despair to the culprit, "O thanklesse wretch thou me shalt see nomore, / But dwell with him, that had thy heart before," after which Satan claims him as one who "vow'd to serve me all his dayes" (signature C 2–2v). The lost soul bewails his misery in hell through some six stanzas of first-person lament. Worst of all, Arundel begins the fourth section of his poem, "Of the joyes of Heaven," with this vindictive exhortation:

> But lift awhile thy cursed eyes on hye,
> And see what joyes, the blessed there possesse:
>   That by the sight, thy torments may increase,
>   And for thy life, thy sorrowes never cease.
>   (signature E 3)

The subsequent description of heaven is imparted less as a goal to be attained than as a further means of punishing the lost soul to whom the "Meditation" is addressed, although the conclusion does urge

> That all these joyes and paines which thou dost see
> May move thy minde, to leade thy life arighte
> ·

30. The typical program is analyzed in chapter 4 of Nancy Lee Beaty's *The Craft of Dying: A Study in the Literary Tradition of the "Ars Moriendi" in England;* see especially pages 163–70 for the "I-thou" relationship between the authors of the treatises and their readers. References to Arundel's "Meditation" follow the text of the Huntington Library's copy of STC 13868.7 unless otherwise noted.

Least thou in vaine dost waile thy wretched state,
When time is past, and wailing comes too late.
(signature G 1v)

Thus, instead of a vivid evocation of the poet's own death and judgment, Arundel fashions a verse treatise that harshly condemns its reader. Where we would expect a meditation stressing penitence and a closer bond with God, we find a powerful exhortation to reform one's sinful life. Of course, the poet might be seen as addressing himself, in the manner of J. Alfred Prufrock, throughout the poem, an approach, however, that would blunt the personal immediacy of the meditation which the treatises so strongly emphasized. The work is likewise out of step as a warning to the earl to mend his ways, since his imprisonment necessarily minimized his opportunities for indulging the worldly vanities excoriated in the poem. As Arundel meditated on the Last Things before he began to write, it apparently struck him that his oppressors' souls were in a far more perilous state than his own. We know furthermore that he recognized individual courtier opponents in Heneage, Walsingham, and Leicester, the more puritanical grandees of the court.[31] His poem took the form, accordingly, of a treatise on the necessity of preparing for one's final reward with the decided implication that little hope remained for a positive outcome.

The "Meditation" not only allowed Arundel to represent the spiritual disasters awaiting his persecutors, he also took the opportunity to snub his sovereign without implying that she too was damned. Four stanzas of the poem were omitted from the 1606 print, no doubt because their exaltation of the Virgin Mary was considered too "Romish" for publication even in Jacobean England. In characterizing the "Quene of heven," Arundel developed a telling contrast with that earthly virgin he had formerly adored even to the neglect of his own wife. Arundel's Mary is blessed "Above al women," and she makes the City of God "drunke . . . with delite," in contrast with the misery inflicted on English Catholics by the Elizabethan regime during the 1580s. The unflattering comparison emerges most pointedly in the assertion that "In glorie she al creatures passeth farre, / The Mone her showes [shoes], the Sunne her garments are," wherein Elizabeth's most personal metaphoric symbols are placed in abject subordination to the Queen of Heaven.[32]

31. Norfolk, *Lives*, 61–62, 124.
32. The unprinted stanzas are edited in Part II from Folger, MS Printed Book, STC 22957.

To some extent, Philip's poetry seems to have benefited as he transformed his "Meditation" from a wholly spiritual exercise into an at least partially vindictive assessment of his enemies' spiritual shortcomings. Among the more vivid descriptions here are the "swords of griefe" with which the sinner's "heart is daily pearst" (signature E 2v), and the fiends

> Whose bloudy mindes thy ruine did conspire,
> Whose neesings seeme, like lightnings for to be
> Whose uglie mouth, doth cast out flames of fire,
>   Whose nostrils smoake, whose eies are glowing red,
>   Whose whole delight by others smart is bred.
>   (signature D 2v)

Yet the topics are too frequently treated in excess of effective limits, and the verse is further hampered by the relentlessly end-stopped lines, pounding rhythms, and trite diction culminating in such alliterative tags as "scalding sighes" and "sobbing sighes" within a few lines of each other. In style, then, the earl's poetry continues to unfold as if Sidney had never written a line, yet the influence of courtier verse on Arundel's work comes into focus when we consider what an innovative anomaly his "Meditation" would be had it been composed by his father, the duke of Norfolk, prior to his execution in 1572. From the subsequent development of courtier verse Arundel gained an acceptance of vernacular poetry as a fit medium for serious religious expression as well as the impetus for creative realization of his subject matter. His creativity does not emerge, of course, in the translations, but it is a prominent feature of the "Meditation," where Arundel imagines Christ rejecting the sinner, along with the horrors with which Satan and his fiends receive him into eternal torment, the lost soul's cursing of his life and fate, and finally, the specific description of heaven. Despite his antiquated poetic style and forms, Arundel is matched among Elizabethan courtiers only by Greville and Essex in his adaptation of fictional elements to devotional verse.

Arundel apparently did not intend for the political dimension of his poem, with its oblique condemnation of his enemies, to be published as were his translations of Lanspergius and Marulus. The "Meditation" seems not to have circulated in court-related channels of manuscript transmission, although its nine extant manuscripts testify to a very wide circulation in Catholic circles. When, by way of contrast, the earl of Essex composed his penitential "Passion" late in February of 1601, there is every indication that he wrote to appease his sovereign as well as to express the deep remorse that seized him shortly after his conviction for high treason.[33]

The "Passion" is a far more sophisticated poem than Arundel's "Meditation" in both style and conception, for Essex drew upon his years of experience as a courtier poet in devising this, his longest poem. He employed the same sixain stanza that Arundel had used but with a technical superiority evident in the greater frequency of substitute feet, feminine rhymes, and enjambment. Devereux's pace is much faster, his lines more image-laden and adorned with similes and biblical allusions. He laments, for example, that his crimes exceed those of a host of sinful figures, including Cain, Judas, the fallen angels, and the Jews who crucified Christ, while his inability to shed true, repentant tears mocks the intensity of the guilt he suffers. The emotional hyperbole of the Elizabethan love lyric is thus transferred to a spiritual lyricism that evokes in its cumulative effect a genuine sense of anguish and depression. Parenthetical remarks, interjections, and above all the colloquial syntax nearly free of strained inversions create a sincere and moving tone. The style is not only beyond Arundel's range, it compares favorably with the very best effects in the Psalms of Philip and Mary.

Coupled with the poetic superiority of Essex's verse there is a second level of meaning similar in purpose to that of Arundel's poem. Robert tended habitually to "evaporate his thoughts in a Sonnet,"[34] and certainly the "Passion" reflects his reliance on poetry to express his innermost feelings. The majority of his extant poems, nevertheless, deal with his relationship to the queen and were no doubt written to influence her directly. When we consider that he apparently believed after the trial that his execution would be delayed,[35] it is clearly consistent with his ordinary practice that this work was intended for both a divine and a worldly audience. Such a strategy would explain the earl's vague and abbreviated allusion to his rebellion at the very end of the poem ("a wretched deede misdone"), as opposed to his lengthy confessions of sexual misprision in the comparisons with King David and Mary Magdalen. Elizabeth did

---

33. For Essex's penitence and the literary and biographical elements in his "Passion," see the commentary to my edition of his poems in *Studies in Philology* (94–106). The text of Essex's "Passion" is reprinted in Part II.

34. Sir Henry Wotton, *A Parrallell Betweene Robert Late Earle of Essex, and George Late Duke of Buckingham*, sig. A3. Wotton served as one of the earl's secretaries during the late 1590s.

35. This belief is established by Edward Doughtie in "The Earl of Essex and Occasions for Contemplative Verse" (363).

not, of course, acquiesce gracefully to rivals for her favorites' affections. She punished Essex when he married in 1590, and later, when he resumed his dalliance with "his fairest B.," the much-admired Elizabeth Brydges, court gossip warned that "Yt cannot chuse but come to 1500 [the queen's] eares; then is he undonne, and all they that depend upon his favor."[36]

Essex seemingly used the "Passion" to apologize for his infidelities to the queen, yet at the same time he threatened to desert her for a far greater rival. It is difficult to believe that Essex, any more than Arundel, treated the Virgin Mary in solely devotional terms. Both poets emphasize her title as Queen of Heaven over her role as mother, virgin, or saint. To the extent that the cult of Elizabeth replaced that of the Virgin in Protestant England, invidious comparisons were unavoidable when courtiers chose to praise the rival cynosure. Essex's stanza on the Virgin Mary (poem 11, lines 25–30) was skillfully calculated to turn the rivalry to his own benefit. As she read its first line, Elizabeth would necessarily suppose that her fallen favorite was addressing her: "And thou faire Queene of mercy and of pittye." After his conviction, royal mercy and pity were the earl's last hope, as Harington observed in an epigram upon the execution: "Thear is no man of worth in all the City, / Will say, 'tis great, but rather little pitty" (epigram 264). The second line of Essex's stanza reveals, however, that he is appealing for mercy from that queen "Whose wombe did once the World's creator carry," thus threatening Elizabeth with his defection to a rival queen. As with Arundel's treatment of Mary, this stanza did not appear in the printed editions of Essex's poem, but whereas Arundel's adoration of the Virgin was germaine to his Catholic faith, Devereux's appeal to Mary and "the Quire of holy Saints" to "preferre my plaints" violates his confirmed Protestantism. Perhaps his invocation of the Virgin was a mere aberration from an otherwise orthodox faith, but even so Essex seems to have exploited its potential for affecting Elizabeth. The stanza implies that he has nowhere else to turn unless Elizabeth can forgive him. Meanwhile, as he seeks mercy from the heavenly Virgin, he necessarily gravitates toward the Church wherein she is preeminently worshiped.

In its utilitarian purpose, Essex's Tower verse is a close devotional equivalent of Ralegh's amorous "Cynthia" poems which were

36. HMC, De L'Isle and Dudley, 2:322, Whyte to Sir Robert Sidney, February 12, 1598. The queen's wrath in this instance was apparently deflected from the earl onto Mistress Brydges.

also composed in the Tower in hopes of allaying the queen's displeasure. There is no evidence that the earl's work, any more than Ralegh's, ever reached Elizabeth—if so, it was equally ineffective. As courtier verse, however, the poems by Essex and Arundel contrast with the "Cynthia" poems in the subtlety with which they carry out their multiple purposes. They provide two of the best examples by Elizabethan courtiers of that penchant for dissimulation and ambiguity which Daniel Javitch hypothesized would be the essence of the courtier's delight in poetry.[37] Although Arundel took no such active delight in verse before his imprisonment, he then used it to condemn his enemies and exalt the Virgin above the queen in a meditation ostensibly designed to prepare him for his own death. Essex's interweaving of penitence with what amounts to a plea for clemency is equally ambiguous and to that extent in sharp contrast as well to his earlier verse in which, as we have seen, the heavy-handed delivery of his meanings, however creatively set forth, lack the subtlety that Javitch had anticipated for courtier verse.

The "Tower verse" written by earlier Tudor courtiers, especially Wyatt and Surrey, differed from that of the Elizabethans by being centered primarily upon translations from the Bible, most notably Wyatt's metrical versions of the seven penitential Psalms and Surrey's translations from Ecclesiastes. These translations nevertheless dilate the sources to emphasize the guilt and crimes of David and Solomon, thus creating a submerged level of meaning similar to that in the meditative poems of Arundel and Essex. No such ulterior motives flavor the metrical Psalms composed by Elizabeth's courtiers, although their translations do reflect the court and are often influenced by the work of other courtier poets. The divine poetry translated by Philip Sidney, the countess of Pembroke, the younger Harington, and Arundel, coupled with the original works of Arundel, Essex, and possibly Greville and the queen as well, testify to the full acceptance of English verse as an appropriate vehicle for even the most solemn subject matter at the late Elizabethan court. Its triumph, all the same, merely restored poetry to the status it had held in the two decades before 1558 when such courtiers as Wyatt, Surrey, Dudley, and Smith had combined biblical translation with verse paraphrase that at times amounted to original meditative verse.

37. *Poetry and Courtliness*, especially chapter 2.

Conclusion to Part I

Courtier verse undoubtedly enriched Elizabethan court culture, although its role, with that of poetry at court in general, is easily exaggerated. It is beyond proof as well as highly unlikely that, after the publication of *Astrophil and Stella* in 1591, "At Court, in polite society everywhere, the latest sonnet was discussed with as much avidity as the latest scandal," or that "All the lords and ladies kept a booklet into which they might transcribe verses that caught their fancy."[1] Many hundreds of individuals attained courtier status during Elizabeth's reign, but only thirty-two of them survive as writers of extant verse, nor are more than a few of the rest charged with writing poetry by their contemporaries. And even if we assume that the works of many other courtiers have perished, what remains can amount to no more than the tip of an ice cube. Something like a "cult of the literary amateur" may have obtained among certain courtiers, but there is no evidence that the practice "pervaded late-Elizabethan court society."[2] A small minority of the queen's courtiers were poets, nor did poetic composition ever become an expected, much less a mandatory, courtly attainment.

If the writing of verse was a recessive accomplishment for courtiers, that need not diminish the importance of poetry within Elizabeth's household, for her poets included many of her most prominent officers, cherished favorites, and trusted members of her immediate circle. Their personal renown as courtiers ensured that their writings exerted a considerable influence on professional authors. At the same time, we gain a telling insight into the nature of courtiership by noting that Elizabeth's courtiers did not take up en masse the writing of poetry as it became known that Secretary Cecil or Lord Oxford, Sidney or Ralegh, Essex or the queen herself did so. Poetry became one among many modes of courtly expression, but it

---

1. Lu Emily Pearson, *Elizabethan Love Conventions*, 104.
2. Michael Brennan, *Literary Patronage in the English Renaissance: The Pembroke Family*, 70.

did so at length and after much resistance, a fact underscored by the vast majority of Renaissance courtesy books which do not recommend or even mention poetic composition.

A more specific examination of those courtiers who were most thoroughly devoted to the muse and those who were the greatest poetic innovators reveals that they were nearly all affiliated with the Sidney family. In addition to Sir Philip, this group includes his friends Greville and Dyer as well as his sister, the countess of Pembroke, his brother Robert, and the "heir" to his courtiership, the second earl of Essex. The younger Harington also belonged to this circle, for he obtained manuscript copies of the *Arcadia* and of *Astrophil and Stella* before their publication, as well as Greville's virtually uncirculated lyrics and the countess of Pembroke's Psalms. Beyond his friendship with Greville and Dyer, he was by the 1590s on intimate terms with Sir Robert Sidney and a partisan of the earl of Essex. These friends and kinsfolk account for most of the finest Elizabethan courtier verse as well as for the great majority of it on a line-by-line basis. Given the degree to which these poets shared each other's works, the variety and originality of their output is all the more remarkable.

This dedication to poetry within the Sidney circle produced its most important results during the last two decades of the reign, yet neither in this output nor in what preceded it can we easily settle on wide-ranging generalizations about what was characteristic of courtier verse. Throughout the reign, courtiers used poetry for certain kinds of communication and display that were never deemed lacking in propriety. The commendatory verses, epitaphs, and encomia produced by Ascham, Cecil, and Wilson during the 1560s find their counterparts through to the last years of the reign in Lady Russell's epitaphs, the elegies for Sidney by Gorges, Ralegh, and Dyer, and the commendatory poems by Drake, Ralegh, and Harington. These occasional works form the most constant element in the courtier tradition and the least interesting one from a strictly literary viewpoint. Two major changes, the shift from Latin to English verse and the introduction of poetic fictions, had to occur before courtiers could make significant contributions to late Renaissance culture.

In retrospect the Latin verse that dominated courtier output during the first decade of the reign seems "uncourtly," yet it grew naturally out of the poets' schooling and their former practice. It harmonized as well with the cautiously conservative atmosphere that prevailed at the court of the new, Protestant queen who ruled a weak and divided people. Most of the courtiers who wrote before 1570 were also government officials who sought an appropriate classical dignity in their public display as poets. Even after English superseded Latin in courtier verse, the efforts of Philip Sidney, Greville, and Lady Pembroke to naturalize quantitative meters testify to the enduring respect for the classics at court, as do the Latin poems of Mildmay, Hoby, Essex, Sir John Harington, and the queen.

The shift away from the older humanism included writing in the vernacular plus the infusion of continental models such as the Italian translations and adaptations by Oxford, both the Sidneys, and Harington, and those from French by Gorges and Pembroke. A significant result of this influence was the emergence of fiction in their works, which previously could boast only of Hatton's contribution to *Gismond of Salern* and the prosopopoeia in Latin verse that Cecil apparently wrote for the queen in 1571. The foremost works of continental inspiration were, of course, Harington's *Orlando* and Pembroke's *Antonie*, as well as the pastoral fictions and poetic forms which Sidney borrowed from Sannazzaro and Montemayor. The love lyrics of the 1570s incorporated Petrarchan conventions and by the 1580s Dyer, Gorges, Ralegh, and Stanley had also written pastorals. Without being too arbitrary about placement on the creative scale that ascends from outright translation through adaptation to independent composition it would be only fair to regard Greville's *Mustapha* and *Alaham* as two of the most ambitious original verse fictions attempted by Elizabethan courtiers.

The court was undoubtedly more receptive to such fictions and to English rhyming generally during the second half of the reign than the first. The external threats of assassination plots and Spanish invasion could not long disrupt the ongoing entertainments, the dances, plays, games, and gambling that took place in the queen's household, on her progresses, and in the tiltyard. The court atmosphere encouraged displays of personal talent, and it came to indulge even trifling, frivolous pursuits for the sake of amusement. The couplets exchanged by Ralegh and Noel illustrate the adaptation of verse to playful socializing at court, as do Lady Cheke's reply to Harington's epigram and the lost poetry which Robert Cecil wrote to be sung to the queen in 1602. The ultimate acknowledgment of poetry as a fully acceptable form of expression comes, however, in the religious works turned out by courtiers during the last dozen years or so of the reign, the Psalm translations and the original prayers and meditations by Arundel, Greville, and Essex. And here, as in the development of significant verse fiction, courtiers produced works undreamed of in Puttenham's philosophy of the courtier as poet.

Within the receptive cultural setting of the court, the fact of a virgin queen elicited specialized forms of poetic address: Wilson's *Diva* became more specifically Phoebe, Diana, and Cynthia in the love poetry addressed to her by Oxford, Ralegh, and Gorges, who were joined by Heneage, Harington, Essex, and Pembroke among those courtiers who tried to influence Elizabeth directly through their verses. In the process, the amorous complaint emerged as a particular specialty of courtier verse for several reasons. As courtiers applied the motifs of love poetry to their relationships with the queen they gravitated naturally toward complaint because the object of their alleged passions was, of course, unobtainable, nor did she always treat her courtiers as they wished. Their lyrics in this vein do in fact employ indirection and pretense, the saying of one thing while meaning another as illustrated primarily in a handful of poems by Oxford, Dyer, Ralegh, and Essex. A corollary to this use of verse to influence the queen is the poetry that directly praises her by Gorges, Heneage, Greville, Sir John Harington, and Lady Pembroke. Here, the hyperbole is often muted and the conventions of love poetry are sparingly if ever employed. Meanwhile, the majority of lovers' complaints stem from purely literary motives such as Gorges's translations from French and Sidney's *Old Arcadia* poems, while a significant remainder was also elicited by disappointments with women other than the queen: Sidney's rejection by Lady Rich, with its apparent influence on Greville's *Caelica*, and Sir Robert Sidney's repulse by one or more ladies-in-waiting.

Within the whole range of Elizabethan courtier verse a number of works lend themselves to variously ambiguous interpretations. Ralegh played upon both meanings of the "faerie queene" in his commendation of Spenser's book, Essex surely directed his "Passion" to his sovereign as well as to his God, and *Astrophil and Stella* must be to some unknowable extent a fictional representation of Sidney's actual devotion to Penelope Rich. For the most part, however, courtier verse achieved well-defined purposes directly enough, even in the poetry most closely connected with courtiership and Elizabeth herself. The exaggerated praise lavished upon her in their works and their equally hyperbolic complaints may be fictions, but they ordinarily fall short of dissimulation. Ralegh's "Cynthia" fragments are emotion-laden barrages of intensely personal associations; as complaints their scope and force of expression, their Sidneian energy, are unsurpassed in sixteenth-century verse. In the context, however, of the disgraced bridegroom who betrayed his aging sovereign by marrying one of her personal attendants the purpose is neither obscure nor subtle, but a stylized, heavy-handed appeal for forgiveness. Courtiers who used poetry to communicate with the queen and compete with rivals apparently realized that a genuinely ambiguous or enigmatic approach might be subject to misinterpretation and hence become a liability rather than an advantage.

In fact, most of the obscurity and ambiguity in courtier verse results from our ignorance of the circumstances that elicited so many poems and the identities of the persons who appear in them under pseudonyms: Myra and Amaryllis, Caelica and Charys, Lynus, Lesbia, and Don Pedro are particularly tantalizing mysteries. The ambiguity is largely dissolved when we crack the code, as with Harington's Paulus epigrams in which the characterization of Ralegh is far from subtle. This is an extreme case, yet it is difficult to argue for a very complex degree of literary sophistication in these plain allegories. Nor would there be much to ponder on the score of multiplicity of meanings if we knew, for example, that Oxford's cry for revenge in poem 10 grew out of the tennis court quarrel with Sidney, or that Cumberland sent poem 1 to Elizabeth during a period of disgrace. Courtiers often wrote for and about an exclusive coterie. Many of the contexts and motives that underlie their works remain as obscure today as they were to contemporary out-of-court readers. The key to solving these mysteries lies in the ongoing study of the court and its personnel.

Courtier verse began to exert a viable influence beyond the court during the 1570s as its texts were disseminated in the printed anthologies and songbooks as well as in manuscript. The impact is easily judged in the case of *Astrophil and Stella*, for such a collection of discrete lyrics in the service of a unified narrative was unknown in English before 1591. A few individual poems were imitated by out-of-court poets, among them "My mind to me a kingdom is" and Dyer's "He that his mirth hath lost" and "The lowest trees have tops." Harington's epigrams were probably helping to popularize this genre by the late 1580s, but since his efforts were modeled on Martial, preceded in English by Heywood among others, and nearly contemporary with the epigrams of John Davies, his impact on the prolific output of English epigrams over the next thirty years lies beyond demonstration. Nor is it possible to define the overall impact of that growing refinement in courtier style which began in the 1580s. Thus the lyrics of Ralegh, Essex, and Sir Robert Sidney are in general more pleasing than those of Oxford, Dyer, and Gorges, while the old-fashioned manner of Arundel's verses is clearly out of step with what most courtiers were producing by the late 1580s. The corresponding improvement of professional poetry must likewise owe something to courtier models albeit the influence cannot be precisely gauged.

It is somewhat less difficult to determine the extent of courtier response to out-of-court developments. Their verse is striking throughout the reign for its relative immunity to the direct influence of either professional writers or the work of courtier peers. This is not to deny that Gorges, Ralegh, and perhaps Lady Pembroke borrowed from Spenser; Gorges undoubtedly copied from Turberville as did Stanley from Kendall. The Sidney circle exchanged motifs and phrasing without sacrificing that creative and philosophical independence which its members in fact studiously asserted. Although Greville revered Sidney unto idolatry, he fashioned his *Caelica* love poems into an ironic negation of the idealism his friend had imparted to *Astrophil and Stella*. Robert Sidney aligned his verse with his brother's genres and phrasing, yet his love poems project an attitude toward extramarital amours at court quite at odds with Philip's guilt-ridden concern for honor. Harington, Ralegh, and Essex deferred to Sidney's example as a poet, but they produced no discernible imitations. Instead, Sidney's closest followers in both prose and verse were the out-of-court, commercial authors who gained respectability by emulating the work of their social superiors.

Courtiers themselves were aristocrats who occupied the uppermost niches of privileged Elizabethan society. They depended ultimately on the queen, and also upon the cooperative esteem of their fellow courtiers, to maintain their status. Their place in the hierarchy generated a self-confident striving for individuality, whether in poetry designed to move the queen, for courtly display, or as private responses to the experience of courtiership. They stood as patterns for the nation at large to follow as well as contributors to the tone and quality of life at court, where a too conspicuous imitation of their peers or anyone else might suggest undue subservience or an unbecoming lack of ability. In its poetry, at least, the Elizabethan court found no one voice or single aesthetic. It developed a chorus of poetic voices only the most utilitarian and famous of which have been heretofore singled out as representative of the whole. But courtiers also translated the Psalms and the *Orlando Furioso*. They wrote facetious narratives and polished love lyrics, sincere elegies and vitriolic personal satires. To later writers, courtiers and professionals alike, they provided both respectability and models for a multitude of poetic endeavors. The lasting contribution of these courtier poets evolved in a disparate profusion, its genres and styles freely shaped by their individual apprehensions, tastes, and circumstances.

PART II

The Courtier Poets
Canons and Texts

Textual Introduction

Most of the Elizabethan courtier poets whose works are treated in Part I are well-known historical figures. Many, however, such as Ascham, Hoby, and Lady Russell, are almost unknown as courtiers, while others such as Cecil, Noel, Wilson, and Wolley have received little or no attention as poets. Sir Francis Drake and Lady Mary Cheke have received scant attention in either capacity. The following alphabetical catalog identifies the thirty-two Elizabethan courtier poets and their works with particular emphasis upon the dual criteria which qualify them for inclusion in this study.

Each poet's credentials as a courtier, along with their periods of courtiership, are set forth below insofar as that seems necessary within the guidelines established in Chapter 1. This focus not only interprets the careers of these men and women from a new perspective but brings to light information about many of them that is not found in previous biographical accounts: the challenge delivered in the Privy Chamber in 1592 by the earls of Cumberland and Essex, for example; the queen's grant of the Walton estate to Heneage in 1578–1579; and her gift of 1,500 pounds to Sir Philip Sidney in 1582. The catalog also specifies the poems written by these individuals during their careers as courtiers. Frequently, these works cannot be dated more precisely than within a range of several years, or before or after a given date. In these cases the list tends to be inclusive rather than exclusive. Bacon and Cordell, for example, may not have written verse after Elizabeth took the throne, and it is possible that some of the works posited here as Elizabethan for Greville, Sir Robert Sidney, and the younger Harington were in fact of Jacobean composition. We are fortunate that Sir Robert, the countess of Pembroke, Gorges, and Greville are among that minority of courtier poets who collected and edited their own output, yet this in fact tends to complicate the assessment of the particular place and flavor of poetry at Elizabeth's court. Greville's modifications of his *Caelica* sequence as late as the 1620s have much to say about his lifelong development as a poet, but they can only obscure the Elizabethan state of his work. Similar problems crop up for Sir John Harington and the countess of Pembroke. In each instance I have tried, in keeping with the historical dimensions of this study, to establish the best Elizabethan state of the author's corpus, while recognizing that this is not always the definitive text.

Ideally, readers wishing to follow the development of courtier verse as it is presented in Part I would need only to acquire the currently edited works of these poets and supplement them with the editions and texts printed in Part II. The selections that follow, however, provide only a representative anthology of courtier verse without filling all the gaps. Reliable modern editions of the works by fourteen courtier poets are readily available. Ascham's three poems in the *Scholemaster* are accessible in William A. Wright's *Roger Ascham: The English Works* and later editions, as are Cordell's two poems in Ruth Hughey's edition of *The Arundel Harington Manuscript of Tudor Poetry*, which also includes Greville's satiric narrative (poem 69). Helen Estabrook Sandison's *Poems of Sir Arthur Gorges* and Ruth Hughey's edition of the elder Harington's verse, *John Harington of Stepney*, provide every known text by these authors. The bulk of Sir John Harington's output is available in his translation of Ludovico Ariosto's *Orlando Furioso*, edited by Robert McNulty (which includes Mildmay's Latin verses); Elizabeth Story Donno's edition of *The Metamorphosis of Ajax* (with its couplets by Hatton and Talbot); Harington's *Tract on the Succession to the Crown*, edited by Clements R. Markham; and the ten poems transcribed in R. H. Miller's article "Unpublished Poems by Sir John Harington." Hatton's contribution to *Gismond of Salern* appears in John W. Cunliffe's edition of the play in *Early English Classical Tragedies*. Lady Pembroke's canon is complete in Geoffrey Bullough's edition of *The Tragedie of Antonie* (in *Narrative and Dramatic Sources of Shakespeare*), J. C. A. Rathmell's edition of her metrical psalms (*The Psalms of Sir Philip Sidney and the Countess of Pembroke*), and Gary F. Waller's of her remaining verse (*Mary Sidney, Countess of Pembroke*). Thomas Clayton's text of Sir Henry Lee's tiltyard poem, "Sir Henry Lee's Farewell to the Court"; Sackville's verse epistle as edited by Rivkah Zim and M. B. Parkes in "Sacvyles Olde Age"; William A. Ringler's *Poems of Sir Philip Sidney* (plus the three Ottley texts transcribed by Peter Beal in "Poems by Sir Philip Sidney: The Ottley Manuscript"); and P. J. Croft's *Poems of Sir Robert Sidney* round out the list of dependably edited and accessible courtier verse not included in Part II.

Equally accessible but in somewhat less satisfactory form are the queen's verses in Leicester Bradner's edition of *The Poems of Queen Elizabeth I*, which omits four of her certain works, three of which are newly edited below. The Elizabethan state of Greville's poems and dramas is at least approximated in the edition of Geoffrey Bullough (*The Poems and Dramas of Fulke Greville*) and Greville's *The Remains, Being Poems of Monarchy and Religion*, edited by G. A. Wilkes. The 1603 version of Sir John Harington's epigrams is likewise approximated in Norman Egbert McClure's edition (*The Letters and Epigrams of Sir John Harington*), which must be supplemented by R. H. Miller's reprint of the poems silently omitted by McClure ("Unpublished Poems by Sir John Harington"). Bacon's "Recreacons" likewise exist in a bowdlerized and relatively scarce edition, yet the uncertainty that any of his poems are of Elizabethan vintage rendered impractical the inclusion of a new edition in this volume.

The poetry interspersed in the following catalog of courtier poets does however fill many of the remaining gaps, with several new and complete editions plus a selection of many other texts which are here printed together for the first time. I reprint my editions of the poems of the earls of Oxford and Essex, and, with one additional work, the earl of Derby. I have completely reedited Sir Edward Dyer's verse in light of the number and quality of manuscript witnesses that have surfaced since Ralph M. Sargent published his *Life and Lyrics of Sir Edward Dyer* (1935), itself a substantial improvement over Alexander Grosart's nineteenth-century edition. I add to the canon established by Sargent Dyer's elegy for Sir Philip Sidney (poem 12) and delete the unattributed elegy which Sargent printed as Dyer's.[1] I provide all fifty lines of poem 3, represented in Sargent's edition by a single couplet (plus four more lines actually written by Sir Arthur Gorges). I demote two lyrics in Sargent's canon to possible status (I and IV), and add two new poems which Dyer may have written (II and III). For the verse common to both editions, the new manuscript evidence permits considerable textual upgrading. I add a previously unknown stanza to poem 6, for example, and correct at least a half-dozen faulty readings in Sargent's text. Poem 2, Dyer's most influential work, varies from Sargent's version in scores of readings, some fifty of which materially alter its tone and meaning.

The anthology also includes the first edited text of Queen Elizabeth's response to Ralegh's "Fortune hath taken thee away," the poems of Lady Mary Cheke and Sir Francis Drake, a text possibly by

---

1. Sargent, *Life and Lyrics*, 198–99.

Sir Henry Lee, Sir John Harington's translation of the Penitential Psalms, devotional verses by the earl of Arundel, and Latin verses by Hoby, Lady Russell, Wilson, and Wolley. The remaining poets' works are collected here in edited reprints for the first time. Poems 1–5 by Heneage, for example, were transcribed from the unique manuscript copy by Bertram Dobell in *The Athenaeum* (1901), while poem 6 was discovered and published in *Modern Language Notes* (1938) by Curt F. Buhler, along with Latin and English verses by the queen to which Heneage's poem responds. All have been reprinted below from the original manuscript sources. The texts by Ascham, Cecil, the earl of Cumberland, and Henry Noel are likewise available in contemporary printed editions or later reprints but are collected here for the sake of convenience. Cecil's birthday verses for his daughter, for example, have not been accurately transcribed in print since 1838.

This anthology of courtier verse in tandem with previous editions nevertheless leaves the works of several courtier poets unedited or inadequately edited. The most glaring omission is a reliable edition of Ralegh's verse, a problem I have admittedly skirted by referring to Michael Rudick's dissertation ("The Poems of Sir Walter Ralegh"), supplemented by Ralegh's verses to the queen as edited below with her response. The earl of Arundel's "Fourfold Meditation" is nowhere available in a critical text, yet its length and poetic quality precluded more than the inclusion here of two unique stanzas. Similarly, only one of Sir Thomas Wilson's six Elizabethan poems appears below; his congratulatory verses on Elizabeth's twelfth accession day are representative of both his courtiership and his attainments as a Latin poet. The *Carmen Gratulatorum* which Lord Burghley may well have composed for the royal visit of 1571 is known only in a unique contemporary print, and Elizabeth's holograph French verses can be read in toto only in manuscript at Hatfield House. In both instances, the obscure circumstances of composition precluded editions of these works in this volume.

At least eight of the courtier poets (Ascham, Cecil, DeVere, Drake, Sir John Harington, Ralegh, Wilson, and Wolley) caused or permitted their verse to appear in contemporary prints. Substantial collections of holograph poetry have survived for Queen Elizabeth (in PRO, SP 12/289, and Hatfield House, MS CP 147), Sir Robert Sidney (BL, Add. MS 58435), and Ralegh (Hatfield MS 144, the "Cynthia" poems). Collections of courtier verse supervised by the authors include Gorges's verse in BL, Egerton MS 3165; Greville's poems and dramas in BL, Add. MSS 54566–54571; the Penshurst Manuscript of the Pembroke-Sidney Psalter; and Sir John Harington's epigrams in BL, Add. MS 12049; his Psalm translations in BL, Egerton MS 2711; and his translation of the *Aeneid*, book 6, in Trumbull, Add. MS 23, in the Berkshire Record Office, Reading. Only two anthologies of verse collected by courtiers are known, the *Arundel Harington Manuscript*, which was compiled by the elder Harington and his son, and BL, Add. MS 38823, a collection of prose and poetry compiled by Sir Edward Hoby. The textual sources of the poems edited in Part II are acknowledged after each poem and in the appended notes. The following bibliography of copy texts for these poems indicates the centrality of the manuscripts to the circulation and survival of courtier verse.

STC IMPRINTS

3191 *Englands Helicon*, 1600 (Noel, poem 2)

3633 *Brittons Bowre of Delights*, 1591 (Stanley, earl of Derby, poem 1)

3679.5 *The passion of a discontented minde*, 1601 (Essex, poem 11)

4607 *Cardanus comforte*, trans. Thomas Bedingfield, 1573 (Oxford, poem 1)

7095 John Dowland, *The second booke of songs or ayres*, 1600 (Lee, poem 1)

7096 John Dowland, *The third and last booke of songs or aires*, 1603 (Dyer, poem 9; Essex, poem III)

7099 Robert Dowland, *A musicall banquet*, 1610 (Clifford, earl of Cumberland, poem 1; Essex, poem 4)

7516 *The Paradyse of daynty devises*, 1576 (Oxford, poems 2–3, 5–7, 9)

7596 *The Queenes Majesties entertainment at Woodstocke*, 1585 (Dyer, poem 1)

13963 *Joannis Juelli Angli, episcopi Sarisburiensis vita & mors*, 1573 (Wolley, poem 1)

14627 Johann Justus Landsberger, *An epistle in the person of Christ to the faithfull soule*, trans. Philip Howard, earl of Arundel, 1595 (Howard, earl of Arundel, poem 1)

19523 Sir George Peckham, *A true reporte of the late discoveries of the Newfound Landes*, 1583 (Drake, poem 1)

20064 Plutarch, *Three morall treatises*, trans. Thomas Blundeville, 1580 (Ascham, poem 1)

21516 *The Phoenix Nest*, 1593 (Oxford, poem 14; Dyer, poem IV)

22541 Sir Philip Sidney, *The Countessse of Pembrokes Arcadia*, 1598 (Dyer, poem 7)

LATER IMPRINTS

The Antiquarian Repertory, ed. Francis Grose and Thomas Astle, vol. 3
     (London, 1780) (Stanley, earl of Derby, poem 4)
John Strype, *Annals of the Reformation*, vol. 3 (1820–1840; rpt., New
     York: AMS, n.d.) (Russell, poem 1)
Sir Henry Wotton, *A Parallell betweene Robert late Earle of Essex, and
     George late Duke of Buckingham* (1641) (Essex, poem 2)

MANUSCRIPTS
Bodleian Library, Oxford

Douce MS 280 (Essex, poem 6)   ·
Douce MS e.16, eighteenth-century transcript of the second edition of
     the *Paradise of Dainty Devices*, 1577 (Oxford, poem 4)
Rawlinson poetry MS 85 (Oxford, poems 12, III; Dyer, poems 8, III;
     Stanley, earl of Derby, poem 3)
Rawlinson poetry MS 148 (Dyer, poem 11)
Tanner MS 304 (Essex, poem 7)
Tanner MS 306 (Oxford, poem 10)

British Library, London

Add. MS 12049 (Sir John Harington's epigram, companion with Cheke,
     poem 1)
Add. MS 17790 (Essex, poem 5)
Add. MS 22583 (Oxford, poem 16)
Add. MS 38823 (Hoby, poems 1–3)
Add. MS 52585 (Essex, poem 10)
Egerton MS 2711 (Sir John Harington, Psalms 6, 32, 38, 51, 102, 130,
     143)
Harleian MS 5353, in Robert Parker Sorlien, ed., *The Diary of John
     Manningham of the Middle Temple, 1602–1603* (Noel, poem 1, and
     companion poem by Ralegh)
Harleian MS 6947 (Essex, poem IV)
Harleian MS 7392(2) (Oxford, poems 8, 11, 15, IV; Dyer, poems 3, 5,
     10, II, III ("Lenvoy")
Lansdowne MS 12/15 (Wilson, poem 1)
Lansdowne MS 104/76 (Cecil, poem 1)
Royal MS 17.B.L. (Essex, poem 8)

Cambridge University Library

MS Dd.5.75 (Dyer, poems 2, 6; Stanley, earl of Derby, poem 2)

Christ Church College, Oxford

Music MS 984 (Dyer, poem 12)

Folger Shakespeare Library, Washington, D.C.

MS V.a.89 (Oxford, poem I; Dyer, poem 4; Ralegh, "Farewell false
   love," companion with Heneage, poem 1)
MS V.a.339 (Essex, poem 1)
MS Printed Book, STC 22957 (Howard, earl of Arundel, poem 2)

Houghton Library, Harvard University, Cambridge, Massachusetts

f MS 1285 (Heneage, poems 1–5)

Huntington Library, San Marino, California

MS EL 11738 (Russell, poem 2)

Inner Temple Library, London

Petyt MS 538.10 (Oxford, poem II)

Marsh's Library, Dublin

MS 183 (Oxford, poem 13)

Pierpont Morgan Library, New York

PML 7768 (Latin verse by Queen Elizabeth with response by Heneage,
   poem 6)

Public Record Office, London

SP 12/254/67 (Essex, poem 3)

The Rosenbach Museum and Library, Philadelphia

MS 1083/15 (Essex, poem I)

John Rylands University Library of Manchester, Manchester

Alexander Grosart, ed., *The Dr. Farmer-Chetham MS.* (Essex, poems
   9, II)

Victoria and Albert Museum, London

Dyce MS 44 (Cheke, poem 1)

Wiltshire Record Office

MS 865/500 (Queen Elizabeth, poem 1, and companion poem by
   Ralegh)

In the texts below *i/j* and *u/v* are normalized, long *s* takes its modern form, and contractions are silently expanded. Other accidentals of the copy texts have been generally preserved but with the silent addition of clarifying punctuation, especially quotation and question marks, apostrophes, and capitalization of proper nouns and of words at the beginnings of lines.

The Courtiers and Their Verse

Ascham, Roger (1515–1568)

This celebrated humanist, secretary of the Latin tongue to queens Mary and Elizabeth, little resembles the stereotype of the blasé, swaggering courtier. Yet Ascham's proximity to the queen conferred upon him a status at court roughly similar to that of his longtime friends Secretary Cecil and John Astley. Although Ascham never became a Privy Councillor, the imperial ambassador paid tribute to his influence with the queen by yoking him with Cecil as her only two advisors who favored the Swedish match.[1] Ascham's description of the famous dinner at Windsor Castle on December 10, 1563, which led to his composition of *The Scholemaster*, also indicates his status at court. The company assembled in Cecil's chamber included Sir William Petre; Sir Richard Sackville, treasurer of the Exchequer; Sir Walter Mildmay, chancellor of the Exchequer; Astley; and Walter Haddon, master of requests. After dinner, Ascham "went up to read with the Queenes Maiestie," and it was to the Privy Chamber that Sackville followed him in order to request that the Latin secretary put his educational theories into writing.[2]

In August of the following year, Ascham sent his servant to court with a message for the earl of Leicester that reveals his close ties with the queen's chief favorite as well as with his sovereign. Ascham explained that he "was every day in the privy chamber and every day in your lordship's Chamber" while the court was at Westminster, but the press kept him from speaking with Leicester. Naturally, he wants to accompany the queen on progress to Cambridge, but his wife is expecting a baby; would Leicester be so kind as to convey his apologies to her majesty? He then mentions his lordship's offer to stand as "my gossip" at the child's christening but suggests that Sir William Pickering could serve as his deputy since Leicester must

1. Lawrence V. Ryan, *Roger Ascham*, 228.
2. Wright, *Ascham*, 177.

continue on with Elizabeth.[3] Subsequently, the earl became god-
father to Ascham's son, Dudley. There can be little doubt that the
Latin Secretary maintained warm, personal ties with his royal pupil
after she became queen, frequented the Privy Chamber when he
attended court, or that he enjoyed the personal friendship of many
prominent courtiers.

Three of Ascham's pre-Elizabethan poems appear in *The Scholemaster*, his elegy for John Whitney and two others that he describes
as written "once" or "long ago."[4] Three other verses, English translations of Strabo, Homer, and Hesiod, appear to have been composed
especially for this treatise. In addition, Ascham contributed commendatory English verses to Blundeville's translation of Plutarch
(reprinted below), and he left unfinished at his death a Latin poem
that he had hoped to present as a New Year's gift to the queen.[5] His
remaining Latin verses, occasional works addressed to Henry VIII
and Prince Edward, a few epitaphs, and his poem to Dr. William Bill
(d. 1561) all seem to predate Elizabeth's accession.

Ascham's interest in contemporary English verse, and his poetic
theories, go far to compensate for his slender accomplishments as a
practicing courtier poet. We know that he read Wyatt and Surrey's
lyrics in Tottel, Golding's translation of Ovid, Phaer's *Aeneid*, and a
number of other contemporary renderings of the classics. He also
encouraged Arthur Hall to undertake the first translation of *The
Iliad* into English verse.[6] His arguments against "barbrous riming"
and for the necessity of adapting English verse to quantitative measures are set forth in some detail in *The Scholemaster*, a book which
saw five Elizabethan editions. Other courtier poets wrestled at
length with these issues throughout the reign.

1

**Roger Ascham Secretory to the Queene's majestie,
for the Latin tongue, in praise of the booke.**

Of English bokes, as I could find,
I have perused many one:

3. J. A. Giles, ed., *The Whole Works of Roger Ascham*, 2:101–2, letter of
August 5, 1564.
4. Wright, *Ascham*, 232, 208.
5. Giles, *Whole Works*, 3:288–93, printed in *Disertissimi viri Rogeri Ascha-
mi* (STC 826) 1576, sig. X 6v-Y 1v. Ascham's translations from Greek are on
pages 199, 228, and 256 of Wright's edition.
6. Ryan, *Roger Ascham*, 243–46.

Yet so wel done unto my mind,
As this is, yet have I found none.

The woordes of matter here doe rise,   5
So fitly and so naturally,
As heart can wishe or witte devise
In my conceit and fantasie.

The woordes well chosen and well sett,
Doe bryng suche light unto the sense: 10
As if I lackt I woulde not lette,
To bye this booke for forty pense.
                              (STC 20064, sig. A2)

Bacon, Sir Nicholas (1509–1579)

Elizabeth appointed Bacon her Lord Keeper of the Great Seal on December 22, 1558. By virtue of this post he was ranked among the lords on the New Year's gift lists where his name takes precedence over all barons. Bacon was also a member of the Privy Council. His thirty-six English poems, entitled "The Recreacons of his age," may well be pre-Elizabethan. The only one which can be confidently dated is entitled "made in Wimbleton in his great sickness in the last year of Queen Mary." This is not the last poem in the sequence, however, as his verses are arranged in the contemporary manuscripts, nor necessarily the last one that he wrote. Thus Bacon is a transitional poet from Mary's reign who may have written a few poems after 1558. His "Recreacons," preserved in several complete manuscripts, were edited in a somewhat bowdlerized fashion by C. H. O. Daniel.[1]

Cecil, William, First Lord Burghley (1520–1598)

Principal Secretary, Lord Treasurer, and Privy Councillor, his position as the queen's trusted and confidential advisor made him the second most influential person in England during most of the reign. Cecil's only surviving English poem, printed below, accompanied his New Year's gift of a spinning wheel presented to his

1. C. H. O. Daniel, ed., *The Recreations of His Age By Sir Nicholas Bacon*. The manuscript texts are Huntington Library, MS HM 1340, and National Library of Wales, MS 10905; others are described in HMC, 4th report, 1:370, MSS of Lt. Col. Carew; and HMC, 12th report, appendix, 9:154, MSS of John Henry Gurney.

daughter Anne in 1567.[1] His Latin verse elegies on Margaret Neville had been published in 1551 in the Brandon brothers' memorial volume organized by his friend, Thomas Wilson.[2] As Lord Burghley, he contributed elegiac Latin verses honoring his friend, Sir Thomas Chaloner; these are printed in the 1579 edition of Chaloner's *De Republica Anglorum* (STC 4938). When the queen visited Cecil at Theobalds on September 21, 1571, she was greeted with "some verses" accompanying a portrait of the house,[3] undoubtedly the *Carmen Gratulatorum* (STC 4896), which is written in the person of Theobalds itself, and which may well have been composed by its owner.

1

To Mistress Anne Cecil

As yeres do growe, so cares encreasse
And tyme will move to loke to thrifte;
Thogh yeres in me worke nothing lesse,
Yet for your yeres, and new yere's gifte
This huswife's toy is now my shifte: 5
To set you on worke some thrifte to feele
I sende you now a spynneng wheele.

But oon thing firste, I wishe and pray
Leste thirste of thryfte might soone you tyre,
Only to spynne oon pounde a daye   10
And play the reste, as tyme require,
Sweat not (oh fy!) fling rocke in fyre;
God sende, who sendth all thrifte and welth
You long yeres and your father helth.
(BL, Lansdowne MS 104/76)

---

1. Thomas Wright set forth a reliable transcription of this poem in his *Queen Elizabeth and Her Times*, 2:73. Less reliable transcripts occur in Violet A. Wilson, *Queen Elizabeth's Maids of Honour and Ladies in the Privy Chamber*, 77, and in Conyers Read, *Mr. Secretary Cecil*, 353–54.
2. STC 25816, 1551, *Vita et Obitus Duorum Fratrum Suffolciensium*. Thomas Park attributes the French verse in BL, Royal MS 16.E.xxviii, to Cecil (*Catalogue of the Royal and Noble Authors of England*, 2:62–63), but this is instead a translation of Queen Catherine Parr's prose tract, *Lamentations of a Sinner* (1547). The apparent attribution to Cecil in this manuscript simply renders in French verse the prose introduction to a commendatory epistle which he prefixed to the queen's book. The manuscript does not appear to be in his handwriting, nor is there other evidence that he was sufficiently fluent in French to have composed these 120-odd pages of verse (see Read's assessment, *Mr. Secretary Cecil*, 24).
3. Nichols, *Progresses*, 1:291.

Notes

The manuscript is not in Cecil's hand but is dotted with crossed-out readings that suggest he dictated the poem to an amanuensis as he composed it.

12 rocke, *Oxford English Dictionary*, the distaff alone, or distaff with wool or flax attached.

Cheke, Lady Mary (d. 1616)

The daughter of Richard Hill, sergeant of the wine cellar to Henry VIII, she married John Cheke about 1547. Her second husband was the pensioner Henry MacWilliam, with whom she received a lease from the crown in 1565 or 1566. Lady Cheke appeared among the extraordinary ladies of the Privy Chamber at Elizabeth's coronation, but as ordinary at her funeral.[1] She was clearly among Elizabeth's most intimate attendants throughout the reign. Her name appears regularly on the New Year's gift rolls, always as Lady Cheke, her rank by her first marriage taking precedence over that of her second husband. In 1562, Cecil appointed her as one of four ladies, the wives of knights, to accompany her sovereign to a proposed meeting with Mary, Queen of Scots.[2] It was probably during the late 1590s that Lady Cheke responded to an epigram by Sir John Harington with a spirited twenty-line poem which advances a strong pro-feminist stance in opposition to Harington's mildly anti-feminist anecdote:

1a

Of a certayn man

Thear was, not serten when, a certayn preacher
That never learnt and yet became a teacher
And having thus in latten read a text
Of *Era quidam homo*, much perplext
He seemd the words with diligence to skan   5
In English thus, thear was a certain man;
"But now" quoth he, "good people, note yow this,
He saith thear was, he doth not say ther is,
For in this age of ours it is most certain
Of promise, oath, word, deede no man is certaine,   10
Yet by my tesh" (quoth he) "this comes to passe
That sewrly once a certaine man ther was;
    But yet I think in all the bible no man

1. PRO, SP 12/166, f. 13; PRO, LC 2/4 (3), f. 54; PRO, LC 2/4 (4), f. 45v.
2. BL, Lansdowne MS 5/37.

Can finde this text: thear was a certain woman."
(Harington, from BL, Add. MS 12049, pp. 192–93)

1

That no man yet could in the bible finde
A certayne woeman argues men are blinde;
Blinde as the preacher whoe had litle learning,
The certeyne cause of his so ill discerning.
A certayne woeman of the multitude   5
Sayde, "Blest be the paps that gave oure Savioure foode."
A certayne woeman too a milstone threw
And from the wall Abimelecke she slew.
There likewise was as holie writ doth say
A certayne woeman named Lydia;   10
Nay more, by men though it be overswayd
The text records there was a certayne mayde,
Which argues there were certayne woemen then
And certayne to, more certayne far then men.
Your preacher then may well stand much perplext   15
To see how grossely he belied the text
And blush his sermon was no better suted
Then by a woeman thus to be confuted;
Yet for his comfort one true note he made
When there was now no certayne man he sayde.   20
        (Victoria and Albert Museum, Dyce MS 44, folio 72v)

Notes

The copy text (D) is collated with versions of the poem in BL, Add. MS 15227, folio 16 (A); Cape Town, Grey MS 7, a 29, p. 157 (G); Rosenbach, MS 1083/16, pp. 16–17 (R); and Yale, Osborn MS b 205, pp. 48–48v (O); not collated are St. John's College, Cambridge, MS U.26 (James 548), p. 116, and University of Nottingham, Portland, MS Pw V 37, p. 172. Lady Cheke's claim to this poem rests upon the attributions of A and O. These manuscripts descend from a common original with G and R which lacked lines 9–10. Conjunctive errors in A-O at line 6, 'be' omitted; line 19, 'had' for 'made'; and line 20, 'here is' for 'there was,' point to a second lost intermediary. D followed an independent line of transmission from the author's original and is here printed without substantive emendation.

Title The Answer to it by the Lady Cheeke A, An answer by the Lady checke O.

1 bible] Screpture G.

2 are] ar *changed to* all R.

3 whoe had] having A O.

4 his so] this his A O; ill] fit O.

6 Sayde . . . paps] Said, Blest the Paps A O, Blessed the papes G, Blest be'th paps R.

7 too a] to a D O, too, a A G.

8 wall] Walles G.

9–10 *om.* A G O R.

11 by . . . overswayd] though wee by men bee overswaide A O, by men thought it be over layd G.

12 The text] A text G.

13 Which . . . were] Which prooves directly A O R; woemen] woman R; then] *om.* G.

14 to, more] maydes, more A O; far] sure A; then men] she G; certayne far then] sure then certein O.

15 *sub.* Noe marvaile then your preacher stood perplext A O, Wel might the preacher then stand much perplext G.

16 the] his A O.

17 blush his sermon] blusht that's sermon R.

19 made] had A O, *om.* G.

20 there was now] here is now A, thatt theres now G, and is now O, there is now R; he sayde] for bred A, *om.* G.

Clifford, George, Third Earl of Cumberland (1558–1605)

Clifford succeeded to the Cumberland title upon his father's death early in 1570. By the mid–1580s he was in regular attendance at court. The queen stood godmother by proxy at the christening of his son in May 1584,[1] and he first exchanged New Year's gifts with Elizabeth the following January. Cumberland was a particularly enthusiastic participant in the court's military spectacles. He appeared as a fellow jouster with Sir Henry Lee and Sir Thomas Gorges in a tournament of April 5, 1587, while he and the earl of Essex were the chief participants in the Accession Day tournament of that year.[2] On Accession Day in 1590 Lee resigned to Cumberland his place as the queen's tiltyard champion, and on the same date in 1592 "ther came two knights armed up into the Privy Chamber, viz. my L. of Essex and my L. of Cumberland, and ther made a challenge that uppon the 26th of February next that they will run with all commers to mayntayne that her M[ajesty] is most wortyest [*sic*] and most fayrest."[3]

Despite his frequent privateering voyages, Cumberland spent a good deal of time at court throughout the 1590s. His reception into the Order of the Garter in 1592 was a mark of particular royal favor. His access to Elizabeth finds eloquent testimony in a letter to Cecil of July 14, 1600, where he reports pressing a suit before her after dinner and attending her afterward in the garden where he "had such gracious usage as I forebore to speak one word touching my business." In August he was urging the queen to grant a pension to

1. PRO, E 351/542, f. 59.

2. G. C. Williamson, *George, Third Earl of Cumberland (1558–1605)*, 18.

3. HMC, 7th report, appendix, 524, Philip Gawdy to Basingbourne Gawdy, December 8, 1592. References in this letter to the Great Carrack and Ralegh's disgrace with the queen establish the year.

Francis Dacre; by early 1602 the earl had received a license to export cloth, although it is not clear that this was the particular favor for which he had pressed Elizabeth a few years earlier.[4]

Cumberland's interest in learning and the muses is not as implausible as his dedication to jousting and piracy might suggest. He had matriculated at Trinity College, Cambridge, at age thirteen in 1571, was in residence until 1574, and took his M.A. degree in 1576. His tutors, John Whitgift and William Whitaker, kept records of the books purchased for young Clifford, and the cost of his dancing lessons, among other expenses.[5] During his ascendancy at court the earl attracted more than a dozen book dedications, including a sonnet by Spenser with the first three books of the *Faerie Queene*. More significant, perhaps, as an indication of patronage, is Robert Greene's dedication to Cumberland of *Pandosto* (1588), source of Shakespeare's *The Winter's Tale*, followed in 1590 by the dedication to a second edition of *Greenes Mourning Garment*.

Several literary fragments connected with Cumberland's tiltyard shows have survived, although it is impossible to be sure that he wrote them. His prose speech to the queen on Accession Day 1600 describes him as a forlorn knight cast upon the shore as a wanderer "after he had throwne his land into the sea"; the earl's considerable investments in voyages of plunder had not turned a profit in the long run.[6] The last poem in Davison's *Poetical Rhapsody* (1602) was sung at a show presented before the queen by the earl "on Maie day last," but this amounts to something less than an outright indication of authorship. However, the attribution to Clifford of the first lyric in Robert Dowland's *Musical Banquet* (1610), as reprinted below, is no doubt reliable, for this songbook provides good texts and attributions of works by three other courtier poets, Essex, Lee, and Sir Philip Sidney. Unfortunately, Dowland's unique version of Cumberland's lyric apparently lacks a line after line 5. Another poem, beginning "My thoughts are winged with hopes," is ascribed to Cumberland in BL, Harleian MS 280, folio 100v, Davison's list of poems in *Englands Helicon*; but Davison's attributions here are quite unreliable, especially with regard to courtier poets. His list credits Dyer, for example, with at least three poems he did not write. This lyric, furthermore, was set to music anonymously as song 3 in John Dowland's *First Booke of Songes or Ayres* (1597) and

4. HMC, Salisbury, 10:234, 291; Huntington, MS EL 2409.
5. Williamson, *Cumberland*, 6–9.
6. Ibid., 243.

culled from that source for inclusion in the *Helicon*, as its subscription there forthrightly acknowledges. Thus the earl's claim to this work is quite doubtful.

1

The Right Honourable *George* Earle of Cumberland.

My heavie sprite opprest with sorrowe's might,
Of wearied limbs the burthen soare sustaines,
With silent grones and hart's teares still complaines,
Yet I breath still and live in life's despight.
Have I lost thee? All fortunes I accurse,   5
Bids thee farewell, with thee all joyes farewell,
And for thy sake this world becomes my hell.
                                             (STC 7099, song 1)

Cordell, Sir William (d. 1581)

A privy councillor under Queen Mary, Cordell was not retained in that capacity by Elizabeth. However, his office as master of the rolls, conferred November 5, 1557, was a lifetime appointment. Sir William's religious leanings may have been suspect, yet at the time of the Northern Rebellion of 1569–1570, he swore obedience to the Act of Uniformity.[1] Cordell was a skilled lawyer. As master of the rolls he served under the Lord Chancellor at the head of the eleven masters of chancery responsible for storing and preserving all patent rolls which passed the great seal.[2] Cordell exchanged New Year's gifts with the queen in every year for which records survive up to and including the year of his death. When Elizabeth visited him on progress at Long Melford, Suffolk, in August of 1578, Sir William is said to have established a precedent for "great feasting" of his sovereign and her train in that shire.[3]

Texts of Cordell's only known poems survive in the *Arundel Harington Manuscript* (ed. Ruth Hughey), and both of them may predate Elizabeth's reign. The first, number 172 in Hughey's edition, is a unique text transcribed just after a poem by Churchyard which was published in his *Chance* of 1580. The second poem, Hughey's numbers 307–8, falls in a section of the anthology devoted to Edwardian and Marian authors: Sir John Cheke, Lord Thomas

1. CSPD, 60/62.
2. Thoms, *Book of the Court*, 261–63.
3. Nichols, *Progresses*, 2:116–17.

Seymour, George Blage, and Lord Vaux (folios 206–18). Other texts of this poem, however, occur in distinctly Elizabethan contexts, for which see Hughey's notes.

Devereux, Robert, Second Earl of Essex (1565–1601)

Essex first exchanged New Year's gifts with Elizabeth in 1584 but recalled having "small grace and few friends" at court so early in his career.[1] His dazzling success as a royal favorite began only after he returned from military service in the Netherlands. He was at court for the Accession Day tilt of 1586 and succeeded his stepfather, the earl of Leicester, as Master of the Horse in the following June. Henceforth until his unlicensed return from Ireland in September 1599 he was a prominent courtier, a leader of English military expeditions to France and Spain, and a minion who absorbed nearly half of all the crown patronage distributed by the queen during the last decade of her reign.[2]

The earl's eleven canonical poems are reprinted below along with four others which he may have written. His earliest work dates from about 1590, while his last and longest poem was composed during his imprisonment in the Tower of London and within four days of his execution there on February 24, 1601.[3]

1

Muses no more but mazes be your names,
When discord's sounde shall marre your concord sweete;
Unkindly now your carefull fancie frames,
When fortune treads your favours under feete;
    But fowle befale that cursed cuckowe's throate,   5
    That so hath crost sweete Philomela's note.

And all unhappie hatched was that byrde,
That parratelike can never cease to prate;
But most untimely spoken was that word,
That brought the world in such a wofull state   10
    That love and likinge quite are overthrowne,
    And in theire place are greife and sorrowes growne.

1. Essex's *Apologie*, STC 6788, sig. A 2v.
2. Lawrence Stone, *The Crisis of the Aristocracy*, 473.
3. For textual notes and commentary see my edition in "The Poems of Edward DeVere, Seventeenth Earl of Oxford, and of Robert Devereux, Second Earl of Essex."

Is this the honour of a hauty thought,
For honour's hate to have all spight at love?
Hath wretched skill this wicked reason taught,   **15**
In this conceite such discontent to move,
    That beauty so is of herselfe bereft,
    That no good hope of ought good hap is left?

O let no phoenix looke upon a crowe,
Nor daintie hills bow downe to dyrty dales;   **20**
Let never heaven an hellish humour know,
Nor fyrme affecte give eare to foolish tales;
    For this in fine will fale to be the troth,
    That filthy water makes unholsome broth.

Woe to the world the sunne is in a cloud,   **25**
And darkesome mists doe overrunne the day;
In high conceite is not content allowed;
Favour must die and fancies weare away.
    O heavens, what hell! the bands of love are broken,
    Nor must a thought of such a thinge be spoken.   **30**

Mars must become a coward of his minde,
Whiles Vulcan stands to prate of Venus' toyes.
Beauty must seeme to goe against her kinde,
In crossinge nature in her sweetest Joyes;
    But oh, no more, it is to much to thinke,   **35**
    So pure a mouth should puddle water drinke.

But since the world is at this wofull passe,
Let love's submission honour's wrath appease.
Let not a horse be meated with an Asse,
Nor hatefull tongue an happy hart disease;   **40**
    So shall the world comend a sweet conceite,
    And humble fayth on heavenly favour waite.
                    (Folger, MS V.a.339, folio 185)

2

And if thou shouldst by Her be now forsaken,
She made thy Heart too strong for to be shaken.
    (Sir Henry Wotton, *A Parallell betweene Robert*
       late Earle of Essex, and George late Duke of
            Buckingham [London, 1641, sig. A3])

3

Seated betweene the olde world and the newe,
A Land there is no other lande may touche,

Where regnes a Queen in peace and honor true;
Storyes or fables doe describe noe suche;
Never did Atlas such a burthen beare   5
As shee, in holding up the world opprest,
Supplying with her vertue every where
Weaknes of friends, errors of Servants best.
No nation breeds a warmer bloud for warre,
And yet She calmes them with her Majesty;   10
No age hath ever witte refyned so farre,
And yet shee calmes them by her pollicie.
To her thy sonne must make his sacrifice,
If he will have the morning of his eyes.
                    (PRO, SP 12/254/67)

4

The Right Honourable *Robert*, Earle of Essex:
Earle Marshall of England.

Change thy minde since she doth change,
Let not Fancy still abuse thee;
Thy untruth cannot seeme strange,
When her falshood doth excuse thee.
　　Love is dead and thou art free,   5
　　She doth live but dead to thee.

Whilst she lov'd thee best a while,
See how she hath still delaid thee,
Using shewes for to beguile
Those vaine hopes that have betrayed thee.   10
　　Now thou seest although too late,
　　Love loves truth which women hate.

Love no more since she is gone,
Shee is gone and loves another.
Being once deceiv'd by one,   15
Leave her love but love none other
　　She was false, bid her adew,
　　She was best but yet untrue.

Love farewell more deere to mee
Then my life which thou preservest;   20
Life, all joyes are gone from thee,
Others have what thou deservest.
　　Oh my death doth spring from hence,
　　I must dye for her offence.

Dye, but yet before thou dye,   25
Make her know what she hath gotten;
She in whom my hopes did lye,
Now is chang'd, I quite forgotten.
    She is chang'd, but changed base,
    Baser in so vilde a place.   30
                    (STC 7099, song 2)

5

To plead my faith where faith hath noe reward,
To move remorse where favor is not borne,
To heape complaints which shee doth not regard
Were frutelesse, bootles, vaine, and yelds but scorne.
I loved her whom all the world admird,   5
I was refused of her that can love none;
And my vaine hopes which far to hie aspird
Are dead and buried, and for ever gone.
Forget my name since you have scornd my love,
And woman-like doe not to late lamente;   10
Since for your sake I must all mischiefe prove,
I none accuse nor nothinge doe repent.
    I was as fond as ever shee was faire,
    Yet lovd I not more then I now despaire.
                    (BL, Add. MS 17790, folio 9)

6

Say, what is love?
A foolishe toye I can well prove,
Some sayes not soe,
And why? because they nothing know,
    They nothinge knowe, that makes me singe hey downe,   5
    A downe, a downe, a downe, hey downe, a downe,
    downe, downe, downe.

In her sweete grace,
I once enjoyed the highest place,
But now not soe,   10
Her frowninge Rage hath wroght my woe,
    Hath wrought my woe, And cast me headlonge downe,
    Hey downe, a downe, a downe, Hey downe a downe,
    downe, downe, downe.
E: Essex Downe.
                    (Bodl., Douce MS 280, folio 67)

7

Happy were Hee could finish foorth his Fate
In some unhaunted Desert, most Obscure;
From all Society, from Love, from Hate
Of wordly Folke! Then should Hee Sleepe Secure;
Then Wake againe, and yield God ever Praise,   5
Content with Hipps, and Hawes, and Brambleberry,
In Contemplation passing still his Daies,
And Change of Holy Thoughts to make him Merry;
    Who when Hee dies, his Tombe may bee a Bush,
    Where Harmeles Robin dwells with Gentle Thrush.   10
                Your Majesty's Exiled Servant,
                    Rob: Essex.
          (Bodl., Tanner MS 304, folio 59v)

8

Verses made by the Earle of Essex in his Trouble

The waies on earth have paths and turnings knowne,
The waies on Sea are gone by needles light.
The birds of th'aire the nearest way have flowne,
And under earth the moules doe cast aright.
A way more hard then these I needs must take,   5
Where none can teach nor noe man can direct;
Where noe man's good for me example makes,
But al men's faults doe teach her to suspect.
Her thoughts and myne such disproportion have:
All strength of love is infinite in mee;   10
She useth the advantage tyme and fortune gave,
    Of worth and power to gett the libertie;
Earth, Sea, Heaven, Hell, are subject unto lawes,
But I, poore I, must suffer and knowe noe cause.
                   R:E:E:
          (BL, Royal MS 17.B.L., folio 2)

9

Ingenium, studium, nummos, spem, tempus, amicos,
Cum male perdiderim, perdere verba leve est.
          (Grosart, *Dr. Farmer-Chetham MS*, 97)

10

I am not as I seeme, I seeme and am the same;
I am as divers deeme, but not as others name;

I am not as I shoulde, I shoulde be as I saye;
In wantinge what I woulde, I must be as I maye.
finis qd Rob: Essex Comes
(BL, Add. MS 52585, folio 72v)

11
The Passion of a Discontented Minde

From silent night, true Register of mones,
From saddest soule, consum'd with deepest sins,
From hart quite rent with sighs and hevy grones,
My wailing Muse her wofull worke beginnes,
    And to the world brings tunes of sad despaire,   5
    Sounding nought else but sorrow, griefe, and care.

Sorrow, to see my sorrowe's cause augmented,
And yet lesse sorrowfull were my sorrowes more;
Griefe, that my griefe with griefe is not prevented,
For griefe it is must ease my grieved sore.   10
    Thus griefe and sorrow cares but how to grieve,
    For griefe and sorrow must my cares releeve.

The wound fresh bleeding must be stancht with teares;
Teares cannot come, unlesse some griefe preceed;
Griefes come but slacke, which doth increase my feares,   15
Feares, lest for want of helpe I still should bleed.
    Do what I can to lengthen my live's breath,
    If teares be wanting, I shal bleed to death.

Thou deepest Searcher of each secret thought,
Infuse in me thy all-affecting grace;   20
So shall my workes to good effects be brought,
While I peruse my ugly sinnes a space,
    Whose staining filth so spotted hath my soule,
    As nought will wash but teares of inward dole.

And thou faire Queene of mercy and of pittye,   25
Whose wombe did once the World's Creator carry,
Bee thou attentive to my painefull dittye,
Further my Sutes deare gracious blessed Mary;
    If thou begin the Quire of holy Saints
    Will all be helping to preferre my plaints.   30

O that the learned Poets of this time
(Who in a love-sicke line so well indite),
Would not consume good wit in hatefull Rime,

But would with care some better subject write:
    For if their musicke please in earthly things,   35
    Well would it sound if straind with heav'nly strings.

But woe it is to see fond worldlings' use,
Who most delight in things that vainest be;
And without feare worke Virtue's fowle abuse,
Scorning soule's rest and al true piety,   40
    As if they made account never to parte
    From this fraile life, the pilgrimage of smart.

Such is the nature of our foolish kinde,
When practiz'd sinne hath deeply taken roote,
The way to penance due is hard to finde,   45
Repentance held a thing of little boote;
    For contrite teares, soule's health, and angels' joy,
    Most men account a meere phantastike toy.

Ill-working Use, devourer of al grace,
The fretting moath that wasteth soule's chiefe blisse,   50
The slie close thiefe that lurkes in every place,
Filching by peece-meale, til the whole be his;
    How many are deceived by thy baite,
    T'account their sinnes as trifles of no waight?

O cursed custome, causing mischiefe still,   55
Too long thy craft my senses hath misse-led;
Too long have I bin slave unto thy will,
Too long my soule on bitter sweetes hath fed;
    Now surfetting with thy hell poysned cates,
    In deepe repent, her former folly hates.   60

And humbly comes with sorrow-rented hart,
With blubbred eies, and hands uprear'd to heaven,
To play a poore lamenting Mawdline's part,
That would weepe streames of blood to be forgiven;
    But (oh), I feare mine eies are drain'd so drie,   65
    That though I would, yet now I cannot crie.

If any eie therefore can spare a teare,
To fill the wel-springs that must wet my cheekes,
O let that eie to this sad feast draw neare,
Refuse me not, my humble soule beseekes;   70
    For all the teares mine eies have ever wept,
    Were now too little had they all bin kept.

I see my sinnes arraign'd before my face,
I see their number passe the moathes in Sunne,
I see that my continuance in this place   75
cannot be long, and all that I have done,
    I see the Judge before my face hath layde,
    At whose sterne lookes all creatures are afraide.

If he be just, my soule condemned is;
And just he is; what then may be expected,   80
But banishment from everlasting blisse?
To live like cursed Caine, base, vile, abjected;
    He in his rage his brother's blood did spill;
    I more unkinde mine owne soule's life doe kill.

O could mine eies send trickling teares amaine,   85
Never to cease till my eternall night,
Till this eye-flood his mercy might obtaine,
Whome my defaults have banisht from his sight;
    Then could I blesse my happy time of crying,
    But ah, too soone my barren springs are drying.   90

Thrise happy sinner was that blessed Saint,
Who though he fell with puffe of woman's blast,
Went forth and wept with many a bitter plaint,
And by his teares obtained grace at last;
    But wretched I have falne of mine accord,   95
    Tenne thousand times against the living Lord.

Yet cannot straine one true repentant teare,
To gaine the blisse from which my soule is banisht;
My flintie heart such sorrowing doth forbeare,
And from my sence all true remorce is vanisht;   100
    For heart and sence are cloyd with dregs of sinne,
    And there's no place for Grace to enter in.

No place (deere Lord) unlesse thy goodnesse please
To pitty him that worst deserves of any,
And in thy tender mercy grant him ease,   105
As thou tofore hast mercy shewd to many;
    Yet none of those doe equall me in sinne,
    O how may I hope mercie then to winne?

The traitor Judas, heire borne to perdition,
Who for a trifle did his Lord betray,   110
In equall doome deserveth more remission,
Then my defaults can challenge any way;

He solde him once, that once for gaine was done;
I oftentimes, yet lesse then nothing wonne.

The bloody minded Jewes, in furie mad,　　　　　　　115
Untill on Christ their cruell rage was fed,
In their fell anger more compassion had
Then I, for whome his harmelesse blood was shed;
　　　Their hellish spite within a day was past,
　　　My sinfull fit doth all my life time last.　　　120

For ev'ry stripe that he from them did take,
A thousand deadly sinnes have I committed;
And ev'ry sin as depe a wound did make,
As did the cordes wherewith my Christ was whipped;
　　　Oh hateful caitife, parricide most vile,　　　125
　　　Thus (with my sinne) his pure blood to defile.

O sinne, first parent of man's ever woe,
The distance large that severs hell and heaven;
Sense's confounder, soule's chiefe overthrow,
Grafted by men, not by the grafter geven;　　　　130
　　　Consuming canker, wasting soule's chiefe treasure,
　　　Onely to gaine a little trifling pleasure.

Happy were man if sinne had never bin,
Thrise happie now, if sinne he would forsake,
But happier farre, if for his wicked sinne　　　135
He would repent, and hearty sorrow make;
　　　Leaving this drosse and fleshly delectation,
　　　To gaine in heav'n a lasting habitation.

There is the place wherein all sorrowes die,
Where Joy exceedes all joyes that ever were;　　　140
Where Angels make continuall harmony,
The minde set free from care, distrust, or feare;
　　　There all receive all joyfull contentation,
　　　Happied by that most heav'nly contemplation.

Now see (alas) the change we make for sinne,　　　145
In steede of heav'n, hel is become our lot;
For blessed Saints, damned fiends we ever winne;
For rest and freedome, lasting bondage got;
　　　For Joy, content, eternall love and peace,
　　　Griefe, dispaire, hate, and jarres that never cease.　　　150

The worme of conscience stil attendeth on us,
Telling each houre, each instant we shall die,

And that our sinnes cannot be parted from us,
But where we are, thither they likewise flie;
    Still urging this, that death wee have deserved,   **155**
    Because we fled from him we should have served.

What greater sinne can touch a humane hart?
What hellish furie can be worse tormented?
What sinner lives that feeleth not a part
Of this sharpe plague, unlesse he have repented?   **160**
    And yet Repentance surely is but vaine,
    Without full purpose not to sinne againe.

And is it not then our plaine follie's error,
To covet that that brings with it contempt,
And makes us live in feare, distrust, and terror,   **165**
Hating at last the thing wee did attempt?
    For never sinne did yet so pleasing taste,
    But lustfull flesh did loathe it when t'was past.

Witnes my wofull soule, which well can tell,
In hiest top of sinne's most fresh delight,   **170**
Although my frailety suffred mee to dwell,
Yet being past, I loath'd it with despight;
    But like the swine, I fed mine owne desire,
    That being cleane, stil coveteth the mire.

So greedy is man's beastly appetite,   **175**
To follow after dunghill pleasures still,
And feede on carrion like the ravening kite,
Not caring what his hungry maw dooth fill,
    But worketh evermore his will's effect,
    Without restraint, controlement, or respect.   **180**

O, why should man, that beares the stamp of heaven,
So much abase heaven's holy will and pleasure?
O, why was sence and reason to him given,
That in his sinne cannot containe a measure?
    He knowes he must account for every sinne,   **185**
    And yet committeth sinnes that countlesse bin.

This to peruse (deere God) doth kill my soule,
But that thy mercy quickeneth it againe;
O, heare me, Lord, in bitternesse of dole,
That of my sinnes do prostrate heere complaine;   **190**
    And at thy feet, with Mary, knocke for grace,
    Though wanting Marie's teares to wet my face.

She, happy sinner, saw her life misse-led,
At sight whereof her inward hart did bleede,
To witnes which her outward teares were shed,   195
O blessed Saint, and O most blessed deede;
    But wretched I, that see more sinnes than she,
    Nor greeve within, nor yet weepe outwardly.

When she had lost thy presence but one day,
The want was such, hir heart could not sustaine;   200
But to thy tombe alone she tooke her way,
And there with sighs and teares she did complaine;
    Nor from her sense once moov'd or stirr'd was shee,
    Until againe she got a sight of thee.

But I have lost thy presence all my dayes,   205
And still am slacke to seek thee as I should;
My wretched soule in wicked sinne so stayes,
I am unmeete to see thee, though I would;
    Yet if I could with teares thy comming tend,
    I know I should (as she) finde thee my frend.   210

Teares are the key that ope the way to blisse,
The holy water quenching heav'ns quicke fire,
The attonement true twixt God and our amisse,
The Angels' drinke, the blessed Saints' desire,
    The joy of Christ, the balme of grieved hart,   215
    The spring of life, the ease of ev'ry smart.

The second King of Israel by succession,
When with Uriah's wife he had offended,
In bitter teares bewailed his great transgression,
And by his teares found grace, and so repented;   220
    He night and day in weeping did remaine;
    I night nor day to shed one teare take paine.

And yet my sinnes, in greatnesse and in number,
Farre his exceede; how comes it then to passe,
That my repentance should so farre be under,   225
And grace's force, deere God, is as it was?
    Truth is, that I, although I have more neede,
    Do not, as he, so truely weepe indeede.

O wherfore is my steely heart so hard?
Why am I made of mettall unrelenting?   230
Why is all ghostly comfort from me bard?
Or, to what end do I deferre repenting?

Can lustfull flesh, or flattring world perswade me,
That I can scape the power of him that made me?

No, no, the secret Searcher of all hearts,   235
Both sees and knowes each deede that I have done,
And for each deede wil pay me home with smart,
No place can serve his wil decreed to shunne;
 I should deceive my selfe to thinke that he
 For sinne would punish others, and not me.   240

Our first borne sire, first breeder of man's thrall,
For one bare sinne was of perfection reft,
And all mankinde were banisht by his fall
From Paradise, and unto sorrowe left;
 If he for one, and all for him feele paine,   245
 Then for so many, what should I sustaine?

The Angells made to attend on God in glorie,
Were thrust from heav'n, and only for one sinne;
That but in thought (for so recordes the Storie),
For which they still in lasting darkenesse bin;   250
 If those, once glorious, thus tormented be,
 I (basest slave) what will become of me?

What wil become of me, that not in thought,
In thought alone, but in each worde and deed,
A thousand thousand deadly sinnes have wrought,   255
And still doe worke, whereat my hart doth bleed?
 For even now, in this my sad complaining,
 With new made sins, my flesh my soule is staining.

O that I were remov'd to some close cave,
Where all alone retired from delight,   260
I might my sighes and teares untroubled have,
And never come in wretched worldlings' sight;
 Whose ill-bewitching company still brings
 Deepe provocation, whence great danger springs.

Ill company, the cause of many woes,   265
The sugred baite, that hideth poysned hooke;
The rocke unseene that shipwrackt soules o'rethrowes,
The weeping crocodile that killes with looke,
 The readiest steppe to ruine and decay,
 Grace's confounder and helle's nearest way.   270

How many soules do perish by thy guile?
How many men without all feare frequent

Thy deadly haunts, where they in pleasure smile,
Taking no care such dangers to prevent?
    But live like Belials, unbrideled or untamed,   275
    Not looking they shall for their faults be blamed.

Alas, alas, too wretched doe we live,
That carelesly thus worke our owne confusion,
And to our willes such libertie doe give;
Ay me, it is the divell's meere illusion,   280
    To flatter us with such sense-pleasing traines,
    That he thereby may take us in his chaines.

This well foresaw good men of auntient time,
Which made them shunne th'occasions of foule sinne,
Knowing it was the nurse of every crime,   285
And Syren-like would traine fond worldlings in;
    Alluring them with shew of musicke's sound,
    Untill on sinne's deepe shelfe their soules be drownd.

But he is held no sotiable man
In this corrupted age, that shall refuse   290
To keepe accursed company now and than;
Nay but a foole, unlesse he seeme to chuse
    Their fellowship, and give them highest place,
    That vildest live, and furthest off from grace.

But better 'tis, believe me, in my tryall,   295
To shun such hel-hounds, factors of the Divell,
And give them leave to grudge at your deniall,
Then to partake with such in sinne and evill;
    For if that God (in Justice) then should slay us,
    From hell and horror, who (alas) could stay us?   300

Good God, the Just (as he himselfe hath spoken),
Should scarce be saved, O terror unremovable;
What then should they that never had a token,
Or signe of grace (soule's comfort most behoveable),
    But gracelesse liv'd, and all good deedes did hate;   305
    What hope of them that live in such a state?

O who will give me teares that I may waile
Both nights and dayes the dangers I have past?
My soule, my soule, 'tis much for thy availe,
That thou art gotten from these straits at last;   310
    O joy, but in thy joy mixe teares withall,
    That thou hast time to say, Lord heare me call.

I might as others (Lord) have perished,
Amid my sinnes and damnable delights;
But thou (good God) with care my soule hast cherished,   315
And brought it home to look on heav'nly lights;
    Ay me, what thankes, what service can I render
    To thee, that of my safety art so tender?

Now doe I curse the time I ever went
In sinne's blacke path, that leadeth to damnation;   320
Now do I hate the houres I have misse-spent
In ydle vice, neglecting soule's salvation;
    And to redeeme the time I have mis-worne,
    I wish this houre, I were againe new borne.

But vaine it is, as saith the wisest man,   325
To call againe the day that once is past,
O let me see what best is for me than,
To gaine thy favour whil'st my life doth last;
    That in the next I may but worthy be,
    Ev'n in the meanest place to waite on thee.   330

I will, as did the prodigall sonne sometime,
Upon my knees with harty true contrition,
And Weeping eies, confesse my former crime,
And humbly begge upon my low submission,
    That thou wilt not of former faults detect me,   335
    But like a loving father now respect me.

Or, as the wife that hath her husband wronged,
So wil I come with feare and blushing cheeke,
For giving others what to thee belonged,
And say, "My King, my Lord, and Spouse most meeke,   340
    I have defil'd the bed that thou didst owe;
    Forgive me this, it shall no more be so."

Yet, for the world can witnes mine abuse,
I'le hide my face from face that witcht mine eies;
These gracelesse eies, that had my bodie's use,   345
Till it be withred with my verie cries,
    That when my wrinckles shall my sorrowes tell,
    The world may say, I joy'd not, though I fell.

And thus will I in sorrowing spend my breath,
And spot my face with never-drying teares,   350
Till aged wrinckles, messengers of death,
Have purchasde mercy and remov'd my feares;

And then the world within my lookes shall read,
The piteous wracke unbrideled sinne hath bred.

And that which was a pleasure to beholde,   355
Shalbe to me an ever-griping paine;
All my misdeedes shall one and one be tolde,
That I may see what tyrants have mee slaine;
    And when I have thus mustred them apart,
    I will display on each a bleeding hart.   360

And lest my teares should faile me at most need,
Before my face I'le fix my Saviour's passion,
And see how his most pretious side did bleed,
And note his death and torments in such fashion
    As never man the like did undertake,   365
    For freely he hath done it for my sake.

If this his kindenesse and his mercy showne,
Cannot provoke me unto tender crying,
Then will I backe againe turne to mine owne,
Mine owne sins, cause of this his cruell dying;   370
    And if for them no teares mine eies can find,
    Sighs shal cause tears, tears make my poore eies blind.

No farre fetcht story have I now brought home,
Nor taught to speake more language than his mother's,
No long done Poem is from Darkenesse come   375
To light againe, it's ill to fetch from others;
    The song I sing, is made of heart-bred sorrow,
    Which pensive Muse from pining soule doth borow.

I sing not *I*, of wanton love-sicke laies,
Of trickling toyes to feed fantasticke eares,   380
My Muse respects no flattring tatling praise,
A guiltie concience this sad passion beares;
    My sinne sicke soule, with sorrow woe begone,
    Lamenting thus a wretched deede mis-done.

FINIS
(STC 3679.5 [1601], from the unique copy in the
Houghton Library)

POEMS POSSIBLY BY ESSEX

I

Courte's skorne, state's disgracinge,
Potentate's scoff, govermente's defacing,

Prince's touch, churche's unhallowinge,
Arte's injury, vertue's debacinge,
Age's monster, honor's wastinge,   5
Beutye's blemmish, favour's blasting,
Witte's excrement, wisdome's vommett,
Physicke's scoomme, lawe's commett,
Fortune's child, nature's defiler,
Justice revenger, freind shippe's beguiler;   10
     Such is the song, such is the author,
     Worthy to be rewarded with a halter.
        (Rosenbach, MS 1083/15, folio 17v)

II

Go Eccho of the minde, a careles troth protest,
Make answere that so raw a lye no stomack can digest.
For why? the lie's discent is over base to tell;
To us it came from Italy, to them it came from hell.
What reason proves, confesse; what slander saith, denye;   5
Let no untruth with triumph passe—but never give the lye.
Confesse in glittering court all ar not goulde that shine,
Yet say one pearle and much fine gould growes in that
     princly mine.
Confesse that many tares do overgrowe the grounde,
Yet say within the fielde of God good corne is to be founde. 10
Confesse som judge unjust the widowe's right delay.
Yet say there ar some Samuels that never say her nay.
Admitte some man of state do pitch his thoughtes to hie;
Is that a rule for all the rest their loyall hartes to trie?
Your wittes ar in the waine, your autumne in the bud,   15
You argue from particulers, your reason is not good.
And still that men may see lesse reason to commend you,
I marvaile most amongst the rest how schooles and artes
     offend you.
But whie pursue I thus the waightles wordes of winde?
The more the crab doth seeke to creepe, the more she is
     behinde.   20
In church and common wealth, in court and country both,
What, nothing good, but all so bad that every man doth loath?
The further that you raunge, your errour is the wider,
The bee sometimes doth hony suck, but sure you ar a spider.
And so my counsaile is, for that you want a name,   25

To seeke some corner in the darke to hide your self from
    shame;
There wrapp the sely flye within your spitefull webbe,
Both church and court may want you well, they ar at no
    such ebbe.
As quarrels once begun ar not so quickly ended,
So, many faultes may soone be founde, but not so soone
    amended.   30
And when ye come againe to give the worlde the lye,
I pray you tell them how to live, and teach them how to dye.
          (Grosart, *Dr. Farmer-Chetham MS*, 118–20)

III

Behold a wonder here,
Love hath receiv'd his sight,
Which manie hundred yeares,
Hath not beheld the light.

Such beames infused be   5
By *Cynthia* in his eyes,
As first have made him see,
And then have made him wise.

Love now no more will weepe,
For them that laugh the while,   10
Nor wake for them that sleepe,
Nor sigh for them that smile.

So powrefull is the beautie
That Love doth now behold,
As love is turn'd to dutie,   15
That's neither blind nor bold.

This Beautie shewes her might
To be of double kind,
In giving love his sight,
And striking folly blind.   20
          (STC 7096, song 3)

IV

**A Poem made on the Earle of Essex (being in disgrace
with Queene Eliz): by mr henry Cuffe his Secretary.**

1. It was a time when sillie Bees could speake,
    And in that tyme I was a sillie Bee,

Who suckt on tyme untill my heart gan breake,
    Yet never found that tyme would favour me;
        Of all the swarme, I onlie could not thrive,   5
        Yet brought I wax and hony to the hive.

2. Then thus I bussed when tyme no sap would give,
    Why is this blessed tyme to me soe dry?
Sith in this tyme the lazie drone doth live,
    The waspe, the worme, the gnat, the Butterfly;   10
        Mated with greefe, I kneeled on my knees,
        And thus complained unto the kinge of Bees:

3. "My leige, god graunte thy tyme may never end,
    And yet voutsafe to heare my plainte of tyme,
Which every fruitles fly hath found a freind,   15
    And I cast downe while Attomyes doe Clime."
        The kinge replied but thus, "Peace, peevish Bee,
        Th'art borne to serve the tyme, the tyme not thee."

4. "The tyme not thee"—this word clipt short my winges,
    And made me wormelike creepe that once did flie;   20
Awefull regard disputeth not with kinges,
    Receaveth a repulse, not askinge whie;
        Then from the tyme I for a tyme withdrew,
        To feede on Henbaine, Hemlock, Nettls, Rue.

5. But from those leaves noe dram of sweet I draine;   25
    Theire headstrong fury did my wittes bewitch,
The juce disperste blacke bloud in every vaine,
    For hony, gall, for wax I gathered Pitch;
        My Combe a Rift, My Hive a leafe must be,
        Soe Changd that Bees scarce tooke me for a Bee.   30

6. I worke on weedes when moone is in the waine,
    Whilst all the swarme in suneshine tast the Rose;
On blacke roote fearne I sitt, and sucke my baine,
    Whilst on the Eglentine the rest repose;
        Havinge too much they still repine for more,   35
        And cloide with sweetness surfit on the store.

7. Swolne fatt with feastes full merelie they passe,
    In sweetned Clustres fallinge from the Tree,
Where findinge me to nibble on the grasse,
    Some scorne, some muse, and some doe pittie me;   40
        And some envy and whisper to the kinge,
        Some must be still and some must have no sting.

8. Are Bees waxt waspes or spiders to infecte?
    Doe Hony bowelles make the sperit galle?
Is this the joyce of flowers to stirr suspecte?   45
    Is't not enough to treade on them that fall?
        What stinge hath patience but a sigheing greefe,
        That stinges naught but it selfe without Releife?

9. True patience, the provender of fooles,
    Sad patience that waiteth at the dore,   50
Patience that learnes thus to conclude in schooles:
    Patience I am, therefore I must be poore;
        Great kinge of Bees, that rightest every wronge,
        Listen to Patience in her dyinge songe.

10. I Cannot feed on Fennell, like some flies,   55
    Nor fly to every flower to gather gaine;
Myne appetite weites on my prince's eies,
    Contented with Contempte, and pleasd with Paine;
        And yet expectinge of an happie hower,
        When he shall saie this Bee shall suck a flower.   60

11. Of all the greefes that must my patience grate,
    There's one that fretteth in the highest degree,
To see some Caterpillers bred of late,
    Croppinge the flowers that should sustaine the Bee
        Yet smiled I for that the wisest knowes,   65
        That mothes doe fret the cloth, Cankers the Rose.

12. Once did I see by flyinge in the feeild
    Fowle beastes to browse upon the lillies faire;
Vertue and bewtie could no succour yeild,
    Al's provender for asses but the aire;   70
        The partiall world of this takes litle heede,
        To give them flowers that should on Thistles
        feede.

13. 'Tis onlie I must draine Egiptian flowers,
    Having noe savor, bitter sapp they have,
And seeke out rotten tombes, and dead men's bowers,   75
    And bite on Lotos growinge by the grave;
        Yf this I cannot have as haples Bee,
        Witching Tobacco, I will flie to thee.

14. What thoughe thou die my longes in deepest blacke?
    A morninge habit suites a sable hart.   80
What thoughe thy fumes sound memorie do Crack,

Forgetfulnes is fittest for my smarte;
   O vertuous fume, let it be carved in Oke,
   That wordes, hopes, wittes, and all the world is
   smoke.

15. Five yeares twise told with promises perfumed,   85
   My hope-stuft head was Cast in to a slumber;
   Sweete dreames of gold, on dreames I then presumd,
   And mongst the Bees thought I was in the number;
   Wakinge I founde Hive hopes had made me vaine,
   'Twas not Tobacco stupified my braine.   90
        (BL, Harleian MS 6947, folios 230–31v)

DeVere, Edward, Seventeenth Earl of Oxford (1550–1604)

As a royal ward in the custody of Secretary Cecil after 1562, Oxford began attending court in his early teens. On August 10, 1564, he was created M.A. at Cambridge University along with sixteen other courtiers who accompanied the queen on her progress thither.[1] He received the same distinction from Oxford University during the progress of 1566. He participated in a court tournament performed on the first three days of May 1571, and with two other courtiers he arranged a parade of harquebusiers before the French ambassador in June of the same year. In December Elizabeth attended the dinner celebrating Oxford's marriage to Anne, daughter of William Cecil, the newly created Lord Burghley. By May of 1573 he was considered one of Elizabeth's foremost favorites.[2] His earliest recorded participation in the New Year's exchange occurred in 1575, with later presentations in 1579, 1580, and 1581. The queen stood godmother to DeVere's daughter, christened July 14, 1575, while Oxford was abroad in the course of a fourteen-month continental tour.[3]

Elizabeth nicknamed the earl her Turk; she held him in very high regard until the revelation in March 1581 of his liaison with Anne Vavasour, one of the maids of honor. By this time as well Oxford had divested himself of most of the family estates that he had inherited with his title. Although Elizabeth pardoned him a few years later (a pardon largely engineered by Ralegh), Oxford never regained his position as a courtier of the first magnitude. But if the queen never

1. Nichols, *Progresses*, 1:164.
2. B. M. Ward, *The Seventeenth Earl of Oxford*, 56; Charles Purton Cooper, *Recueil des Dépêches . . . (Fénelon Correspondence)*, 4:155–56, 315.
3. BL, Add. MS 4827.

granted him a significant post in the household or the nation's service, she did relieve his financial distress in 1586 with a one-thousand-pound annuity. Moreover, the earl was guaranteed a regular if ceremonial degree of prominence at court by virtue of his office as Lord Great Chamberlain of England.

Oxford's sixteen canonical and four possible poems date primarily from his heyday at court during the 1570s. One was printed in 1573, while eight more appeared in *The Paradise of Dainty Devices* and were thus composed before the publication of that anthology in 1576. Another six were cited or in print before 1590, and three of the remaining five had filtered into the printed anthologies within the next four years. There is little reason to suppose that he wrote verse later than the 1580s. For commentary and the textual apparatus see my edition of Oxford's poems in "The Poems of Edward DeVere."

1

The Earle of Oxenforde
to the Reader.

The labouring man that tilles the fertile soyle,
And reapes the harvest fruite hath not in deede
The gaine but payne, and if for all hys toyle
He gets the strawe, the Lord will have the seede.
The Manchet fyne falles not unto his share;   5
On coursest cheat his hungrye stomacke feedes.
The Landlord doth possesse the fynest fare;
He pulles the flowers, the other pluckes but weedes.
The mason poore that buildes the Lordlye halles
Dwelles not in them, they are for hye degree;   10
His Cotage is compact in paper walles,
And not with bricke or stone as others bee.
The idel Drone that labours not at all,
Suckes up the sweete of honnye from the Bee.
Who worketh most, to their share least doth fall;   15
Wyth due desert reward will never bee.
The swiftest Hare unto the Mastive slowe
Oft times doth fall, to him as for a praye;
The Greyhounde thereby doth misse his game we know,
For which he made such speedy hast awaye.   20
So hee that takes the payne to penne the booke
Reapes not the giftes of goodlye golden Muse,

But those gayne that who on the worke shal looke,
And from the soure the sweete by skill doth chuse.
For hee that beates the bushe the byrde not gets,   25
But who sittes still, and holdeth fast the nets.
                        (STC 4607, sig. A4v)

2

Even as the waxe doeth melt, or dewe consume awaie,
Before the Sonne, so I behold through careful thoughts decaie:
For my best lucke leads me, to suche sinister state,
That I doe wast with other's love, that hath my self in hate.
And he that beats the bushe, the wished birde not getts,   5
But suche I see as sitteth still, and holds the foulyng netts.

The Drone more honie sucks, that laboureth not at all,
Then doeth the Bee, to whose most pain, least pleasure doth
    befall;
The Gardner sowes the seeds, whereof the flowers doe growe,
And others yet doe gather them, that tooke lesse paine I
    knowe.   10
So I the pleasaunt grape have pulled from the Vine,
And yet I languish in great thirst, while others drinke the
    wine.

Thus like a wofull wight, I wove my webb of woe,
The more I would wede out my cares, the more thei seme to
    grow.
The whiche betokeneth hope, forsaken is of me,   15
That with the carefull culver climes, the worne and withered
    tree,
To entertaine my thoughts, and there my happe to mone,
That never am lesse idle loe, then when I am alone.
                                          Finis. E. O.
                        (STC 7516, sig. K3-3v)

3

A Croune of Bayes shall that man weare,
    That triumphs over me:
    For blacke and Tawnie will I weare,
Whiche mournyng colours be.

The more I folowed on, the more she fled awaie,   5
As *Daphne* did full long agone, *Apollo's* wishfull praie.
The more my plaints resounde, the lesse she pities me,

The more I saught the lesse I founde, that myne she ment
   to be.

Melpomeney, alas with dolefull tunes helpe than,
And sing *bis* wo worthe on me, forsaken man;   **10**
Then *Daphne's* baies shal that man weare, that triumphs
   over me,
For Blacke and Taunie will I weare, which mournyng
   colours be.

Droune me you tricklyng teares, you wailefull wights of
   woe,
Come help these hands to rent my heares, my rufull happs
   to showe:
On whom the scorchyng flames of love, doeth feede you se,   **15**
Ah, a lalalantida my deare dame, hath thus tormented me.

Wherefore you Muses nine, with dolefull tunes helpe than,
And syng *Bis* wo worthe on me forsaken man;
Then *Daphne's* Baies shall that man weare, that triumps
   over me
For Blacke and Taunie will I weare, which mourning
   colours be.   **20**

An Ancre's life to leade, with nailes to scratche my grave,
Where earthly Wormes on me shall fede, is all the joyes I
   crave;
And hide my self from shame, sith that myne eyes doe see,
Ah, a alantida my deare dame, hath thus tormented me.

And all that present be, with doelfull tunes helpe than: **25**
And syng *Bis* woe worthe on me, forsaken man.
                       Finis. E. O.
                       (STC 7516, sig. I3v–4)

4

Framd in the front of forlorne hope, past all recoverie,
I stayles stand 'tabide the shocke of shame and infamy.
My life through lingring long is lodgde, in lare of lothsome
   wayes,
My death delaide to keepe from life, the harme of haplesse
   dayes;
My sprites, my hart, my witte and force, in deepe distresse
   are dround,   **5**
The only losse of my good name, is of these greefes the ground.

And since my minde, my wit, my head, my voyce and tongue
    are weake,
To utter, moove, devise, conceave, sound foorth, declare and
    speake,
Such pearsing plantes, as aunswere might, or would my
    wofull case,
Helpe, crave I must, and crave I will, with teares upon my
    face: 10
Of al that may in heaven or hell, in earth or ayre be found,
To wayle with me this losse of mine, as of these greefes the
    ground.
Helpe gods, helpe saintes, helpe sprites and powers, that in
    the heaven doo dwell,
Helpe ye that are to waile aye woont, ye howling hounds of
    hell;
Helpe man, helpe beastes, helpe birds and wormes, that on
    the earth doth toile,   15
Helpe fishe, helpe foule, that flockes and feedes upon the salte
    sea soyle;
Helpe eccho that in ayre dooth flee, shril voyces to resound,
To waile this losse of my good name, as of these greefes the
    ground.

FINIS. E. O.

(Bodl., Douce MS e.16, folios 43–44)

5

I am not as I seme to bee,
Nor when I smile, I am not glad;
A thrall although you count me free,
I moste in mirthe, moste pensive sadd.
I smile to shade my bitter spight,   5
As Haniball that sawe in sight
His countrey soile, with Carthage toune,
By Romaine force, defaced doune.

    And *Caesar* that presented was,
With noble *Pompeye's* princely hedd,   10
As 'twere some judge, to rule the case,
A floud of teares, he semde to shedd
Although in deede, it sprong of joye,
Yet others thought it was annoye;
Thus contraries be used I finde,   15
Of wise to cloke the covert minde.

I *Haniball* that smiles for grief,
And let you *Caesar's* teares suffice:
The one that laughs at his mischief,
The other all for joye that cries.   20
I smile to see me scorned so,
You wepe for joye, to see me wo:
And I a harte by love slaine dead
Presents in place of *Pompeye's* head.

O cruell happ, and harde estate,   25
That forceth me to love my foe;
Accursed by so foule a fate,
My choise for to prefixe it so.
So long to fight with secret sore,
And finde no secret salve therefore.   30
Some purge their paine by plaint I finde,
But I in vaine doe breathe my winde.
                    Finis. E. O.
                (STC 7516, sig. K2v–3)

                           6
If care or skill could conquere vaine desire,
    Or reason's raines my strong affection staie,
Then should my sights, to quiet breast retire,
And shunne suche signes as secret thoughts bewraie.
Uncomely love, whiche now lurks in my breast,   5
Should cease my grief, through wisdom's power opprest.

But who can leave to looke on *Venus'* face,
Or yeldeth not to *Juno's* high estate?
What witt so wise, as gives not *Pallas* place?
These vertues rare eche God did yelde amate,   10
Save her alone, who yet on yearth doeth reigne,
Whose beauties' stryng no Gods can well destraine.

What worldly wight can hope for heavenly hire,
When onely sights must make his secret mone?
A silent sute doeth selde to Grace aspire,   15
My haples happe doeth role the restles stone;
Yet *Phebe* faire disdainde the heavens above,
To joye on yearth her poore *Endimion's* love.

Rare is reward where none can justly crave,
For chaunce is choise where reason maks no claime;   20

Yet lucke sometymes dispairyng souls doeth save,
A happie starre made *Giges* joye attaine.
A slavishe Smith of rude and rascall race,
Founde means in tyme to gaine a Goddes' grace.

Then loftie Love, thy sacred sailes advaunce,　　　**25**
My sithyng seas shall flowe with streames of teares;
Amidds disdaine drive forthe my doelfull chaunce,
A valiaunt mainde no deadly daunger feares.
Who loves alofte and setts his hart on hie,
Deserves no paine, though he doe pine and die.　　　**30**
(STC 7516, sig. K1v–2)

7

My meanyng is to worke what wonders love hath wrought,
　Wherwith I muse why men of wit have love so derely
　　bought;
For love is worse then hate, and eke more harme hath doen,
Record I take of those that rede of Paris, Priam's sonne.

It semed the God of slepe had mazed so muche his witts,　　　**5**
When he refused witt for love, whiche cometh but by fitts;
But why accuse I hym, whom yearth hath covered long?
There be of his posteritie alive, I doe hym wrong;

　Whom I might well condempne, to be a cruell judge
Unto myself who hath the crime in others that I grudge.　　　**10**
Finis. E. O.
(STC 7516, sig. K3v)

8

The Lyvely Larke stretcht forth her wynge,
　The messenger of morninge bright,
And with her Chearfull voyce did Singe
　The daye's approache dischanginge Nyght.
When that Aurora blushinge Redd　　　**5**
　Dyscride the guylt of Thetis' Bedd.

I went abroad to take the Ayre, and in the meades I mette a
　knyght,
Clad in Carnation Colour fayre, I did salute this gentle wyght,
　Of him I did his name enquyre,
　　He sighed, and sayd he was desyre.　　　**10**
Desire I did desire to stay, awhile with him I Cravde to talke.

The Courteous knyght said me no nay, but hand in hand
   with me did walke.
   Then of desyre I askde agayne,
   What thinge did please and what did payne?
He smylde, and thus he answerd than, "Desire can have no
   greater payne,   15
Then for to see an other man, that he desirethe to obtayne,
   Nor greater Joy Can be than this,
   Than to enjoy that others mysse."
                  (BL, Harleian MS 7392(2), folio 67)

9

The tricklyng teares that fales along my cheeks,
The secret sighs that showes my inward grief,
The present paines perforce, that love aye seeks,
Bidds me renew my cares without relief,
In wofull song in dole displaie,   5
My pensive harte for to bewraie.

   Bewraie thy grief, thou wofull harte with speede,
Resigne thy voyce to her that causde thy woe;
With irksome cries bewaile thy late doen deede,
For she thou lovest is sure thy mortall foe.   10
And helpe for thee there is none sure,
But still in paine thou must endure.

   The striken Deare hath helpe to heale his wounde,
The haggerd hauke with toile is made full tame,
The strongest tower the Canon laies on grounde,   15
The wisest witt that ever had the fame,
Was thrall to Love by *Cupid's* sleights,
Then waie my case with equall waights.

   She is my joye, she is my care and wo,
She is my paine, she is my ease therefore;   20
She is my death, she is my life also,
She is my salve, she is my wounded sore;
In fine, she hath the hande and knife,
That maie bothe save, and ende my life.

   And shal I live on yearth to be her thral?   25
And shall I sue and serve her all in vaine?
And shall I kisse the stepps that she letts fall,
And shall I praie the gods to kepe the pain

From her, that is so cruell still?
No, no, on her woorke all your will.   **30**

    And let her feele the power of all your might,
And let her have her moste desire with speede;
And let her pine awaie bothe daie and night,
And let her mone, and none lament her neede,
And let all those that shall her se,   **35**
Dispise her state, and pitie me.

Finis. E. O.
(STC 7516, sig. K2–2v)

10

Feyne would I singe but fury makes me frette,
And rage hath sworne to seke revenge of wronge;
My mased mynde in malice so is sette
As death shall daunte my deadly dolors longe.
Pacience perforce is such a pinchinge payne,   **5**
As dy I will or suffer wronge agayne.

I am no sott to suffer suche abuse
As dothe bereve my hart of his delighte,
Nor wyll I frame my self to suche as use
With calme consent to suffer such despyght.   **10**
Noe quiet sleep shall once possesse myne ey,
Till witt have wroughte his will on Injurye.

My hart shall fayll and hand shall lose his force,
But some devise shall pay despight his dewe;
And fury shall consume my carefull coorse,   **15**
Or raze the ground wheron my sorow grew.
Loe thus in rage of ruthfull mind refusd,
I rest revengd of whome I am abusd.

finis Earle of Oxenforde
(Bodl., Tanner MS 306, folio 115v)

11

When werte thow borne desyre?
    In Pompe and pryme of May.
By whom sweete boy werte thou begot?
    By good Conceyte, men say.
Tell me who was thy Nurse?   **5**
    Freshe youthe in sugred Joy.
What was thy meate and dayly foode?

Sad syghes with great Annoy.
What hadste thow then to drinke?
   Unfayned lovers' teares.   **10**
What Cradle werte thou rocked in?
   In Hope devoyde of Feares.
What brought thee then asleepe?
   Sweete speech, that lykte me best.
And wher is now thy dwellinge place?   **15**
   In gentle hartes I rest.
Dothe Company dysplease?
   Yt doth in many a one.
Where wold desire then chuse to be?
   He likes to muse alone.   **20**
What feedethe most your syghte?
   To gaze on Favour styll.
What findste thou most to be thy fo?
   Dysdayne of my goodwill.
Wyll ever Age or Deathe   **25**
   Bringe the unto decay?
NO, NO, DESYER BOTHE LYVES AND DYES,
TEN THOWSANDE TYMES A DAY.
          Finis. LO. OX.
(BL, Harleian MS 7392(2), folios 18v–19)

12

Wing'de with desyre, I seeke to mount on hyghe;
Clogde with myshapp yet am I kept full lowe;
Whoe seekes to lyve and fyndes the waye to dye,
Sythe comforte ebbs, and cares do daylye flowe.
   But sadd despayre would have me to retyre,   **5**
   When smylynge hoape setts forward my desyre.

I styll do toyll and never am at reste,
Enjoyenge least whan I do covet moste;
With wearye thoughtes are my green yeers opprest,
To dawnger drawen from my desyred coast.   **10**
   Nowe crazed with Care, than haled up with Hope,
   With world at will yet wantynge wished scope.

I lyke in harte, yet dare not saye I love,
And lookes alone do lend me cheefe releife.
I dwelt sometymes at rest yet must remove,   **15**
With fayngned joye I hyde my secret greefe.

I would possess yet needs must flee the place
Where I do seek to wyn my cheefest grace.

Lo thus I lyve twyxte feare and comforte toste,
With least abode wher best I feell contente;   20
I seelde resorte wher I should setle most,
My slydinge tymes to sone with her are spente.
    I hover hyghe and soare wher Hope doth tower,
    Yet froward Fate defers my happy hower.

I live abrod but styll in secreat greef,   25
Then least alone when most I seeme to lurke;
I speak of peace, and lyve in endles stryfe,
And when I playe than are my thoughts at worke;
    In person farr that am in mynd full neere,
    Makynge lyghte showe where I esteeme most deere.   30

A mall-content yet seeme I pleased styll,
Braggyng of heaven yet feelynge paynes of hell.
But Tyme shall frame a tyme unto my will,
Whenas in sporte thys earnest will I tell;
    Tyll than (sweet frende) abyde these stormes with me,   35
    Which shall in joys of eyther fortunes be.
            (Bodl., Rawlinson poet. MS 85, folios 48v–9)

13
Love compared to a tennis playe.

Whereas the Harte at Tennysse playes and men to gaminge fall,
Love is the Courte, Hope is the Howse, and Favour serves the
    Ball.
The Ball itself is True Desert, the Lyne which Measure showes
Is Reason, wheron Judgement lookes howe players winne or
    lose.
The Gettye is deceitfull Guyle, the Stopper, Jelouzye,   5
Which hath Sir Argoës' hundred eyes, wherwith to watch and
    prye.
The Fault wherwith fifteen is lost is wante of witt and Sence,
And he that bringes the Racket in, is Double Dyligence.
And loe the Racket is Freewill, which makes the Ball
    rebounde,
And Noble Bewtye is the chase, of every game the grounde.   10
But Rashenes strikes the Ball awrye, and wher is Oversighte?
"A Bandye hoe," the people crye, and soe the Ball takes flighte.

Nowe in the ende Goodlykinge proves
   Content the game and gayn.
Thus in a Tennysse knitt I Love,
   A Pleasure mixte with Payne.
Made by the Earle of Oxeforde.
   (Marsh's Library, MS 183, folio 20)

14

What cunning can expresse
The favor of hir face?
To whom in this distresse,
I doe appeale for grace;
   A thousand Cupids flie,   5
   About hir gentle eie.

From whence each throwes a dart,
That kindleth soft sweete fier,
Within my sighing hart,
Possessed by desier;   10
   No sweeter life I trie,
   Than in hir love to die.

The Lillie in the fielde,
That glories in his white,
For purenes now must yeelde,   15
And render up his right;
   Heav'n pictur'de in hir face
   Doth promise joy and grace.

Faire Cinthia's silver light,
That beates on running streames,   20
Compares not with hir white,
Whose haires are all sunbeames;
   Hir vertues so doe shine,
   As daie unto mine eine.

With this there is a Red,   25
Exceeds the Damaske Rose,
Which in hir cheekes is spred,
Whence every favor groes;
   In skie there is no starre,
   That she surmounts not farre.   30

When Phoebus from the bed,
Of Thetis doth arise,

The morning blushing red,
In faire carnation wise,
    He shewes it in her face,   **35**
    As Queene of every grace.

This pleasant Lillie white,
This taint of roseat red,
This Cinthia's silver light,
This sweete faire Dea spread,   **40**
    These sunbeames in mine eie,
    These beauties make me die.
             E. O.
     (STC 21516, sig. I3v–4)

15

Who taught the first to sighe alas my Harte?
  Who taught thy Tongue the wofull wordes of plaint? } love.

Who fild thine Eyes with Teares of bitter smarte?
  Who gave the grief and made thy Joyes so faynt?
Who first did print with Coloures pale thy face?   **5**
  Who first did breke thy slepes of quiet rest? } Love.

Above the rest in Court who gave thee Grace?
  Who made the stryve in vertue to be Best?
In Constant troth to bide so firme and sure,
  To scorn the world regarding but thy frend, } Love **10**

With pacient mynd each passion to endure,
  In one desire to settle to thy end? }
Love then thy Choyse, wherin such fayth doth bynde,
As nought but death may ever Change thy mynde.
             FINIS .Ball.
    (BL, Harleian MS 7392(2), folio 70v)

16

Weare I a kinge I coulde commande content;
Weare I obscure unknowne shoulde be my cares,
And weare I ded no thought should me torment,
Nor wordes, nor wronges, nor loves, nor hopes, nor feares;
    A dowtefull choyse of these thinges one to crave,   **5**
    A Kingdom or a cottage or a grave.
       (BL, Add. MS 22583, p. 186)

POEMS POSSIBLY BY OXFORD

I

Sittinge alone upon my thought in melancholye moode,
In sighte of sea and at my backe an aunceyent, horye
    woode,
I sawe a fayre yonge ladye come her secreate teares to wayle,
Clad all in colour of a vowe and covered with a vayle.
Yet for the daye was clere and calme, I might descerne
    her face,   5
As one mighte see a damaske rose thoughe hid with
    cristall glasse.
Three tymes with her softe hande full harde upon her
    heart she knockes,
And sighte soe sore as mighte have moved some mercy
    in the rocks;
From sighes and sheadinge amber teares into swete
    songe she brake,
And thus the eccho answered her to every woorde she
    spake.   10

"O heavenes," quothe she, "who was the firste that
    bred in me this fevere?"   vere
"Who was the firste that gave the wounde whose scarre
    I were forever?"   vere
"What tyrant, Cupid, to my harmes usurpes thy golden
    quivere?"   vere
"What wighte first caughte this hearte and can from
    bondage it delivere?"   vere
"Yet who dothe moste adore this wighte? O hollow
    caves tell true;"   yowe   15
"What nimphe deserves his likinge beste? yet doth in
    sorrowe rue?"   yowe
"What makes him not regarde good will with some
    remorse or ruthe?"   youthe
"What makes him shewe besides his birthe such
    pride and such untruthe?"   youthe
"May I his beautye matche with love if he my love
    will trye?"   I
"May I requite his birthe with faythe? then faythfull
    will I dye."   I   20
And I that knewe this ladye well said lorde, how great
    a myracle,

To heare the eccho tell her truthe as 'twere Apollo's
    oracle.   Vavaser.
                (Folger, MS V.a.89, folio 9)

II
In praise of a contented minde

1 My mynde to me a kingdome is, such perfect joye therin I
    finde,
  That it excelles all other blisse that world affordes or growes
    by kind;
  Thoughe much I want which most men have, yet still my
    mynde forbids to crave.
2 No princelie pompe, no welthie store, no force to wynn the
    victorie,
  No wylie witt to salve a sore, no shape to fede eche gazinge
    eie,   5
  To none of these I yelde as thrall; for why? my mynde doth
    serve for all.
3 I see howe plentie suffers ofte, howe hastie Climbers sone
    do fall;
  I see that those that are alofte, mishap doth threaten most
    of all;
  They get with toile, they keape with feare, such cares my
    mynde could never bear.
4 Content I live, this is my staie, I seke no more then may
    suffice;   10
  I presse to beare no hawtie swaie, loke what I lack my
    mynde supplies.
  Loe thus I triumphe like a kinge, Content with that my
    mynde doth bringe.
5 Some have to muche yet still doe crave, I litle have and
    seke no more;
  They are but poore thoughe muche they have and I am
    riche with litle store.
  They poore, I riche, they begge, I give, They lacke I leave,
    they pine, I live.   15
6 I laughe not at another's losse, I grudge not at another's
    gaine,
  No worldly waves my mynde can tosse, my state at one
    doth still remaine;
  I feare no foe nor fawninge friend, I lothe not lief nor dread
    my end.

7 Some weighe theire pleasure by theire luste, their wisdome
    by theire rage of will;
  Theire treasure is theire onely truste, and cloked crafte
    theire store of skill;   **20**
  But all the pleasure that I finde, is to maintaine a quiet
    minde.
8 My welthe is healthe and perfect ease, my conscience clere
    my chief defence;
  I nether seke by bribes to please nor by desert to brede
    offence.
  Thus doe I live, thus will I die, would all did so as well as I.
               (Inner Temple, Petyt MS 538.10, folio 3v)

III

If woemen coulde be fayre and yet not fonde,
Or that there love were firme, not fickll still,
I woulde not mervaylle that they make men bonde,
By servise longe to purchase theyre good will;
  But when I se how frayll those creatures are,   **5**
  I muse that men forget themselves so farr.

To marcke the choyse they make and how they change,
How ofte from Phoebus theye do flee to Pann,
Unsettled still like haggardes willd theye range,
These gentlle byrdes that flye from man to man;   **10**
  Who woulde not scorne and shake them from the fyste,
  And let them flye, fayre fooles, whiche waye they lyste?

Yet for disporte we fawne and flatter bothe,
To pass the tyme when nothinge else can please,
And trayne them to our lure with subtylle othe,   **15**
Till wearye of theyre wiles our selves we easse;
  And than we saye when we theire fancye trye,
  To playe with fooles, oh what a foole was I.
                Finis qd Earll of Oxenforde
        (Bodl., Rawlinson poet. MS 85, folio 16)

IVa

In pescod time when hownd to horne gives eare while Bucke
    is kild,
  And little boyes with pipes of Corne, sit keping beasts in
    field,

I went to gather Strawberies tho when wods and groves wer
    faire,
    And parchte my face with Phebus loe, by walking in
        the ayre.
I lay me down all by a streame and bankes all over head,   5
    And ther I found the strangest dreame, that ever yonge
        man had.

Me thoght I saw ech Christmas game, both revells all and
    sume,
    And each thinge els that man cold name or might by
        fancy cume,
The substance of the thing I saw, in Silence passe it shall,
    Because I lacke the skill to draw, the order of them all;   10
But Venus shall not scape my pen, whose maidens in
    disdayne,
    Sit feeding on the harts of men, whom Cupid's bow hath
        slayne.

And that blinde Boy sat all in blood, bebathed to the Eares,
    And like a conquerour he stood, and scorned lovers' teares.
"I have more harts" quod he, "at call, then Cesar could
    commaund,   15
    And like the dere I make them fall, that overcrosse the
        lawnd."
      (Thomas Churchyard, from BL, Harleian MS 7392(2),
                                   folio 51)

IV

"I do increase their wandring wits, till that I dim their sight,
    'Tis I that do bereve them of their Joy and cheef delight."

Thus did I se this bragging Boy advaunce himself even then,
    Deriding at the wanton toyes, of folyshe loving men.
Which when I saw for anger then my panting breast did beate,   5
    To se how he sate tauntinge them, upon his royall seate.
O then I wishte I had byn free, and cured were my wound;
    Me thought I could display his armes, and coward dedes
        expound.

But I perforce must stay my muse, full sore against my harte.
    For that I am a Subjecte wight, and launced with his darte. **10**
But if that I atchieve the forte, which I have toke in charge,

My Hand and Head with quivering quill, shall blaze his
name at large.

FINIS. L ox.

(BL, Harleian MS 7392(2), folio 51)

Drake, Sir Francis (1541–1596)

Captain Drake conferred with Walsingham, Hatton, and perhaps
the queen as well before undertaking his voyage of circumnaviga-
tion, but only when he returned from this remarkable exploit in
October 1580 did he have time and stature to become a courtier
indeed. Elizabeth granted him a six-hour private audience after he
brought to London a sample of his plunder, laden upon five pack-
horses. On New Year's Day 1581, she wore a crown of emeralds
Drake had given her, and on April 4 she dined with him aboard the
Golden Hind at Deptford, after which she knighted him. Drake
remained at court until the summer of that year in constant attendance upon his sovereign but enjoying as well dinner parties in the
company of such courtiers as the earls of Sussex and Arundel.[1] Sir
Francis exchanged New Year's gifts with Elizabeth in 1587, and on
some other occasion before April 14, 1584, he presented her with an
elaborately sculptured golden salt cellar.[2] Drake apparently frequented
the court with some regularity in 1584–1585, 1587, and during the
early 1590s. He took his place among eleven knights, kinsmen, and
friends at Sir Philip Sidney's funeral on February 17, 1587. He was at
court late in 1592 when it was reported that "Sir Francis Drake
caryethe it away from them all" in the competition for Elizabeth's
favor.[3] Drake's only known poem, reprinted below, was published
among the commendatory verses to Sir George Peckham's *True
Reporte of the Late discoueries . . . of the New found Landes* (1583),
a tribute to Sir Humphrey Gilbert's last voyage of exploration. Along
with Drake, his fellow sea dogs John Hawkins and Martin Frobisher
likewise turned out commendatory poems for this volume.

1

Sir Fraunces Drake
Knight in commendation of this Treatise.

Who seekes, by worthie deedes, to gaine renowme for hire:

1. A. E. W. Mason, *The Life of Francis Drake*, 155, 162; E. F. Benson, *Sir
Francis Drake*, 177–78.
2. Nichols, *Progresses*, 2:420; A. J. Collins, *Inventory of the Jewels and Plate
of Queen Elizabeth I*, 580–81.
3. HMC, 7th report, appendix, 524.

Whose hart, whose hand, whose purse is prest, to purchase
    his desire,
If anie such there bee, that thirsteth after *Fame*:
Lo, heere a meane, to winne himselfe an everlasting name.
Who seekes, by gaine and wealth, t'advaunce his house and
    blood: 5
Whose care is great, whose toile no lesse, whose hope, is all
    for good.
If anie one there bee, that covettes such a trade:
Lo, heere the plot for common wealth, and private gaine is
    made.
Hee, that for vertue's sake, will venture farre and neere:
Whose Zeale is strong, whose practize trueth, whose faith is
    void of feere.   10
If any such there bee, inflamed with holie care,
Heere may hee finde, a readie meane, his purpose to declare:
So that, for each degree this Treatise dooth unfolde:
The path to *Fame*, the proofe of Zeale, and way to purchase
    golde.

                                                Fraunces Drake.
                                   (STC 19523, sig. *4v)

Note
    At line 3, 'thirsteth' corrects the print's 'thristeth,' as at line 8, 'wealth' corrects 'weath.'

Dyer, Sir Edward (1543–1606)

Sargent presents ample evidence that Dyer was in regular attendance at court by the late 1560s. His appointment early in 1570 to the stewardship of the manor and woods of Woodstock, with the rangership and portership of the park, argue that he had progressed from a mere protégé of Leicester to a courtier with independent claims on the queen's attention. The fact that he was described as being out of royal favor for two years in May of 1573 presupposes that he had gained the queen's favor beforehand.[1] Dyer suffered only minor setbacks in his career at court thereafter. He was lodged with the court at Greenwich in 1574, while in September of that year Lady Sidney described him as "the wyse, noble Mr. Dyer" who would know best how to promote her husband's interests at court.[2]

1. Sargent, *Life and Lyrics*, 19–20, 23.
2. BL, Lansdowne MS 18/37; Collins, *Letters and Memorials*, 1:66–67.

In 1576 he received the tanning monopoly and in 1578 exchanged New Year's gifts with Elizabeth for the first time, after which he became a regular on the gift rolls.

By the mid–1570s, Dyer was a close friend of Sir Philip Sidney and Fulke Greville, and he was in close contact later in the reign with such courtier poets as Sir John Harington and the earl of Essex. The dozen poems that can be credited to Dyer with reasonable certainty are edited below, along with four works that may possibly be his. Although Sargent believed that Dyer was writing verse by the 1560s, none of his output can be traced to such an early date, nor is he referred to as a poet before about 1580, when Sidney alluded in *Old Arcadia* poem 9 to a line from Dyer's poem 2. The lyric sung to the queen during the 1575 Woodstock entertainment, "The man whose thoughts against him do conspire," is his earliest datable text. Only two of Dyer's definite works were not in print or referred to in print by 1593.[3] Without evidence to the contrary, it is safest to conclude that Dyer wrote nearly all, if not all of his extant poetry between the mid–1570s and 1590.

The notes to Dyer's poems refer to the following sigla of frequently cited texts:

AH   Ruth Hughey, ed., *The Arundel Harington Manuscript of Tudor Poetry.*
Fo   Folger, MS V.a.89
Ha   BL, Harleian MS 6910
Hy   BL, Harleian MS 7392(2)
Ma   Marsh's Library, MS 183
PN   *The Phoenix Nest* (1593), STC 21516
Ra   Bodl., Rawlinson poet. MS 85
T   Bodl., Tanner MS 306

1

The songe in the Oke

The man whose thoughts against him doe conspire,
In whome mishap her story doth depante:
The man of woo, the matter of desire,
Free of the dead that lives in endlesse plainte:
　　His sprite am I which in this desart wonne　　　　5
　　To rewe his case whose cause I cannot shune.

Dispaire my name who never seekes releife,
Frended of none, unto my selfe a foe,

3. John Lilliat transcribed the unique text of "Amidst the fairest mountain tops" at some time after July 1596 (see Edward Doughtie, *Liber Lilliati*, 157). The unique text of "Where one would be" in Folger, MS V.a.89, f. 12v, could also have been transcribed in the late 1590s or early 1600s.

An idle care mayntayned by firme beleife,
That prayse of faith shall through my tormentes growe,   **10**
    And count the hopes that other hartes doe ease,
    But base conceates the common sorte to please.

I am most sure that I shall not attaine
The onely good wherein my joy doth lye.
I have no power my passions to refraine,   **15**
But wayle the want which nought els may supply.
    Whereby my life the shape of death must beare,
    That death which feeles the worst that life doth feare.

But what availes with Tragical complaint,
Not hoping helpe, the furies to awake?   **20**
Or why should I the happie mindes acquaint
With dolefull tunes, their setled peace to shake?
    O yee that here behold infortune's fare,
    There is no griefe that may with mine compare.
                     (STC 7596, sig. C2v–3)

Notes

The poem is attributed to "Dyer" in Hy, folio 34v, and to "Mr Dier" in Ra. Sargent collated the copy text, *Her Majesties Entertainment at Woodstocke* (1585), with Ha and Ra; thus the readings of Hy below provide a full textual apparatus for this poem. The print (W) descended from Dyer's original with five certain errors. A lost collateral version (X) transmitted the corrupt readings 'spirit' and 'moane' or 'moans' in line 5, 'rise' and 'from whence' at line 14, and 'suffice' at line 16. Hy descends from X, adding faulty readings at line 7, 'ever,' and line 9, 'and.' Intermediate between X and Ra-Ha was Y, with the errors 'mishapp' at line 3 and 'when' at line 16. To these and the misreadings of X, Ra added at least four additional errors, with three for Ha. Thus W provides the copy text with five emendations supplied by unanimous manuscript readings at lines 2, 8, and 14. At line 5 all three manuscripts preserved part of the correct reading, 'which,' but only Ra-Ha retained 'in,' for which Hy substituted 'thus.' At line 7, Hy has the correct verb, 'seekes,' which keeps its third-person inflection in the Ra-Ha verbs 'findes' and 'feeles' (misreading swash s as f). Possibly a few readings of X, which can be reconstructed from the manuscript readings, would be superior to W, especially at line 11, 'others' for 'other,' and line 15, 'sorrowes' for 'passions.'

Title] *in the left margin* W, *om.* Hy Ra Ha.
2 doth Hy Ra Ha] did W.
5 which in Ra Ha] within W, which thus Hy.
7 seekes Hy] seeke W, findes Ra, feeles Ha.
8 a foe Hy Ra Ha] my foe W.
9 An] And Hy.
11 the . . . other] those . . . others Hy.
13 I am most] For I am Hy.
14 wherein] from whence Hy; my Hy Ra Ha] the W; joy doth lie] Joyes do ryse Hy.
15 passions] sorrowes Hy.
16 supply] suffice Hy.
18 that life] which life Hy.

2
Bewayling his exile he singeth thus

He that his mirthe hathe lost, whose comfort is dismayd,
Whose hope is vayne, whose faithe is skornd, whose trust is
    all betrayed,
Yf he have held them dear and can not ceasse to moan,
Com let him take his place by me, he shall not rew alone.
But yf the smallest sweete be mixt with all his sower,   5
Yf in the day, the monethe, the year he feele one lightning
    hower,
Then rest he with himself, he is no mate for me,
Whose feare is fallen, whose succour voyd, whose helpe his
    death must be.
Yet not the wished deathe which hath no playnt nor lacke,
Which making free the better part is only nature's wracke;   10
Oh noe! that were to well, my death is of the mynd,
Which always yeldes extremest pangues but keepes the
    worst behind.
As one which lyves in show but inwardly dothe die,
Whose knowlege is a bloudie feild wher all help slayn dothe
    lie;
Whose hart the alter is, whose spirit a sacrifice   15
Unto the powers whom to appease no sorow may suffise.
My fancies are like thornes on which I goe by night,
Myn argumentes are as an host whom force hath put to
    flight;
My sense my passions' spie, my thoughtes like ruins old
Of famous Carthage or the towne which Synon bought and
    sold,   20
Which still before myn eyes my mortall fall dothe lay,
Whom love and fortune once advanced but now have cast
    away.
Oh thoughtes, no thoughtes but woundes, somtyme the
    seates of joye,
Somtyme the store of quiet rest but now of all anoye.
I sowd the soile of peace, my blisse was in the spring,   25
And day by day I eat the fruict which my lyve's tree doth
    bring.
To nettles now my Corne, my feild is turned to flint,
Wher sitting in the Cypresse shade I read the hyacinthe.
The peace, the rest, the life which I enjoyed of yore,

Cam to my lotte that by my losse my smart might sting the
    more.   30
So to unhappie men the best frames for the worst,
Oh tyme, ohe place, o wordes most dear, sweet then but
    now accurst!
In (was) standes my delight, in (is) and (shall) my woe,
My horrour fastened in the (yea), my hope hanges in the (noe).
I looke for no relief, reliefe would com to late,   35
To late I fynd, I fynd to well, somtyme stood my estate.
Behold suche is the end, what pleasure here is sure?
Ohe nothing els but care and playnt dothe to the world
    endure.
Forsaken first am I, then utterlie forgotten,
And they that cam not to my faith to my reward have gotten. 40
Then love wher is the sawce that makes thie tormentes
    sweete?
What is the cause that many thinke ther death throughe the
    but meete?
The statly, chast disdayn, the secret thankfulnes,
The grace reserved, the common light that shines in
    worthines;
Oh that yt wer not so, or I yt could excuse,   45
Or that the wrathe of Jelousie my judgement did abuse.
Oh frail, inconstaunt kynd, o safe in trust to no man,
No wemen aungels be and lo my maystres is a woman;
Yet hate I but the fault and not the faultie one,
Nor can I rid from me the bonds in which I lie alone.   50
Alone I lie whose like in love was never yet,
The prince, the poore, the yong, the old, the fond or full of
    witte.
Here styll remayn must I, by death, by wrong, by shame,
I cannot blott out of my brest what love wrought in her
    name;
I cannot sett at naught which I have held so dear,   55
I cannot make yt seme so farre which is in deed so neere.
Not that I mean henceforth this straunge will to professe,
As one that could betray suche trothe to build on ficklenes,
For yt shall never faile that my faithe bore in hand:
I gave my word, my word gave me, bothe word and gift shall
    stand.   60
Sithe then yt must be thus, and this is all to yll
I yeld me captive to my curse my hard fate to fulfill.

The solitarie wood my citie shall becom,
The darkest denne shalbe my lodge wherin I rest or runne;
Of eben blacke my boord, the wormes my feast shallbe   65
Wherwith my bodie shalbe fed till they doe feede on me.
My wyne of Niobie, my bed a craggie rocke,
The serpente's hisse my harmonie, the scriching owle my
     clocke.
My exercise nought els but raging agonies,
My bookes of spightfull fortune's foiles and drery trajedies,   70
My walke the pathe of playntes, my prospect into hell
Wher Sisiphus, that wretched wight, in endlesse payn dothe
     dwell.
And though I seeme to use the fayninge poets' stile
To figure forthe my ruthefull plight, my fall and my exile,
Yet is my greife not fained wherin I sterve and pyne,   75
Who feeles his most shall fynd yt least yf his compare with
     myne.
My song, yf any aske whose greivous case is suche,
Die er thou lette his name be knowen, his folie shoes to
     muche;
But best is the to hide and never com to light,
For on the earthe may none but I this accent sound aright.   80
                    (Cambridge University Library, MS Dd.5.75,
                                        folios 25-5v)

Notes

   The pun in line 78 as well as the ascriptions to Dyer in Hy, Ra, and T (folio 173v), confirm his authorship of this popular poem beyond any doubt. Moreover, Sir John Harington referred in his notes to Book 8 of the *Orlando* to "an excellent verse of his [Dyer's] 'the light that shines in worthines,'" an echo of line 44. Several Renaissance poets imitated Dyer's widely circulated verses. Robert Southwell converted its amorous secularism to religious purposes in his "Dyer's Phancy Turned to a Sinner's Complaint." Greville's *Caelica* 83 is modeled on poem 2, while James Murray both copied the text in Cambridge University Library, MS Kk.5.30, folios 5-5v, entitling it "Inglishe Dyare," and wrote his own imitation with the heading, "Murrayis Dyare" (the dialect of both versions obscures their textual value and thus neither was used to establish the critical text). That Dyer's poem was known in Scotland is further substantiated by King James's imitation of it in his lyric beginning, "If mourning might amend" (for which see Part I, Chapter 2).

   Despite Harington's close ties with Dyer since at least his schooldays at Cambridge, he seems not to have received the AH text (Hughey, poem 149) from the author, for it occurs in a section of the manuscript entitled "Certayne verses made by vncertayne autors wrytten out of Charleton his booke" (Hughey, 2:193). The unidentified Charleton was favored with a text of the poem closer than any other to Dyer's original except for its omission, with Ma, of lines 53-56. The versions in Ha, Huntington Library, MS HM 198, vol. 2, folios 43-45 (Ht), and *Poems of Pembroke and Rudyard* (1660) descend from a common original that lacked lines 21-24, 39-40, and 79-80, while sharing the faulty 'O that' or 'O would' of line 46. It is alternatively possible, as Hughey observed (2:207), that the 1660 print was set from the Huntington Manuscript; its text is, at any rate, too corrupt to warrant collation. Versions in Bodl., Ashmole MS 781, pp. 140–42 (A), and the Tanner Manuscript share conjunctive errors at lines 40, 43, and 64, and are thus derived from a lost intermediary as are Ra and Hy with errors in common at lines 30, 52, and 74.

Sargent apparently chose the Ashmole Manuscript as his copy text because it concludes with a couplet found in no other version. These two lines, however, are regular iambic heptameters as opposed to the consistent poulter's measure of the preceding eighty lines. These metrically anomalous lines at the end of one of the most corrupt texts of the poem must be rejected as spurious. As copy text, the Cambridge Manuscript (D) requires six more emendations than would AH but supplies the four lines missing from AH and Ma. These three texts are far superior to the others, followed by the readings of Ht, Ra-Hy, and A-T. Where D receives substantive emendation the preferred reading occurs in both AH and Ma except at lines 2 ('skorn' in all three manuscripts), 19 ('my' in AH Hy Ra Ha Ht), 47 ('safe' in Ma Ra A T), 57 ('Nor' in AH, 'Not' in Ma Hy Ra T), 73 ('fayned' in Ma, 'fayninge" in AH Hy T), and 80 ('the accente' AH, 'this accent' Ma Hy Ra). Sargent collated Ra, Ha, and T, while Hughey collated A, T, Ra, Ha, and Ht against AH. The following collations of D with Hy and Ma along with all emended readings complete the textual apparatus for this poem.

Title] *om.* Ma, secendo vince Hy.

2 is vayne . . . is skornd AH Ma Hy Ra Ht A T] in vayne . . . in skorn D; skornd Hy Ra Ht A T] skorn D AH Ma, voyd Ha.

3 have] hath Hy Ma.

4 his AH Ma Hy Ra Ht Ha A T] a D; rew] morne Hy.

6 one] on D (*as at* 13, 49, 58).

7 with] by Ma.

9 no AH Ma Ra Ha T] not D, ne Hy Ht; nor] ne Hy.

11 death] grief Hy.

12 extremest] thextremest Hy; pangues but] paines and Ma Hy; keepes] leves Hy; worst] leste Hy.

13 which] that Ma Hy; but] and Ma Hy.

15 whose spirit] his spyrit Hy Ma; a] the Ma Hy.

16 sorow] sorrowes Ma; may] can Ma Hy.

17 goe] walke Hy.

18 Myn] my Ma Hy; argumentes are] rusty hope is Hy; as] like Ma Hy; whom] which Ma; force] foes Hy.

19 sense AH Ma Hy Ra Ha A] sent D, sences T; my passions' AH Hy Ra Ha Ht] the passions D, and passions Ma, whose thoughte A, *om.* T; ruins] ruine Ma.

21 myn eyes] my face Hy.

22 but] and Ma Hy; have] hath Ma Hy.

23 seates] seat Ma Hy.

24 store AH Ma Hy] seates D.

26 eat] ate Ma; which] that Hy; lyve's] lyffe Ma, loves Hy; doth] did Ma Hy.

28 read AH Ma Ra Ha Ht A] reap D Hy.

29 which] that Ma Hy.

30 Cam] Come Hy; my losse] ther losse Ma; might] may Hy.

31 men AH Ma Hy Ht T] men *changed to* me D; best] leste Ma; frames AH Ma Hy Ra A T] fares D.

32 wordes most dear] Lookes O WORDES Hy, wordes, o lookes Ma; sweet] deare Ma Hy.

34 horrour] sorow Ma.

35 would] will Ma Hy.

36 I fynd to well] to well To Well Ma; somtyme] to well Hy, *om.* Ma.

37–40 *om.* Hy.

38 Ohe] wher Ma; care and playnt] playnts & care Ma; to] in Ma.

39 then] and Ma.

40 cam not AH Ma Ra A T] were cam D; faith to AH Ma Ra] faith of D; gotten] cropen Ma.

41 Then] Now Hy; sawce] force Hy; thie tormentes] the sower Ma.

42 What] Where Ma Hy; cause] happe Hy, sauce Ma; many thinke] some throw thee Hy, some have thought Ma; death] deathes Ma.

43 chast disdayn] Cawse disdaynes Hy, chaste disdaynde Ma.

44 reserved] deservde Ma, Preferd Hy; light] lyef Hy.

45 that yt] would yt Ma Hy; or . . . could] I could it well Hy.

46 did] myght Ma.

47 frail] false Hy; inconstaunt] unconstant Ma; o safe in Ma Ra A T] a life to D, o fyrme in Hy, oh sure in AH; no man AH Ma Hy Ra A T] wemen D.

48 and lo] ON EARTHE Hy.

49 hate] blame Hy; but] not Hy; and not] But even Hy.

50 Nor] Ne Hy; rid from me] put the thinge Hy, rid me of Ma; bonds AH] bond D, bandes Ma Ra Ht T; in which] wherin Hy.

51 whose . . . love] by Love Whose like Hy.

52 The prince, the poore] The yonge the old Hy; the yong, the old] the prince the poore Hy; or] and Hy.

53–56 *om.* AH Ma.

53 styll . . . I] muste I styll remayne Hy; by death . . . shame] My Love, my Deathe my Shame Hy.

54 what] that Hy; her] his Hy.

55 which I have] that once I Hy.

56 so farre which] farre of that Hy.

57 Not that I Ma Hy Ra T] me yet I D, Nor that I AH A, I doe not Ht; professe] possesse Hy.

58 As . . . could] As one that would Ma, As to betray Hy; betray suche trothe] suche tickle truthes Hy; to build] to bynde Ma, As buyldes Hy.

59 For] but Ma; yt shall never] never shall it Hy; faithe bore] faith bare Ma, word gave Hy.

60 word and gift] gyfte and word Hy.

61 Sithe then] Sith needes Ma, And since Hy; yt must] my choyse Hy; be thus AH Ma Ht T] be this D, is thus Ha, is suche Hy; and this] The which Hy.

62 curse] cares Ma; my hard] myne harde Ma; fate] happe Hy.

63 wood] woodes Ma Hy.

64 wherin . . . runne] wherein I reste and runne Ma, WHERE IS NO LYGHT OF SONNE Hy.

65 boord] BOWER Hy; feast] MEATE Hy.

66 bodie] carcas Ma Hy; till they doe] untill they Ma Hy.

67 My . . . Niobie] MY REST SHALBEE IN MOULDE Hy; a] of Ma, the Hy.

68 The serpente's . . . harmonie] MY HARMONY THE SERPENTES HYSSE Hy, the serpentes hisse myne harmonye Ma; scriching] SCRYKYNGE Hy.

69 My] Myne Ma.

70 bookes] BOOKE Hy.

71 walke] walkes Ma; playntes] playnt Hy.

72 Sisiphus . . . wight] wretched Sysiphe and his feers Ma, SYCYPHO, AND ALL HYS PHEERES Hy; payn] torments Ma Hy.

73 And though AH Ma Hy Ra Ha A T] And yet althoughe D; fayninge poets' AH Hy T] the poetes D, the fayned poets Ma Ha, Poets fained Ra A.

74 plight] playnte Hy; my exile] myne exile Ma Hy.

75 wherin] In which Ma.

76 feeles his] feelethe Ma, feels it Hy; shall] may Hy; his compare] he compare Hy.

77 song] verse Hy; greivous case] Rufull plight Ma, greivous chaunce Hy.

78 his folie] whose folly Hy.

79 But best] yt better Hy; is the to] were the to Ma, is to Hy.

80 on the earthe AH Ma Hy T] on thie deathe D, in the world Ra A; this Ma Hy Ra T] thie D, the AH A.

Subscribed: fynys qd DYER Hy.

3

Before I dy faire dame of me receave my last adieu,
    Acounte my helpelesse grief no Jest, for time shall prove
        it trew;
My Teares were signes of Sorows fytte for all my former care,
    When yet my woes wer very young but now so great they
        are
As all my store consumed quite, that only eyes remayne   5
    Which turninge up their sight to heven lamente their
        master's paine.
With gastly staring lookes, even such as may my death fortell,
    The only meane for me poore Soule to shunne an earthly
        Hell.
But now my deare, for so my love doth make me call thee
    still,
    That Love I say, that luckles Love, which workes mee all
        this yll,   10
This ill wherof sweete Soule, thou art at all no cause,
    Both Hand and hart with francke consent acquytes thee
        of the lawes.
Thou knowste in tender yeeres before my pryme awhyle,
    Cupid at the sight of thee my sences did beguyle.
It was a World of Joyes for me, to live within thy sighte   15
    Thy Sacred presence unto me did give so greate delighte.
It was a Heaven to me to view thy face Devine,
    Wherin besides Dame Venus' stayne great Majesty did
        shine.
These thinges like folishe singed Flye, at first made me my
    game,
    Tyll time and riper yeares cam on, my woes to frame.   20
For at the last I felt it worke and did bethinke me how
    Unproved yet my mystres wold, her servante's love alow.
Thus long in this Conceipt I livde and durst it not bewray,
    Wherby both former Mirth, and Strengthe and Health did
        soone decay.
Thy self didste seme with gracious Eye to pitty my Dystres,   25
    The cause unknown, yet was I far from hope of all redres.
For like the Silly Lambe that makes no noyse untill he Dies,
    Even so I secret kept my tongue, but told it with myn eyes.
Yet this I counted for a Toy, as longe as I myght bee,
    Without suspect of Jelouse heads, in company of thee.   30

But when thy choyse was made and Fortune framde it so,
    As neyther I, nor you nor Hee but did endure som wo,
Then did my Joyes take end, suche force hathe Jelousy
    That both their owne and others to, my harms they
        wroght therby.
Well, this is all my Sute which thou in no case canste deny,   **35**
    When turninge time shall end my dayes, by fatall Destiny,
Which now by open signes I find, comes roundely towards
        mee
    This recompence for all my paynes, I do require of thee;
Vouchsafe to visit for my sake my everlastinge Grave,
    Stay ther untill my latest rites, the Priest performed have   **40**
Thus Charity Commaunds; but somthing yet ther commes
    behinde
    Which if thou graunteste to performe, will argue thee
        more kind.
Eache yeare upon the blessed day, wherin my lyfe toke end,
    Unto my Tombe repaire wher I thy comminge will attend.
Good mystres there confesse, my rare renowmed Love,   **45**
    The Loyall Hart I bare, which Deathe could not remove.
And when thou hast don this, then tell the world from me,
    My suyte at no Time did exceed, the Bandes of Modesty.
Of one thing yet beware, sighe not, and shead no Teare,
    Leste that my Tormentes do renew, when I thy Sorrowes
        heare.   **50**

fynys. DY.
(BL, Harleian MS 7392(2), folios 22v–23)

Note
    Lines 9–10 are quoted in Puttenham's *Arte* as an example of parenthesis "or the Insertour . . . as that of maister Diars very aptly."

    But novv my Deere (for so my loue makes me to call you still)
    That loue I say, that lucklesse loue, that vvorkes me all this ill.
                (169)

The complete text, unique to Hy, was discovered and printed as Dyer's in Bernard M. Wagner's "New Poems by Sir Edward Dyer" (*Review of English Studies* 11 [1935]: 467–68). Dyer apparently shifted from fourteener couplets to poulter's measure at lines 11–14, 17–18, 31–34, and 49–50, but the hexameters that rhyme with preceding heptameters, lines 20 and 46, are probably missing a foot. At line 5 I emend Hy's abbreviation 'ye' as a misreading of 'yt' (that), and at line 49 Hy's 'on' has been emended to 'one.'

4

Wher one woulde be ther not to be
    What is a greater payne,

Or what more greife ther not to be
    Wher thou wouldest be full fayne?

Longe tyme semes shorte when thou arte there   5
    Where thou wouldest gladly be;
Arte thow not there wher thou wouldest be?
    Then eche day semeth three.

Unrippe but that with threede is sowen
    How lothe it dothe departe;   10
Muche lother then must nedes be puld
    The bodye from the hearte.

Then doe thou haste the to the stafe
    With speede thy threde untwyne;
Eche lovinge harte would see his frynde   15
    And soe woulde I doe myne.
           finis Dier
      (Folger, MS V.a.89, folio 12v)

Note
    This text is unique to Fo where the attribution is partially crossed out. This
anthology is generally reliable with regard to Dyer's verse, for it assigns to him texts
of "I would it were not" and "Prometheus when first," while "As rare to hear" is
there anonymous but ascribed to Dyer by Hy and Ra.

5

Devyde my Tymes, and Rate my wretched Howres,
    From Dayes to monthes, from monthes to many yeares,
And then Compare my Sweetest with my Sowres
    To see which more in aequall vyew appeares.
And judge if for my Dayes and yeres of Care,   5
I have but howres of Comfort to Compare.

Just and not muche it were in these Extremes
    So hard a Touch and Torment of the Thought,
For any mynd, that any right estemes,
    To yeld so small Delight, so Dearely bought,   10
But he that Lyves unto his owne Despight,
Ys not to fynde his fortune by his Ryght.

The lyfe that still runnes forth his weary wayes,
    Wyth Sowre to sawce the Daynties of delight,
With Care to Checke the pleasure of his Dayes,   15
    With no Regard those many wronges to quyght,
I Blame and hould such yrksom Tymes in Hate,
As but to Lose, prolonges a wretched State.

And still I Lothe even to behould the Lyght,
    That shines without all pleasure to mine eyes,   20
With greedy wish I wayte for weary night,
    Yet neyther this I find that may suffice,
Nor that I hold the Day in more Delight
But that alyke I loath both Day and night.

The Day I se yeldes but increase of Care,   25
    The night that should by nature serve for rest,
Against his kind denies such ease to Spare,
    As pitty wold afford the mynde opprest.
And broken Sleepes ofte times present in Sight,
A dreamyng wish beguild with false delight.   30

This Sleepe, or els what so for Sleep appeares,
    Ys unto me but pleasure in Despight,
The Flowre of Age, the name of yonger yeares,
    Do but usurp the Title of Delight,
For Carefull thoughtes and Sorowes sundry wayes   35
Consume my youth before myne aged Dayes.

The Touch, the Stinge, the Tormentes of Desire,
    Do stryve beyond the Compas of Restraynt,
Kept from the Reache wherto it wold aspyre,
    Gives cause, alas, to Just to my complaint.   40
Besides the wronge which worketh my distresse,
My meaning is with Silence to Suppresse.

Ofte with miself I enter in Devise
    To reconcile my weary thoughtes to peace,
I treate for Truce, I flatter and entice   45
    My wrangling wittes to worke for their release,
But all in vayn I seke the meanes to fynde
That might appease the discord of my minde.

For when I force a fayned mirth to shoe,
    And wold forget and so beguile my grief,   50
I Can not rid miself from Sorow soe,
    Although I feed upon a false beleef.
For inward touch of uncontented minde
Returnes my Cares by Course unto their kynde.

Weand from my will and thus by Tryall taught,   55
    How far to hold all Fortune in Regard,
Though heare I boast a knowledg dearly bought,
    Yet this poore gaine I reape for my reward,

I know herby to harden and prepare
A ready minde for all assaultes of Care.   60

Wherto (as one even from the Cradle borne,
   And not to loke for better to ensew)
I yeld miself, and wish these Tymes outworne,
   That but remayne my tormentes to renew;
And Leave to those these Dayes of my despight,   65
Whose better Hap may Lyve to more delight.
FINIS Dier
(BL, Harleian MS 7392(2), folios 69v–70)

Notes

   Dyer intentionally limited the number of different rhymes he used in this lyric, for the couplet rhymes of stanzas 1 and 10 are the same as the 'b' rhyme in stanza 5; stanzas 2, 4, 5, and 11 share the same rhyme in the couplet and with the 'b' rhyme in stanza 6; while the couplets of stanzas 8-9 rhyme on the same sound as do the 'b' rhymes of stanzas 4 and 8. Perhaps he was influenced by Sidney's experimentation with difficult rhyme schemes, especially the rhyming sestina of *Old Arcadia* poem 76, yet Dyer's practice here does not seem to form a consistent pattern.

   Both Hy and Ra (folios 40-41) assign the poem to Dyer; the text in PN (sig. M4v–N1v) is anonymous. All three versions are closely related, sharing the conjunctive error 'Not' for 'Nor' at line 23. Ra, the most corrupt text, agrees with Hy against PN in eighteen substantive readings, two of which—'the,' line 16, and 'But,' line 35— are doubtless wrong. No clear stemma seems possible, however, since Ra also agrees with three definite errors in PN: 'No blame to,' line 17, 'sweet,' line 31, and 'To,' line 38. Accordingly, Ra derives from a source contaminated by errors from both lines of descent. 'Touch' in lines 8, 37, and 53 has the sense of *Oxford English Dictionary* substantive 17, "the quality or fact of affecting injuriously; reproach, blemish, stain" (a meaning cited first in a letter of 1567 written by Queen Elizabeth). Hy is emended in only four readings, with the division into stanzas added as well. PN would require at least seven emendations and Ra, eleven. Sargent collated PN against Ra; thus the variants below record only the emendations to Hy.

   16 those PN] the Hy.
   23 Nor] Not Hy PN Ra; in PN Ra] for Hy.
   35 For PN] But Hy Ra.
   FINIS Dier] Finis. Mr Dier Ra.

6

.1. I would yt were not as yt is or that I card not yea or noe,
I would I thought yt not amisse or that amisse might blameles
   goe,
I wishe yt were yet should I not I might be glad yet could I not.

2 Would God desire knew the meane or that the meane desire
   knew,
I would I could my fancie weane from these swete thoughtes
   that do ensew   5
Only to wish is least of all a badge wher bie we know the thrall

3. O happie man that dost aspire to that which thou maist
      semely crave
Twise happie, for thie hart's desire may joyn with hope good
      hap to have,
But woe is me unhappie man whom hope nor hap acquite yt
      can.

4. My life in hope is life with feare and still my foe presents
      his face   10
My fate yf hap the palme did beare unto my hope would be
      disgrace
As diamant in wood were set or Irus' raggs with golden fret.

5. Behold my tired shoulders beare desire's weary baiting
      wings
And at my heele a clog I weare tied on with self-disdaigning
      strings;
My wings to get at gate do hast, my clog doth sinke me down
      as fast.   15

6 Suche is our plight, lo thus we stand, we rise to fall that
      climb to highe.
The youthe that fled King Minos' land may teache the wise
      more low to flie;
What gaind his poynt so neare the sonne? he blames the sea
      his name hath wonne.

7. Yet Icarus more happie was by present death his cares
      to end
Then I who lyve in whom alas ten thousand deathes ther
      pangues do spend;   20
Now love, now feare, now playnt, now spight, long sorow
      mixt with short delight.

8 The pheer and fellow of thy smart Prometheus I am in dede
Uppon whose ever lyving hart the greedie gripe doth tire and
      feede.
And yet no wrong, for whie? we crave the things that gods
      themselves would have.

9. But let them moan and waile ther case that of vild choise
      them selves would blame   25
Let them lament ther faltes' disgrace whose base desires
      worke their shame;
Who hath advanced his hart on hie must be content to pine
      and die.

    (Cambridge University Library, MS Dd.5.75, folio 34v)

Notes

Only Ha (folios 149v–50) and the copy text (D) preserve lines 24–26, the lack of which along with four conjunctive errors reveal the descent from a common ancestor of Hy (folios 23v–24), Fo (folios 6–6v), and Ra (folios 6–6v). The attributions to Dyer in Hy, Fo, and Ra are confirmed by Sir John Harington, who cited the poem's final couplet in his translation of Ariosto, "He that hath plast his heart on hie, / Must not lament althoughe he dies" (sig. L 4v); a marginal note identifies the author as "Master Edward Dier." Harington must have quoted from memory, since no other text resembles his version of these lines. *Oxford English Dictionary* 'bating,' the action of beating wings, explains 'baiting' in line 13; the meaning of line 15, 'to get at gate' is equivalent to getting 'at the gate' (*OED* to get near or close to). Thus, the poet aspires to rise up to the object of his desires, while his "clog" keeps him from doing so.

Ha, Fo, Ra, and Hy are related by their rhyming of 'sought' with 'wrought' in lines 4 and 5, and versions of line 10 quite unlike that of D. Ra, Fo, and Hy are further distanced from Dyer's original by their faulty readings at lines 5 'such sweet,' 8, 'win' for 'joyn,' and 11, 'hope' for 'hap.' They also lack lines 24–26, while their scribes wrestled with an illegible 'advanced his' at line 27; its place is blank in Fo, was misread 'vauntes' in Hy, and 'lyfts' in Ra. D is emended in two instances from Ha alone (lines 11, 26), and in three places by readings from all four of the remaining texts (lines 15, 22). At line 10, the Ra-Fo-Hy reading 'foe' seems clearly preferable to D's 'sore' and Ha's 'feare.' Sargent collated Ra against Fo; in the following collations D is the lemma with Ha and Hy variants plus the emendations to D.

3 wishe] woulde Hy; should] would Ha Hy.

4 Would God] I would Ha Hy; knew] soughte Ha Hy.

5 fancie] fancies Ha; these] those Ha, suche Hy; thoughtes . . . ensew] thoughtes that Love hath wrought Ha, Joyes which love hathe wroughte Hy.

6 Only to] But now Ha; to] my Ha Hy; least of all] leaste at all Ha, lefte at all Hy; we know the] is knowne the Ha, to know a Hy.

8 Twise] Thrise Ha Hy; for thie hart's] man for thy Hy; joyn] winne Hy.

9 hap] helpe Hy; acquite yt] nor quiet Ha, acquiet Hy.

10 My . . . is life] The Birds of hope are starv'd Ha, The budds of hope are starvede Hy; my foe] my sore D, my feare Ha, his foe Hy Ra Fo.

11 fate D] state Ha Hy Ra Fo; hap . . . did] hope . . . shoulde Hy; hope Ha] hap D Hy Ra Fo.

12 diamant] diamondes Ha, diamond Hy; Or] o Ha; with golden fret] with Goulde yfrette Hy.

13 Behold] For loe Hy; baiting] beatinge Ha Hy.

14 at my] on my Ha; heele] feet Ha Hy.

15 wings . . . do] wings to get to gate do Ha, wings to mounte alofte make Hy.

16 Suche . . . plight] This . . . state Hy; thus Ha Hy Ra Fo] this D; we] Theye Ha Hy.

18 poynt] course Ha; blames the sea] blam'd the sea Ha, drownde in seas Hy; name] wracke Ha; hath] had Had, that Hy.

20 who lyve in] that live on Ha, pore mann, on Hy; deathes] cares Ha; pangues] griefs Ha, paynes Hy.

21 love . . . playnt] griefe now plaint now love Ha Hy; sorow] sorrowes Ha.

22 pheer and fellow Ha Hy Fo] scarre and fellow D, pheere and fellour Ra; thy Ha Hy Ra Fo] my D.

23 gripe doth] Grypes do Hy; tire and] allway Ha, gnawe and Hy.

24–26 *om.* Hy.

24 whie] lo Ha; The things that] That which the Ha.

25 vild . . . would] vile . . . may Ha.

26 faltes] fates Ha; desires] desires do Ha; worke their shame Ha] worke the same D.

27 Who hath advanced] But he that vauntes Hy; on] *om.* Hy.

Subscribed FYNIS DY. Hy.

7

E. D.

Prometheus when first from heaven hie,
    He brought downe fire, ere then on earth not seene,
Fond of Delight, a Satyre standing by,
    Gave it a kisse, as it like sweete had beene.

Feeling forthwith the other burning power,   5
    Wood with the smart, with showts and shryking shrill,
He sought his ease in river, field, and bower,
    But for the time his griefe went with him still.

So silly I, with that unwonted sight
    In humane shape, an Angell from above,   10
Feeding mine eyes, the impression there did light,
    That since I runne and rest as pleaseth love,
        The difference is, the Satire's lippes, my hart,
        He for a while, I evermore have smart.
                       (STC 22541, sig. 2R 5v)

Notes

Sargent collates the texts in EH, *Englands Helicon* (1600; sig. 2B2), Ra, Ha, and Fo against that from the copy text, the 1598 *Arcadia*. Ringler (*Poems*, 144–45), adds variants from Hy; Folger MS H.b.i (Cl, the Clifford Manuscript of the *Old Arcadia*); and Bodl., MS e Museo 37 (Bo). The poem also occurs in Ot, National Library of Wales, Ottley MS, folio 3. Fo, Hy, and Ra descend from a lost intermediary with the readings 'outward' in line 5, 'rest and run' in line 12, and 'time' in line 14. Fo and Hy likewise bear witness to a second lost manuscript with 'difference:' for 'difference is' in line 13. The texts in EH, Cl, and Ot share the faulty reading 'shrikinges' at line 6, but these are independent variations from their copy texts rather than evidence of descent from a common ancestor. The EH version of poem 7 derived (as did virtually all the texts in this anthology) from a contemporary printed source, in this case the 1598 *Arcadia* (referred to below as 98). Ot follows six other texts of the poem which read 'delight' at line 3; none of them records 'shrikinges' in line 6, however, except for EH. Cl has 'the light' in line 3, as does Ha, which corrupts an original, singular 'shrieking' into the participial 'a skriching.' Thus the EH, Cl, and Ot scribes worked on collateral lines of descent from Dyer's original. At line 6 they committed identical errors independently, prompted by the plural 'shouts' before 'shrieking' and by elision with the 's' in 'shrill' that follows.

Along with Ot, I provide all substantive variants of Bo and Cl against the lemma, 98, for the choice of the 1598 *Arcadia* as copy text is debatable. Only these four texts and Ha seem to derive from Dyer's original independently, and all are careful transcripts except for Ha, which commits three definite errors plus the wholesale corruption of line 6. Yet Cl-Ha alone read 'Fond of the light' at line 3; all other sources have 'Fond of Delight.' Evaluation of this one reading is crucial to the choice of copy text, given the high quality of 98, Bo, Cl, and Ot. And since the poem is about the fire which Prometheus brought to earth, the satyr's fondness for the light, rather than delight in general, is arguably the preferable reading.

I am unable to conclude, however, that 'delight' is an impossible reading in context and thus a definite error which would then align every text except Cl-Ha in descent from a common ancestor with this faulty reading. With 'Fond of delight' Dyer may have evoked his satyr's hedonism, which disposes him to kiss the attractive novelty, fire. If 'the light' is correct, 98 errs only in this one reading and remains as sound a choice for copy text as Cl, which would still require emendation at line 6. The alternative reading is supported by three of the four most accurate texts of the poem, and its hesitant acceptance weights the choice of copy text toward 98.

Sidney's verse response to poem 7, *Certain Sonnets* 16, refers in line 13 to "thy Satyre deerest Dyer," and Sir Edward is also credited with the poem by the Ra, Hy, and Fo subscriptions. Ringler (*Poems*, 23) dates both Dyer's sonnet and Sidney's response before 1582.

1 when] *om.* Bo
3 Delight] the light Cl Ha
6 shryking] shrikinges Cl EH Ot

<h1 style="text-align:center">8</h1>

Amarillis was full fayre, the goodlyest mayde was she,
From the easte unto the west that heaven's eye could se.
To Diana att her birthe her parents did her geve,
All untouchte a mayden's lyfe duryng her dayes to lyve,
Whose behest she constant kepte and whollye was enclynde   5
To be free to gayne great fame and winn eche worthye mynde:
As there was good cause enoughe so was she honored most;
They that had her seene abroade att home woulde make their
    boaste.
Twoe ther were that her behelde and woulde have done so ever,
Happye men (yea happye thryse) if they had done so never.   10
Coridon and Charimell that longe in deere accorde
Ledd their lyves and neyther wisht of other too be lorde,
All the goods that eche possest of bodye, wealthe, or mynde,
Were employde to other's use as eche by profe did fynde.
They had no cause to envye ought the auncyent worlde's
    prayse   15
Of Damon or of Pytheas and others in those dayes.
Good and sure their freendshipp was tyll Amaryllis fyne
Had the powre, perhapps the will the bande for to untwyne;
Yea, the boye, that blynded god in great despight complaynde
That on earthe alone theye were that his darte quyte
    disdaynde,   20
Wherupon his strongest bowe and arrowes sharpe he hente
And in Amarillis' eyes he slyly pighte his tente,
Wher he lay to watche both tyme and place for his avayll
For the wightes that wiste not yet what foe should them
    assayll:
One of his two shafts was dipte in bitter juyce as gaulle,   25
The other in a pleasant wyne and poyson myxte withall;
As they smackt of dyvers sauce, so dyverslye they wroughte:

By despayre the one to deathe, by vayne hope the other
    broughte.
With the first was Coridon throughe perced to the herte;
Charimell within his brest felte of the second smarte,   **30**
Butt with gould both headed were, which bred a lyke desyre;
Faygne they would within their brestes hyde cloase the
    kyndled fyre,
Butt without it must appeere that burnte so hot within;
Harde it is the flame to hyde that it no issue winn,
And in tyme strange lookes begann that spronge of Jelosye,   **35**
Full of care eche laye in wayghte his felowe to descrye.
In the ende all freendly partes betweene these freendes
    decayde;
Bothe were bente to please themselves, theire freende's case
    nothynge wayde.
Amaryllis' love was soughte with all they could devyse,
Yea, with all the power of mann, and prayer to the skyes.   **40**
All she sawe and herde there moane as Aspis dothe the
    charme;
Now and then she blamde them both as guyltye of theyre
    harme;
Now to the one she woulde geve eare, then putt the other of;
By and by eache did suspect his frind the cause therof,
Butt the trust by tryall paste made them theire doome
    suspende   **45**
And indeed she used there where passione did offend;
He had neede of store of tyme that would his penn prepare
To sett forth theire agonyes, there dredd, hope, joy and care;
Butt in vayne they spente there daies, theire labor all was lost,
She was farthest from theire meed when they foreweened
    most.   **50**
Coridon waxte pall and leane, his younge heares torned hore,
Feates of armes, the horse, the hauke he left and used no
    more;
He had founde that Amaryll soughte glorye more than love,
That she forced not his harmes her bewtye's power to prove;
Yet he could not leave to love, butt yeeldynge to despayre   **55**
Rente his hearte, his corpse fell downe, his goaste flew in
    the ayre.
Charimell thoughte women kynde was apte to change and
    bowe,
And beleeved to please him selfe what fancye did allowe;

But beleefe ne makes the cause, ne weanynge workes the
    webb,
In the tyde his travayll came, he thryved in the ebb: **60**
Att the last his vayne hope him no longer coulde sustayne;
In his longynge he consumde, lyfe coulde not him retayne.
Amaryllis herd of this and pyttye movde withall,
Muche did rue so harde a happ on suche faythe should befall;
To Diana strayghte she hyghes whome wayted on she founde **65**
With a trayne of all the dames whose chast names Fame doth
    sounde.
Unto her in humble wyse she sayde she came to sue
That these two to loving thynges myghte be transformde
    anewe.
In her armes the goddess mylde her darlynge softe did
    strayne:
"What is it that yow" (quoth she) "of me may not obtayne?" **70**
Therewithall Sir Charimell a yellow flowre became,
Sweet of sente and muche esteemde, and Hartes ease hathe
    to name;
Amarillis pluckte the flowre and ware it on her heade,
Somtime she layde itt on her lapp, Sometyme upone her
    bedd.
Charimell, most happye flowre, O most unhappy mann,   **75**
In thy lyfe thou hadst thy deathe, in deathe thy lyfe began.
Coridon, turnde to an Owlle, fledd to the willdernes,
Never flockes butt leades his lyfe in solytarynes;
Nor his eyes can yet behould the deare lyghte of the sunn,
Butt aloofe he stealles his flyghte and in the darke dothe
    runn.   **80**
Amaryllis to the woode att somtyme will repayre,
And delyghtes to here the laye and tune of his despayre.
Well I wott what here is ment, and thoughe a talle yt seeme,
Shadowes have their Bodyes bye, and so of this esteeme;
Ye that chaunce this for to heer and do not prayse their
    speede,   **85**
Geve them thankes, for you by them are warnde to take heed.
                        Finis: E: Dier:
        (Bodl., Rawlinson poet. MS 85, folios 98v–100v)

Notes

Dyer is credited with this poem by three of its four texts, Ra, Hy, and Ma. Its
meter suggests that it was written after 1580, when Sidney first began to experiment
with trochaics. Ra descends with Ma from a lost intermediary in which lines 13–16

followed 17–18, along with definite errors in at least ten substantive readings. Hy and T (folios 174–74v) are similarly derived from a lost version (X), with errors in lines 15, 20, 27, and 48. Hy commits sixteen errors, the same as for the copy text, Ra, but it lacks lines 85–86. The best witness to Dyer's original would be X, and where Hy and T confirm its readings, these take precedence over Ra or Ra-Ma except for the manifest errors in these manuscripts at lines 15, 20, and 48. At line 37, 'partes' has the sense of *OED* substantive 11a, "act or conduct." Sargent collated T against Ra, so that the variants from Hy and Ma below, with the emendations to Ra, complete the textual apparatus for this poem.

4 mayden's] Vyrgins Hy.

6 gayne greate fame Hy T] gett great prayse Ra Ma.

9 and Hy T Ma] who Ra.

10 men Hy Ma] theye Ra, man T; yea Hy T Ma] ye Ra.

11 Charimell T, *also* 30, 57, 71, 75] Charynel Hy, Caramell Ra Ma; that Hy T] Who Ra Ma; in Hy T Ma] with Ra.

13–16 *follow* 17–18 Ra Ma.

13 wealthe Hy T] goodes Ra Ma; or] and Hy.

15 worlde's] words of Hy.

16 or Hy T] and Ra Ma.

18 for] all Hy.

19 Yea Hy T] Butt Ra, *om.* Ma.

20 on earthe] on the earthe Hy Ma; theye . . . darte] ther was Hys love that Hy.

21 arrowes sharpe he Hy T] sharpest arrowe Ra Ma; hente] bente Hy.

22 in] in that Hy; slyly Hy T Ma] lyghtely Ra.

25 juyce Hy T] sauce Ra Ma.

26 The other] Thother Ma.

27 As they] As the Ra Ma, And as they Hy T; smackt Hy T] smacke Ra, smackes Ma.

28 the other] thother Hy Ma.

30 second Hy T] others Ra Ma.

31 which bred a Hy T] And both with Ra Ma.

32 brestes Hy T] brest Ra Ma; hyde . . . kyndled] Have hidden kepte Hy.

34 Hard] For hard Hy.

35 spronge] sprange Hy.

37 al frendly] betwixt those frends Hy; partes Hy T] lookes Ra Ma; betweene these freendes] All frendly partes Hy.

38 please] place Hy; theire] Hys Hy.

40 prayer] prayers Hy.

42 Now and then Hy T] By and by Ra Ma; blamde Hy] blames T, bayed Ra Ma.

43 the one] thone Hy, th'one Ma; then Hy T] Now Ra Ma.

44 *sub.* Allurynge him by courtesye And tauntynge him by scoff Ra, Alluring him by curtesie and taunting this by scoff Ma.

45 the Hy T Ma] that Ra.

46 passione] passions Hy.

48 forth] forth all Hy T; there] They Hy; dredd] dreads Ma; joy and care Hy T] and feare Ra, joy, and feare Ma.

49 daies Hy T] tyme Ra Ma.

50 She] For she Hy; when Hy T] where Ra Ma.

51 leane] wan Hy; heares] heare Hy Ma.

52 the hauke Hy T] and hauke Ra Ma; left] lost Ma.

54 That] But Hy; harmes; power] charmes; pride Hy.

56 flew in Hy T] fledd to Ra Ma.

57 change] bend Hy.

58 what] As Hy.

59 ne weanynge Hy T] nor weanynge Ra Ma.

60 travayll] trubelles Hy; thryved Hy T] torned Ra Ma.

61 coulde] might Hy Ma.

62 retayne Hy T] attayne Ra Ma.

64 did Hy T] to Ra Ma.
65 whome] When *crossed out* where Hy; on] one Ra.
66 names] lyfe Hy, name Ma; doth Hy T] did Ra Ma.
67 sue] showe Hy Ma.
68 That Hy T] For that Ra Ma; to T] *om.* Hy Ra Ma; loving Hy T] lyvyng Ra Ma; thynges] wightes Hy.
70 it Hy T] that Ra Ma; yow Hy T Ma] thou Ra; may Hy T Ma] mayste Ra.
72 hathe to Hy T] caulde by Ra Ma.
73 ware] wore Ma; on Hy T Ma] in Ra.
74 Somtime Hy T Ma] Somtymes Ra; on Hy T Ma] in Ra; sometyme Hy T Ma] Sometymes Ra.
75 most Hy T] o Ra Ma; O] But Hy.
76 in deathe Hy T Ma] In thy deathe Ra.
79 Nor . . . lyghte] Hys eyes cannot abyde The clearnes Hy.
80 stealles] takes Hy; runn] comme Hy.
82 delyghtes Hy T] delighte Ra Ma; laye and tune] tune, And lay Hy.
84 Bodyes Hy T Ma] substance Ra.
Subscription: FYNIS DYER Hy, finis T, G: Dier Ma.

9

The lowest trees have tops, the ant her gall,
   The fly her spleen, the little spark his heat.
And slender hairs cast shadows though but small;
   And bees have stings although they be not great.
Seas have their source, and so have shallow springs,   5
And Love is Love in beggars and in kings.

Where waters smoothest run, deep are the fords;
   The dial stirs, yet none perceives it move;
The firmest faith is in the fewest words;
   The turtles cannot sing, and yet they love.   10
True hearts have ears and eyes, no tongues to speak;
They hear and see and sigh, and then they break.
                 (STC 7096, song 19)

Notes

The only viable attribution to this lyric is that in Rl, Bodl., Rawlinson poetry MS 148, folio 103, where it is subscribed "Mr," corrected to "Sir Edward DIER." This ascription is underscored later in the same manuscript by the title to a poem on folio 106, "The aunswe [*sic*] to Mr: Diers ditie." The text in Tn (Bodl., MS Tanner 169) was transcribed on September 7, 1618, according to its title, which originally attributed the poem to "Mr. Lea." At a later date, "but sithence I did understande that they weare Sr W. Rawleys verses to Queene Elisabeth in the beginninge of his favoures" was crowded into the title. The assertion is too late and too much indebted to casual gossip preceding or following Ralegh's execution to warrant acceptance. Poem 9 was one of the most enduringly popular of all Elizabethan lyrics: it is found in twenty manuscripts and three prints, the latest published in 1662 and reissued in 1682. The textual relationships among the complete copies of this poem are diagrammed on the following page:

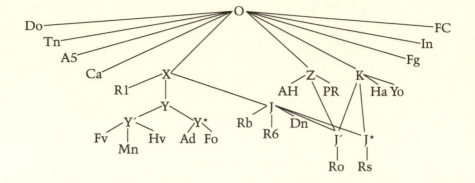

The Rl text, along with versions in Rb (Rosenbach, MS 239/27), R6 (Bodl., Rawlinson poet. MS 206), and Dn (Bodl., Don. MS d. 58) descend from the archetype through a lost intermediary, X, with the error 'floods' (for the rhyme word 'fords') in line 7. Rb, R6, and Dn derive from X through a second lost ancestor, J, with the corrupt readings 'shrubs' in line 1 and 'shores' in line 5. X also gave rise to a third reconstructed text, Y, with errors in lines 5 ('course'), 8 ('though none'), 9 ('fairest'), and 10 ('not love'). Y in turn spawned two hypothetical offshoots: Y' with the faulty readings 'deepest are' at line 7 and 'sweetest' at line 9; and Y*, with 'cleerest' in line 9. Fv (Folger, MS V.a.162), Mn (Bodl., MS Malone 19), and Hv (Harvard, Eng. MS 686) are descendents of Y'. From Y* were derived Ad (BL, Add. MS 22602) and Fo. AH and PR (Davison's *Poetical Rhapsody*, 1602) share conjunctive errors at line 2, 'sparks their,' and line 6, 'as in.' Ha and Yo (Yale, Osborn MS b 200) are likewise related through a hypothetical source, K, that transmitted 'smallest' in line 1, and 'tongue' in line 11. Lost intermediaries contaminated with readings from J, K, and Z were copied into Ro (Rosenbach, MS 1083/15) and from J and K in Rs (Rosenbach, MS 1083/16). The following texts descend independently from Dyer's original: the copy text, Do (John Dowland's *Third Book*), FC (Grosart, *Farmer-Chetham MS.*), In (Inner Temple, Petyt MS 538.10), A5 (BL, Add. MS 52585), Ca (John Forbes's *Cantus*, 1662), Tn, and Fg (Folger, MS V.a.339). The most complete list of variant readings occurs in Hughey's edition of AH (2:306–8), collating AH with Rl Mn Ha Ad Tn Fg Fo Fv PR Do FC. Edward Doughtie (*Lyrics from English Airs*, 521) collates Do against Rb, Ro, Rs, A5 and In. The variants of Ca, Ad, Rl, Ha, Mn, Tn, FC, and the AH transcript in BL, Add. MS 28635, occur in Hyder E. Rollins's edition of *A Poetical Rhapsody* (2:166), along with examples of the responses and additions to the poem. Sargent provides collations for Rl, Ha, Mn, Ad, Tn, FC, and BL, Add. MS 28635. The variants below from R6, Dn, Hv, and Yo complete the textual apparatus for this poem.

The absence in Do, the copy text, of PR errors at lines 2 and 6 argues against Rollins's supposition (2:164) that Do was reprinted from PR. Dowland's songbook version, with only one corrupt reading, is an accurate and independently transmitted text. The emendation at line 11, 'ears and eyes,' aligns these subjects with 'hear and see,' the corresponding verbs in line 12. Only five texts transmit this reading (Rb, Rl, A5, Fg, and Tn), but aside from Fg, with eleven errors, these are superior texts with only two to four certain errors apiece. Only PR with four errors, In with three, and Do with one are comparable in reliability. It thus seems safe to emend the copy text here in accord with these four strong witnesses, given the more orderly sequence of pairings that results for this very orderly poem. (Its final couplet in BL, Egerton MS 2725, folio 168, with "have eyes, have eares" at line 11, is too fragmentary to warrant collation.)

1 lowest] smallest Yo; trees] shrubbs R6 Dn.

2 his] their Yo, its R6.

3 And . . . shadows] The slender haires cast shadowes Yo, Haires cast their shadowes Hv, The slender haires cast shadowes R6; though] though they bee Hv.

4 And] The R6.
5 source] course Hv, shoares R6 Dn; so have] so he R6.
6 and] as Dn.
7 waters] Rivers Yo; deep . . . fords] deeps't . . . floods Hv, deepe . . . floods R6
Dn.
8 yet . . . perceives] though . . . perceive Hv; move] mooves R6.
9 firmest] fairest Hv; in the fewest] not in, e *crossed out* sweetest Hv.
10 cannot sing] sing not Hv.
11 eyes and ears Do Yo Hv] ears and eyes Rb Rl A5 Fg Tn; tongues] tongue Yo Dn.
12 and sigh] and sight Yo.

10

As rare to heare, as seldome to bee seene,
   It cannot be nor ever yet hath been,
That Fier should burne with perfyt heate and flame,
   Wythout some matter for to yeld the same.

A stranger case, yet true by proofe I knoe,   5
   A man in Joy, that lyveth still in woe;
A harder hap who hath his love at liste
   And lives in love, as he all love had miste.

Who hathe ynoughe, yet thinkes he lives withoute,
   To lacke no love yet still to stand in doute,   **10**
What discontent to live in suche desyre,
   To have his will and ever to requyre.

                fynis Dy.
    (BL, Harleian MS 7392(2), folio 23)

Notes
  Hy is free of definite errors and therefore serves as copy text. With Ra and Fo it preserves the "alliterative" state of this poem, for their versions of lines 7, 8, and 10 are substantially different from the less alliterative readings of PN and Ha. None of the PN-Ha variants is necessarily in error in these lines, nor is there further evidence of relationship between these two texts. Rather, Ha agrees in error with Fo at line 5, 'find,' which fails to rhyme with 'woe' in the next line; Ha, however, avoids the second Fo misrhyme, 'loste' for 'liste' in line 7. These differential readings argue either that Ha derives from an ancestor contaminated by both states of the text or that the contamination was the immediate work of the Ha scribe. Both Ra and Hy attribute the poem to Dyer. Sargent collated PN with Ra and Ha; thus, only the Fo variants are given here.
  2 ever] never Fo.
  3 perfyt] perfect Fo.
  5 knoe] fynde Fo.
  8 miste] loste Fo.

11

1. Amidst the fayrest mountayne topps,
   Wher *Zepherus* doth breathe
   The pleasant gale that clothes with floweres
   The valleyes underneath:

A shepparde liv'de that dearely lov'de   5
(Deare Love tyme brought to passe),
A Forrest Nimphe who was as fayre
As ever woman was.

2. His thoughts were higher then the hills
Wherof he had the keepe,   10
But all his actions innocent
As humble as his sheepe.
Yet had he powre; but her pure thoughts
Debard his powers to rise
Higher then kissinge of her handes,   15
Or lookinge in her eyes.

3. One day (I neede not name the daye
Two loovers of their sorrows,
But say as onc a shepperd sayd,
Their mone nightes have no morrows),   20
He from his sheeppcot ledd his sheep
To pasture in the Lease,
And ther to feed while he the while
Might dreame of his disease.

4. And all a lone (if he remayne   25
Alone that is in love),
Unto himselfe aloud he mournd
The passions he did prove.
"Oh heavens" (quoth he) "ar thes th'effects
Of faithfull Love's desarts?   30
Will *Cynthea* now forsake my love?
Have women faythless hearts?"

5. "And will nor witts, nor woords, nor woorks,
Nor time endur'd laments
Bringe to my playnts pitie, or peace,   35
Or to my teares contents?
I, that enchayn'd my Love desires,
From chaunginge thoughts as free
As ever were true thoughts to her,
Or her thoughts falce to me."   40

6. "I, that for her my wandringe sheepe,
Forsooke, forgott, forwent,
Nor of my selfe nor them tooke keepe
But in her love's content:

Shall I like Meads with winter's rayne   45
Be turned into teares?
Shall I of whose true feelinge payne,
These greeves the record beares

7. "Causles be scorn'd, disdayn'd, despis'd?
Then witnes this desire: 50
Love was in women's weed disguis'de,
And not in men's attire."
And thus he said, and downe he lies,
Lyinge as life would part;
Oh *Cynthia*, thou hast Angel's eyes   55
But yet a woman's heart.
  Finis ~~Earle Essex. vel L: Mountjoy.~~ qd Mr dier.
  (Bodl., Rawlinson poet. MS 148, folios 65–66)

Note

The compiler of the Rawlinson manuscript, John Lilliat, at first appended an ambivalent subscription to this poem, then changed it definitely to Dyer. Lilliat copied out the first four lines in a musical setting on folio 112v of his anthology with variants in line 1 Amidst] Amids, and line 3 clothes] cloth'd. In his edition of the Rawlinson manuscript, Edward Doughtie (*Liber Lilliati*, 157) dates the transcription after July 1596, with the change in authorship added, presumably, even later. Yet Dyer had been knighted in April, and Lilliat gives him his title after poem 9, which he entered on folio 103. I follow Doughtie's reconstructed reading at line 27, 'mournd' for the manuscript's 'mourd.'

12

Oh that most rare brest, chrystalin syncere,
Through which like golde thy princelie harte did shine;
O sprite heroique, o valiant, worthi knight,
O Sidney! prince of fame and men's good will,
For thee both kings and princes, lo, do mourne;   5
Thy noble tombe three cities straunge dezirde,
Foes to the cause thy prowes did defend
Bewaile the day that crost thy famous race.
The dolefull debt due to thy herse I paie,
Teares from the Sowle that ay thy want shall moan,   10
And by my Will my life it self wolde yelde
If heathen blame ne might my faith distein;
O heavie tyme! that my daies drawe behinde thee;
Thou dead dost live, thy dier living dieth.
  (Christ Church College, Music MS 984, nos. 60–61)

Note

I am grateful to the late Professor William Ringler for drawing my attention to this text; its punning signature in line 14 resembles Dyer's play on his name in poem

2, line 78, and marks this as almost certainly his work. He had composed it by November of 1587 when William Byrd's *Psalmes, Sonets, and Songs* was entered in the stationers' register; poem 12 was there set to music as song 35, but with 'friend here' substituted for the pun on Dyer's name. The print varies from the manuscript version in two other readings, line 5 princes lo] princesses, and line 12, distein] disdain.

POEMS POSSIBLY BY DYER

I

My mind to me a kingdom is

The critical text appears above under poems possibly by the earl of Oxford. In "The Authorship of 'My Mind to me a Kingdom Is'" (*Review of English Studies* 26 [1975]: 385–94), I present the evidence for Oxford's slightly stronger claim to this poem.

II

Fancy farwell, that fed my fond delight,
  Delight adew, the cause of my distresse,
Distresse adew that dost me such despight,
  Despite adew, for death dothe lend redresse,
And death adew, for though I thus be slayne,   5
  In thy despite I hope to live agayne.

Sweet Hart farwell, whose love hath wrought my wo,
  And farwell wo, that weried hast my wittes,
And farewell wits which will bewitched so,
  And farwell will, soe full of franticke fittes.   10
Franzy farwell whose force I fele to sore,
  And farwell feeling, for I feele no more.

And lyef adew, that I have lovd and loathd,
  And farewell love that makest me loth my lyfe,
Both love and lyfe farwell unto yow both,   15
  Twixt hope and dread, farwell all folishe strife.
Folly farewell which I have fancied so,
  And farwell fancy, that first wrought my wo.
                FINIS. H O. Dyer.
        (BL, Harleian MS 7392(2), folio 51v)

Notes
    Only two of the five texts of this poem are complete, Hy and Huntington Library, MS HM 198, part 2, folio 45v (Hu). A version of the last two stanzas is appended to a sixain beginning "Ceace Sorrow, now! for thou hast done the deede," in *Pieces of*

Ancient Poetry from Unpublished Manuscripts and Scarce Books (F).[4] The first four lines of "Fancy farwell" also occur in Ha, folio 172v, appended to the "Cease Sorrow" stanza, a lyric set to music in Thomas Weelkes's *Madrigals* (1597, song 6), without the addition of any part of the "Fancy farwell" text. The combined text may well be a hybrid created by a scribe who found that the last line of "Cease Sorrow," "Before I dye I singe this Last farewell," invited a continuation that was neatly fulfilled by the "Fancy farwell" poem. It seems rather less likely that the lines doubtfully attributed to Dyer would have become detached from an original preceding stanza, as witnessed by both Hy and Hu. And while the technical form and alliteration are similar in both works, "Cease Sorrow" lacks the persistent anadiplosis of "Fancy farwell." I am grateful to W. H. Kelliher for supplying me with a third fragmentary text of this poem from Cambridge University Library, MS Mm.3.29 (M). This manuscript represents the first twelve lines in two stanzas of five lines each, then adds fourteen lines of what is clearly one or more different verses beginning "Contente am i to lyue in forteune spyhte."

Dyer's claim to the poem rests solely upon the muddled subscription in Hy. I have added the stanza divisions to this text and emended it at lines 2 and 3 from Hu, Ha, and M, and at lines 9 and 10 from Hu, F, and M. In comparison with these four errors, Hu transmits six definite errors and omits line 12, while F omits the first stanza and commits four errors in twelve lines. The M reading at line 8, 'wichede,' is tempting in light of the unanimous 'bewitched' in line 9, yet M preserves two manifest errors besides dropping the last stanza and two of the twelve lines it attempts.

1–6 *om.* F.
1 fed] wrought Hu, fedes M.
2 distresse Hu Ha M] desires Hy.
3 Distresse Hu Ha M] Desires Hy; adew] farewell Ha; that . . . such] that thus dost me Hu, that causd me such Ha, that dideste me this M.
4 for . . . redresse] *om.* M; lend redresse] end distresse Hu, send Release Ha.
5 And death adew] *om.* M; for though] allthoughe M.
6 thy] this Hu.
7 Sweet . . . love] Beauty farewell whose blast Hu, Fancy, farewell! whose love hath wrought F, Falles dame farwelle whoes loue hath wrouhte M.
8 wo] *om.* M; that] which Hu; weried] wichede M; hast] hath Hu M.
9 And farewell wits] *om.* M; wits Hu F] wit Hy; which] that Hu, whome F.
10 soe Hu F] o Hy.
11 Franzy] fancy Hu M, Beauty F; force] fitts Hu, love F; to] full Hu, soe F M.
12 feeling . . . feele] *blank* Hu.
13 adew] farewell Hu; that] which F; I . . . loathd] late I livd but loathd Hu, I have liv'd and loath F.
14 that] which F; makest] made Hu, makes F; my] that Hu.
15 Both] Oh F; farwell unto yow] adieu despised Hu.
16 Twixt . . . all] farewell contempt soe full of Hu, Twixt hope and fare, farewell, all F.
17 which I have] that first I Hu, whome I have F.
18 that first wrought] that didst first work Hu, worker of my F.

III

Fayne woulde I but I dare not,
    I dare but yet I maye not:
I maye although I care not,
    For pleasure when I playe not.

4. (Bristol, 1814), 29. Selections in this part of the volume were printed from an unidentified quarto manuscript of 116 pages; its contents seem to have ranged from late sixteenth- to mid-seventeenth-century verse.

Yow laughe because you lyke not,　　　　　　　　　　　5
    I jest and yet I joye not:
You pearce althoughe you stryke not:
    I stryke and yet annoye not.

I spye whenas I speak not,
    For ofte I speake and spead not;　　　　　　　　10
But of my wounds you wreak not:
    Because yow see they bleed not.

Yet bleed they when you see not,
    But yow the payne indure not,
Of noble myndes they be not　　　　　　　　　　　15
    That ever kyll and cure not.

I see, whenas I viewe not,
    I wishe, allthoughe I crave not,
I serve and yet I sue not,
    I hope for that I have not.　　　　　　　　　　20

I catche, allthoughe I houlde not,
    I burne, allthoughe I flame not,
I seeme, wheras I would not:
    And when I seeme, I am not:

Yours am I, thoughe I seeme not:　　　　　　　　25
    And will be thoughe I showe not,
Myne owtwarde deeds than deeme not,
    When myne intent you knowe not.

But if my servyse prove not
    Most sure allthoughe I sue not,　　　　　　　　30
Wyth-drawe your mynde and love not,
    Nor of my ruyne rue not.
        Finis. W. R.
    (Bodl., Rawlinson poet. MS 85, folio 43v–44)
        Lenvoy. DY
Yf Sweete from Sowre might any way remove:
    What Joy, what Hap, what Heaven, wer like Love
        (BL, Harleian MS 7392(2), folio 22v)

Notes

    "DY," a typical ascription to Dyer in Hy, may apply only to the final couplet or "Lenvoy." It is tempting to convert the initials signed to the copy text to Walter Ralegh and suppose that Dyer provided a two-line response to his poem, a remotely possible scenario. Ha, folios 154–54v, commits errors in lines 13 and 16, and lacks lines 25–32, while Hy errs in readings at lines 13, 14, and 16. Ra, emended at lines 11 and 23, serves as copy text with addition of the unique envoy from Hy.

Wyatt's "Hate whome ye list" follows the same pattern of rhyming 'nots' as poem III and may well have inspired its sing-song effect. A similar poem beginning "Fain I would but o I dare not" in Ferrabosco's *Airs* (1609) largely avoids the insipid "—not" formula and appears to be an essentially independent work that took its cue from this poem's first line. The text in Christ Church College, MS 439, apparently derives from Ferrabosco, although it does add another stanza (see Doughtie's *Lyrics*, 563).

The Hy scribe may have associated this poem with Dyer because it echoes to a degree the first stanza of his poem 6, "I would yt were not," which appears in Hy ascribed to Dyer on the folio following this text.

Title Ferenda Natura Hy.
2 but] and Hy Ha.
6 and yet] when as Ha.
9 whenas] and yet Hy.
11 But] yet Hy; wounds Hy Ha] wound Ra.
13 when] where Ha; see] feele Hy.
14 But] Thoughe Hy; payne] paines Hy.
15 noble] Noble *crossed out* gentle Hy.
16 cure] care Hy Ha.
17 whenas] and yet Hy, wheras Ha.
19 and yet] although Hy.
21 allthoughe] and yet Hy.
22 allthoughe] athoughe Hy.
23 wheras Hy Ha] whenas Ra.
24 when] where Hy.
25–32 *om.* Ha.
32 Nor of] And for Hy.

IV

Alas my hart, mine eie hath wronged thee,
Presumptious eie, to gaze on Phillis' face:
Whose heavenly eie, no mortall man may see,
But he must die, or purchase Phillis' grace;
    Poore Coridon, the Nimph whose eie doth move thee,   5
    Doth love to draw, but is not drawne to love thee.

Hir beautie, Nature's pride, and Shepherd's praise,
Hir eie, the heavenly Planet of my life,
Hir matchles wit, and grace, hir fame displaies,
As if that Jove had made hir for his wife;   10
    Onely hir eies shoote firie darts to kill,
    Yet is hir hart, as cold as Caucase hill.

My wings too weake to flie against the Sunne,
Mine eie unable to sustaine hir light,
My hart doth yeeld, that I am quite undoon,   15
Thus hath faire Phillis slaine me with hir sight:
    My bud is blasted, withered is my leafe,
    And all my corne is rotted in the sheafe.

Phillis, the golden fetter of my minde,
My fancie's Idoll, and my vitall powre;   20

Goddesse of Nimphes, and honor of thy kinde,
This Age's Phenix, Beautie's bravest bowre;
    Poore Coridon for love of thee must die,
    Thy Beautie's thrall, and conquest of thine eie.

Leave Coridon, to plough the barren feeld,   **25**
Thy buds of hope are blasted with disgrace;
For Phillis' lookes, no hartie love doe yeeld,
Nor can she love, for all hir lovely face,
    Die Coridon, the spoyle of Phillis' eie,
    She can not love, and therefore thou must die.   **30**
               (STC 21516 [PN], sig. I3–3v)

Notes

The attribution of this poem in EH (*Englands Helicon*, 1600, sig. L2) to "S. E.
Dyer" also occurs in Davison's list of the anthology's poems in BL, Harleian MS 280,
folio 102. This list, however, gives three other poems to Dyer all of which are by
Thomas Lodge. The *Helicon* repeats Davison's erroneous attributions, and adds a
fourth poem ("Alas, How wander I"), which is also by Lodge. Despite its three
substantive variants from the anonymous PN text, EH doubtless took its version of
poem IV from that print; the *Helicon* was an anthology of works culled for the most
part from previously printed sources, and its version of Oxford's poem 14, which
follows "Alas my heart" in PN, immediately precedes it in EH. Neither its ascription
to Dyer nor that in Davison's manuscript can be taken as strong indication of Dyer's
responsiblity for this lyric. With the *Helicon* editor, I emend the faulty PN reading in
line 3.
    3 may EH] my PN.
    14 eie] eyes EH.
    22 bravest] richest EH.

POEMS WRONGLY ATTRIBUTED TO DYER

In addition to the poems Sargent excluded from Dyer's canon
(*Life and Lyrics*, 219–20), "Silence augmenteth grief" is nowhere
attributed to Sir Edward and cannot reasonably be accepted as his.
It was printed anonymously in PN, then reprinted in *Colin Clouts
Come Home Againe* in 1595 as the work of "a most woorthy
Gentleman." But since scores of worthy gentlemen lamented
Sidney's death in verse it cannot be deduced that this is Dyer's
tribute to his friend; rather, poem 12 was probably his only such
eulogy.

Elizabeth I, Queen of England (1533–1603)

George Puttenham assured readers of *The Arte of English Poesie*
that their sovereign was "the most excellent Poet" of the age, whose
"learned, delicate, noble Muse, easily surmounteth all the rest that

have written before her time or since."[1] Whatever the level of her accomplishment, her interest in the muses was of long standing, for her two Woodstock poems and possibly the verses written in her French Psalter were composed before she took the throne.[2] Her subsequent output shows a steady if infrequent attention to poetry until the last few years of her life.

In addition to the eight original poems accepted as canonical by Bradner, another three works composed during her reign are printed in Part II, as poem 1 below and the Latin and English verses, poem 6a, preceding Heneage's poem 6. Among the poems categorized as doubtful by Bradner, Elizabeth probably should be credited with "When I was fair and young," "Now leave and let me rest," and *"Grata Camena tua est, gratissima dona, Melisse."* Among her translations, the lines from Petrarch apparently date either from very early in the reign or prior to her accession.[3] A Latin quatrain and its translation beginning "A hapless kind of life" were transcribed by Sir Thomas Heneage into his copy of a book published in 1570 and were no doubt composed at some time after that date (these verses and his answering poem are printed with his works below). Although Bradner was skeptical about the authenticity of the queen's Senecan translation, Elizabeth had translated Seneca into prose as early as 1567, while her verses are perhaps referred to in a letter of 1579 from Heneage to Hatton.[4] In 1593 she translated Boethius's *Consolation of Philosophy* to console herself, according to Camden, for the conversion to Catholicism of Henry IV of France. Her translations of Horace and Plutarch date from the fall of 1598.[5] "I grieve and dare not show my discontent" is associated with "Monsieur" and apparently dates from Anjou's departure from England in February of 1582. The queen's response to Ralegh's "Fortune hath taken thee away," edited here in a critical text for the first time, must have been written in 1587. Among the Hatfield House manuscripts are some 270 lines of French verse in Elizabeth's hand-

1. Puttenham, *Arte of English Poesie*, 63.
2. Bradner, *Poems*, 3–4, 13. For the likelihood that the metrical version of Psalm 13, published in 1548 was written by John Bale rather than the Princess Elizabeth see Ruth Hughey, "A Note on Queen Elizabeth's 'Godly Meditation,'" *The Library*, 4th ser., 15 (1934): 237–40.
3. Hughey, *Arundel Harington Manuscript*, no. 320.
4. Elizabeth sent the elder John Harington a prose translation from Seneca in 1567 (*Nugae Antiquae* [1779], 2:304–10); Heneage's reference to her Senecan translation in 1579 could refer to either poetry or prose (Nicolas, *Memoirs*, 127).
5. Camden, *Annals*, 475; BL, Lansdowne MS 253, f. 200, and Bradner, *Poems*, 81.

writing that are almost certainly her original composition.[6] She may also have written an eighteen-line poem on the defeat of the Spanish Armada, sung during her victory procession from Whitehall to St. Paul's Cathedral in December 1588.[7]

1a

A sonnett

Fortune hath taken thee away, my Love,
My live's Joy and my sowle's heaven above;
Fortune hath taken thee away my princess,
My world's delight and my true fancie's mistris.

Fortune hath taken all away from me,   5
Fortune hath taken all by takinge thee;
Ded to all Joyes, I onlie Live to woe,
So Fortune now becomes my fancie's foe.

In vaine mine eyes, in vaine you wast your tears,
In vaine my sighes, the smokes of my despairs,   10
In vaine you serch the earth and heavens above,
In vaine you serch, for fortune keepes my love.

Then will I leave my Love in fortune's hands,
Then will I leave my love in worthlesse bands,
And onlie love the sorrowe Due to me,   15
Sorrowe hencefourth that shall my princess bee.

And onlie Joy that fortune conquers kings,
Fortune that rules on earth and earthlie things
Hath ta'ne my Love in spite of vertue's might,
So blind a goddesse did never vertue right.   20

With wisdome's eyes had but blind fortune seen,
Then had my love my love for ever bin;
But Love farewell, though fortune conquer thee,
No fortune base shall ever alter me.
(Sir Walter Ralegh, from Wiltshire Record Office,
MS 865/500, folio 27)

6. Substantial excerpts from the queen's French verses are transcribed in HMC, Salisbury, 14:324–26.

7. HMC, 12th report, appendix, part 9, "Manuscripts of John Henry Gurney, Keswick Hall, Norfolk," item 21, miscellanea. The Gurney manuscripts have been very widely dispersed, and no other text of this poem seems to have survived.

1

An nanswer

Ah silly pugg, wert thou so sore afrayd?
Mourne not my Wat, nor be thou so dismaid;
It passeth fickle fortune's powre and skill
To force my harte to thinke thee any ill.

No fortune base, thou saist, shall alter thee;   5
And may so blind a wretch then conquer me?
No, no, my pug, though fortune weare not blind,
Assure thie selfe she could not rule my mind.

Ne chouse I thee by foolish fortune's reede,
Ne can she make me alter with such speede,   10
But must thou neads sowre sorrowe's servant be,
If that to try thie mistris Jest with thee.

Fortune I grant somtimes doth conquer kings,
And rules and raignes on earth and earthlie things,
But never thinke that fortune can beare sway,   15
If vertue watche and will her not obay.

Plucke up thie hart, suppresse thie brackish teares,
Torment the not, but put away thie feares,
Thie Love, thie Joy, she loves no worthlesse bands,
Much lesse to be in reeling Fortune's hands.   20

Dead to all Joyes and living unto woe,
Slayne quite by her that never gave wiseman blow,
Revive againe and live without all dread,
The Lesse afrayde the better shalt thou spead.
     (Wiltshire Record Office, MS 865/500, folio 27)

Notes

Texts of poems 1a and 1 occur in the following sources:

W   Wiltshire Record Office, MS 865/500, folio 27 (poems 1a and 1)
B   *The Bagford Ballads*, ed. J. W. Ebsworth (London, 1878), part 2, 4:961
        (poem 1a, lines 13–18, 21–24; poem 1, lines 1–4, 15–20, 23–24)
In   Inner Temple, Petyt MS 538.10, folio 3 (poem 1)
Ma   Marsh's Library, MS 183, folio 30v (poem 1a)
Ph   Phillipps, MS 3602, from the facsimile in Walter Oakeshott's *The Queen
        and the Poet* (London, 1960), facing page 156 (poem 1a)
Pu   Puttenham's *Arte* (poem 1a, lines 9–12, 21–22, 24; poem 1, lines 5–6,
        15–16)

Puttenham assigned his excerpts from Poems 1a and 1 to Ralegh and the queen respectively. Their authorship is also supported by the marginal note to the In text, "per Reginam Walter Rawley," and by the address to "my Wat" in line 2 of Elizabeth's response. L. G. Black's discovery of her reply proves that what Oakeshott took for two poems in the Phillipps Manuscript is actually a single twenty-four-line poem by Ralegh.[8] All twenty-four lines appear together in W and Ma, and are answered by the queen's reciprocal pentameter couplets to equal length. The crisis in Ralegh's career at court which elicited these companion poems is examined above in Chapter 4.

A ballad beginning "Fortune hath taken thee awaye my love, beinge the true dittie thereof" was entered in the stationers' register to William Wright on June 13, 1590. The ballad, "Fortune my foe, why does thou frown on me?" was entered December 14, 1624, and there is notice of a reprint as late as 1675. A ballad entitled "fortune &c the Second parte of" was entered September 22, 1604, to Simon Stafford; this was probably a text of "Ah silly pugg" expanded for popular consumption. Wright had apparently obtained Ralegh's poem by 1590, while Stafford registered a version of the queen's reply in 1604. Meanwhile, either both poems were redacted into the "Fortune my foe" companion ballads or the originals by Ralegh and Elizabeth were grafted onto an earlier ballad. As evidence for this latter possibility, both poems "exactly fit the tune of 'Fortune' on which William Byrd composed keyboard variations." The ballad versions of poems 1a and 1 are preserved in *The Bagford Ballads*, *The Roxburghe Ballads*, and STC 22926.[9]

However the hybrid ballad came about, it is of some textual value for preserving in recognizable form ten lines from Ralegh's poem and twelve from the queen's. Variants from B are given below as the best representative of this state of the text. Both W and In seem to derive from a state of poem 1 that garbled lines 11–12. In puts stanza four after stanza two, then omits line 11 in stanza three but leaves room for a missing line after line 12. The W reading of this couplet may be correct if we construe 'that' as a demonstrative pronoun referring to the queen's immunity to fortune's influence (lines 9–10). Thus Ralegh must needs be sorrow's servant if he tries or tests Elizabeth's susceptibility to fortune, and she responds by jesting with him. The syntax is convoluted, yet no more so than the style of her translations of Boethius and Horace. The readings of In and Pu at lines 6 and 15 are probably errors which reveal their descent from a common intermediary. The Ph, Pu, and B texts of poem 1a probably descend from a lost ancestor with 'frail' in line 24, shared by all three texts and 'sorrows' in line 15 (Ph, B, line omitted by Pu).

Ma, with nine certain errors plus the omission of line 14, is the weakest of the relatively complete texts of Ralegh's poem, while Ph commits nine errors as well, three of which ('hand,' line 13, 'band . . . worldlings,' line 14), are corrected by corresponding passages in Elizabeth's poem, lines 19–20. All five emendations to poem 1a in W follow Ph-Ma except at line 10, where the unique reading of the copy text is replaced with 'my despairs' from Ph, Ma, and Pu. At lines 7 and 21, the aberrant phonetic spellings 'owe' for 'woe' and 'sin' for 'seen' seem to be scribal eccentricities rather than textual corruption, akin to W's rendering of 'An answer' as 'An nanswer.'

POEM 1A

1 thee] *om.* Ph.
2 live's Joy Ph] loves Joy W, lives soule Ma.
4 world's delight] worldes joy Ph, only light Ma; fancie's] fantasies Ph.
5 all] thee Ph.
7 Joyes] joy Ma; woe Ph Ma] owe W.
8 So Fortune now] so ys fortune becomne Ph; fancie's] fantasies Ph, mortall Ma.
9 mine eyes, in vaine] my Eyes, in vayne yee Ph, you eyes you eyes do Ma.

8. L. G. Black, "A Lost Poem by Queen Elizabeth I," *Times Literary Supplement*, May 23, 1968, 535.

9. Edward Arber, ed., *A Transcript of the Registers of the Company of Stationers, 1554–1640*, 2:550. Gerald Abraham, letter to the editor, *Times Literary Supplement*, May 30, 1968, 553, in response to Black's discovery; Rollins, *Analytical Index*, nos. 911, 2569; William Chappell and J. W. Ebsworth, eds., *The Roxburghe Ballads*, 3:192–93.

10 my sighes, the smokes] my sights the smoke Ph, you sighes do smoke forth Ma; of] *om.* Ma; my despairs Ph Ma Pu] mightie feares W.

11 the earth] th'earth Pu; heavens] heaven Ph Ma.

12 you serch] ye seeke Pu; keepes my] rules in Ma.

13 Then will] Thus now Ma; hands] hande Ph.

14 *om. except for* bands Ma; Then . . . worthlesse] My dearest love, in most unconstant B; worthlesse] wordlings Ph; bands] bande Ph.

15 love] serve B; sorrowe] sorrowes Ph B.

16 hencefourth] hereafter thou B; that] it Ma; princess] Mistress B.

17 And onlie Joy] I joy in this Ma; fortune] sometimes B; conquers Ph Ma] conqueringe W.

18 on] the Ph.

19 ta'ne] taken Ph Ma; vertue's] Cupids Ma.

20 goddesse] dame Ma; vertue] cupid Ma.

21 With . . . fortune] If wisdoms eyes blind Fortune had but B; fortune] Cupid Ma; seen Ph Ma B] sin W.

23 But] Then B; conquer] favour B.

24 base shall ever] base nor frayle shall Ph, base or frayle can Pu, frail shall ever B; alter] conquer B.

POEM 1

1 pugg wert] Soul! art B.

2 Wat] dear B; thou] not B.

3 It . . . fortune's] Fortune cannot, with all her B.

4 To force] Enforce B.

5 thou saist, shall] or frayle can Pu.

6 may] can Pu; wretch then] Witche so In Pu.

9 foolish] fickle In.

10 can she make] she shall force In.

11 *om.* In.

12 If that to try thie] But if to try this In.

13 grant] know In.

13–16 *follow* 8 *in* In.

15 But] Never Pu, And B; that] you Pu; fortune . . . sway] fortune can beare the sway Pu In, that Fortune beareth sway B.

16 If . . . not] Where vertues force, can cause her to obay Pu; her not] not her B.

17 Plucke] Pull In; suppresse thie] suppret with B.

18 the] me B; put] take B.

19–20 *om.* In.

19 Thie Love, thie Joy, she loves] Thy Mistress mind brooks B; worthlesse] unconstant B.

20 be] live B; reeling] ruling B.

22 never] nere In.

23 and . . . dread] to faint thou hast no need B.

24 shalt thou] thou shalt In B.

Gorges, Sir Arthur (1557–1625)

Gorges, the son of a gentleman pensioner, was at least marginally connected with the court by 1576, when he was paid for delivering letters to the English ambassador in France. In February 1578 he received payment for another mission to Paris. He was himself serving as a gentleman pensioner by 1580, although his formal appointment seems to have been delayed until 1583. As early as March of the former year, however, he was committed to the Marshalsea, the prison of the royal household, for scuffling in the Presence Chamber with Lord Windsor. In June of 1582 he complained of being insulted "in the Lobbye att the privye Chamber doore" by one of Sir John Scudamour's servants.[1]

In addition to his uncle Sir Thomas Gorges, groom of the Privy Chamber, Arthur held two very promising entrées to favor at court during the 1580s. He was the cousin and close friend of Sir Walter Ralegh, with whom he was apparently lodged at court in 1583,[2] while in 1584 he married into the nobility by taking to wife Douglas Howard, daughter of Henry, Second Lord Bindon. The ceremony was performed at his uncle's house and with the queen's approval, although Lord Bindon was furious.[3] Elizabeth undoubtedly held Gorges in some measure of esteem by the mid–1590s when she considered sending him on an ambassadorial mission to France, but in 1597 he did incur her displeasure by taking for his second wife another noblewoman, Elizabeth Clinton, daughter to the earl of Lincoln. Perhaps Sir Arthur was still attempting to placate his sovereign in November of 1599 when he presented her with a "fair jewel" as she passed by his house in Chelsea.[4] In the following year he struggled to retain the wardship of Ambrosia, his only child by Douglas Howard, a prize that the court of wards had yielded up to the queen. But it was doubted that Elizabeth would profit from her new ward "for that Sir Arthur Gorge . . . doth make greate Meanes to her Majestie, that he may have the Disposing of her before an other."[5] The queen granted Gorges the wardship for one thousand pounds, but when Ambrosia died in 1601, Sir Arthur lost all claim upon her inheritance. In consolation, the crown granted him twelve hundred pounds out of the fine imposed on one of the Essex Rebels.[6] The cumulative portrait here is of a man who served at court on a regular basis, associated with some of Elizabeth's foremost courtiers, and who must have been known to her personally by 1584 at the latest.

    1. Sandison, *Poems*, xv; Tighe, "Gentleman Pensioners," 47; PRO, C 115, box M, letter 7430.
    2. The chamber was assigned to Masters "Greville," "Rawley," "Gordge," and "Cooke." Possibly the pensioners Edward Greville, William Gorges, and Roger Cooke were intended, but it seems more likely that the note refers to the more prominent courtiers Fulke Greville, Walter Ralegh, and Anthony Cooke (Nichols, *Progresses*, 2:402).
    3. Sandison, *Poems*, xvi.
    4. Ibid., xxi; Collins, *Letters*, 1:363; Nichols, *Progresses*, 3:442.
    5. Collins, *Letters*, 2:193, 197.
    6. Sandison, "Arthur Gorges," 653–55.

Sandison's edition of BL, Egerton MS 3165, provides us with Gorges's poems as written out by a professional scribe under the author's supervision. The first one hundred poems in the collection (actually ninety-nine different lyrics, since poems 28 and 55 are identical), plus poem 109 which was sung to the queen "by a Mair-mead as shee past upon the Thames to Sir Arthur Gorges house at Chelsey," represent Gorges's Elizabethan output. Except for poems 98, 100, and 109, all were probably composed between about 1580 and 1587.[7]

Greville, Fulke (1554–1628)

Greville was at court by New Year's of 1577 when he was listed among the untitled gentlemen on a gift roll that does distinguish among "masters." His status at the time of the 1578 exchange is unclear because no "masters" were designated on the roll, but he appears as "Mr. Fulk Greville" on the rolls of 1579, 1581, 1584, 1585, 1597, 1598, 1599, 1600, and 1603. The 1577 exchange may have been motivated as part of his suit for a sinecure on the council of the Marches of Wales which he received that same year.[1] Greville was apparently a protégé of Sir Henry Sidney at this time, yet he must have established an independent rapport with Elizabeth soon thereafter, for upon returning from an unauthorized journey to the Netherlands in the fall of 1578 he was specifically forbidden access to the queen for a matter of months.[2] Greville performed in the tiltyard every year between 1581 and 1586 and thereafter on Accession Day in 1589, 1590, and 1591. He is probably the "Mr Grevell" lodged with Ralegh, Gorges, and Cooke according to a list of court chambers for May 1583.[3] Both Sidney and Greville were stayed by royal command from sailing with Drake's expedition in 1585, and while Sidney obtained a military command in the Low Countries later in the year, Elizabeth kept Greville with her at court. She banished him for six months, however, late in 1587 because he had gone over to France without her permission.[4]

When Greville became secretary to the council of Wales early in 1590 he gained an office which he could not fill by proxy, and Rebholz argues that he may have spent the early 1590s at his post on

7. Sandison, *Poems*, xxx, xxxiii-xxxiv.
1. Rebholz, *Life of Greville*, 21.
2. Ibid., 35.
3. Nichols, *Progresses*, 2:402.
4. Rebholz, *Life of Greville*, 73–74, 79.

the Marches, although he was definitely at court for the Accession Day celebrations in 1590 and 1591.[5] Thus 1592–1593 may constitute Greville's only significant absence from court, for he was again in attendance upon Elizabeth by the spring of 1594, and can be regularly traced at court thereafter until the queen's funeral, at which he figured as a gentleman of the Privy Chamber.[6] According to Sir Francis Bacon, Greville "had much and private access to Queen Elizabeth, which he used honourably, and did many men good."[7]

Rebholz establishes the probable chronology of Greville's works in appendix 1 of his fine biography, which I follow in assigning *Mustapha* to circa 1594–1596, *Alaham* to circa 1599–1601, and the initial work of recasting the choruses from the plays into the *Treatise of Monarchy* to circa 1599–1604. In Chapter 3 I present the evidence suggesting that the order of entries in the *Caelica* Manuscript (BL, Add. MS 54570) is topical rather than chronological. Thus Greville's Elizabethan lyrics here cannot be distinguished from his later ones on the basis of their ordering in that manuscript. For the purposes of this study I exclude from the sequence only poems 78, 93, 101, and 102, which seem to contain definite Jacobean allusions. Greville's Elizabethan canon is also expanded to include a ninety-line poem preserved in the *Arundel Harington Manuscript* (poem 69). Although Ruth Hughey assigned this work to the years 1568–1577, before Greville came up to court, a later date is more likely. The title refers to the "Mr of the Rolles yt nowe is," a distinction which would have been pointless before the death of Sir William Cordell on May 17, 1581, for he had held the mastership since Queen Mary's reign. His successor was Sir Gilbert Gerrard; upon his death on February 4, 1593, the post went to Thomas Egerton, and it was probably within a year or two of one of these turnovers in office that Greville composed this work.[8]

Between roughly 1619 and 1625 Greville employed a scribe to prepare fair copies of his works.[9] These six volumes, formerly in the collection at Warwick Castle, are now BL, Add. MSS. 54566–54571. For all of the Elizabethan works except *Mustapha*, the *Arundel Harington* text, and a few scattered lyrics, these manuscripts repre-

5. Ibid., 89–90.

6. Spedding, *Letters*, 1:298; PRO, LC 2/4 (4), f. 47.

7. James Spedding, *The Works of Sir Francis Bacon*, 13:377.

8. A text of the poem among the Salisbury Manuscripts (Cecil Papers 286) was copied either from the *Arundel Harington Manuscript* or a very close descendent.

9. Kelliher, "Warwick Manuscripts," 111.

sent the earliest extant state of Greville's writings, and while Bullough's edition, *The Poems and Dramas of Fulke Greville*, is based upon the 1633 folio, his commentary provides collations against the Warwick manuscripts.[10] *Mustapha* has survived in several earlier states as represented by two manuscripts: Folger, MS V.b.223, and Cambridge, MS Ff.2.34, plus the surreptitious quarto of 1609. Greville thoroughly revised his play before its transcription into the Warwick manuscript. Rebholz concluded "very tentatively" that the Folger text comprises the earliest and most complete version of the play;[11] this source is cited in Part I but with reference as well to the extensive readings from the Cambridge Manuscript and the 1609 print as set forth in Bullough's commentary to volume 2 of his edition. *Alaham* survives only in the Warwick text and the 1633 folio, both of which represent versions of the play which Greville had revised to an unspecifiable degree at some time after 1601.[12] The *Treatise of Monarchy* probably stands at the furthest remove from its Elizabethan prototype of all of Greville's works. In the Warwick manuscript and the 1670 folio—the only texts—it appears as a polished discourse, although it evolved from Greville's revision of the choruses written for his tragedies. References to the excommunication of Venice (1606) in section 6, Queen Elizabeth's death in section 9, and the death of Henry IV of France (1610) in section 10 indicate that the received text is of Jacobean vintage. Only sections 1–5 are likely to reflect the Elizabethan state of the text and even so, the entire poem was probably revised in response to Greville's experience with the Stuart regime. For the purposes of this study, the most suitable text of the *Treatise* is that edited by G. A. Wilkes from the Warwick manuscript.[13]

Harington, John (d. 1582)

Harington and his first wife, Ethelreda, illegitimate daughter of Henry VIII, entered Princess Elizabeth's service while she was under detention at Woodstock in the spring of 1554.[1] When the princess became queen, Harington prospered as a royal favorite. His second wife, Isabella (born Markham), served as a gentlewoman of the Privy

10. For *Caelica* sonnets 6 and 32 the folio is the only authority.
11. Rebholz, *Life*, 101n.
12. Rebholz offers a reconstruction of the Elizabethan version of this play (Ibid., 132–35).
13. Greville, *The Remains*.
1. Hughey, *John Harington*, 5.

Chamber until her death in 1579.[2] Their son, John, was sponsored by the queen at his christening in 1560. During the early 1560s, Harington received crown leases, was appointed receiver general of the royal revenues in Nottinghamshire and Derbyshire, and became the queen's collector for "obits," presumably, a collector of gifts bequeathed to Elizabeth in her subjects' wills. His name appears regularly on the New Year's gift rolls; he is cited as "Mr. Harington" on the list of 1562 where only fourteen of thirty-nine gentlemen are titled, and he is likewise distinguished from mere gentlemen on the rolls of 1563, 1567, 1576, and 1577.

Harington was an active man of letters during the mid-sixteenth century. He published his translation of Cicero's *De Amicitia* in 1550, and acquired some of the most important manuscript collections of early Tudor verse, including Wyatt's own copy of his poems, BL, Egerton MS 2711, and the *Arundel Harington Manuscript*, which is also an important anthology of Elizabethan verse. Harington wrote several poems relating to his courtship of Isabella Markham along with other occasional verses prior to the reign of Elizabeth. Only the following poems attributed to Harington are likely to have been composed after 1558: "None can deem right"; "Of person rare"; "Such one is ware"; "If duty, wife, lead thee"; "Husband, if you will be"; and "A boy that should content me."[3]

Harington, Sir John (1560–1612)

Ruth Hughey's discovery that the poet was christened on August 4, 1560, established his correct date of birth for the first time.[1] He had probably just begun his studies at King's College, Cambridge, in 1576 when Elizabeth sent him a copy of her speech to Parliament of March 15, addressed to "Boye Jack," and reminding him that "I do thys, because thy father was readye to sarve [serve] and love us in

2. Ibid., 55.
3. The first two poems (part 2, section A, poems 4 and 10, in Hughey's edition) were painted on a portrait of Thomas, Lord Seymour, which Harington is said to have presented to the queen in 1567. The portrait is now at Longleat House. Sir John Harington recalled in his notes to *Orlando Furioso* that his father had written "Such one is ware" for an earl (Ariosto, *Orlando*, 99; Hughey, *John Harington*, part 2, section A, poem 5). The next two poems (Hughey, part 2, section A, poems 16 and 17) were translated from Walter Haddon's Latin verses. The last poem (Hughey, part 2, section A, poem 22) is subscribed "Io. Har." in the *Arundel Harington Manuscript*, and could be of Sir John's composition, although its style and the possibility that it was meant to parody Wyatt's "A face that should content me," suggest the elder Harington instead.
1. Hughey, *John Harington*, 227, n. 205.

trouble and thrall."[2] Harington entered Lincoln's Inn on November 27, 1581. How early he began attending court is uncertain beyond his assertion that it took place after the first twenty years of the reign. He recalled being present at Dr. Launcelot Andrews's sermon at court in February of 1591,[3] but it is entirely plausible that Elizabeth had banished him from court in the late 1580s for reading his translation of the racier passages from *Orlando Furioso* to her ladies there. He endured a similar expulsion in 1596 when he published his *Metamorphosis of Ajax*, an expansive treatise in which he described among other things the construction of the first flush toilet. The queen also rebuked Harington for accepting his knighthood from the earl of Essex while serving in the Irish campaign of 1599, but early in the following year she was reconciled with her godson after granting him a private audience in the withdrawing chamber at Whitehall.[4] Previously, Harington had enjoyed such marks of his sovereign's favor toward him as her sponsorship of his son at his christening on January 22, 1588, and a visit to his house during her progress through Somersetshire in 1592.[5]

Harington is the most prolific of the Elizabethan courtier poets. His canon, much of which awaits definitive editing, falls into three main categories: original English verse, Latin verse, and translations. The first 424 epigrams in McClure's edition (actually, 422 different poems) constitute the bulk of Sir John's original Elizabethan output, granted that more than eighty of them are translated or adapted from Martial and other sources. To these must be added ten English poems in BL, Add. MS 12049, the collection of his epigrams which Harington prepared in 1602 for presentation to King James. These poems have been edited by R. H. Miller, who cites as well the fifteen Latin poems in this manuscript, nine of which are Harington's translations of his English epigrams.[6] The verse letter to King James on pages 208 and 210 of the British Library Manuscript is printed in Thomas Park's edition of *Nugae Antiquae*.[7] Harington

2. *Nugae Antiquae* (1769), 1:148–49.
3. Harington, *Supplie*, 77, 140.
4. *Nugae Antiquae* (1769), 2:25–56.
5. BL, Add. MS 8159; PRO, E 351/542, f. 116v.
6. McClure, *Letters and Epigrams*. Jean McMahon Humez found eighty-odd epigrams derived in whole or part from Martial ("The Manners of Epigram: A Study of the Epigram Volumes of Martial, Harington, and Jonson," 133). R. H. Miller's "Unpublished Poems" (148–58) includes the much-revised text of epigram 292 from this manuscript, while the five epigrams it does not contain (numbers 16, 289, 306, 321, and 343) are probably also Elizabethan.
7. *Nugae Antiquae* (1804), 1:328–31.

apparently also wrote a Latin couplet for his *Succession* tract which is there translated into English as well.[8] BL, Add. MS 12049, apparently represents, in its unrevised readings, Harington's intentions for this collection at the close of Elizabeth's reign; it is therefore the text cited in this study where its substantive readings differ from McClure's edition. The rest of Harington's original English verses are scattered through his publications and family manuscripts; the following list of sources and first lines identifies nine poems having some claim to being of Sir John's own composition.

From *The Metamorphosis of Ajax*[9]

Cease maister anie more, 80
It never yet was deemed a wonder, 153
That still (methinks) he usde a phrase as pliant, 106
The (grace of God) guides well both age and youth, 204
To keep your houses sweet, cleanse privy vaults, 186

From *A Tract on the Succession*

Though plaine my muse, and never superstitious, 121

From the "Briefe Notes and Remembrancer," in *Nugae Antiquae* (1779), vol. 2

Who livethe in Cowrtes muste marke what they saie, 212
Truste not a friende to doe or saie, 213

This is an approximate and doubtless incomplete list of Harington's fugitive pieces. The adages in verse, metrical tags, and rescensions of the poetry of others scattered throughout his prose works defy alignment with the canon. A charming couplet from the *Metamorphosis*, for example, "So we get the chinks / We will bear with the stinks" (128), is cited in Morris B. Tilley's *A Dictionary of the Proverbs in England* as the earliest form of this proverb—but is it original? "Play with me, and hurt me not / Jest with me and shame me not," from the same source, seems to be but a recasting of an older adage which Harington may have adapted from Puttenham's "Iape with me but hurt me not, / Bourde with me but shame me not."[10] Similar adaptations of John Heywood's proverbs, Thomas Tusser's poetic advice on good husbandry, and verses by a number of

8. Harington, *Tract on the Succession*, 115.
9. Donno, *Metamorphosis*.
10. Tilley, *Dictionary*, 184; Puttenham, *Arte*, 254.

others are probably best relegated to our cumulative literary heritage than attached firmly to Harington.

Harington's translation of all forty-six cantos of Ariosto's *Orlando Furioso* (1591) represents his most ambitious literary undertaking. The task was alleviated only by the single stanza composed by his father (canto 19, stanza 1) and the fifty stanzas submitted by his brother, Francis (canto 32, stanzas 1–50). The book also includes Harington's "Briefe Apologie of Poetrie" as its preface, while his notes at the end of each canto provide often elaborate explication of the text along with miscellaneous and quite revealing comments upon a great variety of vaguely related matters. McNulty's edition is the basis for all subsequent references to the *Orlando*.

During the reign of King James, Harington finished his translation of the entire Psalter, sending the complete text to the king about 1612. The project probably occupied him during the closing years of his life, but it seems likely that the seven penitential Psalms transcribed in BL, Egerton MS 2711, folios 104–7, constitute an Elizabethan beginning to the complete translation. Schmutzler has shown that they represent the earliest versions of those Psalms as they appear in the full manuscript texts;[11] they are printed below from the BL, Egerton Manuscript. The first eight lines of Harington's translation of the "Schola Salernitana" appear in the *Metamorphosis*, and while it is possible that he completed this work during Elizabeth's reign, it seems more likely that he did so, as Donno suggests, for dedication to Prince Henry in 1607.[12] The excerpt in the *Metamorphosis* was at any rate substantially revised for the full translation as printed in 1608.

Harington undoubtedly translated book 6 of *The Aeneid* for Prince Henry but was not responsible for a translation of book 4 which also survives in manuscript.[13] The unique manuscript of book 6 is prefaced by an epistle to King James in which Harington explains that a recent visitation of the plague gave him occasion "to revyse a worke I had formerly taken payn in for my sonns better understandinge," indicating that the text is, at best, significantly revised from its Elizabethan state, if any. As a result of these uncer-

11. Schmutzler, "Harington's Metrical Paraphrases," 241–44. Anthony G. Petti accepts a date circa 1600 or even earlier "on purely palaeographical grounds" (*English Literary Hands from Chaucer to Dryden*, 81).

12. Donno, *Metamorphosis*, 156n.

13. Beal, *Index*, vol. 1, pt. 1, 130. Simon Cauchi, "Sir John Harington and Virgil's *Aeneid* IV," 242–49.

tainties about its composition, this translation has been largely excluded from this study.

More than a score of Harington's certain if less ambitious translations survive in his various Elizabethan tracts: in *The Metamorphosis of Ajax* alone he translates Catullus, Persius, Martial, Horace, and Sir Thomas More; in *Orlando Furioso*, Plutarch, Ovid, Martial, Dante, Tasso, a Latin epitaph on Sidney by King James of Scotland, and several of Ariosto's poems which are not part of the *Orlando*. In his *Tract on the Succession*, he adds Vergil, two Welsh poems, and one in French. Omitting translations of a single line, these verses are enumerated below:

From *The Metamorphosis of Ajax*
A bird that hath an angels plume, 148
A builder that will follow wise direction, 87
Alas my head with thy long reading aches, 98
All fortune tellers, Jugglers, and Egyptians, 233
From your confessor, lawyer, and physician, 155
Goodness is best when it is common shown, 192
The men still bear their Masters sin, 198
The Salern school doth by these lines impart, 157
The way from wealth, and store, to want, and neede, 218
Their ears must on the pillory be nailed, 214
Thy dog still licks thy lips, but tis no hurt, 98
Tis noted as the nature of a sink, 161
To break a little wind, sometime one's life doth save, 100
To strive with us it is but vain, 198

From the "Treatise on Play," in *Nugae Antiquae* (1779), vol. 2
Be it virtue, be it fraud, 197
Boyleth thy brest with lucre's base desire? 184
Lyke wandring rogues that have no certaine manger, 163
Stop the first breaches; medcine will not boot, 193
To see a play I call no haynous cryme, 162
Try wee, with glittering blade, not glistening gold, 196
What made Aegistus first a letcher grow? 169

From *A Tract on the Succession*
Both sides have doctors, counsells both alledge, 110
Cause them shake hands as friends by some invention, 113
Christ keep this eighth our rightfull king and true, 122
God grant the fates in order so dispose, 39
The court of France no likeness can express, 80

From *Orlando Furioso* (includes the "Briefe Apologie of Poetrie")
Fly sin, for sharp revenge doth follow sin, 249
Good sir take heed how ear it falls, 557
Lawyers, Hell, and the Chequer are allowed to live on spoile, 4
Our only dying day and end doth show, 275
Take idlenesse away and out of dout, 57
That heav'n is void and that no gods there are, 383
The vile Promoters, foes to peace and enemies to rest, 196
This house is small but fit for me, 576
This may indeed be call'd the age of gold, 239
Thou knowst, the wanton worldlings ever runne, 3–4
Thus I am grown a savage beast and vyld, 57
When Venus saw the noble Sidney dying, 435
While yet my life was in her middle race, 57
Who list to ride about, about may ride, 577
Whose life the fortune of the warres doth save, 420

SIR JOHN HARINGTON'S TRANSLATION OF
THE PENTITENTIAL PSALMS

Psalm 6

1. O doe not Lord correct mee in thy wrath
   Nor chasten mee in fury of thy Choller,
   Though many strypes my fault deserved hath
   That in thy schoole am such a trewant scholler;
2.   My naked soule too tender is, o God,   5
     Too sensible of such a smarting rod.

3. My verie bones are in my body brused,
   Their marrow with this maladie doth melt;
   Let mercie's oyle be to my wounde infused
4. Oh heale my soule of stripes so lately felt,   10
5.   For after death can none record the storie
     Of all thy grace, thy goodnes, and thy glorie.

6. My wofull daies succeed as wakefull nights
   And of my greifs my bed a witnes beares;
   I weepe when I should sleepe with these affrights   15
   In sighs distild I bathe my couche with teares,
7.   My beautie wasts in sight of mine illwillers,
     And of my strength infeebled are the pillers.

8. But gett yee hence from mee yee wicked ones
   For God hath heard the voice of all my weepinge   20
   And giv'n a gracious hearinge to my grones,

9. And now is pleas'd to take mee to his keepinge;
    Now yow my foes that made my greife your game
    Confounded are, put back, and vext with shame.

Psalm 32

1. Thrice blessed hee whose faults such favor wynn
    Hee can by grace conceale his knowne demerit;
2. Thrice blest to whome the Lord imputes no sinne
    Nor fynds no fraud nor falshood in his spirit;
3.   My selfe had once a sore that inward festerd,   5
    But since I found how sore yt sore me pester'd

4. For daies and nights thie heavie hand did presse mee
    And waste my strength like flowrs with summer's
    heate
5. Till halfe inforst I said I would confesse mee
    And open lay my fault both foule and greate;   10
6.   No sooner I perform'd what I decreed
    But thou forgav'st the guilt of my misdeed.

7. Hence learns each man well mynded to apply him
    To seeke by prayer what tyme thou wilt be found,
8. So flowing floods shall fleete and not come nigh him,   15
    For on this rock wee safe may stand and sound
9.   And sing for joy: Let all that seeke instruction
    Come follow mee, I'le save yow from destruction.

10. But be not then like hare-braynd horse or mule
    That strive, and start, and strike, and prone to fall   20
    Whose mouths with bitt and bridle men doe rule.
11. Such willfull wights have woes and ever shall,
    But God will joy, and grace, and peace impart
12.   To faithfull folke and those are true of hart.

Psalm 38

1.   Oh do not Lord in anger mee reprove,
    Nor chasten mee, in tymes of Deep displeasure;
2.   Thy shafts so sticke in mee they will not move,
    Thy heavy hand hath wayght exceeding mesure,
3.   My flesh corrupts, no sowndnes bydes thearin,   5
    My bones want rest by reason of my sinne.

4.   My strength doth fayle soch poyse to undergoe,
    The burden soch that under yt I shrinke,

5.   So taynted ys my flesh from top to toe
    My festring sores, corrupted, inward, stinke;   **10**
6.   My state and staffe of all my strength ys broken
7.   And of sad greefs sad garments are a token.

8.   Though weaknes makes mee mute, smart makes me
           rore,
    My hart ys quyte opprest with inward anguishe,
9.   Thow seest my syghs, o Lord that sentst my sore,   **15**
10. Myne eysyght fayls, my faynting lymbes do languish,
11.   My neyghbors all and frends I hold so deer
       Looke on aloofe, my kyndred come not neer.

12.   And yet my foes as if all this suffiz'd not
    Doe seek eftsoone to draw my vitall bloud;   **20**
       What plot, what practise is yt they devis'd not?
13. Yet like a man both deafe and dumbe I stood
14.   As if that I their fowle reproches hard not,
       Or that to cleere or purge my self I car'd not.

15.   For still I hop't in myds of all this ill   **25**
    That of this question God would make decision,
16.   Nor let my foes be thus insulting still,
    Nor for my plagues to have mee in derision;
17.   I see my sores and know thy justice sent them,
18.   I will confesse my sinns and so repent them.   **30**

19.   And though my foes confirme their wicked faction
    Ungratefully for kyndnes rendring harme,
       And though they seke by slander and detraction
    To weaken my good name and mee disarme,
       Yet Lord thou art my strength and succour cheefe, **35**
       Make haste then I thee pray to my releife.

Psalm 51

1. Have mercie, Lord, of thine aboundant grace,
    Forgive my guilt, that greeveth all my sences,
    Blot owt my blame, my fawlt's record deface,
    With mercye's mayn remitt my mayn offences;
2.   O wash, o rence my sowle withowt, within   **5**
    To make mee clean from this my filthy sin.

3. For well I waygh the poyse of my transgressyon,
    The fowlnes of my fault is still before mee;
    'Gainst thee alone I sin'd, to thee confession

4. Alone I make, that canst alone restore mee,   **10**
     That thou thye doome pronowncinge I obayinge
     May show thee just and cleere in evrie sayinge.

5. In mother's wombe I shaped was in sinn,
6. In sinn conceav'd, yet thou in inward part
     Requirest truths, and earlie did'st beginn   **15**
     To putt a secret wisdom in my hart
7.   With hysop, Lord, then lave my leprous sore
     And so then snow my whitenesse shalbe more.

8. Then shalt thou cause mee know some news of gladnes,
     My bruised bones shall joy that erst did rew,   **20**
9. Then turne thy face from sinn that caus'd my sadnes
10. Make cleane my hart, my sprite aright renew;
11.   O cast mee not from out thy presence quite,
     Nor take fro mee thy sanctifying sprite.

12. To former state of peace reduce my soule,   **25**
     Confirm'd with sprite of princely consolation,
13. So shall my works the wickeds' wayes controule,
     My sample soe may mend their conversation
14.   From cryinge crimes of blood, oh set mee free,
     Thy justice then my Jubile shall bee.   **30**

15. Lord open thou my lipps that shame did close,
     And then my mouth shall publish forth thy praise,
16. Yf sacrifize thee pleas'd (as some suppose),
     I should give holocausts ev'n all my daies;
17.   The sacrifice with thee of greatest merit   **35**
     Is this, a hart contrite, an humble spirit.

     These, these (o Lord), thou never dost despise,
18. Now let with these thy wrath be well appeasd,
     That holy Salem's walls by mee may rise,
     That Sion's hill may fynd thy goodnes pleas'd;   **40**
19.   With offrings pure presented of our parts,
     The calves of lipps on altars of our harts.

Psalm 102

1.   Lord lend thine eare unto my pray'r and crying,
Nor hide thy face when hasty helpe I need;
     I waste as smoke, my bones within are frying,
My stomack faynts, I ev'n forget to feed,
My hart is wither'd like a fading weed,   **5**

My gutts so gryp'd with greivance of my grones
That ev'n my skinn doth cleave unto my bones.

As sparrows skar'd sitt lurking in the thatch,
As desert Pellican or lothed Owle
    With scorned tune doe kepe their nightly watch,   **10**
So I by day doe wake, by night doe howle,
My foes do tawnt mee with reporaches fowle,
    And for my food my bread is earth and ashes,
    And teares the drinke my cupp both fills and
        washes.

So heavie lies on mee thine Indignation   **15**
That lifts mee up to cast mee lower downe,
    As grasse new mowne doth fade, in such a fashion
I shadow-like doe vanish with thy frowne;
But loe, eternitie thy yeares doth crowne;
    Of Salem (Lord) then thinke, thy holy citie,   **20**
    High tyme it is thou take on Sion pitie.

For why, thy servants see with greife and shame
Her monuments thus broken and defac't,
    But tyme will come that heath'n shall feare thy
        name,
Yf earthly kings to honour thee shall haste   **25**
And Sion shall with glory new bee grac't
    When God shall bend his eare to poore men's cries,
    And shall their just petitions not despise.

    This shall be wrote, and kept in safe record
That children after borne, not yet alive   **30**
    May praise thy name, for thow in heav'n, o Lord
Didst ev'n the lowly things on earth contrive,
There thou the bound dost free, the damned reprive
    That nations and their kinges that heare this storie
    May meete at Sion there to give thee glorie.   **35**

    But thou hast quayld my strength amid my waies,
Cut off my yeares and broke my vitall line,
    Oh doe not cut me off at halfe my daies,
Though none can last eternall like to thine;
For thou in heav'n created'st ev'rie signe   **40**
    Thou laid'st of earth the nethermost foundations,
    Thy selfe outlasting all their generations.

The mater dures, but perish shall the creatures
As vestures old that men doe turne and change,
    So shalt thou change the heav'ns and all their
      features   45
And make them new; o works, o worker strange,
Thy selfe alone subjected to noe change;
    But they that in thy service take delight
    Shall see their seed establisht in thy sight

Psalm 130

From horror huge of darke despay'r and deepe
My soule hath cride with seas of sin surrounded;
Oh heare the voice that in thine eare hath sownded
    Both heere, and heed and seeme not, Lord, asleepe;
    Yf thou of sinns a register doe keepe   5
All flesh and bloud for ever were confownded,
    But thou, o Lord, hast grace and mercie store,
    Which makes us feare thee much, but love thee
      more.

Then thow, my soule, abide in expectation
For on his word I sett my rest and stay   10
As they that watch by night expect the day,
    O Israell bee this thy consolation,
His mercies rich thy ransom deere can pay,
His grace is great, then feare wee no damnacon,
    Then Israell, trust in God, for only hee   15
    Redeems thee from thy sinns and sets thee free.

Psalm 143

1. Lord heare my pray'r and crie, respect my ruthe,
   Receave my sute with grace and myld attention,
   I joyntly call thy mercie and thy truthe
2. For if to sitt as Judge be thine intention,
     What flesh can beare soe sharpe a reprehension?   5
   Behould how feirie my foe my soule pursew'th,
     And holds mee heere inclosed in a cave
     In state of those are closed in their grave.
4.   Thus is my hart within my bodie greeved,
   My thoughts present mee woes and desolation,   10
5. Yet I thy words and workes have still beleeved
   Myne exercise with joy and meditation;

6. In them I feele such joys and consolation,
    Like parched lands with tymely raine releeved;
7.   Then hast to helpe, for yf no helpe thou send   **15**
    My daies will draw unto most dolefull end.
8.   O send my soule some glad and joyfull tyding,
    I trust in thee, doe thou direct my way;
9. From force of foes wee have no safer hyding
10. Instruct mee soe as please thee best I may;   **20**
11. Let thy good sprite give mee soe stable stay
    As in these straights may keepe my feete from
        slydinge,
    And of thy grace, o Lord, doe thou destroy
    Such foes as vex thy servant and annoy.
                            finis
                (BL, Egerton MS 2711, folios 104–7)

Note
    Designation of the biblical verses in the left margins of the text is erratic in the
manuscript; I have punctuated these numerals consistently for the sake of clarity.

Hatton, Sir Christopher (1540–1591)

    Hatton was undoubtedly a prominent royal favorite several years
before he composed the fourth act of an Inner Temple play, *Gismond
of Salern*, which was performed at court about 1567. He was admitted to the band of gentlemen pensioners in 1564, and had become a
gentleman of the Privy Chamber by 1572, when he was appointed
captain of the guard. On November 11, 1577, he became Vice-
Chamberlain of the household and was sworn to the Privy Council.
In 1587 he was made Lord Chancellor.
    On June 30, 1564, Elizabeth authorized Hatton's purchase of a
suit of armor from the royal armory, an unusual privilege even if it
were connected with his appointment to the pensioners. In September she sent him to greet the Queen of Scots's envoy, Sir James
Melville, upon his arrival in the capital and the next morning Hatton and Thomas Randolph escorted Melville to a garden audience
with the queen. On November 11, 1565, he joined three other challengers in a court tournament honoring the marriage of Lady Anne
Russell to the earl of Warwick. Among the English representatives at
the christening of King James in December of 1566, Hatton was
described as "greatest in favour" with Elizabeth.[1] In 1568 he was

    1. Eric St. John Brooks, *Sir Christopher Hatton*, 43, 51–52; Melville, *Mem-
oirs*, ed. George Scott (London, 1683), 45–46, 76.

appointed keeper of Eltham Park and the Park of Horne, while in the same year he exchanged his ancestral estate of Holdenby for the Abbey and demesne lands of Sulby, immediately leasing Holdenby from the crown and having it reconveyed to him in fee farm a few years later.[2] Hatton was Elizabeth's "mutton" and her "lids." His name does not appear on the New Year's gift rolls through 1567, but when the records resume in 1572, his name is there as it is regularly thereafter.

The original version of *Gismond of Salern* to which Hatton contributed was edited by John W. Cunliffe in his *Early English Classical Tragedies*.[3] In addition to the fourth act of this play, Hatton may also claim four lines of Latin verse attributed by the younger Harington to "a poore neighbour" of Sir John Spenser who "once dwelt at Holmeby" (that is, Holdenby).[4] The jewel he gave the queen at New Year's in 1578 is described as having "certayne verces written" on the back, evidence, at least, that Hatton used poetry in his personal relationship with Elizabeth.

Heneage, Sir Thomas (d. 1595)

Camden characterized Heneage as "a man for his elegancy of life and pleasantnesse of speech, borne for the Court," while Sir John Harington remembered him as "an old Courtier, and zealous Puritan."[1] Heneage, a gentleman of the Privy Chamber from the beginning of the reign, served as treasurer of the chamber from 1570 until his death. He was knighted in 1577 and had been appointed Vice-Chamberlain of the household by January of 1588.[2] He was sworn to the Privy Council in 1589 and became chancellor of the duchy of Lancaster in the following year. His name appears on every complete New Year's gift roll to 1595. The queen nicknamed Thomas her "Sanguine" and bestowed on him at least eleven grants of land between 1561 and 1595; among the more valuable of these listed in the DNB should be added the lease of the monastery of Walton, valued at 330 pounds annually, which Heneage acquired in 1578–1579.[3]

The intimate personal relations undergirding this steady flow

2. Nicolas, *Memoirs*, 7; Brooks, *Hatton*, 155.
3. Cunliffe, *Early English Classical Tragedies*, 163–216.
4. Donne, *Metamorphosis*, 228.
1. Camden, *Annals*, sig. 2P, 2v; Harington, *Supplie*, 122.
2. BL, Add. MS 8159.
3. PRO, SP 12/166, f. 85v.

of promotions and property are dramatically illustrated by an exchange of messages and gifts occasioned by Sir Thomas's journey to York in July of 1583. In his absence, Heneage sent Elizabeth a jewel with the motto *"amat iste sine fine,"* to which the queen replied that her word to him was "I love *sine fine*." "And besydes that," a servant informed Sir Thomas, "for so gentleye remembring of herr she sent you ten thowsand myllyons of thankes and wyll send you a token agayne before your retorne, which she prayeth may be sone, for she mysseth you all redye." Within a few weeks, Elizabeth sent Heneage a mother-of-pearl butterfly with the explanation that since "her Sanguyne was farre in the colde north countrye where no [butter]flyes weare," he might have this one "to playe with, that he myght allwayes remember her that sent ytt."[4] Heneage today stands very much in the shadow of Elizabeth's flashier favorites such as Leicester, Hatton, and Ralegh, nor is he mentioned by Naunton. Yet he remained on closely affectionate terms with the queen almost throughout her reign.

Heneage had turned to the muses at least as early as 1557 when he composed an elegy for his father-in-law, Sir Nicholas Poyntz, which has apparently survived only in Walter Haddon's Latin translation.[5] Poem 175 in Hughey's edition of the *Arundel Harington Manuscript* is probably one of Heneage's Elizabethan works, although it is not subscribed, but entitled "Hennage," and could thus be a poem addressed to him. The hand which entered it into this anthology also copied number 185, a poem by Edmund Spenser, suggesting that the Heneage poem was also transcribed during Elizabeth's reign.[6] Heneage's six definite poems are edited below; 1 was written to answer verses by Ralegh and 6 responds to verses by the queen.

1a

Farewell false love, thow oracle of lyes,
A mortall foe, an enemye to reste,
An envyous boye from whom all cares aryse,
A bastarde borne, a beaste with rage possest,
A waye of errour, a temple full of treason,   5
In all effects contrary unto reason;

4. HMC, Finch, 1:24–25
5. Haddon's poem is entitled *"ex Anglico clarissimi viri Thomae Henneagii,"* number 72 in Charles J. Lees's *The Poetry of Walter Haddon*. I have discovered no text of the English original.
6. Hughey, *Arundel Harington Manuscript*, 2:253.

A poysoned serpent covered all with flowers,
Mother of sighes and murtherer of repose,
A sea of sorrowes from whence are drawne suche showers
As moysture lends to every greife that growes; 10
A school of guile, a neast of deepe deceipte,
A gilded hooke that holdes a poysoned bate;

A fortresse foyld whom reason did defend,
A syren songe, a fever of the mynde,
A maze wherin affection fyndes no end, 15
A raynge cloude that rones before the winde,
A substance like the shadowe of the sunne,
A goale of greife for which the wysest runne;
 (Sir Walter Ralegh, from Folger, MS V.a.89, folios 7–7v)

1

Most welcome love, thow mortall foe to lies,
Thow roote of life, and ruiner of debate,
An Impe of heaven, that troth to vertue ties,
A soone of choise, that bastard lustes doth hate.
A waye to fasten fancy most to reason 5
In all effects, and enemy most to treason.

A flowre of faith, that will not vade for smart,
Mother of trust, and murderer of our woes
In sorowes' Seas, a Cordiall to the hart
That medcyne gives to every grief that growes; 10
A skoole of witt, a nest of sweet conceit,
A percynge eye, that findes a gilt disceit.

A Fortres sure which reason must defend,
A hopefull toyle, a most delightinge bande,
Affection mazed, that leades to happy ende 15
To raynge thoughtes, a gentle raiginge hande,
A Substaunce such as will not be undonne,
A price of Joye for which the wysest ronne
 (Houghton Library, f MS 1285, folio 72v)

Note
 In the manuscript, "Thomas Heneage" is written in the left margin of poem 1; it is followed by a version of these three stanzas of 1a, attributed to "Mr Raleigh." For the last two stanzas of Ralegh's poem and the evidence that Heneage's verses were written in response to Ralegh's see my "Companion Poems in the Ralegh Canon," *English Literary Renaissance* 14 (1983): 260–73. At 1, line 14, I emend 'amost' to 'a most.'

2

Sir Thomas The markes of thoughtes, and messengers of will
My frend, be wordes, but they not all to trust,
For wordes be good, full oft when thoughtes be ill,
As faire is falce thoughe sometymes sweet and Joste.
Then Friend, to Judge arighte, and skape the scof   5
Trust none till tyme shall putt their vysardes of.
(Houghton Library, f MS 1285, folio 72v)

Note
   'Joste,' line 4, is a scribal variant of 'just,' rhyming with 'trust' in line 2.

3

Sir Thomas Madame, who once in paper puts his thoughte
Doth send to daunger that was safe at home,
And meaninge well, doth make his Judgment naughte
To thrall his wordes he wotes not well to whome,
Yet pullinge backe his penne, he must confesse   5
To show his witt he proves his love the less.
(Houghton Library, f MS 1285, folio 73)

4

Tho. Idle or els but seldome busied best
In Court (my Lord) we lead the vaynest life,
Where hopes, with feares, where joyes with sorrowes rest,
But faith is rare, thoe fayrest wordes be rife.

Heare learne we vice, and look one vertue's bookes;   5
Heare, fine deceit, we hould for courtly skill,
Our care is hear, to waite one wordes and lookes
And greatest worke to follow others' will.

Heare, scorne, a grace, and pride, is present thoughte,
Mallice, but mighte, and fowlest shiftes, no shame;   10
Lust, but delighte, and playnest dealinge noughte,
Whear flattery lykes, and trothe, beares oftest blame;

Yet is the cause, not in the place I finde
But all the fault is in the faulty mynde.
(Houghton Library, f MS 1285, folio 73)

5

Thomas Seldome and short be all our happiest howres
We hear can hold, for why? our hopes and Joies

Failing and falce, their bredinge tyme devowres
Which when we trust, alas we finde but toyes.

Hard to obtaine, but yet more hastly gon   5
Be greatest happ, with grudginge envie matchte.
Of fairest seedes, the fruit is noughte or none
With good and evill, one lyfe so much is patchte

Owr twisted blis, by tyme is soone untwynde
To hope and love, And fear doth gyve a lashe,   10
So change gives checke, to each unstable mynde
To all delight, and daunger gyves the dashe;

    Thus dashte, who yet fast troth to vertew lynckes
    Mak faith to shine, how ever be time shrinckes.
          (Houghton Library, f MS 1285, folio 73)

6a

    Genus infoelix vitae
Multum vigilavi, laboravi, presto multis fui,
    Stultitiam multorum perpessa sum,
Arrogantiam pertuli, Difficultates exorbui,
    Vixi ad aliorum arbitrium, non ad meum.
A haples kynde of lyfe, is this I weare,
Moch watche I dure, and weary toilinge daies
I serve the route, and all therr follies beare,
I suffer pryde, and suppe full harde assaies,
To others' wyll, my life is all addrest   5
And no waie so, as might content me best.
    This above was written in a booke by the Queenes Majestie.
         (Queen Elizabeth, from Pierpont Morgan Library,
                PML 7768, first flyleaf, recto)

6

Madam, but marke the labors of our lyfe
And therewithall, what errors we be in
We sue and seeke, with praiers, sturre, and stryfe,
Uppon this earthe, a happie state to win,

And whilst with cares, we travell to content us   5
In vaine desires, and sette no certaine scope
We reape but things, whereof, we oft repent us
And feede our wylles, with moch beguilinge hope,

We praie for honors, lapt in daunger's handes,
We strive for riches, which we streight forgoe,   10

We seeke delyte, that all in poison standes,
And sette with paines, but seedes of synne and woe
    Then noble lady, need we not to praie
    The lord of all, for better state, and staie?

            Your La: moch bound
                T: Heneage
            (Pierpont Morgan Library, PML 7768,
                        second flyleaf, recto)

Note

Poems 6a and 6 were transcribed into the Pierpont Morgan Library copy of Henry Bull's *Christian Prayers and Holy Meditations* (1570; STC 4029), from whence they were printed by Curt F. Bühler in "Libri Impressi Cum Notis Manuscriptis" (*Modern Language Notes* 53 [1938]: 245–49). I rely on this transcript for the first letters of Heneage's poem in lines 1, 5, 6, 7, 8, and 9, now obliterated in the original volume. Although the texts of both poems appear to be scribal, the signature to poem 6 is holograph. The "noble lady" to whom it is addressed is almost certainly the queen, for which it was intended as a consolatory answer to her own discontented verses.

Herbert, Mary Sidney, Countess of Pembroke (1561–1621)

Mary was first mentioned at court in George Gascoigne's description of the Woodstock entertainment of 1575.[1] Later that year the queen presented her with a gown, and again in 1577 with a "Foreparte" or stomacher from her own wardrobe.[2] She exchanged New Year's gifts with Elizabeth in 1576 and in 1577, the year in which she married Henry Herbert, earl of Pembroke. Thereafter she figures on every complete roll to the end of the reign, usually as the countess of Pembroke junior, to distinguish her from the dowager countess, her mother-in-law. Her brothers, Philip and Robert, addressed their principal works to her, as did a host of Elizabethan writers including Samuel Daniel, Nicholas Breton, Thomas Moffet, and Abraham Fraunce. Her home at Wilton was, to some extent, a center of artistic patronage, to the nurturing of which Mary often sacrificed her attendance at the court of Elizabeth.[3]

The countess may have begun her career as a poet by 1585 in translating the Psalms under Philip's influence. Her works have been reliably edited only in the past few decades, although the tex-

1. Waller, *Triumph of Death*, 2.
2. Janet Arnold, *Lost from Her Majesty's Back*, 53, 56.
3. Mary Ellen Lamb's "The Countess of Pembroke's Patronage" (162–79) offers some useful caveats to overly enthusiastic portrayals of Wilton House as a second English court, and see Brennan, *Literary Patronage*, 72–79. The Herberts patronized a number of writers, thus attracting the plaudits and dedications of many would-be clients.

tual sources have long been known, for she was far from secretive about her poetic undertakings. In 1592 she published her *Tragedie of Antonie*, a translation of Robert Garnier's *Marc Antoine*.[4] The Herbert family's chaplain at Wilton, Henry Parry, affirmed in 1594 that Mary had completed Sir Philip's translation of the Psalms, that is, Psalms 44–150;[5] the latest recoverable Elizabethan state of her work on this project was the manuscript intended for presentation to the queen in 1599, as edited by J. C. A. Rathmell, *The Psalms of Sir Philip Sidney and the Countess of Pembroke*. The countess's dedicatory verses to her brother's memory are edited in Ringler's *Poems of Sir Philip Sidney* and in Waller's *Triumph of Death*.[6] Waller also prints the unique text of her poem dedicating the Psalms manuscript to the queen, verses which were no doubt included in the eight preliminary leaves now missing from the Penshurst Manuscript of the Psalms edited by Rathmell. Waller reprints as well her translation of Petrarch's *Trionfi*, presumably an Elizabethan work, and the pastoral dialogue attributed to the countess in Davison's *Poetical Rhapsody* (1602). The dialogue's title indicates that she wrote these verses "at the Queenes Majesties being at her house at Anno 15   ," although no occasion for the recital of this dialogue has yet been established.

Although Waller accepted "The Dolefull Lay of Clorinda" into the canon, this verse elegy, printed with Spenser's "Astrophel," was no doubt intended as a "prosopopeia," an elegy written in the person of the countess. Spenser explains that he will recite Clorinda's lament, "Which least I marre the sweetnesse of the vearse, / In sort as she it sung, I will rehearse."[7] It is to be a secondhand but faithful rendition of the lament, and it follows in the same stanza and style as the rest of "Astrophel." Its ambiguity as direct quotation is further compromised by Spenser's resumption of the speaker's voice after the sixteenth stanza without pause or break in the verse: "Which when she ended had, another swaine / Of gentle wit and daintie sweet device" continued the eulogy, we are told. If the countess composed the "Dolefull Lay" she coordinated her work in intimate detail with the style and structure of Spenser's verse. Charles G. Osgood found that "Almost every phrase, combination, and mannerism" in the "Lay" "is found elsewhere in Spenser," while H. D.

---

4. Edited by Bullough in his *Narrative and Dramatic Sources*, vol. 5.
5. Brennan, "Date," 434–36.
6. Ringler, *Poems*, 267–69; Waller, *Triumph of Death*, 92–95.
7. Spenser, *Works*, 7:185, lines 215–16.

Rix demonstrated that "Astrophel" was incomplete as a Spenserian elegy without the "Lay" as its "Complaint," and that the distribution of rhetorical figures was proportionately similar in both poems.[8] Moreover, the stylistic alignment of these poems includes their archaic diction, with such rustic phrasing in the "Lay" as "reft from me my ioy," "ne fearing saluage beasts," and "that here in dole are drent" (lines 50, 88, 94). Yet the countess of Pembroke was particularly sensitive to Sir Philip's literary opinions, and she could hardly have overlooked the fact that his praise of Spenser's *Shepheardes Calender* in the *Defence* was qualified by his objection to its archaisms: "That same framing of his style to an old rustic language I dare not allow."[9] It seems unlikely that Mary would have attempted to honor her brother's memory using a poetic diction that he had explicitly rejected. There is, furthermore, no trace of such archaisms in the countess's "Dialogue betweene two Shepheards," where she might have used it with decorum and in less obvious violation of Sidney's pronouncement on the matter.

Hoby, Sir Edward (1560–1617)

The eldest son of Sir Thomas Hoby, translator of Castiglione's *Courtier*, he is presumably the "Mr Hobbye" who exchanged New Year's gifts with Elizabeth in 1581. In May of the following year the queen attended his marriage with Margaret Carey, daughter of Henry, Lord Hunsdon, and on the following day the queen knighted him at Somerset House.[1] Hoby was in close touch with those in the highest circles at court by virtue both of his marriage into the Carey family and the vigilant promotion of his interests by his mother, Lady Elizabeth Russell, Lord Burghley's sister-in-law. Sir Edward wrote Burghley on October 24, 1591, to defend himself from charges of ingratitude, acknowledging the Lord Treasurer's favors to him, and protesting that aside from his Lordship, by "al the frends I have in englonde, I have not benefited one nutshale, more then bare lookes and superficial Countenance." Hoby protested that he could neither sleep nor attend court until he was reconciled with Burghley.[2]

8. Charles G. Osgood, "The Doleful Lay of Clorinda," *Modern Language Notes*, 35 (1920): 90; H. D. Rix, "Spenser's Rhetoric and the 'Doleful Lay,'" *Modern Language Notes* 53 (1938): 261–65.
9. Duncan-Jones and Van Dorsten, *Miscellaneous Prose*, 112.
1. HMC, Rutland, 1:136.
2. BL, Lansdowne MS 68/103.

Sir Edward may have attended court intermittently during the 1580s and early 1590s but with greater regularity toward the end of the reign. He asked Burghley to excuse his absence from court in November 1584, while on April 30, 1595, he claimed not to have been away from court for ten days in the past six months.[3] In 1597 the queen granted him the patent to prosecute and collect the fines of those who exported iron illegally. He participated in the New Year's gift exchanges of 1597, 1598, and 1599, and took his place among the knights of the canopy at Elizabeth's funeral.[4]

Sir Edward followed his father's example in rendering continental renaissance works into English. In 1586 he dedicated to Burghley as a New Year's gift his translation of Martin Coignet's *Politique Discourses*, a book which, incidentally, condemns poets on the primordial charge of being liars, and assembles precedents both classical and biblical for ostracizing them.[5] In the following chapter, jugglers and stage players are likewise condemned, so that we may wonder, assuming that Hoby shared these opinions, whether his subsequent invitation to Sir Robert Cecil to an entertainment at which King Richard would "present himself" necessarily refers to a dramatic performance of any kind.[6] In 1597 Hoby published his translation of Bernard de Mendoza's *Theorique and Practise of Warre*, with a dedication in Spanish to his friend Sir George Carew, master of the ordnance.

Hoby's only known poetry is printed below from his personal anthology of letters, notes, miscellaneous prose, and verse.[7] On folio 48 he copied out his Latin epitaph for his stepfather, John, Lord Russell, who died in 1584; these lines were likewise inscribed on Russell's monument in Westminster Abbey.[8] There follows in the manuscript a letter of eight folios to his brother-in-law, Sir George Carey, dated March 6, 1586, "stilo antiquo" (1587). The letter is actually a brief tract in the "praise of contraries" tradition wherein Hoby argues that childless men are happier than those with issue. The subject was most appropriate for Sir Edward, who had no chil-

---

3. CSPD, 175/7; HMC, Salisbury, 5:193.

4. Huntington Library, MS EL 2290; PRO, LC 2/4 (4), f. 46v.

5. Chapter 35, sig. L2–3.

6. HMC, Salisbury, 5:487. I. A. Shapiro questioned the nature of Hoby's allusion in "*Richard II* or *Richard III* or . . . ?," *Shakespeare Quarterly* 9 (1958): 204–6.

7. BL, Add. MS 38823.

8. Printed from the inscription in John Dart's *Westmonasterium; or, The History and Antiquities of St. Peters Westminster*, 1:115, and J. R.'s *The Antiquities of St. Peter's; or, The Abbey-Church of Westminster*, 1:46.

dren by Margaret, but it no doubt spoke to Carey as well, who lacked a male heir, his only child being his daughter Elizabeth, born in 1572. In the course of supporting his thesis, Hoby translated several lines of Greek verse into English, a couplet each from Hesiod's *Works and Days*, lines 170–72 (poem 2) and Aratus's *Phaenomena*, lines 123–25 (poem 3).

1

In obitum Iohanni Domini Russelli, Edwardi Hoby
    militis Epicedium 1584

Mors Russelle tibi somno suffudit ocellos
    Mens tamen in caelis nescia mortis agit
Qui vitam sanctam meliori fine peregit
    Vivet, et evicta morte superstes erit.
Quis, qualis, quantus, fueris tua stemmata monstrant   5
    Integra vita docet morsque dolenda probat
Stat sit Privigno posuisse hoc lige carmina pauca,
    Tu sibi mente parens, Filius ille tibi.
               (BL, Add. MS 38823, folio 48)

2

To live in this first age o what ill hap had I,
Before or after to be born, great gain had come thereby.
               (BL, Add. MS 38823, folio 53)

3

Now since the golden age alas, what change is founde?
And yet your childeren will, in greater sinnes abounde?
               (BL, Add. MS 38823, folio 53)

Howard, Saint Philip, First Earl of Arundel (1557–1595)

Howard was styled earl of Surrey until February 25, 1580, when he became Lord Arundel upon the death of his maternal uncle. In his farewell letter to the queen of April 1585, he mentions coming up to court some nine or ten years before, a reckoning which coincides with his first appearance on the New Year's gift rolls in 1577. Thereafter he exchanged gifts with Elizabeth in 1579, 1581, 1582, 1583, and 1585. On August 20, 1578, the queen dined with the French ambassadors at Howard's house in London.[1] He participated with

1. Pollen and MacMahon, "Venerable Philip Howard," 23.

the earl of Oxford, Thomas Howard, and Lord Windsor in a Shrovetide show presented at court in 1579, and at about this time allegedly became so favored by the queen that he began to neglect his
wife.[2] Arundel was a frequent performer in the tiltyard; among his
many appearances there, he jousted during the Anjou marriage
negotiations in the tournaments of January 22, April 25, and May
15–16, 1581. In the latter spectacle he joined Lord Windsor, Philip
Sidney, and Fulke Greville as a challenger under the collective title
of "the four Foster Children of Desire."[3]

Arundel's wife, Ann, daughter of the exiled, recusant earl of
Westmorland, was a staunch Catholic. Philip himself was placed
under house arrest late in 1583 under suspicion of communicating
with Mary, Queen of Scots, and with Thomas, Lord Paget, who had
recently fled to the continent. Following his release from confinement in April of 1584, Arundel was converted to Catholicism and
made plans to escape to France; but when the attempt was actually
undertaken almost a year later, he was intercepted at sea and sent to
the Tower of London on April 25, 1585.[4] Arundel remained a prisoner there until his death except for two trips to and from Westminster, for his Star Chamber trial in May 1586 and his attainder in April
1589. He was canonized in 1970 by Pope Paul VI.

During his imprisonment Philip engaged in a number of devotional tasks. When a fellow prisoner, the Jesuit Henry Walpole, was
interrogated about the earl's doings, he confessed only to hearing
that Arundel "had written verses."[5] Some of them he composed as
he translated Lanspergius's Latin *Epistle of Christ* and Marcus Marulus's "*Carmen De Doctrina Domini nostri Jesu Christi pendentis
in Cruce*," both of which were published before 1595, the year in
which a revised edition appeared, attributed simply to "one of no
small fame."[6] The edition of 1610 identified the translator as Philip,
late earl of Arundel. Two poems on signature A3v of the 1595 edition
are clearly an editor's preliminaries written to introduce the printed
translation. On signatures A4–6v Arundel's thirty-six iambic heptameter couplets, reprinted below, provide a close translation of
Marulus's seventy-eight lines of Latin verse; indeed, the introduc-
tory woodcut depicting Christ on the cross may have been modeled

2. Lodge, *Illustrations*, 2:146. Norfolk, *Lives*, 13–14.
3. HMC, Salisbury, 13:199; Pollen and MacMahon, "Venerable Philip
Howard," 22–23.
4. Pollen and MacMahon, "Venerable Philip Howard," 41–44, 56, 109.
5. Ibid., 324.
6. STC 14627.

upon that in the 1586 Paris edition of Marulus's works which is likewise followed by the verses.[7] Four other poems in the 1595 print also appear in Folger, MS Z.e.28, folios 9v, 59v–62, and in the modern facsimile reprint of an undated edition of the *Epistle* published as volume 56 of the *English Recusant Literature* series.[8] The following signatures locate the poems in this reprint: "Use ever silence in thy tongue," sig. C2; "Have speciall care to rule thy tongue," sig. 2H1; "Almighty Lord whose love to us," sig. 2H2v–2I2; and "O Christ the glorious crowne", sig. 2I2v–2K1.

Arundel composed two original works in verse, one of them probably but not certainly a product of his years in the Tower. A fifty-six line prayer beginning "O Christ my lord which for my sinnes" is headed in the "Sydenham Prayer-Book," "Earle of Arundle's Verses."[9] His most ambitious poetic undertaking is his 756-line "Fourfold Meditation," which survives in a 1606 print (New STC 13868.7) and at least nine manuscripts. Its attribution to Robert Southwell, as H. J. L. Robbie first argued, was no doubt motivated by commercial considerations, for three of the manuscripts assign it to Arundel.[10] The poem's title in Folger, MS Printed Book, STC 22957, asserts that the earl wrote these verses "after his attaindour" (1589), but it is more specifically described as "written against Christmas: 1587" in Folger, MS Z.e.28. The complete copy of the 1606 print in the Huntington Library provides a sound text of the "Meditation" except for the four stanzas printed below as poem 2 which are preserved only in the manuscripts. These stanzas are replaced in the

7. *M. Maruli Spalatensis Dictorum Factorumque Memorabilium Libri sex*, sig. +7v–8v, BL, shelfmark 4807.bbb.29.

8. The anonymous "Monk of Parkminster" who edited Arundel's translation as *An Epistle of Jesus Christ to the Soul That is Devoutly Affected Towards Him*, discovered three poems by Lanspergius in the edition of 1547 (xxix), thus establishing that the poems at the end of Arundel's work were translations. The edition of 1610 omits all but the "Use ever silence" couplet within Lanspergius's text.

9. John Hungerford Pollen, ed., "Bedingfield Papers . . . The Sydenham Prayer-Book," 129–30. The text of this poem in Bodl., MS Tanner 118, f. 53v, is printed in Louise Imogen Guiney's *Recusant Poets*, 227–28.

10. H. J. L. Robbie, "The Authorship of 'A Fourefold Meditation,' " 200–202. Robbie studied the texts in Bodl., MS Rawl. poet. 219, ff. 1–14, the "Crowcombe Court" MS (now Folger, MS Z.e.28, ff. 73–82); Bodl., MS Tanner 118, ff. 44–53, with one folio misplaced in MS Tanner 80, f. 155; and the Oscott College MS, case B.II, ff. 109–24, the first two of which bear attributions to Arundel. He is also credited with the poem in the manuscript text on folios 51–86v following Folger, Printed Book, STC 22957. The remaining anonymous texts are in Folger, MS V.a.198, ff. 30–44v; Harvard University, Houghton Library, MS Eng. 749, ff. 101–16v; and Yale University, Osborn MSS a.5 and a.6.

print by two stanzas which deal with the status of saints and the twelve Apostles (the last stanza on sig. E4v and the first stanza on sig. F1). These lines were no doubt contrived by the printer or editor to substitute for the most blatantly Catholic passage in Arundel's work.

If Arundel wrote poetry while a courtier in good standing with the queen, it is unknown today. All of his extant verse was inspired by his conversion to Catholicism and the imprisonment eventuated by that decision. Both his translated and original poetry were probably turned out between 1587 and the early 1590s; they are works of a courtier fallen from favor but not necessarily in isolation from the court and all that it represented.

1

Christian.

Sweet soveraigne God, why mortall limmes
    Upon thee didst thou take,
And slyding downe from toppe of skye,
    In earth thy dwelling make?   5

Christ.

That earthly man, whom error foule,
    Had fondly led a stray:
By me might learne how he to heaven,
    Might take the readie way.   10

Christian.

What forced thee, who alway wert,
    From every sinne so pure,
Such grievous paines, and death with all,
    So gladly to endure?   15

Christ.

The love I bare to man that him,
    Whom sinne had clogged so,
Our blood (by clearing well) might make
    Above the stars to goe.   20

Christian.

Why be thy armes so spred abroad,
    And streched out so farre?
And what's the cause (sweet Christ) thy feete,
    So close eonjoyned are?   25

Christ.

Cause everie where from every coast

I divers nations call,
And in one faith, with stedfast league
   I do conjoyne them all.   30
        Christian.
But why with bended necke dost thou
   So bend thy selfe likewise,
And so on earth fast fixed cast,
   Thy countenance and eyes?   35
        Christ.
I monish men that they may shun
   With pevish pride to swell,
And humbled necks, with sacred yoake,
   To daunt and governe well.   40
        Christian.
Why is thy body naked so?
   And wherefore is thy hue
So dry and leane? and all thy limmes
   So stiffe and starcke to vew?   45
        Christ.
I would that ryot of the world,
   should hatefull seeme to thee,
And that thou wouldst feele hunger, thirst,
   And pore estate with me.   50
        Christian.
But whitish veyle thy slender loines
   Doth compasse round about;
Doth hidden part admonish ought?
   Resolve I pray this doubt.   55
        Christ.
Learne thou hereby that bodies chaste
   Doo greatly me delight,
And that I loath that lawles love
   Disclose foule thinges to sight.   60
        Christian.
What doo thy blowes, bespettinges, tauntes,
   And cruell scourgings tell,
With Crowne of thornes, and (of the Crosse)
   The other torments fel?   65
        Christ.
That he must suffer each offence,

And offer no annoy,
Which quiet peace above the stars
   Desireth to enjoy.   **70**
Life is but short, the labour light,
   Most wished is the pay,
The benifit is infinite,
   Which never shall decay.
But now if great rewards doo not   **75**
   At all with some prevaile,
Yet let them feare the banishment,
   Of ever during Gayle.
The quenchlesse fire, the uglie darke,
   Which never shall abate,   **80**
The gnawing worme for aye, for aye,
   The bitter, wretched state.
The griesly groanes, the sorrowes sharpe,
   The wofull weal-aday;
The endles plaints, the cursed ill,   **85**
   Which never will away.
For such paines rest for those whome now
   Lewd lust (which lasts small while)
Enjoy, and with false flattering snares,
   Deceitfully beguile.   **90**
To greedy wretches vaunting wealth,
   To slouthfull sluggards ease,
And cursed Venus' chamber worke,
   The wanton crew to please.
Sweet wine and daintie cates to such,   **95**
   As in their panch delight:
Pompe to the proude, and spoiles to such,
   As hardie are in fight.
The haplesse route inticed thus
   With these decaitfull traines,   **100**
Mindlesse of saving health doo fall
   To utter wracke and paines.
And neyther heare my counsayle good,
   Nor seeke to follow me,
And to conclude feare not my doome,   **105**
   How sharp so e're it be.
But dreadfull doome, when e're at last,
   That dismall day befall,
That day of wrath, that day of wrake,

And hugie storme with all.   110
When of the shaken firmament,
    The hideous clashing sound
Shall trouble starrs with tumblings swift,
    And dash their globes on ground.
When as the moone with blood-red lampe   115
    The people shall affright,
And globe of Sunne draw in his beames
    Depriving men of light.
When all shall dread, and all the world
    At once shall shaken be,   120
So as the quiers Angelicall
    Men may amazed see.
Fire shall consume the world with noyse,
    And crackling flash of flame;
And earth and sea, and burning lampe,   125
    Of fierie lump shall frame.
Straight waies with dreadfull majestie,
    With powre and vertue great
Come I, and on a glistering cloud
    Will sit in judgment seate;   130
There many thousands shall of Saints
    Roundly inviron me:
Yea there of glorious Angels bright
    Shal many thousands be.
Forthwith the Trumpet from above   135
    Shall gastlie noise sound out,
Renting the earth, and raysing up
    The low, infernall rout.
Then by and by shall al the dead,
    All up together rise,   140
Whome earth so great, in womb so wide,
    Did heretofore comprise.
The multitude revived shall
    Before my throne be prest,
Expecting there, with trembling feare   145
    My dreadfull doome and hest.
For nothing shall be undiscust
    Nor hid, nor secret ought;
No not the thing which any have
    Committed in their thought.   150
There shall desert receave reward,

The life which lives for aye;
Or els the death which never more
    Shall have a dying day.
Go too then wretches, whom as yet,   155
    lewd error fettereth close,
Whilst that you may of fettered feete
    The gives and chaines unloose;
Watch well that deadlie sleepe do not
    Your waking eyes oppresse,   160
Lest endles day of latest time
    You slumbring do possesse.
Behold with how swift course the times
    Doo slip and slide away,
And how the flying houre admits   165
    No manner let or stay.
Happie is he who still his life
    Doth well and Godly spend,
And thinks withall it shall forthwith
    And in a moment end.   170
    Convertanter qui
        oderunt Syon.
          (STC 14627, sig. A4–6)

Note
    Line 23, 'streched,' and line 130, 'judgment,' correct the print's 'sterched' and 'indgment.'

2

The Angels then are next in their degree,
Whose orders rise in number to be nine;
No hart can thinke what joy it is to see
How al these troupes like lampes in glorie shine:
The joy is more then writing can expresse,   5
O happie eies that may this joy possesse.

Above them al the Virgin hath a place,
Which made the world with comfort to abound;
The beames do shine in her unspotted face,
And with the starres her head is richely crown'd: 10
In glorie she al creatures passeth farre,
The Mone her showes, the Sunne her garments are.

O Quene of heven! o pure and glorious sight!
Most blessed thou above al women art;

This Citie drunke thou makest with delite,   **15**
And with thy beames revivest ev'ry hart:
Our blisse was lost, and thou did'st it restoare,
The Angels al and Men do thee adore.

Loe here the looke which Angels do admire;
Loe here the Spring from whom al goodnes flowes;   **20**
Loe here the sight which men and Sainctes desire;
Loe here that Stalke on which our comfort growes;
Loe this is she whom heven and earth imbrace,
Whom God did chose, and filled ful of grace.
   (Folger, MS Printed Book, STC 22957, unfoliated)

Note
   A preliminary analysis of the texts of Arundel's "Meditation" suggests that all the manuscripts descend from a lost ancestor, X, and two hypothetical sources derived from it, Y and Z. The Folger, MSS, STC 22597 (F) and Z.e.28, descend from Y, the versions in Tanner, MSS 80 and 118, and Folger, MS V.a.198, from Z. Both descendants of Z are significantly corrupt states of the poem while F is perhaps superior to the print and is accordingly the copy text for the stanzas printed here. I have not consulted the Osborn or Oscott College manuscripts in arriving at these tentative conclusions.[11]

Lee, Sir Henry (1533–1611)

Sir Henry may well have come to the queen's attention by the twelfth year of the reign (1569–1570), when he received the manors of Spillbury and Shipton by lease from the crown, perhaps as a reward for his service against the Northern Rebellion.[1] Chambers suggests that he may have founded the tradition of the Accession Day tournaments as early as 1570. In the tournament of May 1571, he joined Lord Oxford, Hatton, and Charles Howard as the challengers, and he became recognized as Elizabeth's personal champion in the subsequent Accession Day spectacles.[2] Burghley's letter of August 10, 1572, apparently addressed to Howard of Effingham, Lord Privy Seal, attests eloquently to Lee's high standing with the queen. Burghley enclosed a bill which she had signed for Sir Henry and which she "meaneth to bestowe upon him unwares to him self."[3] Perhaps this was his patent as master of the leash, a post he obtained no later than 1574; in any event, it confirms his personal

---

11. A rather corrupt version of these four stanzas, apparently derived from the Oscott College manuscript, was printed as Robert Southwell's in *The Fovre-Fovld Meditation*, edited by Charles Edmonds, stanzas 95–98.
   1. PRO, SP 12/166, f. 56v.
   2. Chambers, *Lee*, 38; HMC, Rutland, 1:92.
   3. PRO, SP 12/89/3.

ties with Elizabeth by the early 1570s. He exchanged New Year's gifts with her every year from at least 1575 through 1587. He was appointed master of the armoury in 1580, was at court actively pressing the queen for some crown office as late as 1595,[4] and was received into the Order of the Garter in 1597.

Two of the three poems most likely to have been written by Sir Henry are of Elizabethan vintage, and both are connected with his retirement from competition in the tiltyard. Thomas Clayton has presented the case for Lee's authorship of "His golden locks," which was recited before Elizabeth during the Accession Day tilt of 1590, when Lee surrendered his position as queen's champion to the earl of Cumberland.[5] Clayton establishes a modern spelling text of this lyric, and notes that poem 1 below, printed anonymously in John Dowland's *Second Book* (1600), is attributed to Lee in Bodl., Rawlinson poetry MS 148. Chambers proposed that Lee may also have written eight lines of verse inscribed in a prayer book at Ditchley, and it seems equally likely (if quite beyond proof) that he composed verses beginning "Reason in Man cannot effect such love" which accompany his portrait with a dog.[6]

1

Time's eldest sonne, olde age, the heyre of ease,
Strength's foe, love's woe, and foster to devotion,
Bids gallant youths in marshall prowes please,
As for himselfe, hee hath no earthly motion,
But thinks sighes, teares, vowes, praiers, and sacrifices,   5
As good as showes, maskes, justes, or tilt devises.

Then sit thee downe, and say thy *Nunc Demittis*,
With *De profundis, Credo*, and *Te Deum*,
Chant *Miserere*, for what now so fit is,
As that, or this, *Paratum est cor meum*?   10
O that thy Saint would take in worth thy hart,
Thou canst not please hir with a better part.

When others sings *Venite exultemus*,
Stand by and turne to *Noli emulari*,
For *quare fremuerunt* use *oremus*,   15
Vivat Eliza, for an *ave mari*,

4. Chambers, *Lee*, 43, 48; Collins, *Letters*, 1:385.
5. Clayton, "Henry Lee's Farewell," 268–75.
6. Chambers, *Lee*, 42, 83.

And teach those swains that lives about thy cell,
To say *Amen* when thou dost pray so well.

(STC 7095, songs 6–8)

Note

The poem is entitled "In yeeldinge up his Tilt staff: sayd," and subscribed "Qd Sir Henry Leigh" in Bodl., Rawlinson poetry MS 148, folio 75v. The subscription is rendered suspect by the fact that the manuscript text is a hybrid which adds to this poem the last stanza of "His golden locks." These lines, moreover, are about Sir Henry and could not so easily be adapted to first-person performance as could the former poem. Nevertheless, Lee could have composed this lyric for some member of his retinue to sing before the queen at the Accession Day tournament or a related occasion. The Rawlinson attribution permits its classification as a poem possibly by Sir Henry. In the print, the second and third stanzas are designated "Second part" and "Third part." At line 18 the "Basso" text reads 'sing' for 'say.'

Mildmay, Sir Walter (1520–1589)

Mildmay became Elizabeth's chancellor of the Exchequer on February 5, 1559, and on July 7, 1566, he was sworn to the Privy Council.[1] His name appears regularly on the New Year's gift rolls from the beginning of the reign through 1589. In his will Mildmay stipulated that his executors, Francis Walsingham, Edward Carey, and William Dodington, purchase a jewel worth one hundred pounds "as a remembraunce of my dutie to her Highnes . . . whiche ought to have byne farr greater in respect of her favour and goodnes ever shewed unto me."[2] Beyond this witness to Mildmay's rapport with the queen, his place at court is confirmed by his other bequests to such friends as Hatton, Burghley, Sir Francis Knollys, and Thomas, Lord Buckhurst.

Sir John Harington recorded in his notes to book 22 of *Orlando Furioso*,[3] that Mildmay had presented him with a "litle volume" of "his writings and sayings" when Harington was enrolled at Eton College. Harington also affirmed that the collection had been published after his death, but this print has not been discovered; thus the only relic of Sir Walter's muse, and one not certainly written after Elizabeth's accession, is the quatrain of Latin verse quoted and translated into English by Harington.

Noel, Henry (d. 1597)

Noel may well be the "Hen No" who collaborated with Hatton and three others on the original version of *Tancred and Ghismond;*

1. Stanford E. Lehmberg, *Sir Walter Mildmay and Tudor Government*, 48.
2. Lehmberg, *Mildmay*, 305.
3. Ariosto, *Orlando*, 249.

there is no evidence however that Noel was established at court as early as 1567. In May of 1581 he participated in the "Fortress of Perfect Beauty" tournament held in honor of the Anjou marriage negotiations, and his name appears as well on every list of Accession Day tilters from 1583–1591 and 1593–1595. George Peele described Noel's conduct in the Accession Day jousts of 1590 and 1595.[1] He exchanged New Year's gifts with Elizabeth in 1584 and 1586, and in October of the latter year he reported to Walsingham on what seems to have been a less than memorable audience with his sovereign. Her Majesty, he wrote, "told me she would determine with your Honour touching my brother's stay or going into Flaunders. Some answer she made me therof, but through other occasions of more note to me that then hapned I have forgotten there effect"—he begs Walsingham to find out just what conclusion Elizabeth had reached on the matter.[2] Noel apparently attended to his own "occasions" with greater diligence. In 1584 he was granted the patent to search out concealed lands to the value of one hundred marks, and in 1593 he gained a monopoly to import stone pots, bottles, and heath brush. In March of 1592 the queen had reimbursed him for some unspecified losses sustained in her service to a total of over 658 pounds.[3] The DNB, probably following Fuller, describes Noel as a gentleman pensioner, but there is no record of his appointment to or service in the band. Clearly, however, he was a most successful courtier by the early 1590s. His death, Fuller reports, was occasioned by a fatal fever contracted after playing at balloon with an Italian; Elizabeth arranged for his burial in Westminster Abbey.[4]

Noel was a more famous wit and probably a far more prolific man of letters than his scant literary remains suggest. Harington remembered him as "one of the greatest Gallants" of the early 1590s.[5] Bacon credited him with the witty comparison "That courtiers were like fasting-days; They were next the holydays, but in themselves they were the most meagre days of the week." Noel belonged to Ralegh's circle of friends by at least 1578 when he embarked on Sir Humphrey Gilbert's voyage of exploration accompanied by Walter but aboard the ship commanded by his brother, Carew Ralegh. He

1. Roy Strong, *The Cult of Elizabeth*, 206–9. *Polyhymnia* (1590), *Anglorum Feriae* (1595), both in Horne, *Life*, 234, 274.

2. PRO, SP 12/194/50, October 19, 1586.

3. Huntington Library, MSS. EL 1328, 1349; Price, *English Patents*, 143; BL, Add. MS 22924, f. 50v.

4. Thomas Fuller, *The Worthies of England*, 318–19.

5. Harington, *Supplie*, 141.

was also on good terms with Henry, ninth earl of Northumberland, one of the more intellectual Elizabethan peers.[6] Noel patronized the poet Thomas Watson, while the musician, John Dowland, recalled that his "old Master and Frend," Noel, had informed him in 1596 that he might gain a post at court if he would return to England from the continent.[7]

Noel must have had some limited reputation as a poet, for the scribe of Bodl., Rawlinson poetry MS 85, attributed to him a copy of Sidney's *Certain Sonnets* 21. Noel's only extant poems, however, are his well-known companion to Ralegh's rebus on his name and a lyric in *Englands Helicon*.

1a

(Noe L)

The word of deniall, and the Letter of fifty
Makes the gentleman's name that will never be thrifty.
[Sir Walter Ralegh]

1

(Raw Ly)

The foe to the stommacke, and the word of disgrace
Shewes the gentleman's name with the bold face.

Note

Both couplets are from BL, Harleian MS 5353, as edited by Sorlien, *Diary of John Manningham*, 161–62. Poem 1 is attributed to Noel (or by derivative error to Dr. Noel) in three other manuscripts, Folger, MS V.a.103, folio 69; Bodl., MS Malone 19, folio 53; and Houghton, MS Eng. 686, folio 17v.

2

Of disdainfull Daphne.

Shall I say that I love you,
    Daphne disdainfull?
Sore it costs as I prove you,
    Loving is painfull.

6. Spedding, *Works*, 13:379. G. R. Batho, ed., *The Household Papers of Henry Percy, Ninth Earl of Northumberland*, record the earl's borrowing fifty pounds from Noel in April 1586 and twenty-one pounds in the following month (62). These accounts also record gratuities to Noel's servants who brought gifts to the earl (63).

7. Watson dedicated his *Amyntas* (1585) and his *Compendium Memoriae Localis* (1585?) to Noel. Dowland's reminiscence is cited in Edward Doughtie's *Lyrics from English Airs, 1596–1622*, 44. Noel's death was commemorated by other musicians, including Thomas Weelkes and Thomas Morley.

Shall I say what doth greeve mee?   5
    Lovers lament it:
Daphne will not releeve mee,
    Late I repent it.

Shall I dye, shall I perrish,
    Through her unkindnes?   10
Love untaught love to cherrish
    Sheweth his blindnes.

Shall the hills, shall the valleyes,
    The fieldes, the Cittie,
With the sound of my out-cryes,   15
    Move her to pittie?

The deepe falls of fayre Rivers,
    And the windes turning,
Are the true musique givers,
    Unto my mourning.   20

Where my flocks daily feeding,
    Pining for sorrow:
At their maister's hart bleeding,
    Shot with Love's arrow.

From her eyes to my hart-string,   25
    Was the shaft launced;
It made all the woods to ring
    By which it glaunced.

When this Nimph had usde me so,
    Then she did hide her;   30
Haplesse I did *Daphne* know
    Haplesse I spyed her.

Thus Turtle-like I waild me,
    For my love's loosing:
Daphne's trust thus did faile me,   35
    Woe worth such chusing.
      FINIS. *M. H. Nowell.*
        (STC 3191 sig. 2A1–1v)

Note

    Despite the questionable reliability of *Helicon* attributions, this poem, unlike Dyer's poem IV, is at least not compromised by having been previously published anonymously.

Ralegh, Sir Walter (1554–1618)

Although Ralegh styled himself *"de Curia"* as early as December 17, 1577, and as "one of the extraordinary Esquires of the Bodye of the Queen's Majesty" by February 3, 1581, he seems not to have gained genuine courtier status before 1582.[1] His elder half-brother, Sir Humphrey Gilbert, provided Walter with an entrée to court during the late 1570s; by 1579 he was named among the earl of Oxford's retainers and, a few months later, in the train of the earl of Leicester.[2] It is probably to one or the other of these noble patrons, rather than to Elizabeth, that he owed his appointment as esquire extraordinary. In August of 1580 he arrived in Ireland at the head of a company of Lord Grey's forces. In December of that year he returned to London with papers taken from the Catholic troops massacred at Smerwick. Late in 1581 he again brought letters post from Ireland to the Privy Council. The latter journey, at least, brought him to the queen's attention. She had consulted with him by the first of January, although the earliest reference to his success is Roger Manners's report of October 14 that "Mr Raleigh is in very good favour." Later that month Elizabeth found it necessary to reassure Hatton that, despite her fascination with her new favorite, she still cherished her older pets, her mutton and other *"pecora campi."*[3]

For almost a decade Ralegh enjoyed an exalted status among the queen's most favored courtiers. He received a patent for licensing wine sales in 1583 and one to export broadcloth a year later. He became Lord Warden of the stannaries and steward of the duchy of Cornwall in 1585, was knighted in the same year, and was appointed captain of the guard circa 1586. Still, his name never appears on the New Year's gift rolls during all these years of his most brilliant success at court, for his only recorded exchange occurred in 1603, Elizabeth's last New Year's Day. Not until the summer of 1592 when she sent him to the Tower for his clandestine marriage with Elizabeth Throckmorton, did Ralegh's star suffer eclipse. For the next five years, until June of 1597, and despite his retention of his offices in the west and as captain of the guard, he was denied access to the queen and her court.[4] From then until the end of the reign, he resumed his place as a prominent courtier, although he could hardly

---

1. Eccles, "Brief Lives," 110; Latham, "Birth-Date," 245.
2. Pierre Lefranc, *Sir Walter Ralegh Écrivain*, 29.
3. Lodge, *Illustrations*, 2:186. HMC, Rutland, 1:142; Nicolas, *Memoirs*, 277.
4. McClure, *Letters of John Chamberlain*, 1:31.

have hoped to rekindle the intensely warm relations he had formerly known with Elizabeth.

Ralegh's poetry presents one of the most difficult editorial problems of the English Renaissance. The best available edition is Michael Rudick's unpublished doctoral dissertation, the basis for my analysis of Ralegh's achievement as a courtier poet.[5] With Rudick I accept the following poems as constituting Ralegh's canon during his years as a courtier from circa 1582 to 1603:

> Calling to mind mine eye went long about
> Farewell false love, thou oracle of lies
> Go soul, the body's guest
> If Synthia be a Queen, a princess and supreme
> Like truthless dreams so are my joys expired
> Me thought I saw the grave, where Laura lay
> My body in the walls captived
> My days delights, my spring time joys foredone
> Nature that washed her hands in milk
> Now we have present made
> Sufficeth it to you, my joys interred
> The praise of meaner wits this work like profit brings
> To praise thy life or wail thy worthy death

The text of "Farewell false love" referred to in this study is edited in my "Companion Poems in the Ralegh Canon." Pierre Lefranc's discovery of a seventy-eight-line version of the "Petition" to Queen Anne may well restore a fragment of Ralegh's Elizabethan verse, for this new text begins with the first two stanzas of "My days delights," and it seems likely that the next ten to twelve stanzas represent the original state of the poem.[6] In addition to these works, Ralegh's "Fortune hath taken thee away" is edited above with Queen Elizabeth's response. A couplet assigned by Rudick as tentatively Ralegh's has also been received into the canon for this study. The companion to Noel's rebus on Ralegh's name, printed above with

5. Rudick, "Poems." Rudick's arguments for ejecting from the canon the unattributed poems from *The Phoenix Nest* are set forth in his "The 'Ralegh Group' in *The Phoenix Nest*," 131–37.

6. Steven W. May, "Companion Poems in the Ralegh Canon," *English Literary Renaissance* 13 (1983): 267–68; the first three stanzas of "Farewell false love" are printed above before Sir Thomas Heneage's response, Poem 1. Lefranc transcribes the new text of "My days delight" in "Une Nouvelle Version de la 'Petition to Queen Anne,' de Sir Walter Ralegh," 60–62. For further analysis of the "Petition," with a transcription of the text, see my *Sir Walter Ralegh*, 45–46, 116–20.

Noel's couplet, is attributed to Sir Walter in seven manuscript texts, and while Rudick is properly cautious given the lateness of these attributions, the scale is tipped in favor of authenticity by the fact that Ralegh and Noel belonged to the same circle of friends from at least 1578. Of the remaining poems which Rudick classified as possibly Ralegh's, three were probably composed between 1582 and 1603: "Conceipt begotten by the eyes," "Lady farewell, whom I in silence serve," and "Passions are likened best to floods and streams."

Russell, Lady Elizabeth Cooke Hoby (circa 1540–1609)

Elizabeth's first husband was Sir Thomas Hoby, the translator of Castiglione's *Cortegiano*. When he died during an ambassadorial mission to France in 1566, the queen wrote Lady Hoby to assure her of continuing royal favor. After returning to England, Lady Hoby apparently spent most of her time managing the family estates from her house at Bisham, Berkshire, and it was there in 1574 that she wed John, Lord Russell, heir to the earl of Bedford and carver to the queen.[1] Her years of active courtiership apparently date from her marriage into the nobility, and continue intermittently into the reign of King James. In 1575 the queen stood godmother to Elizabeth, Lady Russell's firstborn child by her second husband. She appears as Baroness Russell on the New Year's gift rolls for 1576 and 1584. Lord Russell's death in 1584 occasioned Sir Edward Hoby's poem 1, the Latin epitaph for his stepfather.

Through her connections at court, particularly with her brother-in-law, Lord Burghley, and her nephew, Sir Robert Cecil, Lady Russell long exerted a benign influence on behalf of her family and friends. Lady Dorothy Perrott, the earl of Essex's sister, begged her to intervene with Lord Burghley to prevent her husband's ruin in June of 1592, while Sir Henry Unton acknowledged her good efforts on his behalf to alleviate the queen's displeasure. Queen Elizabeth visited Lady Russell at Bisham in mid-August during the progress of 1592.[2] Lady Russell's poor health may often have kept her from court during the 1590s, and she may have faced financial problems

1. For the year of Lady Russell's birth and other biographical information I rely on Sheridan Harvey's "The Cooke Sisters: A Study of Tudor Gentlewomen." The queen's letter is printed in Ellis, *Original Letters*, 1st ser., 2:229–30. Lord Russell's household post is recorded in the 1576 subsidy roll, PRO, E 179/69/93; his name appears on the New Year's gift lists for 1578 and 1581.

2. HMC, Salisbury, 4:214, 362; Nichols, *Progresses*, 3:130–36, prints the queen's entertainment at Bisham; for the date see PRO, E 351/542, m. 166.

as well, yet her self-portraits in the Cecil correspondence as deaf, blind, and bankrupt cannot be taken at face value. Illness may have kept her from the Privy Chamber at New Year's in 1595, but she went personally to court in the spring of 1600 to extricate her daughter Ann from serving the queen as a maid of honor, in preparation for one of the grandest weddings of the Elizabethan age.[3] The ceremony took place at the Blackfriars with Queen Elizabeth in attendance for two days of celebration. In the wake of this triumphant occasion, Lady Russell protested to Cecil that she was so far in debt that she could neither keep nor hire horses for her coach. As a further indication of the relative tenor of her poverty, she had begged Cecil less than a year before the grand wedding to establish her in some poor lodging at court since she had disbanded her household more than a year before and now struggled along with the help of only six servants. In the same year, moreover, she recalled giving the queen thirty pounds in gold as a New Year's gift plus an additional five hundred pounds in gifts toward securing a crown lease for her eldest daughter.[4]

Lady Russell was quite as accomplished a Christian humanist as the other three daughters of Sir Anthony Cooke, and she appears to have continued her study of the classics well into her seventies. One of her letters to Sir Robert Cecil, for example, is bulwarked with quotations from the *Epistles* of Horace and from two books of the *Aeneid*.[5] She had translated from French and in 1605 published an unidentified tract entitled *A Way of Reconciliation* (STC 21456), with dedicatory verses to her daughter, Lady Ann Herbert. Her Elizabethan poetry, however, is entirely funereal. She wrote verse epitaphs in English and Latin for Sir Thomas Hoby; for his brother, Sir Philip; for her neighbor, Thomas Noke; and for her daughters by Sir Thomas, all before she began to frequent the court. Her courtier verse consists primarily of the epitaphs she prepared for other members of her family. These include two Latin verse inscriptions for Lord Russell and one for their son, Francis, who died in infancy, plus two more epitaphs for Lord John, one in Greek and the other in

---

3. HMC, Salisbury, 6:546. Lady Russell assured Cecil that she had agreed to nothing with regard to Ann's marriage with Lord Herbert until she had gained her Majesty's consent (April 21, 1600, HMC, Salisbury, 10:121). Ann departed from court on June 9 in a procession of eighteen coaches: "the like hath not bene seen amongest the maydes," Whyte reported to Sidney (HMC, De L'Isle and Dudley, 2:468).

4. HMC, Salisbury, 10:412, 9:339, 10:52.

5. HMC, Salisbury, 9:384.

English. To these may be added a Greek epitaph for her sister, Katherine Killigrew,[6] and the Latin verses she sent to Lord Keeper Egerton in condolence for the loss of his son, Thomas, who was killed in 1599 while serving under Essex in Ireland. This poem and the English epitaph for Lord Russell are printed below.

1

Right noble twice, by Virtue and by birth:
Of heaven lov'd, and honour'd on the earth:
His country's hope, his kindred's chief delight,
My husband dear, more dear than this world's light.
Death hath me reft: but I from death will take   5
His memory, To whom this tomb I make.
John was his name. Ah! was; wretch, must I say,
Lord Russel once, now my tears' thirsty clay.
      (John Strype, *Annals of the Reformation*, 3:402)

2

Hunc Deus Altitonans Caelesti Numine Favens
*   Eripuit Terris, Vivat ut ipse sibi*
Insignem Forma Iuvenem, et Fulgentibus Armis
*   Abstulit Atra Dies, Surget ac ille Deo*
Mittatur Thomas qui non Virtutis egentem   5
*   Post patriae liguit spemque Decusque Suae.*
            E Russella Douager
          (Huntington, MS EL 11738)

Sackville, Thomas, Lord Buckhurst, First Earl of Dorset (1535 or 1536–1608)

Sackville was perhaps the most talented English poet to span the reigns of Mary and Elizabeth Tudor. His father, Sir Richard Sackville, was a Privy Councillor and the queen's cousin through his mother, Margaret Boleyn. Thomas thus enjoyed a superb entrée to court, although he seems not to have attended there regularly until after his father's death in April 1566. That event recalled him from

6. Elizabeth's earlier verse is printed in Elias Ashmole's *The Antiquities of Berkshire*, 2:465–71, 491. The first Latin epitaph for Lord Russell along with the one in English are printed in John Strype's *Annals of the Reformation*, pt. 1, 3:402. Texts of the epitaphs from the Russell tomb are printed in Dart's *Westmonasterium*, 1:115–16, and J. R.'s *Antiquities*, 1:47–49. The Killigrew elegy is printed in George Ballard's *Memoirs of Several Ladies of Great Britain*, 206–7.

the continental tour he had begun in 1563. He first exchanged New Year's gifts with Elizabeth in 1567, and while his will states that she created him Baron Buckhurst "ymediately after my father's decease,"[1] that honor was bestowed more than a year later, on June 8, 1567. Previously the queen had presented a gift at the christening of Sackville's son on November 24, 1561, but the earliest sure sign of her personal regard for Thomas is her grant to him of the manor of Knole in June 1566. Thus began the period of Sackville's "younger yeres," when Elizabeth required his "contynewall private attendance upon her owne person."[2] In addition to land and title, the queen sent him as her ambassador extraordinary to France in 1571 and appointed him to the Privy Council early in 1586. Despite many months of disfavor in 1587–1588, he was received into the Order of the Garter in 1589. After Burghley's death, Buckhurst became Lord Treasurer, an office he retained upon the accession of King James. He died peacefully during a meeting of the Privy Council on April 19, 1608.[3]

During Mary's reign, Sackville had composed the "Induction" and the "Complaynt of Henry Duke of Buckingham" for *The Mirror for Magistrates*. His commendatory sonnet for Hoby's translation of Castiglione's *Cortegiano* appeared in 1561, and *Gorboduc*, to which he contributed the last two acts, was performed at court on Twelfth Night in 1562. Sackville's only extant courtier verse, however, is the poem entitled "Sacvyles olde age," recently discovered and printed by Rivkah Zim and M. B. Parkes. The poem is a verse epistle dated by its editors circa 1566–1574, and addressed to Dr. Thomas Francis, physician in ordinary to the queen.

Sidney, Sir Philip (1554–1586)

Sidney's career as a courtier began in the summer of 1575 when he returned to England from his three-year continental tour. In the

---

1. Arthur Collins, *The Peerage of England*, 2:182.

2. Paul Bacquet, *Un Contemporain d'Elisabeth I: Thomas Sackville L'Homme et L'Oeuvre*, 49; Collins, *Peerage*, 2:182. Sackville's name appears on every extant New Year's roll from 1567–1603 except for the years from 1581–1585.

3. Sackville stated in the will he drew up August 11, 1607 that he was sworn to the Privy Council after his embassy to the Low Countries (1587), and "after fourteen yeres service to the queen, and tenne yeres following her courte" (Collins, *Peerage*, 2:182). Yet Buckhurst was an acting Privy Councillor by February 1585 or 1586 at the latest, by which time he had followed the court for some twenty years, rather than ten. See HMC, Buccleugh and Queensberry, 3:26, for a Privy Council order of February 19, 1586, signed by Buckhurst, and HMC, Rutland, 1:189, and HMC, Salisbury, 3:137, for reports of his appointment.

decade following he spent most of his time at court or with his family at Ludlow Castle and Wilton House but with absences abroad to Ireland in 1576 and to Germany in 1577. By May of 1576 he had succeeded his father as cupbearer to the queen; he exchanged New Year's gifts with her in 1578, 1579, 1580, 1581, 1583, and 1584. Late in 1581 Elizabeth agreed to ease the burden of Philip's debts by granting him a portion of the income from forfeited Papists' goods, and in June following she gave him an outright gift of 1500 pounds.[1] In 1583 he began assisting his uncle, the earl of Warwick, as joint master of the ordnance, although his patent for this office was not signed until 1585. Meanwhile, during the spring of 1583, Elizabeth expressed her displeasure concerning the proposed marriage between Sir Philip and Frances Walsingham; she was finally reconciled to the match, which was solemnized on September 21. The queen was present as godmother at the christening of Sidney's daughter in November 1585, by which time the father was probably in the Low Countries.[2] Sir Philip spent the last months of his life as governor of Flushing and in the active military service of his country that he had so long desired.

Sidney is the preeminent Elizabethan courtier poet, yet his poetic canon and text were not well defined until the publication of Ringler's Clarendon Press edition in 1962. The main components of the Sidney canon are the verses from his "Lady of May" entertainment presented before the queen at Wanstead in 1578, the poems and eclogues from the *Old Arcadia*, the thirty-two *Certain Sonnets*, the 108 songs and sonnets of *Astrophil and Stella*, and his translation of Psalms 1–43. In addition, Ringler prints seven works ("Other Poems"), unconnected with any of these titles, and classifies another five as "Possibly by Sidney."

Ringler dismissed thirty poems as wrongly attributed, yet four of these had sufficiently compelling attributions to warrant editing.[3] AT 19 and 21 deserve reconsideration in light of Peter Beal's discovery of the "Ottley Manuscript" in the National Library of Wales.[4] These six leaves contain excellent texts of forty-one poems from Sidney's *Old Arcadia* and *Certain Sonnets*, works he had completed no later than 1582,[5] plus AT 19, 21, and a unique text beginning

---

1. Ringler, *Poems*, xxiv; the 1500 pound gift is recorded in PRO, E 403/2559, f. 190.
2. PRO, E 351/542, f. 84; BL, Harleian MS 1641, f. 36.
3. AT 5, 14, 19, and 21; Ringler, *Poems*, 354–58.
4. Beal, "Poems," 284–95.
5. Ringler, *Poems*, 365, 423.

"Waynd [weaned] from the hope which made affection glad." These three poems were apparently written for recitation during an Accession Day show in the tiltyard. Unfortunately, the Ottley Manuscript is not exclusively by Sidney but preserves as well verses by the queen and two anonymous texts not otherwise connected with him. Still, the appearance here of AT 19 and 21, both attributed to Sir Philip in BL, Harleian MS 7392, provides strong circumstantial evidence for their admission to the canon. To summarize Beal's arguments, the protagonists of AT 19 are Sidney's *Old Arcadia* characters, Philisides and Menalchas, the texts of all forty-one definite poems are substantive, the Ottley transitions between the poems are in the first person ("aftr that I had passed the Tilt with my rusticall Musick"), and the manuscript contains Sidney's "Nota" on quantitative verse which is known otherwise only from the St. John's College, Cambridge, Manuscript of the *Old Arcadia*.[6] All three of these interconnected poems are treated as canonical in this study.

Sidney, Sir Robert (1563–1626)

Sir Philip's younger brother had been mentioned as a poet only in a few nineteenth-century booksellers' catalog until 1973 when P. J. Croft identified his manuscript of poems. Rowland Whyte claimed that Robert had attended court "ever since you were 18 yeare old, and never away, but when her Majesties imploiements occasioned yt."[1] Sidney must have joined the queen's entourage in his eighteenth year, shortly after returning from his continental tour in March 1582. In May of 1584 he participated in a court tournament but was in Wales that September where he married the heiress Barbara Gamage, daughter of Sir Walter Ralegh's cousin, John Gamage. Robert joined Sir Philip in the Netherlands late in 1585 and fought at Zutphen where his brother was fatally wounded. On October 7, 1586, he was knighted by his uncle, the earl of Leicester. Sidney became governor of Flushing in July 1589 but was absent from his post for months or years at a time throughout the remainder of Elizabeth's reign.

Sir Robert had first exchanged New Year's gifts with the queen in 1589, and his name appears on the rolls of 1597 and 1599. Elizabeth

6. Beal, "Poems," 289.
1. BL, Add. MS 58435; P. J. Croft, *Autograph Poetry in the English Language*, vol. 1, no. 22; Croft, *Poems*, 6–7; HMC, De L'Isle and Dudley, 2:218.

stood godmother to one of Sidney's daughters in February of 1593.[2] During one of his leaves from Flushing, he apologized to Barbara for not joining her at home, since "Yesternight I was til 2 aclock with the Queene and she commanded me to wayte again this day."[3] Sidney was a respected if intermittent courtier from about 1582 and took his place among the seventeen knights of the canopy at Elizabeth's funeral.[4]

Sir Robert copied his sixty-seven lyrics into the Additional Manuscript from another source, then revised them in a number of sittings thereafter according to Croft, who argues that their composition was inspired by events in the author's own life between about 1595 and 1598.[5] The first state of the text as transcribed in Croft's edition is no doubt Elizabethan and, with the correction of purely scribal slips, stands as the version of the poems used in this study.

Stanley, Ferdinando, Lord Strange, Fifth Earl of Derby (circa 1559–1594)

Ferdinando was styled Lord Strange from 1572 until his succession to the earldom upon his father's death on September 25, 1593. The fifth earl enjoyed his new honors for only a few months, dying in his house at Lathom, Lancashire, the following April. His will includes an unusual and quite pathetic appeal to Elizabeth, indicating his close ties with his sovereign.[1]

The queen had summoned Ferdinando to court as early as 1571; in 1573 she presented him with a "remnant" of cloth of gold and silver in excess of nine yards of material. He exchanged New Year's gifts with her in 1575 and 1576, but the absence of his name from the five complete rolls of the 1580s suggests that he was not regularly at court for the Christmas season during these years. He often came to London, however, and may simply have spent his Christmas holidays in the north, as he certainly did, for example, in 1587–1588

2. PRO, E 351/542, f. 185.
3. HMC, De L'Isle and Dudley, 2:152, April 13, 1594.
4. PRO, LC 2/4 (4), f. 46v.
5. Croft, *Poems*, xiv and commentary passim.
1. PRO, PCC, 69 Dixy. Stanley begs the queen to see to the welfare of his wife and children "sithence it hath pleased god soe to call me unto his mercy in the yeares of my youthe." He requests that "therefore it would please her most excellent majesty of her princelie and ever to me wardes most favorable and gracious disposicion to continue and transferr hir gracious goodnes from me her faithfull and loyall subjecte unto my wife and my said younge childeren."

when Lord and Lady Strange arrived at Knowsley from London on November 4 and celebrated New Year's there with Sir Henry Lee, and Edward, Lord Dudley, among other aristocratic guests.[2] Stanley figured prominently in military entertainments before the court, including the Accession Day tilts of 1588–1591 and a military show during the progress of 1591 in which he "became an Hermytt and ran the course of the field for her Majesty's sake."[3] Lord Strange must have been an accomplished jouster, for Sir John Harington likened him to Sir Charles Brandon "for armes and cavallarie" in his notes to *Orlando Furioso*.[4]

Stanley's patronage of the arts was praised by Thomas Nashe and by Spenser, who mentions his poetry in *Colin Clouts Come Home Againe*. He also patronized an acting troupe from at least 1576, and it is likely that Shakespeare was affiliated with these players by the early 1590s. John Bodenham listed Stanley among the poets represented in his *Belvedere* (1600), although no excerpts from his works have been identified in that anthology. Three of Ferdinando's four poems were assigned to him in contemporary manuscripts; a fourth, poem 1 below, is assigned to him by virtue of the punning internal reference to its authorship in lines 20–21.[5]

1

Of his unhappie state of life.

If ever man did live in *Fortune's* scorne,
Whose joyes do faile that feele distresse in minde:
Whose yeres with cares, whose eies with teares beswolne
That in each part, all parts of griefes doth find
To grace his ill, send such a man to me,   5
That am more haplesse then himselfe can be.

For good desart that is unkindly used,
For service, love, and faith that findeth hate:
Who in his Mistresse eyes is most refused,
Whose comforts faile, whose succours come too late;   10
     If that man live that in his life findes this,
     Know hee my chance, for my hap harder is.

2. Arnold, *Lost*, 46; F. R. Raines, ed., "The Stanley Papers," 31:41–47.
3. Strong, *Cult*, 207–8; see also Peele's *Polyhymnia*, in Horne, *Life and Minor Works*, and University College, London, Ogden MSS. 7 [41], ff. 12v–13v.
4. Ariosto, *Orlando*, 369.
5. For Spenser's praise of Stanley and the backgrounds to his poems 2, 3, and 4, see my "Spenser's 'Amyntas': Three Poems by Ferdinando Stanley, Lord Strange, Fifth Earl of Derby," 49–52.

If damming vowes be but as dreames regarded,
And constant thoughts as shewes of custome taken:
If any man for love be thus rewarded,   **15**
And hath his hopes for these unrights forsaken,
    Let him see me whose like hath never beene,
    Kilde by these wrongs, and yet by death unseene.

Then by this rivall of my such dispise,
With much desire shall seeke my name to know;   **20**
Tell him my lines *Strange* things may well suffice,
For him to beare, for me to seeke them so.
    And 'twas inough that I did finde such evils,
    And 'twere too much that Angels should be divels.
               (STC 3633, sig. D1v–2)

Note

    The copy text, from *Brittons Bowre of Delights* (1591) appears corrupt at line 19, where the first word in the line should perhaps be 'Thereby.' Variants from the edition of 1597, printed in Hyder Edward Rollins's facsimile edition of the 1591 text, show the normal deterioration of reprinting.

2

A restless life by losse of that I love
    I doe endure whose torment none can tell.
A graved soul as well these lines may prove
    Desyring death but spendes not half so well.
        A mazed mynd wherin affection dies,   **5**
        A wounded hart that still for mercie cries

A wofull man in prison bound by greefe,
    Ransackt by love, condemned by disdayn,
A wayting death yet fyndes no suche relief
    But nedes must lyve to linger out in pain,   **10**
        Whose terrour none but I my selfe can shew,
        That do the terrour best of any know.

Let this suffise to gyve the world a gesse
    Of my estate, of whence and what I am,
And let these lines to my last love expresse   **15**
    When first and how, for what these tormentes cam,
        And if that this move not in the relent
        Then kill the heart which conquered dies content.
             ferd. Strange.
          (Cambridge, MS Dd.5.75, folio 32v)

3

My Mistress in hir brest dothe were
Two apples bryghte that shyne
And eke those appeles strawberryes bere
In bosome hers devyne;
Hir goddess' brests for apples goe   5
Hir nypples be the berryes,
The one doth shyne as whyte as snowe
The other as redd as cherryes.
Love came and suckte and I did see
The bewty of hir breste;   10
Yea happy I but happiest hee
Thatt founde suche place of reste:
Butt yet unhappy Mistress you
Thatt suffered thus the blynde
To sucke the sapp that's justlye due   15
For an unspotted mynde:
For love is but a shorte delyghte
A lyfe that deathe dothe urge:
A sea of teares, of noble wites
An everlastynge scourge: 20
A glass for foolles to looke into
A labyrinthe of smarte
A deadlye wounde which pearcethe throughe
The sinewes of the harte:
A youthe whose tender chylldishe heade   25
His mother's hand hath bounde
An angrye boye, in all the worlde
His lyke maye nott be founde:
Regarde sweet Mistress then his faulte
And loe in my behove   30
Some difference make betwyxte a man
And suche a chyllde as love.
                    finis
               Lo: St[ra]nge:
(Bodl., Rawlinson poet. MS 85, folios 76v–77)

Note

   Stanley based lines 1–10 on a poem from Timothy Kendall's *Flowers of Epi-grammes* (1577), which purported to be translated from an Italian original.

4
A Sonnett by Ferdinando
Earle of Derby.

There was a sheppard that did live,
 And held his thoughts as highe,
As were the mounts where on his sheepe
 Did hourely feed him by.
He in his youth, his tender youth,   **5**
 That was unapt to keepe,
Or hopes or feares, or loves or cares,
 Or thoughts but of his sheepe,
Did with his dogg, as sheppards doe
 For shepheards fale in witt,   **10**
Devise him sports, though foolish sports,
 Yett sports for shepheards fitt.
Who free from cares, his only care
 Was where his flocke did goe,
And that was much to him that knewe **15**
 Noe other cares but soe.
This boye, which yet was but a boye,
 And soe desires were hid,
Did growe a man, and men must love,
 And love the shepheard did.   **20**
He loved much, none can to much
 Love one soe high devine,
As but her selfe was never none
 More fayre, more sweet, more fine.
One day, as young men have such dayes **25**
 When love the thought doth thrall,
Since wishes be but bare desires
 Of things not gott withall;
And he had wished oft and still,
 And every wish in vayne,   **30**
And but to wish gave little ease,
 Nor never endeth paine;
He vowed by his shepherd's weed,
 An oath which shepherds keepe,
That he would followe Phillis' love **35**
 Before a flocke of sheepe.
Soe from his sheepe, his gentle sheepe,
 Ungentlye he did goe,

Not caring whose cares might them keepe,
    Or car'd for aye or noe.   40
Leaving the playnes, the playnes whereon
    They playd and hourelye fed,
The plaines to them, they to the plaines,
    From plaines and them he fledd.
Yet fledd he not, but went awaye   45
    As one that had free scope,
Oft loath to leave and yet would leave
    His quiet for his hope.
But leave he did his snow white flocke,
    To seeke a nymphe as fayre   50
As is the dew be-sprinkled rose,
    Or brightness of the ayre.
And first he sought the rivers sweet,
    Whose runings every where,
In silent murmure did complaine   55
    That Phillis was not there.
And as he sawe the fishes leape
    Before him for the flye,
Soe did the shephard's harte for hope
    That Phillis should be nye.   60
But finding that his hopes were vaine
    And but as dreames to him,
He lean'd unto a tree that grew
    Fast by the river's brim.
And there he writt his fancye's thought,   65
    Love is a sweet intice,
Gainst whom the wisest witts as yett
    Have never found devise.
And thus he left the streames to hide
    The kisses they did hold,   70
And went awaye as whoe should saye
    Love cannot be controul'd.
His thoughts were swifter then his feete,
    Yet they did slownes shunn,
But men's desires have winges to flye,   75
    Whose leggs can only runne.
Loe thus drawne on by spedy pace,
    Ledd forth with Phillis' fame,
Unto a wood that grew thereby
    The gentle shepheard came.   80

Where hee approaching shady groves,
    Sweet groves for moone shine night,
Where as the sunne was bard his force,
    But not debar'd his light.
Whereas the birds, the pretty birds,   85
    That or could chirp or singe,
In consort of well tuned noats
    Did make the woods to ringe,
Even double pleased in the place
    Soe long he there did staye,   90
As night grewe on which forced him
    To tarrye for the daye.
When not a bird stir'd in a bush,
    But still the shepheard demed,
The sweet comander of his thoughts   95
    Was neerer than shee seemed.
Thus wearye with his former toyle
    He could not further goe,
But rested there as they doe rest
    Whome love possesseth soe.   100
Possest he was with thoughts of love,
    High thoughts for shepheard's brest,
Were not there shepheards in their love
    As well as monarchs blest.
Blessed he was but 'twas in thoughts,   105
    And thoughts be blessings hidd,
And hidden blessings are noe blisse,
    And then he slumber did.
Whome length of time and high desires
    In suche a dumpe had cast,   110
As ravisht with his thoughts he slept,
    As he had slept his last.
But as all quiets have their dead,
    And every slepe his wake,
Now here to hope, now there to feare,   115
    Now fancye, then forsake:
Soe had the shepheard restles dreames
    Amyd his tyme or rest,
Which forced him to wake for feare,
    And prove his dreames a jest.   120
And though that feare be nothing else
    But as the fearefull deme,

Yet waking, every bush to him
    A savage beast doth seeme.
Which made him start, as men doe start   **125**
    Whose resolucions breed
A quicknes, yet a carelesnes
    Of that which maye succeed.
Frighted he was but not afraide,
    For love makes cowards men,   **130**
And soe the bushes seemed them selves
    And were but bushes then
Which his faint eyes did quickelye fynd,
    Fill'd full with faithfull streams,
And soe he lay'd him by his dogg   **135**
    That barkt not at his dreames.
And there he rested till the daye,
    And only said thus much,
My dogg is happyer then my selfe,
    Whom theis cares cannot touch.   **140**
    (*The Antiquarian Repertory*, 3:133–38)

Notes

    Lines 1–12, 17–24, and 33–36 were set to music in Robert Jones's *The Muses Gardin for Delights* (1610), song 9, with the following variants:

3 sheepe] flockes.
5 in] from.
6 That] which.
10 fale in] wanting.
11 him] some.
17 This boye, which] The boy that.
18 desires] desir's.
20 the] this.
23 was never none] none but her selfe.
24 More . . . fine] So faire, so fresh, so fine.
34 which] that.
35 Phillis' love] Phillyday.

At line 25 I substitute 'One' for the print's 'On.'

Talbot, Gilbert, Seventh Earl of Shrewsbury (1553–1616)

Gilbert was styled Lord Talbot from 1582 and inherited the Shrewsbury title upon his father's death in 1590. He was received into the Order of the Garter in 1592 and sworn to the Privy Council in 1601. Long before coming to the earldom, however, Talbot and his wife had attended court, for Gilbert was relaying court gossip to his father as early as 1573. He exchanged New Year's gifts with the queen every year from 1584 through 1588 as well as in 1597, 1599, and 1603. Elizabeth was godmother to his daughter, christened in December 1584. At the beginning of that year his favor with the queen is noted in a newsletter from the court, while Talbot himself wrote on July 14, 1585, that "It hath pleased her Majestie to intertayne me with very great favore and care of my heal[t]he as may be."[1]

Given Talbot's intense and lengthy feuds with his neighbors and members of his own family, it is reassuring to know that he also cultivated close friendships with his fellow courtier poets Fulke Greville, Edward Dyer, and Sir John Harington.[2] It is to Harington that we owe the only known text of a poem by Talbot, a couplet which he addressed to their mutual friend, Thomas Markham, as printed by Harington in The Metamorphosis of Ajax.[3]

Wilson, Dr. Thomas (circa 1523–1581)

Wilson received an excellent humanist education at Cambridge under John Cheke and Sir Thomas Smith. He published his Arte of Rhetorique in 1553, then went into exile on the continent during the reign of Queen Mary, joining the Protestant community at Padua in the company of Cheke, Francis Walsingham, and Thomas and Philip Hoby. He took his Doctor of Laws degree at the University of Ferrara in 1559 but returned to England by late 1560. He was appointed one of the masters of requests in 1561, sworn to the Privy Council in 1577, and was secretary of state jointly with Walsingham by 1578.[1] Wilson exchanged New Year's gifts with Elizabeth in 1575, 1578, and 1581; we know, furthermore, that he presented the queen with

1. PRO, E 351/542, f. 70v; HMC, Rutland, 1:157; 1:176, letter of July 14, 1585.
2. A lengthy poem in praise of Shrewsbury and his wife, apparently written by Harington's son, John, in both Latin and English is preserved in BL, Add. MS 12049, pp. 196–201. For Gilbert's artistic interests see David C. Price, "Gilbert Talbot, Seventh Earl of Shrewsbury: An Elizabethan Courtier and His Music," 144–51.
3. Donno (Metamorphosis, 241) cites Harington's ascription in the Lumley-Folger copy to "The Erl of Shrowsbery," presumably the current title holder rather than his father, who died six years before The Metamorphosis was published. Gilbert is also suggested in light of his ties with Thomas Markham, for which see Wallace MacCaffrey, "Talbot and Stanhope: An Episode in Elizabethan Politics," 76–79.
1. DNB, s.v. "Wilson, Thomas (1525?–1581)"; recent biographical information about Wilson is summarized in the introduction to Thomas J. Derrick's Arte of Rhetorique by Thomas Wilson. Wilson retained the requests post through at least 1576 (PRO, E 179/69/93). Walsingham mentions "my Fellowe, Mr. Secretary Wylson," in a letter of January 20, 1578, while Wilson is credited with that office on the New Year's gift roll for 1578 (Collins, Letters, 1:234; Nichols, Progresses, 2:74).

his prose *"Oratio de Clementia"* on New Year's Day 1567.[2] In 1571 the queen granted him a one-hundred-pound annuity. Although Wilson included an original English couplet and the translation of a few lines from Juvenal in his *Rhetorique*, his Elizabethan verse is entirely in Latin and consists of: the poem he sent to Sir William Cecil upon Cecil's recovery from an illness in August 1568;[3] a congratulatory poem sent to the queen on the twelfth anniversary of her accession, November 17, 1569 (printed below); commendatory verses before Nicholas Carr's Latin translation of Demosthenes' *Olynthiacae orationes tres*, 1571 (STC 6577), a work which Wilson had translated the year before into English; an epitaph on Bishop John Jewel published in the biography edited by Lawrence Humphrey in 1573 (STC 13963, also preserved in BL, Lansdowne MS 377, folio 5v); commendatory verses before Bishop John Parkhurst's *Ludicra sive Epigrammata Juvenilia* 1573 (STC 19299); and commendatory verses in praise of Roger Ascham included in the posthumous publication of his letters (STC 826, 1576).

1

Ad sacratissimam Elizabetham, Dei gratia Angliae,
Franciae, et Hyberniae Reginam, fidei Defensorem.
  etc. annum Regni eiusdem Reginae
Thomae Wilsoni Epigrama in Duodecimum
  xvii Novembris .1569. etc.

Ecce duodecimus Regni nunc incipit annus,
  Quem tibi, quem Regno det Deus esse sacrum.
Hactenus est series foelix, talisque videtur
  Qualis in Elysiis dicitur esse locis.
Quae superest series, sit par, vel laetior esto,   5
  Si modo fata dari Prosperiora queant.
Talis es ut merito valeas, regnesque beata,
  Regno nempe tuo stella salutis ades.
Nescio si Dea sis, mihi numen haben videris,
  Iam bene nos Anglos Diva benigna regis.   10
Quod si sola potès sine sensu viven mortis
  Sola sis, eternum vivere digna solo.
Sed licet ex caelo es, mortali in corpore vivis,

---

2. BL, Royal MS 12.A.1.
3. PRO, SP 12/47/25; the disease was described as a "fever ague" in late July. Cecil had shaken it off by the second week in August (Read, *Mr. Secretary Cecil*, 407).

Ortaque temporibus, tempori cuncta cadunt.
Pignon sed vives ter foelix mater adulto,   **15**
  Sic potes eternam vivere Diva, Vale.
                    (BL, Lansdowne MS 12/15)

Wolley, Sir John (d. 1596)

Upon Ascham's death in 1568, Wolley succeeded to his post as
Latin Secretary. The fair copy letterbook of his official correspondence for the queen between 1569 and 1586 is preserved in Cambridge University Library.[1] He became a Privy Councillor in 1586,
was appointed chancellor of the Order of the Garter in 1589, and was
knighted in 1592. Elizabeth visited his house at Pyrford, Surrey, in
1576. He exchanged New Year's gifts with her in 1578, 1580, 1581,
1584, 1585, 1588, and 1589. Wolley exerted considerable influence
at court and with the queen. With Robert Cecil he assisted Lord
Burghley in carrying out the duties of secretary after Walsingham's
death, thereby forestalling the appointment of a principal secretary
until after his own death, when Cecil obtained the post.[2] Lord
Buckhurst, suffering royal displeasure in the autumn of 1587, tried
to regain "access to her presence" through the intervention of "my
cousin Wolley." A few months later, the earl of Rutland's correspondent at court informed him that he was "specially indebted to Mr.
Wolley" for his appointment as lieutenant of Nottinghamshire.[3]
Wolley's Latin sixain in memory of Bishop Jewel, printed below,
appeared with Wilson's elegy among more than two dozen such
laments appended to Humphrey's 1573 biography; a manuscript
copy of this poem occurs in BL, Lansdowne MS 377, folio 5v.

1

Ioannes Wollaeus, in lingua
Latina R. M. Secretarius.

Hei mihi quam celeri fugiunt mortalia cursu,
  Quaeque minus debet surripit atra dies.

1. MS Dd.3.20; A. E. B. Owen, "Sir John Wolley's Letter-Book as Latin Secretary to Elizabeth I," 16–18.
2. Florence M. Greir Evans, *The Principal Secretary of State*, 54–55.
3. HMC, Salisbury, 3:283–84; HMC, Rutland, 1:232.

Vivere tu longo fueras dignissimus aevo:
    Flende mihi nimium chare Iuelle iaces.
Moribus, ingenio, doctrina, relligione,   5
    Nulla ferent talem saecula longa virum.
                    (STC 13963, sig. M3v)

Selected Bibliography

The Antiquarian Repertory. Edited by Francis Grose and Thomas Astle. 4 vols. London, 1775–1784.

Antiquaries, Society of. *A Collection of Ordinances and Regulations for the Government of the Royal Household.* London, 1790.

Arber, Edward, ed. *A Transcript of the Registers of the Company of Stationers, 1554–1640.* 5 vols. London and Birmingham, 1875–1894.

Ariosto, Ludovico. *Orlando Furioso.* Translated by Sir John Harington. Edited by Robert McNulty. Oxford: Clarendon Press, 1972.

Arnold, Janet. *Lost from Her Majesty's Back.* Wisbech: Costume Society, 1980.

Ashmole, Elias. *The Antiquities of Berkshire.* 3 vols. London, 1723.

Attridge, Derek. *Well-Weighed Syllables.* Cambridge: Cambridge University Press, 1974.

Axton, Marie. *The Queen's Two Bodies: Drama and the Elizabethan Succession.* London: Royal Historical Society, 1977.

Axton, Marie, and Raymond Williams, eds. *English Drama: Forms and Development, Essays in Honor of Muriel Clara Bradbrook.* Cambridge: Cambridge University Press, 1977.

Aylmer, G. E. *The King's Servants: The Civil Service of Charles I, 1625–1642.* New York: Columbia University Press, 1961.

Bacquet, Paul. *Un Contemporain d'Elisabeth I: Thomas Sackville L'Homme et L'Oeuvre.* Geneva: Droz, 1966.

Ballard, George. *Memoirs of Several Ladies of Great Britain.* Edited by Ruth Perry. Detroit: Wayne State University Press, 1985.

Batho, G. R., ed. *The Household Papers of Henry Percy, Ninth Earl of Northumberland.* Camden Society Publications, 3d ser., vol. 93 (1962).

Beal, Peter. *Index of English Literary Manuscripts*, vol. 1, pts. 1, 2. London and New York: Mansell Publishing, 1980.

———. "Poems by Sir Philip Sidney: The Ottley Manuscript." *The Library*, 5th ser., 33 (1978): 284–95.

Beaty, Nancy Lee. *The Craft of Dying: A Study in the Literary Tradition of the "Ars Moriendi" in England.* New Haven: Yale University Press, 1970.

Beauchamp, Virginia Walcott. "Sidney's Sister as Translator of Garnier." *Renaissance News* 10 (1957): 8–13.

Bednarz, James. "Ralegh in Spenser's Historical Allegory." *Spenser Studies* 4 (1984): 49–70.

Benson, E. F. *Sir Francis Drake.* New York and London: Harper and Brothers, 1927.

Bentley, Gerald Eades. *Shakespeare: A Biographical Handbook.* New Haven: Yale University Press, 1961.

Berdan, John M. *Early Tudor Poetry.* New York: Macmillan, 1920.

Bergeron, David M. *English Civic Pageantry, 1558–1642.* Columbia: University of South Carolina Press, 1971.

Birch, Thomas. *Memoirs of the Reign of Queen Elizabeth.* 2 vols. 1754. Reprint. New York: AMS, 1970.

Black, L. G. "A Lost Poem by Queen Elizabeth I." *Times Literary Supplement*, May 23, 1968, 535.

Bradner, Leicester. *The Life and Poems of Richard Edwards.* New Haven: Yale University Press, 1927.

———. *Musae Anglicanae: A History of Anglo-Latin Poetry, 1500–1925.* New York: Modern Language Association of America, 1940.

———, ed. *The Poems of Queen Elizabeth I.* Providence: Brown University Press, 1964.

Brennan, Michael. "The Date of the Countess of Pembroke's Translation of the Psalms." *Review of English Studies*, n.s., 33 (1982): 434–46.

———. *Literary Patronage in the English Renaissance: The Pembroke Family.* London: Routledge, 1988.

Brooks, Eric St. John. *Sir Christopher Hatton.* London: Jonathan Cape, 1946.

Brown, Carleton, ed. *Poems by Sir John Salusbury and Robert Chester.* Early English Text Society, extra ser., 113 (1914).

Brydges, Sir Samuel Egerton. *The British Bibliographer.* 4 vols. London, 1810–1814.

Bullough, Geoffrey, ed. *Narrative and Dramatic Sources of Shakespeare.* 8 vols. New York: Columbia University Press, 1957–1975.

———, ed. *The Poems and Dramas of Fulke Greville, First Lord Brooke.* 2 vols. Oxford: Oxford University Press, 1945.

Bülow, Gottfried Von, ed. "Journey Through England and Scotland Made by Liupold Von Wedel in the Years 1584 and 1585." *Transactions of the Royal Historical Society*, n.s., 9 (1895): 223–70.

Buxton, John. *Sir Philip Sidney and the English Renaissance.* 2d ed. London: Macmillan, 1964.

Camden, William. *Annals.* Translated by R. N[orton]. 3d ed., London, 1635.

———. *Remains Concerning Britain.* Edited by Leslie Dunkling. 1870. Reprint. East Ardsley, Yorkshire: EP Publishing, 1974.

Castiglione, Baldassare. *The Book of the Courtier*. Translated by Sir Thomas Hoby. London: J. M. Dent and Sons, 1974.

Caudhi, Simon. "Sir John Harington and Virgil's *Aeneid* IV." In *English Manuscript Studies, 1100–1700*, edited by Peter Beal and Jeremy Griffiths, 242–49. Oxford: Basil Blackwell, 1988.

Chambers, E. K. *The Elizabethan Stage*. 4 vols. Oxford: Clarendon Press, 1923.

———. *Sir Henry Lee: An Elizabethan Portrait*. Oxford: Clarendon Press, 1936.

Chappell, William, and J. W. Ebsworth, eds. *The Roxburghe Ballads*. 10 vols. Hertford: Ballad Society, 1871–1899.

Clapham, John. *Elizabeth of England: Certain Observations Concerning the Life and Reign of Queen Elizabeth*. Edited by Evelyn Plummer Read and Conyers Read. Philadelphia: University of Pennsylvania Press, 1951.

Clayton, Thomas. " 'Sir Henry Lee's Farewell to the Court': The Texts and Authorship of 'His Golden Locks Time Hath to Silver Turned.' " *English Literary Renaissance* 4 (1974): 268–75.

Cokayne, George Edward. *The Complete Peerage of England, Scotland, Ireland, Great Britain and the United Kingdom*. Edited by Vicary Gibbs. 13 vols., in 14. London: St. Catherine Press, 1910–1959.

Collins, A. J. *Inventory of the Jewels and Plate of Queen Elizabeth I*. London: Trustees of the British Museum, 1955.

Collins, Arthur. *Letters and Memorials of State*. 2 vols. 1746. Reprint. New York: AMS, 1973.

———. *The Peerage of England*. 9 vols. London, 1779.

Connell, Dorothy. *Sir Philip Sidney: The Maker's Mind*. Oxford: Clarendon Press, 1977.

Cooper, Charles Purton, ed. *Recueil des Dépêches, Rapports, Instructions et Memoires Des Ambassadeurs de France En Angleterre (Fénelon Correspondence)*. 7 vols. Paris and London, 1838–1840.

Croft, P. J. *Autograph Poetry in the English Language*. 2 vols. London: Cassell, 1973.

———. *The Poems of Robert Sidney*. Oxford: Clarendon Press, 1984.

———. "Sir John Harington's Manuscript of Sir Philip Sidney's *Arcadia*." In *Literary Autographs*, edited by Stephen Parks and P. J. Croft, 37–75. Los Angeles: William Andrews Clark Memorial Library, 1983.

Croll, Morris W. *The Works of Fulke Greville*. Philadelphia: J. B. Lippincott, 1903.

Cunliffe, John W., ed. *The Complete Works of George Gascoigne*. 2 vols. 1907. Reprint. New York: Greenwood Press, 1969.

———. *Early English Classical Tragedies*. Oxford: Clarendon Press, 1912.

Daiches, David. *A Critical History of English Literature*. 2 vols. New York: Ronald Press, 1960.

Daniel, C. H. O., ed. *The Recreations of His Age By Sir Nicholas Bacon.* Oxford: privately printed, 1919.

Dart, John. *Westmonasterium; Or, The History and Antiquities of St. Peters Westminster.* 2 vols. London, 1742.

Dasent, J. R. *Acts of the Privy Council of England.* 32 vols. London: His Majesty's Stationery Office, 1890–1897.

Derrick, Thomas J. *The Arte of Rhetorique by Thomas Wilson.* New York: Garland, 1982.

Donno, Elizabeth Story. *Sir John Harington's "A New Discourse of a Stale Subject, Called the Metamorphosis of Ajax."* London: Routledge and Kegan Paul, 1962.

Doughtie, Edward. "The Earl of Essex and Occasions for Contemplative Verse." *English Literary Renaissance* 9 (1979): 355–63.

———. *Liber Lilliati.* Dover: University of Delaware Press, 1985.

———. *Lyrics from English Airs, 1596–1622.* Cambridge, Mass.: Harvard University Press, 1970.

Duncan-Jones, Katherine. " 'Rosis and Lysa': Selections From the Poems of Sir Robert Sidney." *English Literary Renaissance* 9 (1979): 240–63.

Duncan-Jones, Katherine, and Jan Van Dorsten, eds. *Miscellaneous Prose of Sir Philip Sidney.* Oxford: Clarendon Press, 1973.

Eccles, Mark. "Brief Lives: Tudor and Stuart Authors." *Studies in Philology,* Texts and Studies (1982).

Edwards, Edward. *The Life of Sir Walter Ralegh.* 2 vols. London: Macmillan, 1868.

Ellis, Sir Henry. *Original Letters Illustrative of English History.* 11 vols. 1825. Reprint. London: Dawsons, 1969.

Elton, G. R. "Tudor Government: The Points of Contact III. The Court." *Transactions of the Royal Historical Society,* 5th ser., 26 (1976): 211–28.

Evans, Florence M. Grier. *The Principal Secretary of State.* Manchester: Manchester University Press, 1923.

Falls, Cyril. *Mountjoy: Elizabethan General.* London: Odhams Press, 1955.

Feuillerat, Albert. *John Lyly.* 1910. Reprint. New York: Russell and Russell, 1968.

———, ed. *The Prose Works of Sir Philip Sidney.* 4 vols. 1912. Reprint. Cambridge: Cambridge University Press, 1962–1965.

Fisken, Beth Wynne. "Mary Sidney's *Psalmes:* Education and Wi[sd]om." In *Silent But for the Word,* edited by Margaret Patterson Hannay, 166–83. Kent: Kent State University Press, 1985.

Fuller, Thomas. *The Worthies of England.* Edited by John Freeman. London: George Allen and Unwin, 1952.

Giles, J. A., ed. *The Whole Works of Roger Ascham.* 4 vols. London, 1864.

Goldwyn, Merrill Harvey. "Notes on the Biography of Thomas Churchyard." *Review of English Studies* 17 (1966): 1–15.

Gouws, John, ed. *The Prose Works of Fulke Greville, Lord Brooke.* Oxford: Clarendon Press, 1986.

Greenblatt, Stephen Jay. *Sir Walter Ralegh: The Renaissance Man and his Roles.* New Haven: Yale University Press, 1973.

Greville, Fulke. *The Remains, Being Poems of Monarchy and Religion.* Edited by G. A. Wilkes. Oxford: Clarendon Press, 1965.

Groos, G. W., trans. *The Diary of Baron Waldstein.* London: Thames and Hudson, 1981.

Grosart, Alexander, ed. *The Dr. Farmer-Chetham MS., Being a Commonplace Book in the Chetham Library, Manchester, Temp. Elizabeth, James I, and Charles I.* Chetham Society Publications, 89–90. Manchester, 1873.

Guiney, Louise Imogen. *Recusant Poets.* New York: Sheed and Ward, 1939.

Hamilton, A. C. *Sir Philip Sidney: A Study of his Life and Works.* Cambridge: Cambridge University Press, 1977.

Hannay, Margaret P. " 'Doo What Men May Sing': Mary Sidney and the Tradition of Admonitory Dedication." In *Silent But for the Word*, edited by Margaret Patterson Hannay, 149–65. Kent: Kent State University Press, 1985.

Harington, Sir John. *A Supplie or Addicion to the Catalogue of Bishops to the Yeare 1608.* Edited by R. H. Miller. Potomac, Md.: Studia Humanitatis, 1979.

———. *A Tract on the Succession to the Crown (A.D. 1602).* Edited by Clements R. Markham. London, 1880.

Harvey, Sheridan. "The Cooke Sisters: A Study of Tudor Gentlewomen." Ph.D. diss. Indiana University, 1981.

Hasler, P. W. *The House of Commons, 1558–1603.* 3 vols. London: History of Parliament Trust, 1981.

Hay, Millicent V. *The Life of Robert Sidney, Earl of Leicester (1563–1626).* Washington, D.C.: Folger Shakespeare Library, 1984.

Heal, Felicity. *Of Prelates and Princes.* Cambridge: Cambridge University Press, 1980.

Helgerson, Richard. *The Elizabethan Prodigals.* Berkeley: University of California Press, 1976.

Horne, David H., ed. *The Life and Minor Works of George Peele.* New Haven: Yale University Press, 1952.

Hudson, Winthrop S. *The Cambridge Connection and the Elizabethan Settlement of 1559.* Durham: Duke University Press, 1980.

Hughes, Paul L., and James F. Larkin, eds. *Tudor Royal Proclamations.* 3 vols. New Haven: Yale University Press, 1969.

Hughey, Ruth. *John Harington of Stepney.* Columbus: Ohio State University Press, 1975.

———, ed. *The Arundel Harington Manuscript of Tudor Poetry.* 2 vols. Columbus: Ohio State University Press, 1960.

Humez, Jean McMahon. "The Manners of Epigram: A Study of the Epigram Volumes of Martial, Harington, and Jonson." Ph.D. diss. Yale University, 1971.

Hunter, G. K. *John Lyly: The Humanist as Courtier.* Cambridge, Mass.: Harvard University Press, 1962.

Javitch, Daniel. "The Impure Motives of Elizabethan Poetry." *Genre* 15 (1982): 225–38.

———. *Poetry and Courtliness in Renaissance England.* Princeton: Princeton University Press, 1978.

Jaeger, C. Stephen. *The Origins of Courtliness: Civilizing Trends and the Formation of Courtly Ideals, 939–1210.* Philadelphia: University of Pennsylvania Press, 1985.

John, Lisle Cecil. "Roger Manners, Elizabethan Courtier." *Huntington Library Quarterly* 12 (1948): 57–84.

Kelliher, W. Hilton. "A Manuscript of Poems by Robert Sidney: Some Early Impressions." *British Library Journal* 1 (1975): 107–44.

Kelliher, W. H., and Katherine Duncan-Jones. "The Warwick Manuscripts of Fulke Greville." *British Museum Quarterly* 34 (1970): 107–21.

Kendall, Timothe. *Flowers of Epigrammes.* Spenser Society Publications, no. 15. 1874. Reprint. New York: Burt Franklin, 1967.

Kenny, Robert W. *Elizabeth's Admiral: The Political Career of Charles Howard, Earl of Nottingham, 1536–1624.* Baltimore: Johns Hopkins Press, 1970.

Krueger, Robert, ed. *The Poems of Sir John Davies.* Oxford: Clarendon Press, 1975.

Lamb, Mary Ellen. "The Countess of Pembroke's Patronage." *English Literary Renaissance* 12 (1982): 162–79.

Lanspergius, Joannes. *An Epistle of Jesus Christ to the Faithful Soul.* Translated by Philip Howard, Earl of Arundel. English Recusant Literature, edited by D. M. Rogers, vol. 56. Menston: Scolar Press, 1970.

———. *An Epistle of Jesus Christ to the Soul That is Devoutly Affected Towards Him.* Translated by Philip Howard, 19th earl of Arundel. Edited by a Monk of Parkminster. New York: Benziger Brothers, 1926.

Latham, Agnes M. C. "A Birth-Date for Sir Walter Ralegh." *Etudes Anglaises* 9 (1956): 243–45.

Lees, Charles J, ed. *The Poetry of Walter Haddon.* The Hague: Mouton, 1967.

Lefranc, Pierre. "Une Nouvelle Version de la 'Petition to Queen Anne' de Sir Walter Ralegh." *Annales de la Faculté des Lettres et Sciences Humaines de Nice* 34 (1978): 57–67.

———. *Sir Walter Ralegh Écrivain.* Paris: Librairie Armand Colin, 1968.

Lehmberg, Stanford E. *Sir Walter Mildmay and Tudor Government.* Austin: University of Texas Press, 1964.

Lewis, C. S. *English Literature in the Sixteenth Century Excluding Drama.* Oxford: Clarendon Press, 1954.

Litt, Gary L. "'Images of Life': A Study of Narrative and Structure in Fulke Greville's *Caelica."* *Studies in Philology* 69 (1972): 217–30.

Loades, David. *The Tudor Court.* Totowa, N.J.: Barnes and Noble, 1987.

Lodge, Edmund. *Illustrations of British History, Biography, and Manners.* 3 vols. 1838. Reprint. Westmead, U.K.: Gregg International, 1969.

M., D. F. R. de. *An Answer to the Vntrvthes, Pvblished and Printed in Spaine.* Translated by J[ames] L[ea]. London, 1589.

MacCaffrey, Wallace. "Place and Patronage in Elizabethan Politics." In *Elizabethan Government and Society: Essays Presented to Sir John Neale,* edited by S. T. Bindoff, et al., 95–126. London: Athlone Press, 1961.

———. "Talbot and Stanhope: An Episode in Elizabethan Politics." *Bulletin of the Institute of Historical Research* 33 (1960): 73–85.

Maclean, John, ed. *Letters from Sir Robert Cecil to Sir George Carew.* Camden Society Publications, vol. 88. 1864. Reprint. New York: AMS, 1968.

Mares, F. H., ed. *The Memoirs of Robert Carey.* Oxford: Clarendon Press, 1972.

Mason, A. E. W. *The Life of Francis Drake.* 1941. Reprint. London: Hodder and Stoughton, 1950.

May, Steven W. "The Authorship of 'My Mind to me a Kingdom Is.'" *Review of English Studies,* n.s., 26 (1975): 385–94.

———. "Companion Poems in the Ralegh Canon." *English Literary Renaissance* 13 (1983): 260–73.

———. "The Poems of Edward DeVere, Seventeenth Earl of Oxford, and of Robert Devereux, Second Earl of Essex." *Studies in Philology,* Texts and Studies, 1980.

———. *Sir Walter Ralegh.* Boston: Twayne Publishers, 1989.

———. "Spenser's 'Amyntas': Three Poems by Ferdinando Stanley, Lord Strange, Fifth Earl of Derby." *Modern Philology* 70 (1972): 49–52.

Maynard, Winifred. "*The Paradyse of Daynty Deuises* Revisited." *Review of English Studies,* n.s., 24 (1973): 295–300.

McClure, Norman Egbert, ed. *The Letters and Epigrams of Sir John Harington.* 1930. Reprint. New York: Octagon, 1977.

———, ed. *The Letters of John Chamberlain to Dudley Carleton.* 2 vols. Philadelphia: American Philosophical Society, 1939.

Melville, Sir James. *The Memoirs of Sir James Melville.* Edited by George Scott. London, 1683.

Miller, Edwin Haviland. *The Professional Writer in Elizabethan England.* Cambridge, Mass.: Harvard University Press, 1959.

Miller, R. H. "Unpublished Poems by Sir John Harington." *English Literary Renaissance* 14 (1984): 148–58.

Montrose, Louis Adrian. "Celebration and Insinuation: Sir Philip Sidney and the Motives of Elizabethan Courtship." *Renaissance Drama*, n.s., 8 (1977): 3–35.

———. "Of Gentlemen and Shepherds: The Politics of Elizabethan Pastoral Form." *English Literary History* 50 (1983): 415–59.

Moore, Dennis. *The Politics of Spenser's "Complaints" and Sidney's "Philisides" Poems*. Salzburg: Institut für Anglistik und Amerikanistik Universität Salzburg, 1982.

Motley, John Lothrop. *History of the United Netherlands*. 4 vols. London, 1869.

Murdin, William. *A Collection of State Papers*. 2 vols. London, 1759.

Naunton, Sir Robert. *Fragmenta Regalia*. Edited by John S. Cerovski. Washington, D.C.: Associated University Presses, 1985.

Nichols, John. *The Progresses and Public Processions of Queen Elizabeth*. 3 vols. 1823. Reprint. New York: AMS, n.d.

Nicolas, Sir Harris. *Memoirs of the Life and Times of Sir Christopher Hatton*. London, 1847.

Norfolk, Duke of. *Lives of Philip Howard, Earl of Arundel, and of Anne Dacres, His Wife*. London, 1857.

Nugae Antiquae: Being a Miscellaneous Collection of Original Papers in Prose and Verse. 3 vols. London, 1769. Reprint, edited by Henry Harington. London, 1775, 1779. Reprint, edited by Thomas Park. 2 vols. London, 1804. Reprint. New York: AMS, 1966.

Orgel, Stephen. *The Jonsonian Masque*. 1967. Reprint. New York: Columbia University Press, 1981.

Owen, A. E. B. "Sir John Wolley's Letter-Book as Latin Secretary to Elizabeth I." *Archives* 11 (1973): 16–18.

Park, Thomas. *Catalogue of the Royal and Noble Authors of England*. 5 vols. 1806. Reprint. New York: AMS, 1971.

Pears, Steuart A. *The Correspondence of Sir Philip Sidney and Hubert Languet*. London, 1845.

Pearson, Lu Emily. *Elizabethan Love Conventions*. Berkeley: University of California Press, 1933.

Pegge, Samuel. *Curialia; or, An Historical Account of Some Branches of the Royal Household*. London, 1782.

Pellegrini, Giuliano. *Un Fiorentino alla Corte d'Inghilterra nel Cinquecento, Petruccio Ubaldini*. Turin: Bottega d'Erasmo, 1967.

Pemberton, Caroline, ed. *Queen Elizabeth's Englishings*. Early English Text Society, o.s., 113 (1899).

Petti, Anthony G. *English Literary Hands from Chaucer to Dryden*. Cambridge, Mass.: Harvard University Press, 1977.

Phillips, James E. "Elizabeth I as a Latin Poet: An Epigram on Paul Melissus." *Renaissance News* 16 (1963): 289–98.

Pieces of Ancient Poetry from Unpublished Manuscripts and Scarce Books. Bristol, 1814.

Plett, Heinrich F. "Aesthetic Constituents in the Courtly Culture of Renaissance England." *New Literary History* 14 (1983): 597–621.

Pollen, John Hungerford, ed. "Bedingfield Papers . . . The Sydenham Prayer-Book." Catholic Record Society, *Miscellanea* 6 (London, 1909): 1–245.

Pollen, John Hungerford, and William MacMahon. "The Venerable Philip Howard, Earl of Arundel, 1557–1595." Catholic Record Society 21 (London, 1919).

Prescott, Anne Lake. *French Poets and the English Renaissance.* New Haven: Yale University Press, 1978.

Price, David C. "Gilbert Talbot, Seventh Earl of Shrewsbury: An Elizabethan Courtier and His Music." *Music and Letters* 57 (1976): 144–51.

Price, William Hyde. *The English Patents of Monopoly.* Boston: Houghton Mifflin, 1906.

Puttenham, George. *The Arte of English Poesie.* Edited by Gladys Doidge Willcock and Alice Walker. Cambridge: Cambridge University Press, 1936.

R., J. *The Antiquities of St. Peter's; or, The Abbey-Church of Westminster.* 2 vols. 5th ed. London, 1742.

Rabelais, François. *The Histories of Gargantua and Pantagruel.* Translated by J. M. Cohen. Harmondsworth: Penguin Books, 1955.

Raines, F. R., ed. "The Stanley Papers." Part 2. Chetham Society Publications, 31. Manchester, 1853.

Rathmell, J. C. A., ed. *The Psalms of Sir Philip Sidney and the Countess of Pembroke.* New York: New York University Press, 1963.

Read, Conyers. *Mr. Secretary Cecil and Queen Elizabeth.* London: Jonathan Cape, 1955.

Rebholz, Ronald A. *The Life of Fulke Greville, First Lord Brooke.* Oxford: Clarendon Press, 1971.

Rees, Joan. *Fulke Greville, Lord Brooke, 1554–1628:, A Critical Biography.* London: Routledge and Kegan Paul, 1971.

Rich, Townsend. *Harington and Ariosto: A Study in Elizabethan Verse Translation.* Yale Studies in English 92 (1940).

Ringler, William A., Jr., ed. *The Poems of Sir Philip Sidney.* Oxford: Clarendon Press, 1962.

Robbie, H. J. L. "The Authorship of 'A Fourefold Meditation.' " *Review of English Studies* 5 (1929): 200–202.

Rollins, Hyder Edward. *An Analytical Index to the Ballad-Entries (1557–1709) in the Registers of the Company of Stationers of London.* 1924. Reprint. Hatboro, Pa.: Tradition Press, 1967.

———, ed. *Brittons Bowre of Delights 1591.* Cambridge, Mass.: Harvard University Press, 1933.

———, ed. *The Paradise of Dainty Devices.* Cambridge, Mass.: Harvard University Press, 1927.

————, ed. *A Poetical Rhapsody, 1602–1621.* 2 vols. Cambridge, Mass.: Harvard University Press, 1931.

Rudick, Michael. "The Poems of Sir Walter Ralegh: An Edition." Ph.D. diss. University of Chicago, 1970.

————. "The 'Ralegh Group' in *The Phoenix Nest.*" *Studies in Bibliography* 24 (1971): 131–37.

Ryan, Lawrence V. *Roger Ascham.* Stanford: Stanford University Press, 1963.

Rye, Constance E. B. "Queen Elizabeth's Godchildren." *The Geneaologist,* n.s., 2 (1885): 292–96.

Rye, William Brenchley. *England as Seen by Foreigners in the Days of Elizabeth and James the First.* 1865. Reprint. New York: Benjamin Blom, 1967.

Sandison, Helen Estabrook. "Arthur Gorges: Spenser's Alcyon and Ralegh's Friend." *PMLA* 43 (1928): 645–74.

————, ed. *The Poems of Sir Arthur Gorges.* Oxford: Clarendon Press, 1953.

Sargent, Ralph M. *The Life and Lyrics of Sir Edward Dyer.* Oxford: Clarendon Press, 1968.

Schmutzler, Karl E. "Harington's Metrical Paraphrases of the Seven Penitential Psalms: Three Manuscript Versions." *Papers of the Bibliographical Society of America* 53 (1959): 240–51.

Segar, William. *The Booke of Honor and Armes.* London, 1590.

Seneca, Lucius Annaeus. *The Seconde Tragedie of Seneca.* Translated by Jasper Heywood. London, 1560.

Sidney, Sir Philip. *The Countess of Pembroke's Arcadia.* Edited by Jean Robertson. Oxford: Clarendon Press, 1973.

Smith, Alan G. R. *Servant of the Cecils: The Life of Sir Michael Hickes, 1543–1612.* Totowa, N.J.: Rowman and Littlefield, 1977.

Smith, G. C. Moore. *Gabriel Harvey's Marginalia.* Stratford-upon-Avon: Shakespeare Head Press, 1913.

Smith, Lacey Baldwin. *Henry VIII: The Mask of Royalty.* Boston: Houghton Mifflin, 1971.

Smuts, R. Malcolm. *Court Culture and the Origins of a Royalist Tradition in Early Stuart England.* Philadelphia: University of Pennsylvania Press, 1987.

Sorlien, Robert Parker, ed. *The Diary of John Manningham of the Middle Temple, 1602–1603.* Hanover: University Press of New England, 1976.

Southall, Raymond. *The Courtly Maker.* New York: Barnes and Noble, 1964.

Southwell, Robert. *The Fovre-Fovld Meditation.* Edited by Charles Edmonds. London: Elkin Mathews, 1895.

Spedding, James, ed. *The Letters and the Life of Francis Bacon.* 2 vols. London, 1861.

————, ed. *The Works of Francis Bacon*. 15 vols. 1860. Reprint. St. Clair Shores, Mich.: Scholarly Press, 1977.

Spenser, Edmund. *The Works of Edmund Spenser: A Variorum Edition*. Edited by Edwin Greenlaw, et al. 11 vols. Baltimore: Johns Hopkins University Press, 1932–1945.

Starkey, David. "Introduction: Court History in Perspective." In *The English Court: From the Wars of the Roses to the Civil War*, 1–24. New York: Longman, 1987.

Stone, Lawrence. *The Crisis of the Aristocracy*. Oxford: Clarendon Press, 1965.

————. *An Elizabethan: Horatio Palavicino*. Oxford: Clarendon Press, 1956.

Strong, Roy. *The Cult of Elizabeth*. 1977. Reprint. Berkeley and Los Angeles: University of California Press, 1983.

Strong, Roy, and V. J. Murrell. *Artists of the Tudor Court*. Over Wallop, Hampshire: Thames and Hudson, 1983.

Strype, John. *Annals of the Reformation*. 4 vols. 1824. Reprint. New York, Burt Franklin, 1966.

Tennenhouse, Leonard. "Sir Walter Ralegh and the Literature of Clientage." In *Patronage in the Renaissance*, edited by Guy Fitch Lytle and Stephen Orgel, 235–58. Princeton: Princeton University Press, 1981.

Thomas, David. "Leases in Reversion on the Crown's Lands, 1558–1603." *English Historical Review* 30 (1977): 67–68.

Thoms, William J. *The Book of the Court*. 2d ed. London, 1844.

Tighe, William. "The Gentleman Pensioners in Elizabethan Politics and Government." Ph.D. diss. Cambridge University, 1983.

Tilley, Morris P. *A Dictionary of the Proverbs in England in the Sixteenth and Seventeenth Centuries*. Ann Arbor: University of Michigan Press, 1950.

Turberville, George. *Epitaphes, Epigrams, Songs and Sonets (1567)*. Introduction by Richard J. Panofsky. Delmar, N.Y.: Scholars' Facsimiles and Reprints, 1977.

Van Dorsten, Jan. "Literary Patronage in Elizabethan England: The Early Phase." In *Patronage in the Renaissance*, edited by Guy Fitch Lytle and Stephen Orgel, 191–206. Princeton: Princeton University Press, 1981.

Vere, Sir Francis. *The Commentaries of Sr Francis Vere*. Cambridge, 1657.

Wagner, Bernard M. "New Poems by Sir Edward Dyer." *Review of English Studies* 11 (1935): 467–68.

Waller, Gary F. *Mary Sidney, Countess of Pembroke: A Critical Study of Her Writings and Literary Milieu*. Salzburg: Institut für Anglistik und Amerikanistik Universität Salzburg, 1979.

————. " 'This Matching of Contraries': Calvinism and Courtly Philosophy in the Sidney Psalms." *English Studies* 55 (1974): 22–31.

———. *The Triumph of Death and Other Unpublished and Uncollected Poems by Mary Sidney, Countess of Pembroke (1561–1621)*. Salzburg: Institut für Englische Sprache und Literatur Universität Salzburg, 1977.

Ward, B. M. *The Seventeenth Earl of Oxford*. London: John Murray, 1928.

Waswo, Richard. *The Fatal Mirror: Themes and Techniques in the Poetry of Fulke Greville*. Charlottesville: University Press of Virginia, 1972.

Westcott, Allan F., ed. *New Poems of James I of England*. 1911. Reprint. New York: AMS, 1966.

Whipple, T. K. *Martial and the English Epigram from Sir Thomas Wyatt to Ben Jonson*. University of California Publications in Modern Philology, no. 10. Berkeley and Los Angeles: University of California Press, 1925.

Whitney, Geffrey. *A Choice of Emblemes*. Edited by Henry Green. 1866. Reprint. New York: Benjamin Blom, 1966.

Williams, Clare. *Thomas Platter's Travels in England, 1599*. London: Jonathan Cape, 1937.

Williams, Neville. "The Tudors: Three Contrasts in Personality." In *The Courts of Europe*, edited by A. G. Dickens, 147–67. New York: McGraw-Hill, 1977.

Williams, Penry. "Court and Polity under Elizabeth I." *Bulletin of the John Rylands University Library of Manchester* 65 (1983): 259–86.

Williamson, G. C. *George, Third Earl of Cumberland (1558–1605)*. Cambridge: Cambridge University Press, 1920.

Wilson, Jean. *Entertainments for Elizabeth I*. Totowa, N.J.: Rowan and Littlefield, 1980.

Wilson, Violet A. *Queen Elizabeth's Maids of Honour and Ladies of the Privy Chamber*. New York: E. P. Dutton, 1922.

Wotton, Sir Henry. *A Parallell Betweene Robert Late Earle of Essex, and George Late Duke of Buckingham*. London, 1641.

Wright, Pam. "A Change in Direction: The Ramifications of a Female Household, 1558–1603." In *The English Court: From the Wars of the Roses to the Civil War*, 147–72. New York: Longman, 1987.

Wright, Thomas. *Queen Elizabeth and Her Times*. 2 vols. London, 1838.

Wright, William A., ed. *Roger Ascham: The English Works*. 1904. Reprint. Cambridge: Cambridge University Press, 1967.

Yates, Frances A. *Astraea: The Imperial Theme in the Sixteenth Century*. London: Routledge and Kegan Paul, 1975.

Young, Alan. *Tudor and Jacobean Tournaments*. London: Sheridan House, 1987.

Zim, Rivkah, and M. B. Parkes. " 'Sacvyles Olde Age': A Newly Discovered Poem by Thomas Sackville, Lord Buckhurst, Earl of Dorset (c. 1536–1608)." *Review of English Studies*, n.s., 40 (1989):1–25.

Index

Index of First Lines of Poems Edited in Part II